D0860751

PRESENTED BY

_____

DATE

Strength
for Service

TO GOD AND COUNTRY

PSALM NINETY-ONE

You who live in the shelter of the Most High, who abide in the shadow of the Almighty, will say to the Lord, "My refuge and my fortress; my God, in whom I trust."

For he will deliver you from the snare of the fowler and from the deadly pestilence; he will cover you with his pinions, and under his wings you will find refuge; his faithfulness is a shield and buckler.

You will not fear the terror of the night, or the arrow that flies by day, or the pestilence that stalks in darkness, or the destruction that wastes at noonday. A thousand may fall at your side, ten thousand at your right hand, but it will not come near you. You will only look with your eyes and see the punishment of the wicked.

Because you have made the Lord your refuge, the Most High your dwelling place, no evil shall befall you, no scourge come near your tent. For he will command his angels concerning you to guard you in all your ways. On their hands they will bear you up, so that you will not dash your foot against a stone. You will tread on the lion and the adder, the young lion and the serpent you will trample under foot.

Those who love me, I will deliver; I will protect those who know my name. When they call to me, I will answer them; I will be with them in trouble, I will rescue them and honor them. With long life I will satisfy them, and show them my salvation.

—NRSV

Strength
for Service

TO GOD AND COUNTRY

Daily Devotional Messages for
Those in the Service of Others

Edited by
NORMAN E. NYGAARD

Revised edition
compiled by
EVAN HUNSBERGER

Providence House Publishers
PROVIDENCE PUBLISHING CORPORATION
FRANKLIN, TENNESSEE

Printed in the United States of America

06   05   04   5   6   7   8

Library of Congress Catalog Card Number: 2002108885

ISBN: 1-57736-266-7

Unless otherwise marked, Scripture quotations in 1942 edition devotions are from the HOLY BIBLE, King James
Version.

Scripture quotations in 2002 edition devotions and others
marked NRSV are from the New Revised Standard Version
Bible, copyright 1989, Division of Christian Education of the
National Council of the Churches of Christ in the United
States of America. Used by permission. All rights reserved.

PROVIDENCE HOUSE PUBLISHERS
an imprint of
Providence Publishing Corporation
238 Seaboard Lane Franklin, Tennessee 37067
www.providencepubcorp.com
800-321-5692

INTRODUCTION TO THE NEW EDITION

Strength for Service to God and Country is a book with a remarkable heritage. Well over 1 million copies of its early editions were published soon after the December 7, 1941, attack upon Pearl Harbor and distributed to armed services personnel during World War II and the Korean conflict. American soldiers carried it with them during the invasion of Normandy, the Battle of the Bulge, and other military campaigns of the 1940s and '50s.

One sailor held on to that book for many years and gave his tattered, underlined copy to his fifteen-year-old grandson, a Boy Scout named Evan Hunsberger. For his Eagle Service Project, Evan decided to honor his grandfather's memory by introducing this powerful collection of devotions to a new generation of American military personnel and public servants. Evan secured permission from the original publisher and gathered new meditations from a diverse group of contemporary spiritual leaders.

The General Commission on United Methodist Men assisted Evan in the development and fundraising for the publication. Providence House Publishers shared the vision and began working with the team to publish a new edition. As a testimony to the ecumenical nature of the project, the United Methodist Men gave Evan, a Roman Catholic, its Good Samaritan Award for his exceptional work on this initiative.

Although this edition was well underway when America was attacked by terrorists on September 11, 2001, this book has taken on new meaning in light of that tragic day. Just as the shock of December 7, 1941, launched the nation into war, this new threat is placing the members of our armed forces in harm's way. Spiritual concerns are a priority as our faithful soldiers are separated from family and friends, and a devotional resource such as Strength for Service to God and Country becomes for them the Light shining in the darkness.

These writings from a broad spectrum of the Body of Christ are free of denominational or doctrinal teachings, yet they boldly bear witness to the timeless truth. Yielding to the infinite power of almighty God, trusting in the promises of scripture, and living in the victory of our salvation in Jesus Christ offers any who will believe the peace that passes understanding and the assurance of eternal life.

This new edition is offered to all the individuals who guard the institutions of democracy and help protect the people of the world in times of danger. Military personnel, firefighters, police officers, paramedics, and a host of others bravely sacrifice their own security so that their brothers and sisters might be safe from harm. Thank You and God bless.

EDITOR'S NOTE: New devotions from contemporary Christian leaders are included between each month of the original devotions and are indicated by a cross (†). Jewish and Muslim devotions are located in the "Special Devotions" section at the back of this book.

KEEPING POWER

Who are kept by the power of God through faith unto salvation, ready to be revealed in the last time.—1 Pet. 1:5

As a young man I read in the First Epistle of St. Peter, at the fifth verse, the words: "Kept by the power of God through faith." It expressed a philosophy or rule of life that I might make my own. Every year I write these words on the first page of my diary.

I have lived a long and eventful life, traveled much in the Old World and the New, been privileged to know many of the great men and women of my time, and read many books; but in all the strange and changing circumstances and trials of life I have clung to this verse and made it the guide and assurance of my life. Every day as I go forth to my tasks I have been conscious of the truth that my life is kept and preserved by the power of God. It may be a simple faith, but it has proved adequate and sustaining. I have found no substitute for it. I would not part with it for all the wisdom I have found in the great books that men have written.

If we live by this word of comfort and assurance, we can with sure confidence face all the exigencies and trials of life. There is no other power, no other strength equal to it. Live by it and you will know that life has meaning and purpose, and that no matter what comes to you, you are "kept by the power of God." I know it, for I have tested it.

DEAR HEAVENLY FATHER, may I begin this day of life as in Thy presence. In all my ways may I acknowledge Thee, and do Thou direct my paths. Keep me ever true to Thee; increase my faith, and guide me in every thought and word and act. Prepare me that I may be ready to meet each trial and temptation that may come to me, and make me worthy of Thy protecting care. In humility and unfailing trust I make this, my daily prayer, in the name of Jesus Christ, my Redeemer. *Amen.*

JAMES E. FREEMAN
Bishop of Washington, D.C., Episcopal

THE OVERRULING PROVIDENCE

The Lord shall preserve thy going out, and thy coming in, from this time forth, and even for evermore.—Ps. 121:8

What a gracious promise! What a comforting assurance, especially for those of us who have been called to walk in new paths and to face new and untried experiences! In these experiences there may be elements of danger, but if our lives have been committed to the Lord Jesus Christ, the result is sure. He shall preserve—forever.

As a chaplain in the last war, I remember leaving my wife and three small children at the railroad station, wondering whether I would ever see them again. As I sat in the train, I began reading a letter from a friend, at the close of which he said, "May the Lord preserve thy going out, and thy coming in." I lifted my heart to God and said, "Lord, do this for me for the sake of those whom I love." Then I took out my Bible and read this great thing: "The Lord *shall* preserve thy going out, and thy coming in."

I still remember the joy of it and the wondrous sense of security it brought. That, of course, didn't mean that I was coming back, but it did mean that God was going to watch over me and care for me and hold all that affected me in His control. It means the same thing for you today if you belong to Him. Every life committed *to* Him is cared for *by* Him.

LORD, give to us a sense of Thy nearness and "stay our minds upon Thee," that we may have Thy "perfect peace." *Amen.*

T. Roland Philips
Arlington Presbyterian Church, Baltimore, Md.

BEHAVING VALIANTLY

Be of good courage, and let us behave ourselves valiantly for our people, and for the cities of our God; and let the Lord do that which is good in his sight.—1 Chron. 19:13

We behave valiantly when we are stronghearted. We are not truly Christian till we behave valiantly. What is involved?

First, *receive* whatever comes, good or bad, as a part of life; do not try to *reject* trouble as though it were an intruder. Happiness comes not from avoiding hard situations but from overcoming them. A desperate opposition and strength to win—that is real joy, the joy Christ promised: "My joy I give unto you!"

Second, *respond* to whatever comes; do not *react*. Whenever we merely react mechanically, we function on a subhuman level. As persons we can respond; that is, we can project into any situation something that is the unique contribution of a personality, something spiritual, creative. This is obviously what the Master had in mind when He spoke of returning good for evil. This is the redemptive power of the Cross.

Third, *rejoice* in whatever comes; do not *rebel*. In these dark hours—rejoice (a) that we are matched with such a supremely significant age as this. Rejoice (b) that we now have an unusual chance to test the validity of our Christian principles. Rejoice (c) that we shall discover what we ourselves are actually made of. Rejoice (d) that we shall be able to discover how tribulations bring patience, patience experience, experience hope—which means we shall be living deeply, richly, greatly. Rejoice (e) that we shall have revealed to us the necessity and availability of God.

INFINITE FATHER, we would open our hearts to Thee willingly: confidently, completely. Whatever comes to us, teach us how to receive it, respond to it, and rejoice in it valiantly, and thus transform tragedy into triumph, as did Thy Son. *Amen.*

HENRY H. CRANE
Central Methodist Church, Detroit, Mich.

THE POWER THAT SUSTAINS

The eternal God is thy dwelling-place, and underneath are the everlasting arms.—Deut. 33:27 ARV

O ne of the most beautiful concepts of religion is that of the Everlasting Arms of God. Many are the people in dangerous times who have been helped by these words. In times of anxiety they have given us confidence that God knows. When haunted by insecurity, they have given us a feeling of confidence in the Eternal. With Whittier we may sing:

> I know not what the future hath
> Of marvel or surprise,
> Assured alone that life and death
> His mercy underlies.

Psychologists tell us that one of the fundamental fears of an infant is that of physical insecurity. A baby fears lack of support. But the support underneath of the arms of a father or mother sets the child at ease. While we are not babies, that need for a power to sustain lives with us throughout life. The knowledge that God is our strength and that "underneath are the everlasting arms" is basic for heroic, courageous living.

How much mental suffering and torture of anxiety we might save ourselves if only we were to trust in God! How much richer our lives would be if we were to live in the security of the Everlasting Arms!

ETERNAL FATHER, as Thou hast led men and women of the past through darkness to light, through despair to hope, through tragedy to triumph, we place our confidence in Thee, sure that as always Thou wilt keep that which we commit unto Thee. Into Thy hands daily we commit our lives. Make us to feel the sustaining power of Thy Everlasting Arms underneath us. *Amen.*

VICTOR M. RHEIN
Pilgrim Congregational Church, Oak Park, Ill.

THE WILL OF GOD

Thy will be done in earth, as it is in heaven.—Matt. 6:10

God wills it that all people should have life and have it more abundantly. Ours is an enterprise in arms, which prospers only as it deals out death and destruction. Can this be to do God's will? Only if we, who fight, shall see to it that out of this death-dealing comes a world filled with life and peace, not for our nation only, but for our present enemies as well. Only so can this war be blessed of God.

Let us remember that God's will is done even now, as always, everywhere except here on this tiny earth. God has not been overthrown by the follies that bred this war. Once, at least, each day let us remember that. Then, even though death crashes around us, we shall know it for what it is, our share in the penalty that must be paid for having been so long disobedient fools, resistant to the divine law of mutual sacrifice. God still reigns. It is we who fail.

God's will is now done in heaven. It must be done in earth as well, in that world which will emerge at last. We who fight now—how shall the world be built by us when these war days are done? Any better than our fathers built it a generation ago? If not, then our sons and daughters will in their day have to deal out death and bear the pain of all this dreadful business, paying for our sins as now we pay for the sins of our ancestors. God forbid! This war is but a prelude. Our lifework will begin when the guns at length are silent.

ALMIGHTY FATHER, guide us that we may bring all nations to the doing of Thy will, that we may establish that peace which is the fruit of mutual goodwill and a shared compassion, that Thy Kingdom may come on earth and all Thy children share in life abundant, through Jesus Christ. *Amen.*

BERNARD IDDINGS BELL
St. John's Cathedral, Episcopal, Providence, R.I.

THE PEARL OF GREAT PRICE

The kingdom of heaven is like unto a merchantman, seeking goodly pearls; who, when he had found one pearl of great price, went and sold all that he had, and bought it.—Matt. 13:45–46

So far as I know, the pearl is the only gem which is formed by a living organism. A grain of sand or some other irritating substance finds its way into the shell of an oyster. Very soon a smooth, beautiful coating covers the foreign body. Over a long period of time countless layers are added, and a priceless pearl is formed.

Here Christ gives us an accurate picture of the way the most valuable things in human life are produced. An irritation, an injury, a wrong is met by a person who is in living, spiritual fellowship with God. (Remember, only a living oyster can make a pearl out of a sharp grain of sand.)

That very injury becomes the means of greatly enriching the individual injured. There is no circumstance in the world so bad that it cannot be the means of a great blessing. No truer words were ever spoken than the words of Paul when he said, "All things work together for good to them that love God."

FATHER, may we have a living faith in Thee which will enable us not only to endure injuries and disappointments, but to transform them into treasured experiences. Do not take from us the irritating conditions surrounding us until we have learned all we can from them. In Jesus' name we pray. *Amen.*

KARL P. BUSWELL
Chaplain, U.S. Naval Reserve

THE SAFEST PLACE IN ANY RAID

He that dwelleth in the secret place of the Most High shall abide under the shadow of the Almighty.—Ps. 91:1

While walking through Hyde Park in London just before the outbreak of World War II, I saw the efforts being made to build great underground air raid shelters. From thinking of this, and of the dangers of war, the words of this psalm have come to mind, with the suggestion that here is the only safe shelter for us.

The description of terrors by night, pestilence walking by day, destruction at noonday, and so on, almost uncannily fits the situation in which many have found themselves. While we may be in great physical danger and must seek for safety, yet we must remember that there is a spiritual danger which is greater. We cannot run away from God, and we should not, for in Him alone do we find the place of perfect safety.

"He that dwelleth in the secret place of the Most High shall abide under the shadow of the Almighty." Here is the place of safety and the path by which this place may be found. It is a secret belonging to God, and yet made plain through that One who said, "I am the Way." Following Him, we come to the shadow of the Almighty and there find refuge. Finding is not enough; we must dwell in this place of safety.

For whatever experience may confront you, may I suggest out of the experiences of my own life during the days of the last world war, plus that of millions of others, that in Him there can be found this place of perfect safety.

FATHER IN HEAVEN, give light on the pathway that leads to this secret place of safety. Help each one who seeks to find and, in finding, to dwell in Thy shadow. Thy shadow is, to those who find, like the shadow of a great rock in a weary land. Lead us, through Jesus Christ, who is the Way, the Truth, and the Life. *Amen.*

C. Gordon Brownville
Tremont Temple Baptist Church, Boston, Mass.

THE CHARACTER OF GOD

Our God is a consuming fire.—Heb. 12:29

These are days when men and women, both those in the armed forces and civilians, are making great sacrifices to secure victory. This experience should enable us to see more clearly the true nature of the God whom Jesus reveals.

There is an old legend that the devil tried to disguise himself as Christ and tempt a disciple; but the disciple said, "Show me the print of the nails in your hands," and the devil had to sneak away because he had no marks of sacrificial love. Jesus reveals that at the heart of the universe there is Love which triumphs through sacrifice.

This spells peace and hope and joy to all that is unselfish within us, but God is a consuming fire to all that is self-centered. If we try to build our society on self-will, war will follow war until civilization crashes in misery. This war will not have been in vain if our men and women in the service, out of the new insights gained through their experience, will lead us to work and sacrifice for a Christian world order.

LORD GOD OF HOSTS, stretch forth, we pray Thee, Thine almighty arm to strengthen our soldiers and sailors. Keep them temperate in all things, and grant that they may serve without stumbling and without stain. For their homes, give them steadfast loyalty through all the days of separation; for their Church, give them reverence and devotion; and grant that, returning with greater insight into Thy purpose, they may lead us into greater service in Thy Kingdom, through Jesus Christ our Lord. *Amen.*

OLIVER J. HART
Bishop Coadjutor of Pennsylvania, Episcopal,
on leave as Chaplain, Fort Dix, N.J.

A YOUNG MAN'S HIGH PURPOSE

Daniel purposed in his heart that he would not defile himself with the king's dainties, nor with the wine which he drank.—Dan. 1:8 ARV

Daniel was a military captive in a totalitarian state ruled by the dictator Nebuchadnezzar. It has always been dangerous to oppose a dictator, but Daniel dared to do it. "He purposed in his heart that he would not defile himself." He would be true to the highest and the best that he knew even under the debasing conditions in which he was forced, as a captive, to live.

Surrounded by influences calculated to destroy every fine ideal he had learned at home and at the temple in Jerusalem, he was determined not to yield, and he did not yield. He kept himself strong and clean for the service ahead—for God and country.

Today, as never before in America, we need Daniels who will purpose in their hearts, men and women who will highly resolve to do right and to keep clean though the heavens fall. Daniels are needed in the armed forces. To serve my country and my God most effectively, I shall need to keep my mind steady, my heart true, and my body fit. I must:

Dare to be a Daniel,
Dare to stand alone,
Dare to have a purpose firm!
Dare to make it known!

FATHER GOD, help me to be ever true to the highest and best that I know, through Jesus Christ, our Lord. *Amen.*

ARTHUR BRADEN
Wilshire Christian Church, Los Angeles, Calif.

WHAT RELIGION CAN DO FOR US

God is our refuge and strength, a very present help in trouble. Therefore we will not fear, though the earth be removed, and though the mountains be carried into the midst of the sea.—Ps. 46:1–2

Religion should do for us what Edwin Markham had in mind when he wrote the poem called "Man-making."

> We are all blind until we see
> That in the human plan
> Nothing is worth the making if
> It does not make the man.
> Why build these cities glorious
> If man unbuilded goes?
> In vain we build the work, unless
> The builder also grows.

Religion is not intended to make life an escape from hardships, but to make us the kind of people who can turn difficulties into opportunities. When we rise from our prayers, we know that we are not lost orphans in an alien world, but God is the guardian of our common life.

Religion gives meaning and purpose in life. In these days of broken promises and deferred hopes, of war and world upheavals, we all need desperately the poise and stability which religion can give us. Even though the storms of an upside-down world rage around us, let us retain our poise and sanity. Religion can help us here.

OUR FATHER GOD, help us to follow Christ in His comprehensive understanding of human needs and in His courageous facing of difficult situations. Make us heroic enough to decide our problems in His Spirit. We look to Thee for help, strength, and courage to choose the right way as revealed in Christ. *Amen.*

JACOB J. SESSLER
First Reformed Church, College Point, N.Y.

OUR GREATEST CONTRIBUTION

I thank my God . . . for your fellowship in the gospel, from the first day until now.—Phil. 1:3–5

A father and mother were having some difficulty in interesting their little daughter in the study of geography. They schemed to help her by purchasing for her a jigsaw puzzle map of the United States. They were sure that this would be a valuable geographical project. To their amazement she was able to assemble the map in a remarkably short time. They asked her how she did it, and she explained that on the opposite side of the map was a picture puzzle of the face of George Washington. This further word from her was especially thought-provoking: "When you get the man put together right, the United States comes out all right."

There is a deep truth in that child's comment. The best way to put things together as they should be, in society, in the nation, and in the world, is for us to have our separate and individual lives put together properly. The whole is made up of the sum total of its individual parts. There is primarily no more important part which we can play today as individuals than to present to the nation and the world a good life.

The finest and most successful way to achieve this good life is to have our lives inspired and molded daily after the example, purpose, and teaching of Jesus Christ. He has been the source of the noblest and most useful living the world has ever known. Let us keep our eyes day by day upon the King.

OUR FATHER IN HEAVEN, we thank Thee for Jesus Christ. By His Spirit help us to prove in our daily lives that He did not come to us and live with us and die for us in vain. Inspire us to say "Yes" to His claims on our lives. *Amen.*

JOSEPH MARQUIS EWING
First Presbyterian Church, Fresno, Calif.

VICTORY

This is the victory that overcometh the world, even our faith.
—1 John 5:4

Just being a person of faith in a difficult time is itself a victory. Anybody can give up. Anybody can despair. But it is not easy to keep one's faith when things go to pieces around one.

In the hardest hour of His life Jesus told the disciples they need not be afraid because He had "overcome the world." He had refused to be overcome by adverse conditions. He had not given in to pressures which would lead Him to doubt God's control of the world.

When an individual keeps clear in his or her own mind the assurance that the right does win because it is held in God's will, that the wrong does fail because it is against God's will, that one's life is safer in God's hands than anywhere else, that the people one loves are safer there also—that is a victory in itself. A person always wins in that spirit.

DEAR GOD, help me to realize that there are greater victories in life than those which are won on the battlefield. Help me to be true to my best self. And wilt Thou, I pray, govern that self that it may be empowered and directed by Thine own self.

Keep the loved ones at home safe from harm. Help them to keep home fires burning, fires of love and faith. Be with them to share good and bad news, Thou who dost weep with those who weep and who dost rejoice with those that do rejoice. And strengthen us all to do Thy will. For the Master's sake. *Amen.*

CLELAND B. MCAFEE
Noted Bible Teacher, Former Moderator, Presbyterian General Assembly

THE DESTRUCTION OF HATE

But now abideth faith, hope, love, these three: and the greatest of these is love.—1 Cor. 13:13 ARV

The history of human society has recorded the futility of hate. Hate dies with itself. At the longest it survives through only a few generations.

Hate cannot destroy hate, but love can and does. Not the soft and negative thing that has carried the name and misrepresented the emotion, but love that suffers all things and is kind, love that accepts responsibility, love that marches, love that suffers, love that bleeds and dies for a great cause—but to rise again.

"Love your enemies" is advice from Jesus that is difficult to understand; but surely no one truly loves his or her enemies who, to escape a bitter test, refuses to deny and resist the enemies' evil purposes. I would not love my enemies, I would not "do good to them that hate me," nor would I love God, if I consented to the destruction of freedom and democracy. If we save freedom and democracy for ourselves, they shall be for our enemies as well.

OUR HEAVENLY FATHER, we do not ask to be delivered from dangers and burdens, but we do pray for wisdom, courage, and power. Strengthen us as is our need. May we be good citizens and true Christians in all things. May we be loyal to the royal in our own spirits. Throughout our lives may we be precious in Thy sight and received then unto Thyself. In Christ's name. *Amen.*

DANIEL A. POLING
Baptist Temple, Philadelphia, Pa.

GOD NEEDS YOU

As my Father hath sent me, even so send I you.—John 20:21

In the temple once, long ago, Isaiah beheld the holiness and majesty of God. As a result, his own heart and lips were cleansed, for this happens when we see Him. Then he heard God's voice: "Whom shall I send, and who will go for us?" And the thought filled his mind—"God needs me; God needs *me*." Pushed forward by it, he volunteered—"Here am I, send me." And God sent him, to comfort us, to give us great ideals, to preach the judgments of a just and holy God.

Christ needs you. In certain places even He must fail unless you are true to Him. E. Stanley Jones, his schooling completed, bade his sick mother good-bye and went to India, impelled by one idea—"Christ needs me." Today Christ would mean little to thousands of people, if He had not had E. Stanley Jones. "Christ needs me," said Albert Schweitzer. He resigned his professorship at Strassburg University, took a four-year medical course, then went down to Lambarene, in the French Congo in Africa. Here Christ had meant nothing to multitudes until Albert Schweitzer came.

Does Christ need you and me? He does, right where we are. And faithfully trying to serve Him, we shall hear the whisper, "Fear thou not, for I am with thee; be not dismayed, for I am thy God."

O LORD, be with me this day, and help me to contribute worthily to the beauty and the moral triumph of the lives around me. *Amen.*

SAMUEL W. MARBLE
Trinity Methodist Church, Denver, Colo.

A SACRAMENTAL PERSONALITY

And for their sakes I dedicate myself.—John 17:19 (CENTENARY)

To live hopefully and courageously today is not easy. To do so, a man must dedicate himself to something beyond his own little self. After all, a life that ends with self has a belated and shallow philosophy upon which it is founded. These are hours in which eternities are compressed, and none of us can afford to live superficially.

In a conversation with a patient who had been desperately ill in a great city hospital, one of the highest tributes was paid a young Christian gentleman who moved about the city with quiet dignity. The patient said something like this: "It was necessary for me to have a transfusion of blood. My husband, whose blood had been used before, being too far away for the immediate need, Mr. W— generously gave his blood to save my life. If I were to choose the person whose blood should go into my veins to bring new life, I know of no one whose blood I had rather have than his. His Christian life has been an inspiration and his influence a benediction."

What compensation for having lived a pure life! What convincing proof that it pays to keep one's life well poised and properly disciplined. All real men and women are now being called upon to make sacrifices that cost. In the ultimate, whatever one's gift may be, the sum total will be worth no more than the inner qualities of one's personality.

> God, give me sympathy and sense,
> And help to keep my courage high;
> God, give me calm and confidence,
> And—please—a twinkle in my eye. *Amen.*
> —MARGARET BAILEY

HOWARD P. POWELL
Dilworth Methodist Church, Charlotte, N.C.

OUR CONFIDENCE IN GOD

Have not I commanded thee? Be strong and of a good courage; be not afraid, neither be thou dismayed: for the Lord thy God is with thee whithersoever thou goest.—Josh. 1:9

These words came to Joshua in a crucial hour. *Command:* "Have not I commanded thee?" Joshua was entrusted with a great mission. God commanded him to face the perils and opportunities of the present, to go forward and possess the land. He was told to read the Bible, meditate daily upon its truth, and "to do according to all that is written therein."

Courage: "Be strong and of a good courage." God gives courage. Moral courage and spiritual intrepidity are even more important than physical bravery. Such courage is rooted in faith in God. The person who has committed his soul, his sins, his life, his destiny into the keeping of Jesus Christ, the Captain of his salvation, has a fighting courage, a Christian optimism, and a victorious faith. Christ will give us courage to confess Him, to do our duty, and overcome ourselves and the world.

Companionship: "For the Lord thy God is with thee whithersoever thou goest." Jesus said: "I am with you always." He is above us—to guard. He is underneath us—to support. He is before us—to lead. He is at our right hand—to protect. He is within us—as Companion and Comforter. He never leaves us nor forsakes us. He is faithful who promised. "He is here. I know Him. He knows me. It is the realest thing in the world."

ALMIGHTY GOD, our heavenly Father, we thank Thee for life; and that in Jesus Christ, Thy Son, we have spiritual life, abundant and eternal. Help us to put our whole trust in Thee. Forgive our sins and make us more than conquerors. Grant us courage to do Thy will, in Jesus' name. *Amen.*

FRANCIS SHUNK DOWNS
First Presbyterian Church, Berkeley, Calif.

A CHALLENGE TO YOUTH

Remember now thy Creator in the days of thy youth.—Eccles. 12:1

The preacher of the Book of Ecclesiastes was an unusual man, and I think not very popular in his generation, at least for most of his days. He was not a preacher in the modern sense in any case; he was a thinker, a philosopher, a writer. In his own early days he seems to have tried all manner of pleasure and to have found very little happiness as a result. His conclusion, as a result of his experiences, was, "Vanity of vanities; all is vanity." He tried this business of eat, drink, and be merry, and to hang with morals and religion. The only trouble with the formula, he discovered after a while, was that he wasn't merry—he was anything but merry.

So this man turned back to God; and, having turned back, he found happiness which had escaped him heretofore. In the last lovely chapter of Ecclesiastes you have some of the finest prose poetry in the Bible. Yes, and you have some of the soundest religion. Youth is the time to remember God and to find strength and blessing and happiness in Him.

The fear of God is that which makes a man unafraid in the face of every peril and danger that life has to offer. The Puritans of old England were the greatest fighting men of their generation. No enemy ever saw the backs of Cromwell's Ironsides, because those psalm-singing, Bible-reading soldiers feared God and Him alone. In His fear is wisdom, strength, and courage for time and for eternity.

GRACIOUS GOD AND FATHER, strengthen the arms and warm the hearts of all those who turn unto Thee in humility and with sincerity. Create in the hearts of young men and women an abiding love of Thy truth, a steadfast courage to defend Thy law, a loyal devotion to Thy Son, our Lord. In His name we ask it. *Amen.*

JOHN CURRY WALKER
Second Congregational Church, Waterbury, Conn.

TO GREET THE MORN

*My voice shalt thou hear in the morning, O Lord; in the morning will
I direct my prayer unto thee, and will look up.*—Ps. 5:3

Every Christian finds at least three suggestions in these words for his own practice of the presence of God—namely, a time, a manner, and an attitude.

When the day is fresh and new, before the common cares have placed their burdens upon me, and before the daily temptations have lessened the sensitiveness of my soul, I come into the vitalizing atmosphere of the fellowship of the Father. "My voice shalt thou hear in the morning."

It is a serious matter to come into the presence of God. Believers will organize their minds that they may be definite and exact as they present their petitions to the Creator of all. Careful selection should be made that their words may be well chosen. This is rifle work. The target must be clearly defined. They will not choose carelessly, but, "I will direct my prayer unto thee."

My privilege does not end when I have chosen the morning hour and have directed my prayer to God. The answer is yet to come. With my heart full of confidence, "I will look up," or, as the Revised Version gives it, "I will keep watch." These three valuable suggestions will make my devotional moments most valuable. I am responsible for my time, my manner, and my attitude in the presence of God.

BLESSED LORD, may we remember that our prayers will avail when Thou art graciously willing to "consider my meditation." Thou hast no pleasure in wickedness; therefore, we humbly repent of all sin. We are conscious of the multitude of Thy mercies; therefore, we express our gratitude. May the prayer we voice to Thee be definite; may we look up with expectation; and may we be guided in thy righteousness. In Jesus' name. *Amen.*

E. C. McCOWN
Mount Lebanon United Presbyterian Church, Pittsburgh, Pa.

FIGHTERS ARE NOT HATERS

Love your enemies, bless them that curse you, . . . and pray for them which despitefully use you.—Matt. 5:44

If we believe that Jesus Christ is our Lord and Savior, everything He has to say has a meaning for us. Yet it may seem strange, in the midst of war, to read what He has to say about hating others, particularly our enemies. But read again what He says in the text above. Can we do that and still be soldiers? We can.

First, because we are not fighting people; we are fighting ideas, ideas which are evil and which cannot exist in the same world in which the ideas that made America are to be found.

Second, because one of the greatest soldiers this country ever produced did it. That was Robert E. Lee. Shortly after the Civil War ended he was telling of the grief he felt over the spirit of hatred that possessed so many of those in the South. He was asked, "But did you never feel resentment toward the North?" The answer came in quiet tones, "I believe I may say, looking into my own heart, and speaking as in the presence of God, that I have never known one moment of bitterness or resentment."

Certainly he proved a soldier, one of the best that his country ever produced. The men who fought against him as well as the men who fought under him testify to that. But he also showed that a soldier can be a Christian and not hate, even those against whom he must wage battle.

OUR FATHER, as I go into battle help me to fight as bravely as the heroes of old. Help me to meet treachery with coolness, to wage war against evil with the spirit of goodwill. Help me to be generous to fallen foes whether or not they would be generous to me. Keep me from rashness, and especially keep me from hate. This do I ask in the name of my Captain, Jesus Christ. *Amen.*

WILLIAM E. BROOKS
First Presbyterian Church, Morgantown, W.Va.

ESTABLISHED PEOPLE

He shall not be afraid of evil tidings: his heart is fixed, trusting in the Lord.—Ps. 112:7

Are you established like the North Star? Sailors find their way across trackless seas because this star is fixed. Families, peoples, nations find their ways through periods of unrest, uncertainty, and tragedy because some people's hearts are fixed.

Our God is the Father of Lights with whom there is no variableness, neither shadow that is cast by turning. Those whose hearts are fixed, "trusting in the Lord," are established people. Can you say this minute with the sweet singer of the Fifty-seventh Psalm: "My heart is fixed, O God; my heart is fixed"? How do you suppose his heart got that way? It was captured by the goodness and greatness and compassion of the Eternal God. To know God is to love Him: and to "love the Lord thy God with all thy heart, and with all thy soul, and with all thy mind, and with all thy strength" is to be established and therefore unafraid of evil tidings.

Take time right now, therefore, wherever you may be, whatever the circumstances, to give God your whole heart. Then you will know what the psalmist knew when he said, "God is our refuge and strength." It is such a short way to God if you go down the right road. That which will make you a great soldier or sailor or flyer will be the putting on of the whole armor of God and having done all to stand. Be an established person by closing in with the Eternal God.

O ETERNAL GOD, our Rock in a weary land, our Fortress, our great High Tower, we turn now to Thee. Thou hast sought us and Thou hast found us. We need Thy love and Thy calm breath in our souls to be a fountain of strength. Give unto us to be established in eternal truth and righteousness. *Amen.*

PAUL CALHOUN
First Presbyterian Church, Spokane, Wash.

THE PURE ARE STRONG

Blessed are the pure in heart: for they shall see God.—Matt. 5:8

When a young girl left home to attend an art school, her mother gave her just one bit of advice. "Mary," she said, "always love beauty." Think what it means to love beauty in speech, in friendship, and in reading. If that were always true, vulgarity would disappear, wrong companions would automatically be ruled out, and at least one half of the current magazines would go out of print. "Who walks with beauty has no need of fear."

It is a current practice to poke fun at purity as though it were something of which to be ashamed. It is not a mark of weakness but of strength. Tennyson wrote that purity multiplies our strength by ten. "The pure heart is the strong heart, because it is not weakened by inner compromise."

It should be noted that purity is more than innocence. We have to grow in purity. Growth there is of greatest importance. Our problems come not from weakness of mind but of morals.

Purity is your most valuable possession. Never let life rob you of that. Cyrano de Bergerac met many temptations, and that is what makes his last speech so significant:

> Yet, in spite of you,
> There is one crown I bear away with me.
> One thing without stain,
> One thing unspotted from the world, in spite of doom
> Mine own! And that's—My white plume.

FATHER IN HEAVEN, Source of beauty, strength, and truth; help me by Thy Holy Spirit to be pure in heart, that I may see Thee. In the name of Jesus Christ. *Amen.*

ROY L. MINICH
First Church in Malden, Malden, Mass.

FAITH FOR OUR TIMES

Father, if thou be willing, remove this cup from me: nevertheless, not my will, but thine be done.—Luke 22:42

There are three ways to meet the experiences ahead of you. First, in a dull stupor, letting apprehension wear you down. "He came unto the disciples, and found them sleeping for sorrow." You can steel yourselves until you have no feeling toward anything that comes your way.

Or, you can run away from unpleasantness; like Scarlett O'Hara in *Gone with the Wind*, you can say in each crisis, "I will not think of this today; I will think of it tomorrow." "Then all the disciples left him, and fled." Fear is the most devastating of emotions. It makes the pit of the stomach hollow; it drives sleep from our eyes; it exhausts us like a fever.

There is a third way to meet life, however difficult it may be: you can pray that it may be as pleasant as possible. "Father,. . . . let this cup pass from me." Then you can take each event in faith—"not my will, but thine, be done"—and make it an instrument of discipline to bring out the best in you, like a hard workout on the parade ground. You can say in all honesty, "I would not deliberately choose this way; but, since it has come, I will be its master and not its slave. I will let God do something for me in it." The Lord of life can turn floods into fertility and storms into refreshment for dry and thirsty ground.

Faith is the secret of this third way, which is the way Christ followed, and by which He turned His cross into a throne from which He rules in our Hearts.

HEAVENLY FATHER, Thou canst strengthen me for every experience; I am resolved to rely upon Thee, to believe even where I cannot see, to say, "Thy will be done," and in that prayer to be content. *Amen.*

CHARLES GERLINGER
First Congregational Church, Sioux Falls, S.Dak.

THE SECRET OF COURAGE

*Fear thou not; for I am with thee: be not dismayed; for I am thy God:
I will strengthen thee; yea, I will help thee; yea, I will uphold thee with
the right hand of my righteousness.*—Isa. 41:10

Personal courage is the positive manifestation of an inward alertness to the presence of God. The immensity of our lives depends upon the intensity of our faith in the power of God to see us through. In life's darkest moments, in the darkest moments of history, God has always spoken to those who were in tune with His infinite will. He is greater than any power which exists outside of His holy realm. The wicked way of humans may claim the battle today, and tomorrow, but the third day belongs to Him. The tragedy of the Cross is finally swallowed up in the victory of the Resurrection.

Wherever you may be this hour, be still for a moment. Listen to that voice which speaks with supreme authority; it is saying, "Fear thou not; for I am with thee: be not dismayed; for I am thy God: I will strengthen thee; yea, I will help thee; yea, I will uphold thee with the right hand of my righteousness." Yes, God is by your side; His spirit is anxious to dwell within you.

When you have found the secret of His presence, you are at the source of power which manifests itself through your life as courage. A courageous life is one that knows and accepts God's presence, and gives Him absolute right of way every day. His way, His will, is always the right way; it is the way up and out.

OUR FATHER, Thou hast made us for Thyself. We dare not try to live without Thy Holy Presence. Increase the spark of faith within us: that our lives may be guided by Thy wisdom, strengthened by Thy Spirit, and made victorious through the triumphant Kingdom. In the name of Thy Son. *Amen.*

O. JAMES SOWELL
University Place Christian Church, Oklahoma City, Okla.

WHAT GOD KNOWS

He needed not that any should testify of man; for he knew what was in man.—John 2:25

Nothing written of Jesus is more significant than this verse. Moffatt gives it: "He required no evidence from anyone about human nature; well did he know what was in human nature."

Yes, let us be sure, this is one thing Christ knows, or, if you please, God knows; He knows human nature. Jesus knew people, as a result of His own divine nature, and also as a result of His own struggle with life in His own temptations—a victorious struggle, to be sure, but nonetheless a struggle. Yes, God knows people. Perhaps Jesus had our base possibilities in mind when He said, "There will be wars and rumors of wars." No doubt He had our spiritual possibilities in mind when He said, "Pray . . . Thy Kingdom come. Thy will be done in earth, as it is in heaven."

Many modern playwrights and novelists have written only of the base human nature. A few have maintained the "Pollyanna" attitude toward it. But Jesus knew what was in us; He knew the depths to which we could sink, and He knew the heights to which we could rise. Let us be sure this present war is the result of our own thinking and living. God did not send this war. We brought it upon ourselves. Nevertheless, as long as we are human, there is still hope of a better world. For we are capable of goodness, mercy, and sacrifice. There is still hope. Begin in yourself. Think highly, live nobly, carry no spirit of revenge toward your enemies. As one person you may now begin to prepare for the world which is in the making.

OUR FATHER, Thou dost know what is in me. I cannot hide from Thee. Forgive the sins which always separate me from Thee, and which betray my best self. Inspire in me the courage to be that which by Thy grace is possible for me. *Amen.*

GEORGE R. DAVIS
First Christian Church, Chickasha, Okla.

THINK TO THANK

I will give thee thanks with my whole heart.—Ps. 138:1

The difference between the words "think" and "thank" is only a vowel. The two words are vitally related. One must "think" to "thank." Ingratitude is always the result of thoughtlessness.

There are several channels through which we may express our gratitude. First, there is the channel of prayer. God waits today for intercessors. The grieved amazement of heaven is expressed in that startling statement: "And he saw that there was no man, and wondered that there was no intercessor" (Isa. 59:16). What a challenge! God is willing, but He waits for intercessors.

Second, there is the channel of contentment. Among the products of the human mind there are no richer gems than those which have emanated from darkness. Some of the world's foremost books smell of prison damp. More than half of the great epistles of Paul were written from a dungeon. "Weeping may tarry for the night, but joy cometh in the morning" (Ps. 30:5).

Third, there is the channel of worship. We need a new vision of the greatness of God. Well for us if the passing of all that can pass will drive us to Him who cannot pass! The passing of the earthly for the receptive soul oftentimes means the dawn of the heavenly. Such a vision is needed today. We have lifted ourselves so high that we cannot see the Lord "high and lifted up." And because God is not thus lifted up today, worship and respect for the Sanctuary has become cheap and wearisome.

O LORD, look in pity upon our world today and heal its desolations. Send Thy comfort to those who suffer, whose lives are so devastated by war. Bear up the prisoners and the wounded, and have mercy on the dying. And grant to Thy people everywhere the gift of merciful love, that they may minister in Thy name to all the needy of the earth. *Amen.*

J. GEORGE DORN
Hollywood Lutheran Church, Hollywood, Calif.

SUNSET AND EVENING STAR

Jesus said unto her, I am the resurrection, and the life: he that believeth in me, though he were dead, yet shall he live.—John 11:25

In my seminary days, when I commuted between San Francisco and San Anselmo, seeing the sun set on the Golden Gate would put me in a pensive mood, and I often said to myself, "That evening star is rising yonder in the Philippines. Farther west lie Japan, China, Korea." I had never visited those lands. From personal contact I could not say that they existed. But I had missionary friends who had lived in them. I had their word for it that such countries existed beyond my sunset.

Now turn from earth's geography to heaven's horizon. Is there a land beyond life's sunset? This is an age-old question. We cannot escape the thought of death and life beyond. The keenest minds of all ages have held that there must be a land beyond life's sunset. The facts of life demand it. But not until Jesus came, died, and rose again could we be sure.

"I am the resurrection, and the life," He said; "he that believeth in me, though he were dead, yet shall he live." And again: "In my Father's house are many mansions . . . I go to prepare a place for you." We have His life, words, and resurrection for it. We know Him well enough through personal experience to trust Him fully. Let us live in the light, joy, and peace of our immortal hope through Jesus Christ our Lord.

ALMIGHTY GOD, our heavenly Father, from whom we come and unto whom we return, and in whom, while we tarry here, we live and move and have our being; we thank Thee for Jesus Christ, Thy Son our Savior, who hath brought life and immortality to light through the Gospel. Help us so to live that when our sunset comes we may "hope to see our Pilot face to face, when we have crossed the bar." *Amen.*

GEORGE HUNTER HALL
First United Presbyterian Church, Los Angeles, Calif.

THUS FAR—NO FARTHER

Blessed is the man that walketh not . . . —Ps. 1:1

Christianity is positive and negative. It could not be one without being the other. There is a strong "againstness" in every worthy character. Those who are "for" something must necessarily be "against" its opposite. Our religion makes us confront choices between good and evil, and we cannot cast our vote for one without being negative toward the other. Those who say that they want only positives to live by fail to realize that every positive has its reverse side.

This is the discipline of Christian experience. It is always saying to us, "Thus far and no farther." Even the Ten Commandments are largely negative warnings; and the Master's teachings in the Beatitudes and in the whole Sermon on the Mount bring out God's great positives by showing what God is opposed to.

There have been as many definitions of character as there are definitions of religion. One collector gathered together a thousand such definitions. While they were marked by great variety, the one thing in common was this element of the negative. All great and strong people you can think of are known by the things they oppose. Their honesty means that they do not lie, cheat, or steal. Their purity means that they refrain from the counsel of the ungodly. Their positive acts of goodwill mean that they resist tendencies toward ill will. They are, in short, as negative as they are positive. As liberal-minded people they may go "thus far"; but as a people of sound Christian virtue they honor the sign, "no farther."

O LORD, keep our hearts from evil, and our lips from speaking guile. Help us to watch and pray lest we enter into temptation. And guide us in the way of all truth. In Jesus' name. *Amen.*

GEORGE M. GIBSON
United Church of Hyde Park, Chicago, Ill.

WILL YOU BREAK OR BEND?

I have learned the secret both to be filled and to be hungry, both to abound and to be in want.—Phil. 4:12 ARV

In a great art gallery in Europe I saw a famous painting of a frightful oncoming storm before which fled both horrified man and terrified beast. It reminded me of a fierce storm I had seen in the Rockies. The lightning flashed, the thunder roared, and torrents poured down upon the wind-swept forest. Some of the trees swayed and crashed under the strain, while others yielded to the wind but rose again when the storm was over. The former had broken; the latter had only bent.

Today fierce storms of greed and selfishness, war and famine, suffering and death, are sweeping over all the earth. Under the strain some will break, while others will only bend. Paul said that he knew how to bend: "I know how to be abased, and I know also how to abound: in everything and in all things have I learned the secret both to be filled and to be hungry, both to abound and to be in want." And he tells us the secret: "I can do all things in [Christ] that strengthened me." We can do that also, for "my God shall supply every need of yours according to his riches in glory in Christ Jesus."

In these testing days our faith in God's sustaining power will give us confidence; and, although we may bow to the inevitable, we shall not break.

The Lord's our Rock, in Him we hide,
A shelter in the time of storm.

O GOD, our gracious heavenly Father, we are grateful for the many blessings which Thou hast so lovingly lavished upon us. Today we need Thy love in our hearts so that, whatever may befall us, Thy peace "which passeth all understanding" may guard our "hearts and minds through Christ Jesus." *Amen.*

JOHN NEWTON GARST
First Baptist Church, Schenectady, N.Y.

THE WAY OF LIFE

Incline your ear, and come unto me: hear, and your soul shall live; and I will make an everlasting covenant with you, even the sure mercies of David.—Isa. 55:3

God made us for Himself. Estranged from Him, deprived by our own selfishness of His companionship, we are never going to feel at home. We shall be swept by recurring tides of loneliness and restlessness. We may wander far, we may exhaust ourselves with labor or excesses, but we shall not find peace.

We shall seek for satisfaction and shall find it not. There is no satisfaction for the river save in the ocean, no satisfaction for the finite save in the arms and care of the Infinite. Hence there can be neither joy nor happiness apart from God. The apples of appetite and pleasure turn to ashes in our grasp.

God made us for Himself. He made us to live in an infinite world, to catch gleams of new glory and hear new tones of wonder, and every day to find something new and entrancing. True life finds its real meaning and glory in a daily companionship with Christ, the Eternal Word. He is for all people the Way, the Truth, the Life.

O CHRIST OF GOD, grant us this day a sense of Thy presence. May we know that Thou art with us. In this companionship may we find strength for our tasks, safety from evil, courage for the day, and a divine splendor for the road we must travel. *Amen.*

WILLSIE MARTIN
Wilshire Methodist Church, Los Angeles, Calif.

THE TELLTALE MARKS OF A CHRISTIAN

Whatsoever things are true, . . . honest, . . . just, . . . pure, . . . lovely, . . . of good report; if there be any virtue, . . . any praise, think on these things.—Phil. 4:8

A scientist once intrigued the art world by declaring that certain paintings accredited to Leonardo da Vinci were not from his brush. Students, after the custom of the day, would inscribe the name of their master, with no thought that patrons of art would ever care. The scientist later discovered that the genuine canvases bore intricate insignia which became the telltale marks of a real da Vinci.

The telltale marks of a Christian are not superimposed insignia, but inextricable parts of life itself. The apostle Paul has listed them. "Whatsoever things are true." In the long run, it matters little what others say or think; it matters a great deal whether or not truth stands. "Whatsoever things are honest." A Laconian maid, being sold as a slave, was approached by a prospective buyer. "If I purchase you," he asked, "will you be honest?" "I'll be honest whether you buy me or not," she replied. "Whatsoever things are just, pure, lovely." That which is just will be pure, and that which is pure is bound to be lovely. "Whatsoever things are of good report." It is easy to destroy by evil and by wrong reporting. It is noble to extend the influence of goodness by bearing witness to it.

What we think, we are. Paul knowingly said, "If there be any virtue, any praise, think on these things."

O LORD, clear our vision, open our ears, and awaken our minds that we may see Thee, hear Thee, and know Thy voice. May the wondrous thought that we can dwell in Thee by faith never cease to excite our minds. And by the power of noble thinking, may we be transformed into reflecters of divine light. *Amen.*

WENDELL L. MILLER
University Methodist Church, Los Angeles, Calif.

THE STRENGTH THAT COMES FROM GOD

It is God that girdeth me with strength, and maketh my way perfect.
—Ps. 18:32

As never before, the world needs strength that binds us together in a full consciousness of victory. The apostle Paul speaks of that spirit when he says, "I can do all things through Christ which strengtheneth me." Likewise, the psalmist says, "It is God that girdeth me with strength." Without that consciousness of the power of God in our lives we cannot but fail, but with it we rise to our full height.

Yea, we rise to the height of the Man Christ Jesus, and go out to tackle the task of the day in the fullest assurance that we shall win a triumph in our own life over every impediment that stands in our way. Moreover, as never before do we need an awareness that God is binding us together with all others of like spirit for the winning of a victory for humankind. It is in that strength that we look to God today for courage and faith.

To be sure, it is not always easy to recognize the presence of God and the perfect way of life. The clouds of doubt eclipse this vision at times, but in the strength of prayer and in that faith that was Christ's we see beyond these dark moments to the day of our deliverance. We look for that time of peace and victory through Him who is our eternal Strength. Our prayer, then, for the day is that we may sense God girding us with His power, and revealing to us a way of service and happiness.

ETERNAL GOD, we look to Thee for Thy girding strength and for the revelation of the perfect way in this day of service. Enable us to maintain a calm and steady faith in ourselves because we believe that Thou art our Guide. We trust not in our own unaided judgment but look to Thee for that guidance which cometh from above. Make us strong in our attitude of trust; and in utmost simplicity may we cast ourselves on Thee. *Amen.*

THOMAS R. NIVEN
First Presbyterian Church, Omaha, Neb.

I HEARD THE VOICE OF THE LORD SAYING . . .

Then I heard the voice of the Lord saying, "Whom shall I send? And who will go for us?" And I said, "Here am I. Send me."

—Isa. 6:8 NIV

I used to think this verse was about a special call spoken only to the chosen few. God called her; she went. God called him; he said, "Yes." Then I wondered, "How many people were in the temple that day?" And I imagined hundreds, maybe more. In addition to the priests and Levites, people were in the temple night and day. To just be there was no big deal; to hear from God was something entirely different.

Then there was Isaiah. Not only was he there, physically present in the temple, but he really listened for God. Jacob said, "Surely the Lord is in this place, and I was not aware of it" (Gen. 28:16 NIV). How often are we in the presence of the One True God speaking to us, and we don't even hear His voice?

You see, God showed up—God was in the house!—and no one but Isaiah was aware of it! The question isn't, "Why doesn't God choose me?" but rather, "When God calls me, will I be listening?"

MY GOD, teach me to hear Your voice. It is You I desire—nothing and no one else. Let me hear You so I can say, "Yes," too! *Amen.*

STEVE VENABLE
Director of Ministry
Ceta Canyon Methodist Camp and Retreat Center, Happy, Tex.

✝

ON PEACEMAKERS AND PEACEKEEPERS

Blessed are the peacemakers, for they shall be called the children of God.—Matt. 5:9

Peacekeeping is an important task often assigned to those who serve in the armed forces. In a world as fractured and tension-filled as ours, peacekeepers are vital to the protection of human life. Peacemaking, however, if we hear Jesus' invitation in the Beatitudes, is the vocation of all God's children. To claim our membership in God's human family, we are invited to be peacemakers and not simply peacekeepers.

Peacekeepers often stand between fighting factions, persons at odds with weapons and words, to preserve order. Peacemaking, on the other hand, arises first from God's grace within our human hearts and spirits. Peacemakers don't keep others apart—quite the contrary, peacemakers embody God's own invitation to relate, to work at communication, to acknowledge mutual and interdependent perspectives.

As children of God, we must honor our call to be peacemakers wherever we find ourselves each new day.

GOD OF PEACE AND RECONCILIATION, help me to acknowledge Your gift of deep peace in my own life by working for reconciliation among my sisters and brothers wherever I am. Give me courage to risk the security of my own space, that others might find safety in sharing themselves. And if it is Your will, grant the gift of reconciliation's peace to those who today live in fear and isolation. This I ask in Your Holy Name. *Amen.*

R. GERALD TURNER
President, Southern Methodist University, Dallas, Tex.

A GOD WHO LONGS FOR OUR RETURN

For my son was dead, and is alive again. . . .—Luke 15:24

The most wonderful short story in all of literature is the parable of the Prodigal Son. It is the story of a boy who thinks that he knows more about life than his father. The boy leaves home for the good life, only to find himself in a pigpen. The parable tells us many wonderful truths, but perhaps the most important is the image of God that Jesus gives to us.

God is not the one who is going to get us when we are bad. God is a loving, caring Father whose heart is broken when we leave and who is always eager for us to return home. I can picture the old father standing by the road, looking over the next hill with hope that this might be the day when his son will return home. And when the boy does come home, the father runs down the road to welcome him and to give him the symbols of family.

Hear the Good News. God loves us when we are sinners and always longs for our return.

LOVING FATHER, may I always know Your love for me and Your broken heart when I sin. In my times of wandering, may I always know Your eagerness for me to return to Your love. *Amen.*

WILLIAM P. MULLINS
St. Luke's United Methodist Church, Memphis, Tenn.

CHRISTIANITY IS AN ALL-OUT AFFAIR!

Amaziah did that which was right in the sight of the Lord, but not with a perfect heart.—2 Chron. 25:2

That was what they said of King Amaziah. He was a good king. He held the throne of Judah for twenty-nine years—a long enough reign for any king! But something was missing from his rule, some indefinable quality of character which left a mar upon those years. What was it? He had good intentions. He could work hard, and he did. But he never quite came up to the standard of royalty. He never mastered the art of decisive action. Whenever he set out upon a course of action, he was hounded by a question mark. "Amaziah did that which was right in the sight of the Lord, but not with a perfect heart."

Certainly this probes to the very heart of our modern dilemma. Are we not our own worst enemy? Are we, too, not pursued by old doubts whenever we try to do anything decisive? The greatest calamity that can strike our lives is the division of our loyalties, the undermining of our moral and spiritual certainties.

So pull yourself together! Make up your mind! Get a fast hold upon the things you believe, and then wade out into the day's tasks. No glances backward, no lingering regrets! Life, if it is worth living at all, is worth living valiantly, forthrightly, and with resolution. That's the way Christ lived it, and we still gasp for breath at the things He did. He stood for something, and all of Him was in it. What about you?

O GOD, grant this day, that I may take hold upon Thee; that so I may come away from the day's work with joy and victory in my heart. If today I must face physical pain, or strained nerves, or moral temptation, or spiritual distress, may I be strengthened by these, life's teachers. Thus, may I reach the sunset a stronger, kinder person, a worthier child of God. *Amen.*

EUGENE M. AUSTIN
Toga Baptist Church, Philadelphia, Pa.

STANDING UP UNDER THE PRESSURES OF LIFE

The Lord is my light and my salvation; whom shall I fear? the Lord is the strength of my life; of whom shall I be afraid?—Ps. 27:1

How can a man live under tension? How can he face difficulty, pain, and uncertainty with faith that does not fail, with convictions that do not compromise, and with courage that stands up under the strain of life?

As Christians we have a sense of being bound up with a divine goodness and love more potent and more lasting than the troubles that environ us. Christians have found God to be a divine reality, a precious companion, and therefore we can face anything that can happen to us in the universe. This is the essence of all genuine religious experience.

How can one do this? Find some affirmation of your Christian faith that you honestly believe. "The Lord is my light and my salvation; the Lord is the strength of my life." When you waken in the morning, let that statement be your first thought. Repeat it again and again, then and during the hours that follow, let it be the motif of your day's activities, the unlowered banner of your day's striving. Let it be the last thought before you sleep at night. This is not vain repetition. This is actually the procedure by which the faith you profess becomes the prevailing pattern of your inner emotional life. Just as repeated exercise strengthens your muscles, so repeated affirmations of faith give character to your life. Thus you can stand up under the pressures of life.

O GOD, who art man's refuge and strength, grant me insight to discern Thy will and courage to live as a child of Thine. May no inner impulse drive me to unworthy action and no pressure deflect me from loyalty to Thee. Grant me grace to face the future, and all that it holds, with faith. *Amen.*

HAROLD LEONARD BOWMAN
First Presbyterian Church, Chicago, Ill.

OUR ANCESTORS' GOD

Blessed is the nation whose God is the Lord.—Ps. 33:12

One of the really great heritages of the American people is the heritage of noble ancestry. It is with a spirit of just pride that we point to their achievements in the growth and development of our democracy. They blazed a new trail in a wilderness. This was done, not only with their axes as they carved roadways across the continent from the eastern seaboard to the Pacific Ocean, but also with their freedom-loving minds. They blazed a new trail with mind and heart as they laid the firm foundation for our "land of the free and home of the brave."

We must never lose sight of the fact that these men and women whom we honor were enabled to do great deeds because they had great faith. Their faith was in God. Belief in a God of justice and righteousness, a God of mercy and love, moved them to heroic deeds in the cause of freedom and liberty.

If we would preserve, extend, and perpetuate the ideals for which our fathers and mothers gave their all, then we too must be inspired by faith in their God. If the day should ever come when we should lose our God, if enough of the people of our land should definitely turn aside from His teaching, then would we also lose our own and our children's freedom. May the God of our ancestors inspire our lives to loyal service in protecting their ideals for those who shall come after us.

OUR ANCESTORS' GOD, Author of liberty—to Thee we pray. Give to us the courage of heart and will, the integrity of mind and soul, the drive of vision and purpose, with which Thou didst inspire those noble founders of our nation. May we, by the guidance of the Holy Spirit, give ourselves as completely to the work of preserving freedom and liberty as they gave themselves to the task of establishing it. *Amen.*

I. LYND ESCH
First United Brethren Church, Los Angeles, Calif.

BIFOCAL SOULS

*The Lord's compassions fail not. They are new every morning; . . . It
is good that a man should both hope and quietly wait for the salvation
of the Lord.*—Lam. 3:22–23, 26

I used to have two pairs of glasses. With one of them I could read fine
print, but when I looked up the vision was blurred. With the other I
could safely drive my car, but could not make out bold letters on a page.
Now I have bifocals. I am deeply grateful to Benjamin Franklin, who first
invented them. My sense of awe at this discovery will wear dim as I grow
older, but I hope never to lose my determination to live a bifocal life. I
want to be able to look down into all the harsh realities of life; but I want
to be able to look up toward the eternal purposes of God.

There was once a man named Jeremiah who had a bifocal soul. He
surrendered his life to the cause of the right. He turned away from family,
from fortune, from friendship, and spoke out boldly as from the Lord. They
burned his writings, lashed his back, pilloried him in the stocks, cried out
that he preached just what their enemies approved. For forty-one years he
bravely kept on in the midst of this spiritual conflict. No miracle came to
support his claims; no fulfilled prediction justified his words; but he kept
on, winning only a handful of believers.

Jeremiah was not afraid to look down. But he knew how to look up.

Join the ranks of those who live bifocal lives. Look down, frankly and
boldly, into all the trouble of the world. Spare yourself no part of terrible
reality. Then look up. Hope, and wait patiently, for the salvation of the Lord.

O Lord, Grant us courage for the conflict,
　　　Patience for the long striving,
　　　Love enough to forgive. *Amen.*

BERNARD C. CLAUSEN
First Baptist Church, Pittsburgh, Pa.

IN THE NAME OF CHRIST

*Whatsoever ye do, in word or in deed, do all in the name of the Lord
Jesus, giving thanks to God the Father through him.*—Col. 3:17 ARV

Christ is set forth as a way of life for us all. Christ dies again in every
person who dies to the lusts of the world; He is buried again in every
person for whom uncleanness, passion, covetousness cease to exist; He is
resurrected again in every person who lives the unselfish life, the life of
service, the life of love. The moral and spiritual life becomes for us not
merely an ethical effort on our part but the living presence of Christ in us.

Christ Jesus is an experience and not a mere historical figure. A vast
multitude of men, women, and children bear witness to that fact. They have
put their trust in Christ, not in themselves; they have let Him enter their
lives and, to their amazement, they have found that He has entered theirs
as a great tide comes into the bay and lifts every ship to higher levels.

Who of us does not need strength for the struggle of life? It is our
common experience that what we would do, we do not; what we would
not, that we do. Peter the Great said that he could conquer cities but was
unable to conquer Peter. Paul, the follower of Jesus, after uttering the same
thought concerning his own need for self-mastery, exclaimed in gratitude
for victory: "I thank God through Jesus Christ our Lord."

O GOD, who alone can uphold our wills, consecrate our lives to Thy will,
giving us such purity of life, such strength of faith, such steadfastness of
purpose that we do not fall, or having fallen may rise again and stand erect
as children of God and brothers and sisters of Jesus Christ. *Amen.*

JOHN HOWARD MELISH
Church of the Holy Trinity, Episcopal, Brooklyn, N.Y.

OUR PRAYER AND GOD'S ANSWER

Draw nigh to God, and he will draw nigh to you.—Jas. 4:8

In less fearful hours than these, we could perhaps think of prayer as something to be argued about, or to be remembered wistfully but kept carefully back among childish things. Now it becomes overnight something to live by and to die by. How long is it since you really prayed? Or waited wordlessly in the silence for a wordless but wondrous answer to your barely breathed desire? You may need strength, courage, calmness in amazing measure; and you may need them very suddenly. I suggest that you get on speaking terms with God at once—not so much that He may hear your cry, as that you may recognize His answer.

His answer will be to give us inward assurance that we are really safe in Him. In these days what we really need is not so much refuge from outward hurt as it is refuge in the deep security of God. A letter came to me some years ago. It bore this declaration: "If we're safe on the inside, we're safe on every side." It is true. Those who "dwelleth in the secret place," those who are "under the shadow of the Almighty"—they are really safe. Let your life be hid in the life of God. The person has not been born and the weapon has not been forged that can harm your life if you hide it there. "Father, into thy hands I commend my spirit." If faith anything like that can be ours, all will be well.

O GOD, increase the spirit of neighborliness among us, that in peril we may uphold one another, in calamity serve one another, in suffering tend one another, and in homelessness, loneliness, or exile, befriend one another. Grant us brave and enduring hearts, that we may strengthen one another, till the disciplines and testings of these days be ended, and Thou dost give again peace in our time. Through Jesus Christ our Lord. *Amen.* (Used in England during the fearful experiences of 1940.)

BOYNTON MERRILL
The Second Church, Congregational, West Newton, Mass.

I WILL LIFT UP MINE EYES

I will lift up mine eyes unto the hills, from whence cometh my help. My help cometh from the Lord, which made heaven and earth.—Ps. 121:1–2

The psalmist was living through trouble-filled times much like these through which all of us are now passing. In the text above he calls to his own soul, and to the souls of his embattled, tempted, and bewildered people, to look up toward the strength, the help, the keeping power which never failed nor was ever diminished, and which no circumstance or condition could overwhelm. It was a power adequate for every need, and always available to all men. "I will lift up mine eyes unto the hills"—yes, and beyond the hills to Him who "made heaven and earth," for "my help cometh from the Lord." Nothing can defeat one with such a source of power.

The chief business of all of us is to keep life "unspotted from the world," "to walk uprightly" to be worthy of Him "who loved us and gave himself for us." To do this we need to lift up our eyes, our hearts, and our minds, above the surrounding temptations to Him "who was tempted in all points like as we, yet without sin." We need to see Him who is "our rock and our salvation."

And how many and how valuable the promises that He makes. "He will not suffer thy foot to be moved." "The Lord is thy keeper." "He shall preserve thy soul." "The Lord shall preserve thy going out, and thy coming in." Our resolve should be to lift up our eyes, our souls, our faith, and our love, to the Lord from whom cometh our help, for victorious living. Prove Him. Put Him to the test. He has never failed those who in faith come unto Him.

O LORD, it is for this day's needs we pray. Tomorrow, when it becomes today, we will repeat this petition. So, Lord, only for today would we pray. Keep us today, fit for life at its best, fit to be numbered in Thy family as Thine own children. *Amen.*

JOHN H. COWAN
Westminster Presbyterian Church, Cincinnati, Ohio

HOPE FOR THE FUTURE

He will smite the ruthless with the rod of his mouth.
—Isa. 11:4 (SMITH-GOODSPEED)

In the eleventh chapter of Isaiah there is expressed the longing of humanity for an order of society in which justice, fair dealing, cooperation, and peace shall prevail. This seems almost an idle dream in such a time of war as this. But we are engaged in this struggle in order that such a dream may be brought closer to realization.

We are fighting against injustice, oppression, and cruel exploitation. And if we will only open our eyes and look around us, we will realize that even in the midst of war, peoples who have largely been strangers to each other have been drawn together as allies in the common struggle. Citizens of many countries are united in a common purpose to stop aggression and create a more just social order in the world.

Never before in the history of the world have so many people stood side by side in a great endeavor. The number of those who are with us is far greater than those who are against us. We are now united because we fight the same enemy. If the newly united force is to prevail and continue cooperation after the war, we must be held together by a common religion and a common morality. Even as we struggle we must pray that the knowledge of God, the Father of all people, shall cover the earth as the waters cover the sea. And someday even our present enemies may be included in that unity.

GOD, give to us hope as we struggle, that we may be made sure that our struggle is not in vain. May our fight for the downtrodden bring freedom and justice for the masses of earth as well as ourselves. *Amen.*

GORDON POTEAT
Crozer Theological Seminary, Chester, Pa.

THE HERO IN THY SOUL

Finally, my brethren, be strong in the Lord, and in the power of his might.—Eph. 6:10

In times like these we have need of words that will sound the trumpets within our souls. What better words than those of Nietzsche: "I charge thee, throw not away the hero in thy soul."

But we need more than courageous words. Without God all this talk about heroism amounts to little more than an attempt to lift ourselves by our own bootstraps. The encouragers of the race, by handling their own lives well and by working for a better world in face of the most stubborn opposition, have been those who like the psalmist could say of the Eternal, "He restoreth my soul," or like Paul, "Not that we are sufficient of ourselves . . . but our sufficiency is of God."

People are sometimes led to overlook this important fact because it is not so obvious as the heroic deeds themselves. The church has so magnified the cross on Calvary's hill where a heroic deed was done that many people have lost sight of Gethsemane where our Lord tapped the resources of inner power. No Gethsemane, no Calvary!

"I charge thee, throw not away the hero in thy soul"—great words those; but when we are looking for help that will enable us to express the latent hero in our soul, we would do well to look, not to Nietzsche, who was an unbeliever, but to a man like Paul whose secret was best expressed; "Finally, my brethren, be strong in the Lord, and in the power of his might."

O LORD, Thou knowest how weak and cowardly we can be when confronted with new tasks and surrounded by dangers which appear the more threatening because uncertain. Breathe into us thine own Spirit, O God, and make us strong. We pray in His Spirit who was more than conqueror. *Amen.*

HERBERT C. KIMMEL
First Congregational Church, Janesville, Wis.

COURAGE THAT CONQUERS

*Fear thou not; for I am with thee: be not dismayed; for I am thy
God.—Isa. 41:10*

Following a summer conference a college girl remarked, "I have gained
hundreds of new ideas; what I want now is courage to put a single one
of them into operation in my life." We all know what she meant.
Knowledge is one thing, but the power to turn fine learning into great
living is something else.

Yet if we are to be true to our best selves and become supremely useful
to our generation, we must all find such courage somewhere. Something
deep within us says that William James was right when he said: "Mere
ideals are the cheapest things in life. The more ideals a man has the more
contemptible he is if the matter ends there, if there is no courage shown,
no privations undergone, no scars contracted in the effort to get them
realized." Scars and danger for freedom's sake many of us are now risking,
with our patriotism kindling the needed courage.

So devotion to God breeds indispensable spiritual courage. "When they
saw the boldness of Peter and John . . . they took knowledge of them, that
they had been with Jesus." *With Jesus*—the secret lay there! Strong faith nour-
ished by vital fellowship with Him made them fearless; and with such courage
born of communion we too, against our foes of the spirit, can win today.

O GOD OUR FATHER, we thank Thee for the unseen Power upon
which people of faith have called and become strong. Thou knowest the
fears which often rob us of poise, the weakness which often undermines
our will to serve Thee. Into Thy hands we give our spirits; nerve us for
those inward battles which make us stronger when we win them. Keep us
steadfast and true because in fellowship with Christ we have felt the pull
of His searching eyes and the glory of His incorruptible nature. *Amen.*

J. H. MARION JR.
Grace Covenant Presbyterian Church, Richmond, Va.

A SAFE REFUGE

The Lord is good, a stronghold in the day of trouble; and he knoweth them that trust in him.—Nah. 1:7

In speaking of Christ as the "Rock of Ages," the hymn writer Toplady says,

Other refuge have I none;
Hangs my helpless soul on Thee.

Three major ideas are to be found in the text:

First, "The Lord is good." Who can doubt the goodness of Him who has given us seedtime and harvest, who has painted the blue sky, the purple mountains, the green fields? Evil comes through humankind's transgression of God's laws. But God is able to save people and nations when they turn to Him and live in obedience to His precepts.

Second, "a stronghold in the day of trouble." We are safe when the Lord has a strong hold on us. He is a fortress into which we may retreat when we are beaten, from which we may sally when He has given us new courage.

Third, "he knoweth them that trust in him." He knows us by name among the countless millions of people whom He has created. The very hairs of our head are all numbered. What a wonderful Savior He has proved Himself to be. This day we believe that "the Lord is good, a stronghold in the day of trouble; and he knoweth them that trust in him."

OUR HEAVENLY FATHER, lead us through these perilous times into the safety zones which Thou hast established for those who follow Thee. Teach us to walk day by day in the ways of righteousness for His name's sake. *Amen.*

MYRON E. HAYES
First Methodist Church, Keokuk, Iowa

FOR PEOPLE LIKE THESE

And these all, having obtained a good report through faith, received not the promise: God having provided some better thing for us, that they without us should not be made perfect.—Heb. 11:39–40

It is a refreshing American custom to celebrate. It is good to pause even in critical times to celebrate the birthday of that crisis-created character, Abraham Lincoln.

Do not say, "He should be alive today." He is alive today! I have seen Abraham Lincoln in the solemn eyes of young America. I have seen Abraham Lincoln in the swinging stride of American leadership. I have heard Abraham Lincoln's throbbing voice in a radio address.

Ask a thoughtful person why we have to go down into the pit again to wrestle "against principalities, against powers, against the rulers of the darkness of this world, against spiritual wickedness in high places." He or she will answer, "For people like Abraham Lincoln." Their faithfulness and their dreams we must not forsake.

The old truth comes freshly to our new day. People like George Washington and Abraham Lincoln cannot without us be made perfect. The "certain inalienable rights" must be continually contested in order that our day and our coming day may be safe for "people like these."

Faith, the faith of our ancestors, is not something which we can be content merely to celebrate. It must be lived. Our ancestors' God must be rediscovered as our God, or all history will become profane. So, in days rich with promise but beset by adversaries we pray for personal and national faith and its first fruit—righteousness.

OUR ANCESTORS' GOD, Author of liberty, to Thee we sing; long may our land be bright with freedom's holy light; protect us by Thy might, great God, our King. *Amen.*

FREDERICK W. CROPP
Chaplain, Headquarters, Fort Monmouth, Red Bank, N.J.

YOUR LIFE A GIFT OF GOD

Stir up the gift of God, which is in thee.—2 Tim. 1:6

We all have unexplored riches within ourselves. Our Christian faith asserts that an individual is of value even to God. What powers are there unexplored? What possibilities lie there unexpressed? If we regard ourselves as "heels," we imprison these potentialities.

If we are willing to get by with mediocre effort, we have narrowed the channel of our service. Whatever may be one's condition in life, environment is not all there is to possibilities. There is the unmined ore of the inner life that may yield the gold of brilliant achievement and sturdy quality. These gifts are from God. Stir up the gift that is within you.

O GOD, who dost know us better than we know ourselves; teach us to trust Thy faith in us, that daily we may stir up the gift within which Thou hast made to us with such generosity. *Amen.*

MILTON M. MCGORRILL
Fountain Street Baptist Church, Grand Rapids, Mich.

OUR GOODLY HERITAGE

The lines are fallen unto me in pleasant places; yea, I have a goodly heritage.—Ps. 16:6

When it comes to riches and marvels of native land, when it comes to benefits and blessings, when it comes to rights and privileges, and when it comes to opportunities and possibilities, we, the people of these United States, have a goodly heritage—something we are in danger of forgetting, unless we remind ourselves of it from time to time, especially in view of the fact that there are some among us who are always finding fault with our country. We would be wiser and better citizens if we would spend more time in evidencing our appreciation of what we have and less time in complaining about what we do not have.

We have a goodly heritage geographically, vast oceans removing us from the rest of the world; a goodly heritage industrially, possessing abundant natural resources and productive factories; a goodly heritage racially, being a combination of many races and nationalities; a goodly heritage politically, being a democratic people with a democratic form of government, a goodly heritage culturally, knowing the value of good books, the fine arts, and good manners; and a goodly heritage spiritually, consisting of courage and faith and fortitude.

Our goodly heritage deserves the best defense we can accord it, the best industrial defense, the best political defense, the best moral defense, and the best spiritual defense. We shall do our best to prevent the crucifixion of our goodly heritage upon a totalitarian cross.

OUR HEAVENLY FATHER, we thank Thee for our country, for life, and liberty, and the pursuit of happiness: in a word, for our goodly heritage. May we be worthy of it. Help us to hand it down enriched and untarnished to those who shall come after us. In the name of Jesus. *Amen.*

OTTO C. SEYMOUR
First Presbyterian Church, Joplin, Mo.

ORDERS FROM HEADQUARTERS

Then the Spirit said unto Philip, Go near, and join thyself to this chariot.—Acts 8:29

"Then the Spirit said unto Philip, Go near, and join thyself to this chariot." It was an order from the Commander to a faithful soldier of Christ. Travel directed is necessary in the King's business. An old believer with rich experience once wrote: "God never sends any man forth at his own charges." Philip may have felt distressed to be called from a spiritually prosperous work to a desert, loneliness—and—nobody.

But notice how the desert has a man, one man, though a stranger, and a foreigner. He is the designated objective. Many of us are being pulled up and sent south, east, north, and over the sea. Let us remember that God has orders for each servant.

Notice that the stranger was prepared for Philip. God set the stage for Philip's dramatic arrival. So it was when Ananias was sent to Saul of Tarsus. "Behold, he prayeth" (Acts 9:11). There is more reason in our unanticipated movements and more preparation than we realize. Philip was sent on a "blind date." But the all-seeing eye of God was looking into the desert, and the man to meet Philip came.

He was reading God's word about the Savior. The ground was prepared. Beginning at that passage in Isaiah (chapter 53) Philip preached unto him Jesus, the Lamb of God, that taketh away the sin of the world. The stranger heard the divine call, accepted his Atoning Savior, and was baptized. He went away glad. Philip was ordered on. So God uses us in many places.

O LORD, grant that I may study Thy will in Thy Word and cheerfully do my duty as in Thy holy sight. Make me watchful for opportunities to tell others of Thy saving power in Christ my Savior. *Amen.*

STEWART M. ROBINSON
Editor, **The Presbyterian,** *Philadelphia, Pa.,*
Former Chaplain, U.S. Army

FORM YOUR BATTALIONS

Fear not; for they that be with us are more than they that be with them.—2 Kings 6:16

We are living in times that are disquieting and even terrifying. Our present civilization seems shaky and insecure. The world is constantly changing. Yet change is our hope as well as our danger. In a changing world so much depends upon the kind of people we are, the character we reflect. Dean Wickes of Princeton said, "It is well that this crisis should urge us to make the world over, but long before we can do this we can let this crisis make us over into the sort of people the world is going to need."

The need of the present hour has been challengingly expressed by one of the greatest of all Americans, Oliver Wendell Holmes. Alexander Woollcott tells of a visit which President and Mrs. Franklin D. Roosevelt made to the aged justice on the occasion of his ninety-second birthday, March 8, 1933, just after Mr. Roosevelt had been launched upon his first term as president. The retired justice was asked what advice he would give in view of the chaotic conditions. Mr. Holmes replied, "You're in a war. I have been in a war. There is only one thing to do in a war. Form your battalions, and carry the fight to the enemy." In just this same spirit we must mobilize every resource of God and humankind to ensure the coming of the Kingdom to earth.

ETERNAL GOD, in the midst of the ever-shifting human scene, teach us how to live in and with the strength of Christ. Help us to realize that beyond the near things that distract lie the eternal things that endure. Direct us in prayer to the place of vision that we may renew our faith and regain our power and poise of spirit. Grant us strength to defeat temptation and evil, thus helping to build a highway where all Thy people may walk together in liberty and virtue. In Thy holy name. *Amen.*

FORREST L. RICHESON
Portland Avenue Christian Church, Minneapolis, Minn.

BE STRONG

I am come that they might have life.—John 10:10

Once upon a time, says an old story, a young man left the village of "Nowhere" to be off to "Somewhere." He reached another village. He asked, "Is this Somewhere?" The villagers replied, "No, to get to Somewhere you must have a dream in your eye."

The ancient of the village put a dream in his eye, and he went on. Again he came to a village. "Is this Somewhere?" he asked. "No, if you are going Somewhere, you are on the road, but this is not Somewhere. You have a dream in your eye, but you must also have a voice in your ear."

The ancient of the village added a voice in the ear. The voice told him the great things that the ages had accumulated. On he went. Another village appeared on the horizon, and he quickened his pace. He asked the same question, "Is this Somewhere?" And the answer came back, "No, this is not Somewhere. Yet we see that you have a dream in your eye and a voice in your ear. Yet you still need a sword in the hand. With the sword you will win your way to Somewhere." The ancient of this village gave him a sword and he went on.

At the next village, which also proved not to be Somewhere, he was told that he was on the road but that he needed one last thing before he could really find Somewhere. He needed a song in the heart. So the ancient of that village gave him a song in the heart, a lilt for the road. He set forth and, equipped as he was, finally reached Somewhere.

To get Somewhere, to do something with our lives, vision, knowledge, and faith are all needed, and the courage that sings.

GOD, give us vision to see the magnitude of living and strength to meet the implications of our vision. In Jesus' name. *Amen.*

M. Joseph Twomey
North Orange Baptist Church, Orange, N.J.

THE LIGHT THAT NEVER FAILS

I am the light of the world.—John 8:12

Kipling's famous story *The Light That Failed* will last as long as our language is spoken. It tells of the artist Dick Heldar, who had been a war correspondent. In consequence of an old wound his eyes had been affected, and he was steadily going blind. He had only a few months in which to finish his masterpiece. Feverishly he bent himself to his work. There was no time to waste. In spite of the acute pains shooting through his head, the occasional lights flashing before his eyes, he kept doggedly on. Then one day the painting was complete. But things suddenly became dark. He asked his friend to turn on the lights, unwilling to admit what he knew had happened. Yet the blow had fallen. He was blind; the light had failed.

In another way, that is what seems to have happened to the world. We have seen one light of hope after another slowly go out. Some people, who have little faith in humankind and less in God, have abandoned all thought of a better time. We know differently. Christ is the Light of the World. The radiant light of His presence is seen by those who believe in His divine purpose and in His eternal grace. They are spending themselves to bring in that better day in which the darkness of despotism and tyranny shall be dispelled. Meanwhile, their own way is illuminated by the presence of the Great Comrade. They shall have light for their task. Christ cannot break faith. He is the Light that never fails.

O CHRIST, who art the Light of humankind, grant us the dear guidance that Thou alone canst give, that this day we may be kept true to Thee and to our duty. Through Thy Grace. *Amen.*

J. W. G. WARD
First Presbyterian Church, Oak Park, Ill.

A MATTER OF INTEREST

Where your treasure is, there will your heart be also.—Matt. 6:21

To many of us, Christianity's goals seem beyond our reach. "World peace" seems too high for us to reach by frontal attack. Suppose we come at it indirectly by taking an interest in people around us.

That was the significant thing about the Good Samaritan. He took an interest in a wounded man by the roadside. The priest and the Levite of the story were not bad people. They were disinterested men. Jesus' point seems clearly to be that His followers must take an interest in the welfare of others.

Our interests, then, are what make the wheels go round. Our "treasure" may be our country, our home, our spouse and children, the friend beside us. Whatever the treasure is, our interest in it will decide what we do. Our interests will also determine the kind of men and women we shall become.

For one thing, our interest in the welfare of others will bring out the best in ourselves. Heroes are those who are so interested in others that they forget themselves.

Again, people's interests indicate what they have chosen to live or die for. The most powerful interest is the interest in the welfare of people. Richard Cobden saved his friend John Bright at a time of great sorrow, when he said, "There are thousands of homes at this moment where wives, mothers and children are hungry. . . . I would advise you to come with me, and we will never rest until the Corn Law is repealed."

A life worth living is a matter of interests worth having.

O GOD, give us the will to seek Thee and the mind to know Thee, that finding Thee, we may serve Thee in ways which Thou wilt make plain before us, in Jesus Christ. *Amen.*

NORRIS L. TIBBETTS
Riverside Church, Baptist, New York City, N.Y.

THIS IS THE VICTORY

This is the victory that hath overcome the world, even our faith.
—1 John 5:4 ARV

The apostle Paul expended himself in tireless exertions for the Christ whom he had seen on the Damascus road, and for His sake endured hardships, shipwrecks, imprisonments and, at the last, death itself. His dauntless spirit was that of the conqueror who allowed nothing to down him. "I can do all things through Christ who strengtheneth me." Christ was the unseen Companion of his way, and Paul's faith never wavered.

Paul's faith was practical, enlisting head, heart, hand, and will. It was a faith by which to live, giving him singleness of purpose, songs in the night of prison, courage in the face of danger and death. His last word was one of victory, "I have fought the good fight, I have finished the course, I have kept the faith."

A worthwhile life is never easy. To conquer oneself, to win spiritual victory, to maintain courage and cheer in the face of disappointment, discouragement, and danger, is not easy. But such victory can be won through faith in the sustaining presence of Christ, "our refuge and strength, a very present help in trouble." He will never leave you nor forsake you. Keep the faith, for that is victory.

DEAR LORD, may I not be one who says, "Lord, Lord," and then fails to obey Thy command. Strengthen my faith that I may win the victory over temptation. Help me to live for Thee "a life that is true, striving to please Thee in all that I do." Bless my loved ones, and provide all things needful for them. *Amen.*

A. W. WEBSTER
First United Presbyterian Church, Pasadena, Calif.

TOUGHNESS

Keep alert, stand firm in your faith, be courageous, be strong.
—1 Cor. 16:13

Sometimes people speak of Christianity as though it were soft and weak. But usually they have not known Christians nor read the New Testament. For Christianity is not a way of dodging danger and suffering; it is a way of accepting hardship and calls for sacrifice. It is not so much a way of escape as the assurance that God is with you in the day of trouble. Jesus accepting silently the unjust sentence of death and the cruel abuse of the mob, Paul unwavering in his work for Christ in spite of beatings and prisons—these are models of manliness from the New Testament.

There have been others with courage to stand fast in their faith and be strong. In 1555 Nicholas Ridley and Hugh Latimer were burned at the stake because they would not change their faith as the court changed. As the executioner made ready, Latimer said to his friend, "Be of good cheer, Master Ridley, and play the man; we shall this day light such a candle in England by God's grace as shall never be put out." Kagawa, a Japanese Christian of our time, was arrested because of his Christian work. At first the police spoke of him as of any other prisoner; later they called him "Dr. Kagawa." He won their respect.

Holding to our deepest convictions, keeping our honor bright and our record clean in spite of everything, is a part of Christian toughness.

O STRONG SON OF GOD, help me to stand fast in my faith, to hold firmly to the right, to do my duty well, to be strong, that I shall never need to be ashamed before others or in Thy presence. *Amen.*

WILLARD W. STRAHL
First Presbyterian Church, Minot, N.Dak.

FIRST IN THE HEARTS OF HIS COUNTRYMEN

Let us lay aside every weight . . . and let us run with patience the race that is set before us.—Heb. 12:1

An inscription at Mount Vernon, the home of George Washington, reads:

Washington, the brave, the wise, the good,
Supreme in war, in council, and in peace.
Valiant without ambition, discreet without fear,
Confident without assumption.
In disaster, calm; in success, moderate; in all, himself.
The hero, the patriot, the Christian.
The father of nations, the friend of mankind,
Who, when he had won all, renounced all, and sought
In the bosom of his family and of nature, retirement,
And in the hope of religion, immortality.

Not all these statements may legitimately be applied to you and me. We won't be "supreme in war, in council, and in peace," or "father of nations." But in our own sphere we can come to merit the more important valuations of character: "the brave, the wise, the good"; "the hero, the patriot, the Christian"; "the friend of mankind."

Our American inheritance of great people is rich. Think also of Jefferson and of Lincoln—we have the privilege of following their high example. But let us go on to find our hero in the Greatest Example of all, "looking unto Jesus the author and finisher of our faith."

OUR FATHER, we would take as our example and our ideal Thy Son. Grant to us some measure of His courage and strength, His humility, His unselfishness, His faith in Thee. *Amen.*

MERRIMON CUNINGGIM
Emory and Henry College, Emory, Va.

GLORIFYING GOD IN SUFFERING

If any man suffer as a Christian, let him not be ashamed; but let him glorify God on this behalf.—1 Pet. 4:16

The Christian life is not an easy life. It may involve many kinds of experiences which are unpleasant and at times painful. It is this failure to see suffering as normal to discipleship which has caused many to doubt the worth of their faith. Jesus said, "Come unto me, and I will give you rest," and we come—for rest. He said, "I will not leave you comfortless," and we come—for comfort. Again He said, "These things have I spoken unto you . . . that your joy might be full," and we come—for joy.

But Jesus also said, "If any man will come after me, let him deny himself, and take up his cross, and follow me"—and then we hesitate. The Scripture says, "Christ also suffered for us, leaving us an example, that ye should follow in his steps." Suffering in itself is not necessarily virtuous. Peter says, "If ye suffer for righteousness' sake, happy are ye." An old spiritual gives expression to sound religion:

> Nobody knows the trouble I've seen,
> Glory hallelujah!

When suffering comes to us, whether it be in the form of loneliness, temptation, or physical distress, let us not be resentful, but rather thank God for the privilege of using our discomforts to grow by grace more into the likeness of Him who suffered upon the cross that we might be saved.

O CHRIST, when we see Thee agonizing in Gethsemane, suffering the humiliation of the crown of thorns pressed upon Thy sacred brow, and dying upon the cruel cross for our redemption, we pray that we may be more worthy of the privilege of following Thee. In Thy dear name we pray. *Amen.*

WILLIAM L. YOUNG
President, Park College, Parkville, Mo.

BEYOND FAILURE

I will lift up mine eyes unto the hills, from whence cometh my help. My help cometh from the Lord, which made heaven and earth.—Ps. 121:1–2

Jesus did not always win an immediate victory. When He led people to the hard upward path, some "went back, and walked no more with him." Jesus sometimes lost. But Jesus knew how to look unto the hills of difficulty and defeat and draw from these very hills strength of character and of purpose. His life was a constant series of crises. So is ours. A great ascending trail leads ever onward over mountains of trial and temptation.

To seek the valley of easy victory is to miss life's deepest meaning. It is to reject the enlargement of vision, the consciousness of new powers, the knowledge of our own limitations, the necessity of cooperation, and the flaming faith of dependence on God.

These come only from facing the hills of failure and frustration. If we desire to be men and women after the pattern of Jesus, our greatest help forward to that stature is not the valley of ease, but the hills of difficulty.

FATHER, we return thanks for the noble ideals which were established in this land by our forefathers; for the determination with which they sought to make those ideals permanent; for the heritage of free speech which they bequeathed to us; for the united nation which they preserved to their posterity; and for those towering figures whose lengthened shadow reaches even to the feet of those now living. Grant unto us, we beseech Thee, such a sense of the eternal values of our national ideals that we shall hasten to obey Thy voice, which calls us to render service for the preservation of these ideals in the earth. Lead us to be true stewards of our national trust, that we shall transmit this nation to our descendants not only not less, but far greater than it was transmitted to us. In Christ's name we pray. *Amen.*

HENRY DAVID GRAY
Oneonta Congregational Church, South Pasadena, Calif.

THE VOICE OF GOD

Speak, Lord; for thy servant heareth.—1 Sam. 3:9

Gallaudet College in Washington, D.C., was founded for the education of the deaf and mute. I have played football against that college. In the game when Gallaudet had the ball, all of the Gallaudet players looked at the quarterback and watched him signal with his fingers. When we had the ball our players listened to the quarterback and heard him signal with his voice. The Gallaudet players heard with their eyes. We heard with our ears. Both quarterbacks "spoke," but through a different medium.

So God speaks to us in different ways. Joan of Arc heard "voices"—even the voice of God—with her ears. Must we deny the experience of Joan of Arc simply because we have not heard God with our ears? Many people have heard God's voice through their eyes—they have seen a gardenia. Surely Joan of Arc would not deny the truth of their statement merely because she had heard Him with her ears.

We may say, then, that God speaks to us through our various senses—seeing, hearing, tasting, smelling, and feeling. We differ in the sense used, but the "Voice" is real.

We cannot deny these voices. This sentence by an unknown author appeals strongly: "If you and I cannot speak out of the richness of our spiritual experience to confirm this voice, surely we ought not to speak out of the poverty of our spiritual experience to deny it."

O DIVINE MASTER, grant that I may not so much seek to be consoled as to console; to be understood, as to understand; to be loved, as to love; for it is in giving that we receive, it is in pardoning that we are pardoned, and it is in dying that we are born to eternal life. *Amen.* (St. Francis of Assisi.)

ALBERT BUCKNER COE
First Congregational Church, Oak Park, Ill.

THE GUIDED LIFE

Our steps are made firm by the Lord, when he delights in our way.
—Ps. 37:23 NRSV

For generations people have believed that God guides His children through the days of life. This is the reason for morning devotions. A variety of experiences come to us in the course of a day, some of them delightful, some tragic. Thoughtful people begin each day conscious of possibilities.

Our God is the Creator of heaven and earth. And yet He is interested in all of His creatures. His greatness does not keep Him from considering the details of life; rather, it makes Him to plan the very steps of a person. "The eyes of the Lord run to and fro throughout the whole earth." Jesus said that the hairs of my head are all numbered, that not even a sparrow falls to the ground without the knowledge of our Father. If this be true, then may we not believe that God has a plan for each day? And we will be happy only in proportion as we fit into that plan.

What advantage we gain once we learn to live a day at a time. President Calvin Coolidge had a motto which he followed religiously: "Do the day's work." Do what lies at hand. Remember that each day will open its own program. God leads us day by day, and the duties of life come in divine order. Duties never conflict. The schedule of a Christian's life is so divinely perfect that it is beyond human explanation.

HEAVENLY FATHER, direct my steps this day that I may bear testimony for the Savior, that I may bring honor and glory to Thy name, that I may bring peace and comfort to the heart of some discouraged friend. In Jesus' name. *Amen.*

WALTER E. McCLURE
Memorial Presbyterian Church, St. Louis, Mo.

SOUL DEPTH

Deep calleth unto deep.—Ps. 42:7

As men and women in service we face reality. Shallow thinking does not catch our imagination. In these days of "do or die" it is the "hero in the soul" that, once more, must fight against all the enemies of the human spirit.

For such a conflict we may be undergirded with unusual strength. We are made courageous when under pressure. Science tells us that deep sea fish, two thousand feet down, endure a pressure of a thousand pounds per square inch. But they are made for it. When they escape to shallow waters they die. Souls who gird themselves with the armor of God can withstand great pressure and, in turn, display creative genius. "Deep calleth unto deep."

The extra pressure of these days calls for soul depth as well as for military skill. Whole-souled individuals never give such an excellent account of themselves as they do under pressure. If they try to escape, they lose their heroic strength. Our example is Jesus, "who, for the joy that was set before him, endured the cross," the deep sea pressures of life.

As strong children of God we strive for a new world order. Deep within our hearts we know that a new philosophy of life must come. We know that a new attitude toward other nations and races must come. The whole of humanity must become a single family of God. In these trying days we may draw added strength from the deep wellsprings of eternal life, and we will fight the more courageously on all fronts.

O THOU who hast been our strength in all the generations, outlasting the armed hate of many centuries; may Thy Holy Spirit fill our souls to their very depths, that no outer force may be able to defeat our spiritual purposes. Grant to us this very day strength to live, and courage to dare. *Amen.*

GEORGE C. PULLMAN
First Congregational Church, Sioux City, Iowa

CONTENTMENT

I have learned, in whatsoever state I am, therewith to be content.
                                                        —Phil. 4:11

Contentment is a quality of the soul, a regal adornment of noble minds. It is not the exclusive possession of the wealthy, nor is it reserved for the learned and the great. Like the brightness of sunshine or the freshness of the day in spring, it is available for all. The humblest toilers may claim it, and, if they have found its secret, though they be bound like slaves to their menial tasks, they will walk the earth like royalty. Those on the street may possess it, and though the world be cruel and inhospitable, their life will be a song.

Contentment arises from proper adjustment to one's environment. It will not dwell with those who harbor jealousy, envy, or hatred in their hearts. Worry and fear will destroy it; selfishness and uncontrolled ambition will bring it to naught.

Life is all too short to grumble over every misfortune. If we cannot change the circumstances which surround our lives, at least we may be master of them. Contentment is not a gift; it is an achievement. It is not a legacy to be conferred, but a prize to be won!

HEAVENLY FATHER, grant that I may live this day in peace and calm serenity. Help me to meet whatever life has to offer with an unfaltering trust in Thee, and may I find assurance and contentment in Thy eternal love. *Amen.*

ALFRED GRANT WALTON
Tompkins Avenue Congregational Church, Brooklyn, N.Y.

GOD'S MYSTERY

. . . He made known to us the mystery of his will . . . which he purposed in Christ . . . to bring all things in heaven and on the earth together under one head, even Christ.—Eph. 1:9–10

There is mystery in the heavens. We look up, we wonder, and we hope. Jim Horsley, a retired Blue Angels pilot, once observed, "Hope is hearing God's music for the future. Faith is daring to dance to it today." If we knew everything about God, what might be our response? Would we dance?

It might be best not to know everything we would like to know. Christian author, Lynn Anderson, once recounted this story: James Irwin, Apollo astronaut, said that standing on the surface of the moon was one of the most profoundly disillusioning moments of his life: "All my life I have been enchanted by the romance and the mystery of the moon. I sang love songs under the moon. I read poems by moonstruck poets. . . . But that day when I stepped from the capsule onto the lunar surface and reached down at my feet, I came up with nothing but two handfuls of gray dirt. The romance and mystery were stripped away. There will be no more moon in the sky." I believe the answer to some mysteries may disappoint us, just as I am confident some mysteries will delight us.

In our obedience to God, we dance. As we express the joy we can feel as a consequence of faith and hope in our lives, we dance. In Christ, the focus is not on the rationale for our faith—although it is rational; it is not about the proof—although there is proof; and it is not about the occasional gaps and doubts—we all have them. If we could explain the mystery of Christ simply, perhaps He did not need to die for us. But we can't, and He did.

FATHER, we trust in You. We hope in You. We hear Your word and want to do Your will. Give us the confidence to allow the mystery of the gift of Your Son to take hold of our lives. Give us hope. Give us courage. Give us grace. In the name of Christ we pray. *Amen.*

ANDREW K. BENTON
President, Pepperdine University, Malibu, Calif.

A PERSONAL CALL

I have called you by name. You are mine.—Isa. 43:1

A friend of mine gave me a picture with this verse on it. It reminds me that God personally calls me to something more. He knew my name before I was born and had a plan laid out for me. This is not an exact itinerary of what my life will be, but rather a rough outline of where it is headed. I have the ability to make decisions in my life, good and bad, but knowing that He has called me by name, I tend more and more to follow His lead. It is comforting to know how much God cares for me, and that I am His. The more I listen to His call, the stronger our relationship becomes and the easier it is to do the right thing. This verse is not only given to me—it is a personal call to each one of us.

LORD GOD, help me to listen to Your voice more and more each day, so that in the good times and the bad times I will always know that You are near. Thank You for calling me by name. *Amen.*

JAMES RIES
Parochial Vicar, St. Norbert Catholic Church, Orange, Calif.

ROUTINE

And he must needs go through Samaria.—John 4:4

Life in the armed forces is often monotonous. There may be times of extreme danger during which we commit ourselves to God, but what of His presence in the routine days? They are our "Samaria." Jesus was thinking of Galilee, where His real work was to be done; Samaria merely had to be passed through in order to reach it. Notice, then, the wells which He found to refresh Him on the way:

First, the old well said to be dug by Jacob, from which many generations had drawn. When we are uprooted from our home and put into strange surroundings, it is refreshing to discover ancient and much-used inspirations at hand—a church service, our Bible, prayer which takes us directly to God.

Second, the well of another's need. We find ourselves refreshed when we are of help to anybody. When the Samaritan woman questioned our Lord, and He opened up for her "living water" to make new her life, He was Himself renewed. He told His disciples, "I have meat to eat that ye know not of."

Third, the well of the confidence which men expressed in Him. Not only did this woman give Him the story of her life and let Him help her; but her neighbors came out to see Him, and afterward declared: "We have heard Him ourselves, and know that this is indeed the Christ, the Savior of the world." When we are trusted, we have the strongest incentive to be trustworthy. Through the faith of men in us, we begin to realize what God expects of its. We dare not disappoint Him.

O GOD, in whose hand are our lives, keep us faithful both in the crises and in the routine of our days, through Him who is our unfailing Life, even Jesus Christ. *Amen.*

HENRY SLOANE COFFIN
President, Union Theological Seminary, New York City, N.Y.

BEHOLD MY HANDS

Reach hither thy finger, and behold My hands.—John 20:27

The hand," said Galen, "is the instrument of instruments." In prayer we lift the hands; in bargains we clasp them; in blessings we place them on the head; in taking an oath we lay them on the Bible; in matrimony we join them; and in death we rest them side by side on the bosom. The hand is an instrument of sacrifice, suffering, service, and victory.

To Thomas, His prejudiced disciple, Jesus presented His hands with the nailprints as the badges of His identity. "Behold my hands!" Indeed, "we shall know Him by the prints of the nails in His hands." Said an old saint to an impostor, "You are not the Christ! You haven't any nailprints in your hands." The scars have a message for Jesus as well as for us. They keep the experience of the Cross before Him forever.

When I was a lad my mother frequently had me tie a string on my finger when she wanted me to remember something. Why on the finger? Easy enough. The hand is never out of sight. A string there is a constant reminder. Yes, the prints of the nails which He ever sees, regardless of the position of the hands, tell Him over and over again the story of Calvary.

Further, they are the blessed forget-me-nots of His own. We are engraved in the scars in His hands. Wherever we are, at home or abroad, on land or sea, at the battlefront or in the S. O. S., we are assured that He is mindful of us. The nailprints keep us constantly before Him. "Behold my hands!"

OUR HEAVENLY FATHER, Thou hast loved us and brought us through the sacrifices of Thy dear Son. We rejoice in Thy love. To know that in Christ Thou art always mindful of us gives us strength in what would otherwise be the hour of our weakness. Constantly watch over us and bless us in Jesus' name. *Amen.*

FRED B. WYAND
First Methodist Church, Williamson, W.Va.

ASSURANCE ALWAYS

Thou wilt keep him in perfect peace, whose mind is stayed on thee; because he trusteth in thee.—Isa. 26:3

If in the adventures of life we always had the assurance we needed, our often wavering courage would be stabilized. And we may have courage. Beyond our meager resourcefulness, our never-failing God assures us that we shall be kept, and that on the basis of our humble trust in Him. And He is known as "the one who cannot lie." What confidence may be ours!

There are many times when we are plagued by doubts. We sometimes say to ourselves, "What's the use?"

> I've tried in vain a thousand ways,
> My fears to quell, my hopes to raise.

That, surely, is the golden moment when "man's extremity is God's opportunity." Through the chilling darkness of fear and doubt, when

> My soul is night, my heart is steel—
> I cannot see, I cannot feel;
> For light, for life, I must appeal
> In simple trust to Jesus.

He, our ever-near Companion, will still "stake" us; for He has said, "I will not forsake you; I will be with you *all* the way." Then lo, our darkness is turned to light, our failures to success, and our doubts are resolved into His "perfect peace."

OUR FATHER, we thank Thee for Thy unchanging compassion for Thy children. In ways we cannot always now fathom, Thou dost answer our cries to Thee. Help us, in our proneness to err, implicitly to trust in Thee, our Redeemer. *Amen.*

HENRY F. WIDEN
First Baptist Church, Glasgow, Mon.

THE ETERNAL AND CHANGELESS

Therefore, my beloved brethren, be ye steadfast, unmoveable, always abounding in the work of the Lord.—1 Cor. 15:58a

It may well seem presumptuous for one who still dwells amid the familiar and peaceful surroundings of civil life to offer any word of counsel to you who have been thrust into this new and unwanted life of military service to answer your country's need. But there is one experience we share in common—the piercing of grim realities through that selfish complacency in which we were so comfortably cushioned to the uncovering of our souls. And in such a time we find ourselves face to face with the spiritual values which we have so long forgotten. It is only these that offer us anything that can survive all shock and struggle and sorrow. They are made available to us in that inner temple of the spirit in which we can commune with God. And in that great Book in which we find God most clearly revealed, I call attention to a little couplet in Deuteronomy 33:27, whose two lines form the theme of the ninetieth and ninety-first psalms:

> The eternal God is thy refuge,
> And underneath are the everlasting arms.

In the dizzy shifting of the daily scene and the changing panorama of life there is something eternal and changeless—the refuge of God's overshadowing love. And in that heartless world of sudden death and bloodshed in which war has involved you, there still remains the everlasting tenderness of God, as close and warm as a mother's encircling arms.

ETERNAL GOD, in whom we live and move and have our being, shadow us with Thy protecting love, and encircle us with Thy comforting arms. For Christ's sake. *Amen.*

HENRY KENDALL BOOTH
First Congregational Church, Long Beach, Calif.

SELLING THE SOUL

And cinnamon, and odours, and ointments, and frankincense, . . . and souls of men.—Rev. 18:13

The apostle John, the author of the Book of Revelation, was a good reporter. Newspaper reporters tell me a good reporter just is or "ain't." As to that, I cannot say, but I maintain John was a good reporter because he could see what everyone else could see and that additional bit more which marks the difference between mediocrity and preeminence.

When he looked at the city of Babylon and saw the city tumbling in ruin and the merchants weeping for lack of customers, he narrated all the things they had to sell, and he saw something that was bought and sold in Babylon that would have escaped all except the expert eye. These merchants sold gold, silver, precious wood and ivory products, and even slaves; but John saw that they sold the "souls of men."

How can you sell a soul? Can you put it on a scale and sell it at so much a pound? No—but you can sell a soul! You can sell your own by being less than you know you can and ought to be. No one who fully understands the worth of his or her soul will sell it for any price; for after all it is the most essential part of you—in fact it is you. It is your life.

Now if you do not care enough to guard your own soul, can you really condemn others if they hold it in slight value and treat your soul as if it were of no value? Do not lament if someone tries to cheapen your soul. Make it your main objective to see that this does not happen!

OUR FATHER IN HEAVEN, preserve the soul of Thy servant, clean, strong, and pure until the daybreak and the shadows flee away, through Jesus Christ my Lord and Elder Brother. *Amen.*

GEORGE H. TALBOTT
First Presbyterian Church. Passaic, N.J.

LIVING BY OUR DEEPEST PERSUASIONS

I am persuaded.—Rom. 8:38

We often hear each other say, "I am convinced." It may be of "this" or "that," but in any case it represents a persuasion. Let us, then, consider the convictions, the deep persuasions, by which we all live.

Persuaded, as we are, that the Eternal God cares, and has a personal stake in our performance, we find life never completely levels off until in our hearts we feel His care and know that our performance is in line with His divine purpose.

Persuaded, as we are, that personal honor, nobility of character, and ethical conduct are the supreme values, we remain uneasy in conscience until we are sure that all our striving is directed toward achieving these goals. We can all give thanks that Jesus did not say, "Blessed are the righteous," but rather, "Blessed are they which do hunger and thirst after righteousness." For, although none of us would claim complete righteousness, we would claim to be trying desperately for it.

In the Bible reading above you will discover a man utterly persuaded that God is dependable. To him there was nothing in life nor death that could destroy the certainty of God's love. There was no outward circumstance and no inner turmoil that could shatter his faith or dispel his courage. The human mind could not imagine a situation in which he could not be aware of the love of God. There is nothing you can do to someone who lives by such persuasions.

DEAR FATHER IN HEAVEN, give me faith made strong for today, and courage to live by my deepest convictions. Help me to be true to the high hopes my loved ones have for me, and not to fail my best self in any thoughtless moment. *Amen.*

A. WARD APPLEGATE
Society of Friends, Wilmington, Ohio

THE SPONTANEOUS THINGS IN LIFE

As he thinketh in his heart, so is he.—Prov. 23:7

The spontaneous things in life have the longest history." What we do in an emergency usually reveals who we are at rock bottom. By our thoughts and habits over the years we have been unconsciously determining our conduct in that particular situation. When Daniel Webster made his famous reply to Hayne in Congress, the emergency merely called out in Webster what his thought and reading had been storing up for years. The speech, seemingly so spontaneous, had a long preparation.

Habit makes us what we are. Every act and every thought grooves the path which we shall take when the emergency leaps out from the ambush upon us. For this reason it is critical for us to prepare for the event before it arrives. It's too late to get insurance when the house is afire.

Donald Hankey, who fell in the First World War, once said: "Religion is betting your life that there is a God." There is more to religion than that, but such a belief is necessary to vital religion. If we begin with that, and practice it, God becomes real to us. Not only that, we will feel that we have an ally that cannot be defeated. It will give us something to nail to when the emergency hits us. It is like laying up money in the bank for a rainy day. The reserve will be there when the crisis comes.

O GOD, who art more ready to give than we are to receive, help us to make it possible for Thee to help us. May we open our hearts to Thy influence, in quiet confidence that Thou art near to every child who earnestly seeks Thee, and art willing to sustain us in every time of need. Forgive us that we so often defeat ourselves by not calling on Thee for strength, and that we plod along a lonely road when the Divine Companion is so near at hand. *Amen.*

HOWARD J. CHIDLEY
First Congregational Church, Winchester, Mass.

FAITH—A SHIELD

Above all, taking the shield of faith, wherewith ye shall be able to quench all the fiery darts of the wicked.—Eph. 6:16

Faith is a prominent word in the vocabulary of the American people at this time. It is usually mentioned in reference to faith in democracy and the need of ever keeping it in mind. It is more than faith in our Constitution and institutions, for it is faith in the people and their willingness to rule themselves by their own form of government. This is the kind of democracy we have faith in and for which we fight, hoping that all the world may benefit by its privileges.

This faith is vital when its origin is with the individual and indicates the influence of religious faith in mind and heart. It increases the worth of the individual in service to the country in war and peace.

Paul taught this truth in the text in Ephesians, where he made use of the soldier's equipment as an illustration of this religious lesson. The shield of faith gave protection against danger and kept the soldier strong and efficient in every demand.

This faith is not visionary or merely idealistic in utterance. It is real religious faith, coming from Christ and becoming the model of faith and practice in meeting all conditions of the world. It illuminates the mind so that it is possible to see the world as it is and fortifies the heart for the fight for the right. It is the means of sensing the purpose of God in calling us to His service of righteousness. Take this shield of faith now!

ALMIGHTY AND EVERLIVING GOD, revealed through the love and grace of our Lord Jesus Christ, bestow Thy divine blessing upon the men and women in the service of our nation, and equip them in body, mind, and soul for their heroic duty and sacrifice, for Christ's sake. *Amen.*

FRANK M. KERR
Christ's First Presbyterian Church, Hempstead, N.Y.

SEEING THROUGH

For the things which are seen are temporal; but the things which are not seen are eternal.—2 Cor. 4:18

Do you have X-ray vision? Can you not only see the things before you, but also see them in relation to all behind them?

A drawing "in perspective" represents things as they appear to the eye with objects in right relationship. So tasks should be seen set in their whole pattern, revealing relative values and importance. The order-of-the-day, the assignment, or the objective is related to the entire campaign, and to the final purpose.

"What are you doing?" was asked of three laborers working together. "Carrying mortar," answered the first; "Earning four dollars a day," the second; "Building a cathedral," the third.

So blood, sweat, and tears are for all; but for some they are discerned against a background of humanity freed, civilization restored, God's will done. They are not interested in merely stopping the enemy, or removing barriers; they do both that others may go on and up into the fullness of the good life. So "things seen" are related to the "unseen," to that better day of faith, imagination, and determination.

Some merely obey orders. Others have, back of their obedience, the wisdom of what it is all about, and serve with conviction and consecration. In the ranks of the latter are found those who receive medals and are promoted to higher ranks. Most folks see only God's acts or deeds; while others like Moses, discerning His ways or purposes, become leaders.

O LORD, keep clean and clear my vision; enable me to see through the dust and fog of the moment all things as Thou dost see them, and never to lose sight of the eternal. *Amen.*

CHARLES W. FLINT
Bishop, Syracuse, N.Y. Area, Methodist

A FORWARD-REACHING SPIRIT

Reaching forth unto those things which are before, I press toward the mark
for the prize of the high calling of God in Christ Jesus.—Phil. 3:14

Not in many years has Lent seemed so suited to our need as now. Its call to penitence and humility, to self-examination and self-denial, to prayer and devotion, finds us in a more than responsive mood. For the thing that is most deeply wrong with us is that we do not know the meaning of things. We have so largely lost sight of what life is for. Our need is for some basic and compelling idea with which to come to grips with the world.

For such an idea we are falling back upon religion because we cannot help ourselves. But it is not a return to such a religion as we have experienced that will suffice. Our need is for something the force of which we have never fully felt before.

Lent speaks to our need now, for it celebrates the fasting and prayer of Jesus in the wilderness, an experience which carried Him not backward in religion but forward, to the discovery of the Will of God on a deeper level than humankind had ever known it before. The God we see has gone out ahead of us. He is even now fashioning the world after His own purposes before our very eyes. Our tragedy is that we do not see what He is doing. Yet if we follow Christ in His forward-reaching spirit and by the selfsame discipline He knew, we shall not fail to find as He did the faith and hope in which the heart can rest.

O LORD, who hast breathed into us the breath of life, and endued us with an immortal spirit, upon whom we depend for the prevailing strength of all our highest purposes; grant, we beseech Thee, that we shall the more surely come to know, receive, and perform Thy Holy Will. Through Jesus Christ. *Amen.*

A. HERBERT HASLAM
Ashland Avenue Baptist Church, Toledo, Ohio

CHEER UP!

Cheer up, men! I believe God.—Acts 27:25 (Moffatt)

These words come out of a situation where shipwreck and death stared at Paul, the sailors, and their captain. On that ship were trouble, hatred, persecution, uncertainty, hopelessness. How like these days and our own situation! Yet Paul could say to his comrades, "Cheer up, men!"

But how could he do this? The answer lies in the next words, "I believe God." We must believe God before we can cheer up. With that faith we can bear anything, face anything, endure anything. Without it we are done for.

We need a faith in God which will surmount physical suffering, adverse circumstances, world hatred. Paul's life is a good example. Jesus' life is the supreme example. Good people are not spared suffering, torture, pain, loss. But their faith enables them to use these adverse circumstances for high and spiritual purposes. Suffering is inevitable in life. We need not, however, be confused. We are not alone if God is with us.

In the midst of a world situation in which ships are going down and the anguished cry out to heaven, in which life is cheaply esteemed, may we hear these meaningful words, "I believe God!" Our resources are all-sufficient in Him. With this unshakable faith in God we are strengthened from day to day and are able to face anything. Though the earth be moved, and though the mountains be shaken, yet will we *not* fear. "The Lord of hosts is with us." "Be of good cheer; I have overcome the world." "Cheer up, men! I believe God."

ETERNAL GOD, our Father, from everlasting to everlasting the same; give me an unshakable faith in Thee, so that in the midst of shipwreck, suffering, and death, I may be of good cheer. I believe, O God; help Thou mine unbelief. *Amen.*

HERMANN WALTER KAEBNICK
Secretary, Board of Christian Education, Evangelical Church, Somerset, Pa.

LIFE AS A PROPER NOUN

I came that they may have life, and may have it abundantly.
—John 10:10b ARV

When Jesus spoke of "life," He thought of it in terms of a proper noun. It was more than one of a number of desirable things. It was the most desirable of all. Jesus said He came to give humankind life and give it abundantly.

Many of us make our mistakes by putting the emphasis upon the wrong things. We do not pray because prayer for us has become lost in the shuffle. We cease to be honest because honesty is only a policy and there are also other policies. So it has gone with other great values. Life finally becomes sour and tiresome because we have capitalized the wrong things and they have failed us.

We live in a day when many challenges are flung at us. "Buy this!" "Read that!" "Go to something else!" These invitations yell at us from the radio and TV and glare at us from advertisements. They come from every side, and if we do not take care, they will have us dizzy. In our confusion we are likely to lose that which is best of all. Our Master said we should seek first the Kingdom of God and His righteousness, and the other things would be added in their proper order.

A person can bring a penny so close to his eye that it shuts out the entire sun. We must see that the truly biggest things are kept in their proper place. In doing this we shall make sure that "life" is a proper noun.

O GOD, help us to keep the different values of life in their true places. May we put first things first and keep them there. Amid the tumult and shouting may we continue to hear one clear, small voice urging us upward to the heights. *Amen.*

PAUL E. BECKER
Bethany Christian Church, Lincoln, Neb.

READ THE BIBLE

All scripture is given by inspiration of God, and is profitable for doctrine, for reproof, for correction, for instruction in righteousness.
—2 Tim. 3:16

For cleansing, for comfort, and for command, the Bible has no equal. It is the moral radium of the world. It is Everbody's Book. Coffins and cradles, glories and glooms, comedies and tragedies, all the ups and downs of human experience are in the Bible.

The Bible is the most hopeful book in the world. It is full of the spirit of the morning. It has splendid "eyes for the dawn." No literature matches it for pure sunniness. It snatches the crepe from the door of death. It looks for the latent good in bad people. It has a Gospel for the gutter. It peoples eternity with singing men and women.

The Bible is the most helpful book in the world. It teaches how to think about life—feeds the heart with vision and ideal and reveals the superb pattern of humanity in Jesus. It is a lantern for our feet in any situation in life. It gives valor to our dreams of good and maps the road to a civilization of unity among all people. Its religious truths are essential to our health in character, our hope in service, and our triumph in death. It is a telescope through which we can see the living God.

ETERNAL GOD, whose presence can never be changed to absence, and whose Spirit mingles with ours as the sunshine mingles with the morning air, we thank Thee for the bracing climate, the cool springs, the quiet valleys, and the snow-clad summits of the Bible. Lead us into its wonderland of wisdom and beauty, and help us to find companionship and inspiration for our souls in all the moods and experiences of life. *Amen.*

HUGH ELMER BROWN
First Congregational Church, Evanston, Ill.

A DAY WITH GOD

In the beginning God. . . .—Gen. 1:1a

In the beginning God. . . ." With these majestic words the Bible opens. They constitute a sublime affirmation of faith, a penetrating challenge to every life. The truly great persons of all ages have placed God in the beginning of their lives' enterprises. In the beginning of each day's plan and purpose they have looked first to God for guidance. Daniel looked to God thrice a day and defied a pagan king; the prophets sought God's will and then went forth unafraid; Jesus, in His temptation, in His ministry, in Gethsemane, and on Calvary, incarnated the principle of "In the beginning God. . . ." and Jesus overcame all evil. No great Christian ever lived who did otherwise.

In contrast, how often we begin and live our days as we please. We give God almost no place in our plans or in our purposes for living. Then, in the evening, we pray: "Bless, O God, what we have done this day; establish Thou the work of our hands." And, when God cannot put the blessing of His approval upon what we have done, we are cross with God, and petulantly declare, "There's nothing to prayer." Why not try, "In the beginning God. . . . ?"

HEAVENLY FATHER, it is good to know that Thou art available. A new day lies before me. That I may go forth strong and ready, let me breakfast at Thy table. Lend to me for this day some of Thy wisdom and courage and goodwill. Fashion the plans of my life for this day. Establish the purposes of my life, and give unto me the assurance of Thy companionship. Then no way will be too difficult, no trail too steep. When this day is over may I rejoice in the knowledge that I have not departed from the purpose true and lovely loaned of Thee at break of day. *Amen.*

LOUIS H. KAUB
Centenary Methodist Church, Beatrice, Neb.

THE RESOURCES OF GOD

All things therefore whatsoever ye would that men should do unto you,
even so do ye also unto them: for this is the law and the prophets.
—Matt. 7:12 ARV

Note particularly the word "therefore." Jesus, the world's supreme authority on our relationship to God, speaking out of His own marvelous experience with Him, has just declared that the resources of God are available for those who seek them. Nine times He emphasizes this fact. Count them: (1) "Ask, and it shall be given you"; (2) "seek, and ye shall find"; (3) "knock, and it shall be opened unto you"; (4) "every one that asketh receiveth"; (5) "he that seeketh findeth"; (6) "to him that knocketh it shall be opened"; (7) "what man is there of you, who, if his son shall ask him for a loaf, will give him a stone"; (8) "or if he shall ask for a fish, will give him a serpent?" (9) "How much more shall your Father who is in heaven give good things to them that ask him?" *Therefore*! since the resources of God are available to those who really seek them, since you have God to help you, you can live a godly life. Therefore, do unto others whatsoever you would that they should do unto you. The Golden Rule is possible through fellowship with God.

O GOD, our Father, grant that we may live in intimate fellowship with Thee today and so have the desire and the strength to do unto others as we would have them to do unto us. In Christ's name we ask it. *Amen.*

J. L. CUNINGGIM
President, Scarritt College, Nashville, Tenn.

GOD SAVE US FROM HATE

Love your enemies.—Matt. 5:44

In time of war it's hard not to hate. There are some things that we ought to hate—we ought to hate war itself; we ought to hate the evils that produce war, and the evil ideologies that lead to war. But we do not need to hate the people of the countries that we fight. After all, they are people very much like ourselves. They are not essentially different from ourselves. Fundamentally, people are the same the world over. They are all the children of God. And I am sure that we Christians must valiantly strive to maintain an attitude of goodwill toward all of them, for all of them are the children of God and brothers and sisters of our own.

That is a difficult thing to do, but it is not impossible. Chiang Kai-shek did it. Once a Canadian was visiting in the home of Chiang Kai-shek. He was invited by the Generalissimo and his wife to join them in family worship. He said that he will never forget the prayer that Chiang Kai-shek prayed that night. He said, "The most amazing thing in his prayer was a plea that God would help him to help China not to hate the Japanese people. He prayed for the Japanese Christians and all the suffering multitudes of Japan whose impoverishment was making the war on China possible." Well, that's Christianity! That's loving your enemies. And if Chiang Kai-shek did it, you and I ought to be able to do it, too.

O GOD, Thou who art the Father of all people, help us not to hate the people who are Thy children and our brothers and sisters. Help us to remember that "enemies" are still people, and that they too belong to the Family of God. *Amen.*

STODDARD LANE
Plymouth Congregational Church, Des Moines, Iowa

THE GOSPEL OF PERSONAL RESPONSIBILITY

Then he said, Who shall begin the battle? And he answered, Thou.
       —1 Kings 20:14 ARV

The directness of this thrust makes one wince. Even a king cannot escape personal responsibility. Neither can we. Life as a conflict is not a new thought. The children of light wage an unremitting fight against the overwhelming forces of the children of darkness. Always we are assured in this conflict that with God can "one chase a thousand, and two put ten thousand to flight."

Moses appears before Pharaoh saying, "Let my people go." Elijah on Mt. Carmel faces the four hundred priests of Baal shouting, "Choose you this day whom ye will serve." Amos appears at Bethel and denounces the king and his corrupt court. The whole goodly company of apostles and martyrs throughout the centuries sound a note of defiance. They bear witness to their part in the "insurrection against a pagan world." In this warfare the tide of battle is turned even against overwhelming odds as the individual accepts responsibility. "Who shall begin the battle? And he answered, Thou."

That challenge comes to the Christian today. It is a warfare not only of flesh and blood but of the "hosts of wickedness in heavenly places." It is a conflict of ideas. The battle lines are drawn. We cannot evade the Spirit's voice—"Thou."

O GOD, my heavenly Father, do Thou stand by me this day. Keep me continually aware of my personal responsibility to fight the good fight, to finish the course, to keep the faith, that I may be not only true and valiant in my country's service, but a good soldier of Jesus Christ as well. *Amen.*

CLARENCE A. SPAULDING
First Presbyterian Church, River Forest, Ill.

REMEMBER

"Then Peter remembered. . . ."—Mark 14:72 (MOFFATT)

You lose yourself every time you forget who you are or to whom you belong. When Peter in the inn, with the awful pressure of the crowd around him, denied Jesus, he had forgotten who he was and to whom he belonged. The moment he remembered—he found himself and became the greatest of the soldiers of the Cross.

How easy it is for us amidst the great crowds of our cities and our armies to forget who we are and to whom we belong; and, forgetting, lose ourselves; and, losing ourselves, lose our cause, our heritage, our task, our God. In remembrance we are saved!

Remember that you are the child of your mother. Remember your father. Remember the name you bear and the honor of that name. Remember that you have a home, and that a light burns for you, and that prayers are lifted to God for you. Remember that people are sacrificing for you. Remember that there's a teacher who is counting upon you, and that some boy or girl is looking up to you.

Remember that you belong to God. Remember that you came from Him and that you are going to Him. Remembering this—never forget to act accordingly.

In remembrance of all that we are and of all that we must do and of all who are counting upon us, we are saved. I say unto you: Remember, and remember, and remember!

OUR FATHER, help me and my friends to be reverent in our behavior, to use our liberty as befits followers of Christ, and to take our stand with the true, and the clean, and the brave. *Amen.*

RAYMOND A. WASER
First Plymouth Congregational Church, Denver, Colo.

THE FRUIT OF THE CHRISTIAN LIFE

The fruit of the Spirit is love, joy, peace, longsuffering, gentleness, goodness, faith, meekness, temperance: against such there is no law.
—Gal. 5:22

Many times the question arises in our minds: "Why should we try to be good? Why make the effort to grow spiritually? Why not have a good time? We only live once. Why be hampered and restrained?" But the more we think it over, the more we come to the place where we are ready to say: "That's right, we only live once. How can I make the greatest investment?" Really, life becomes adventurous when we realize that Christian living has more satisfaction per square inch than any other kind of living. Sin may seem to have lots of fun about it, but there soon comes a day when we wake up to the fact that we have been wasting our time and have not left the world any richer for our being here.

Think of the list of the fruit of the Spirit: "love, joy, peace, longsuffering, gentleness, goodness, faith, meekness, temperance." The only way we will know about them is to live a thoughtful, prayerful life under God and then see how each one of these fruits is found in our life. There is nothing that can take the place of such great thoughts as these words express. The times are not easy, but the Christian faces them, and with victory. We live so to develop our life in Christ that the fruits are ours.

O MASTER, teach us to live day by day that we may be able to give Thee the best in our life. We desire to have the fruits of the spirit and not the fruits of the flesh. It is not easy to be faithful in cultivation, but show us the way to live victoriously every day, and we shall give Thee thanks for ever and ever. In Jesus' name. *Amen.*

HAROLD R. MARTIN
Second Presbyterian-First Congregational Church, Bloomington, Ill.

REQUIREMENTS FOR VICTORY

Watch ye, stand fast in the faith, quit you like men, be strong.
—1 Cor. 16:13

In this conflict in which we are engaged we are anxious that our cause shall be victorious. Defeat is something from which we inevitably shrink. That would mean the loss of much that has meant the enrichment of life.

It is possible for us to help to bring victory to our cause and yet suffer personal defeat. It is of tremendous importance that we come out of this struggle as personal victors. There are powerful, deceptive foes lurking in our path, and we must be prepared to meet them.

Important battles have been lost because of surprise attacks. Many strong people have failed because temptation came to them at some weak point that was left unguarded. When we are in the midst of enemies we must constantly be on watch.

If the morale of the American people is to be so strong that nothing can make us falter, we must have faith in our cause. It is faith that will give us the victory in our personal conflicts. We need faith in God, faith in loved ones, and faith in ourselves.

If we quit ourselves as Christians under all circumstances, we will have nothing to regret. Studdert-Kennedy, writing from the trenches during World War I, said the first prayer he wanted his son to learn to say for him was not, "God keep Daddy safe," but, "God make Daddy brave and keep him true." That is the spirit that we all need to make us strong.

O GOD, who knowest the secrets of our hearts, help us to have high ideals and to be true to them. Help us to be worthy followers of Him in whose name we pray. *Amen.*

A. W. FORTUNE
Central Christian Church, Lexington, Ky.

PREPARE FOR TOMORROW

*He restoreth my soul: he leadeth me in the paths of righteousness for
his name's sake.*—Ps. 23:3

Has life given me a bad deal? The answer is not a simple "Yes" or "No."
All of us have failed in recent years to give enough time and devotion to building a world of goodwill. We have tried to break the laws of
unity, and instead we have broken ourselves. Our judgment is here.

But as for me, whatever requirements are laid upon me now, I can
always know that a better way and a brighter day will come. Deep in our
souls are the seeds of a new springtime. I must not forget that. Even
while it is dark and while chill winds sweep the world this new life can
germinate.

Whatever else happens I shall keep alive in my soul a faith in springtime.
I shall live and think more deeply than ever before in order that my truer,
better self may be prepared for the days of creative peace that lie ahead.

I shall not allow the bitterness of hate to dwarf my life, nor the blight
of pessimism to kill my faith. When the day for constructive goodwill
comes again I shall be ready. Knowing how often I have needed forgiveness from others, I too shall forgive and remember that only by following
the way of Jesus of Nazareth can the generations that follow escape the
cruelties of conflict. For that day I shall live and prepare, and when it comes
I shall build. So help me God!

O GOD OF SPRING, let me not forget that only Thy way, as seen in
Jesus, can finally win. Sharpen my faith and deepen my devotion to the
new day which must come to earth. I enlist for the glad enterprise of
peace. *Amen.*

ERROL T. ELLIOTT
First Friends Church, Indianapolis, Ind.

ON GOD'S SIDE

Lo, I am with you always, even unto the end of the world.
—Matt. 28:20b

It is one thing to have God on our side. It is a very different thing for us to be on God's side. The latter is the true goal of every Christian, for it means an orientation of one's whole life and not simply a temporary adjustment for some immediate crisis.

One of the important things we must learn is that we live in the presence of God. That all of our life, with its successes and failures, its joys and sorrows, its virtues and sinfulness, is lived in that Presence is both terrifying and inspiring to contemplate. Once we arrive at the point where we approach every phase of life as an expression of our relationship to God, we will have gone most of the way towards accomplishing the personal task that is set before us as Christians.

We are apt to put things into different compartments and to feel that therefore they have no relationship one to another. We create zones of life which are sacred, others that are secular. We find it hard to appreciate that our business dealing, our patriotism, our social relations, our international outlook, all are affected by our conception of our relation to God. When we finally realize that we live continually in God's presence, the partitions break down, and the whole of our life becomes a demonstration of our faith in Him.

O GOD OF PEACE, who hast taught us that in returning and rest we shall be saved, in quietness and in confidence shall be our strength; by the might of Thy Spirit lift us, we pray Thee, to Thy presence, where we may be still and know that Thou art God. Through Jesus Christ our Lord. *Amen.*

HERBERT VERNON HARRIS
Trinity Episcopal Church, Los Angeles, Calif.

I'M PROUD OF MY FAITH

I am not ashamed of the gospel of Christ: for it is the power of God unto salvation, to every one that believeth.—Rom. 1:16

I am not an atheist or an agnostic; I am a Christian and proud of it. I believe in a Christlike God, such a God as is revealed in the life and in the teachings of our Lord. I believe in a Christian civilization, where every person is looked upon as possessing transcendent and eternal value, and where everyone is to be accorded full rights and privileges to live the most useful and most meaningful life possible. I believe in a God who will give me power to triumph over temptations and discouragements that would tend to drag me down.

I believe it is eminently worthwhile to contend for righteousness, justice, and truth in the world; and that Heaven will reward those who thus take their stand. I am so thoroughly convinced of the presence of the ever-living God in the affairs of humankind that I refuse to become panic-stricken when the sins and selfish ambitions of the usurpers of authority bring about destructive wars and international chaos. So sure am I of the life eternal that even death is robbed of its sting, and I go forward with courage undaunted.

I am so proud of this faith that is mine that I shall not hesitate to declare it anywhere, in any environment, by my deeds, by my words, by my attitudes, and by every outward manifestation of my life.

O LORD, increase my faith in the eternal truths that have been taught me from my early childhood, and help me to remain true to Thee even amid the most trying circumstances. I ask it in the name of our Christ. *Amen.*

ARBA MARTIN
Trinity Methodist Church, Portsmouth, Ohio

THE STILL SMALL VOICE

A still small voice.—1 Kings 19:12

In the British Navy "The Still" is blown when there is a sudden disaster. It means, "Prepare to do the wise thing." Observing this moment of calm has averted many catastrophes.

Long ago the psalmist wrote: "Be still and know that I am God" (Ps. 46). He was pointing out the secret of poise when we face an attack from the world about us. Only those who dwell in the secret place of the Most High find the shelter of the Almighty.

Worry and fear are twin enemies that attack us. The still, small Voice ever calls us to a love that will cast out worry and a faith that makes fear mere folly.

The fiery doubts of temptation come at the most unexpected moments. The apostle Paul describes the secret of defense as the life "hid with Christ in God" (Col. 3:3).

Many voices clamor for our attention in these days of chaos and confusion, but to the wise no greater gift for guidance need be given than the calm to tune in the still small Voice of the Eternal God.

O MOST LOVING FATHER, preserve us from faithless fears and earthly anxieties. We would cast all our care upon Thee, for Thou carest for us.

> Drop Thy still dews of quietness,
> Till all our strivings cease;
> Take from our souls the strain and stress,
> And let our ordered lives confess
> The beauty of Thy peace.

We ask in the name and for the sake of Jesus Christ, our Lord and only Savior. *Amen.*

CLARENCE ALBERT KIRCHER
Westminster Presbyterian Church, Sacramento, Calif.

I WANT WINGS

If ye then be risen with Christ, seek those things which are above.
—Col. 3:1

This is the last generation of earthbound people, a speaker at a convention of school administrators once avowed. The next generation will have wings. Earthbound people are doomed. God's children, on the other hand, never earthbound, have always been air-minded. Risen with Christ, they seek the things which are above. They have always wanted and had wings. David, overwhelmed with horror because of the voice of the enemy, cried, "Oh for the wings of a dove!" The wings of escape! Thank God they are provided.

Were there no means of escape from bloodshed, hatred, fear, monotony, loneliness, who could retain sanity? How often have we escaped from our impossible life situations on the magic wings of faith and prayer and roved awhile through the beautiful corridors of the Word of God, felt the sweep of eternal purposes in it, caught visions rare and beautiful, and returned fresh and ready to meet the demands of the day before us!

Then we were ready to exchange the wings of a dove for the wings of eagles. Isaiah said, "They that wait upon the Lord shall renew their strength; they shall mount up with wings as eagles." Wings of escape gain strength to become wings of aspiration and achievement when we wait on the Lord. We feel a strange welling up of power within us and say with Paul, "I can do all things through Christ which strengtheneth me."

FATHER, I praise Thee, for the sweet hour of prayer that calls me from a world of care and bids me claim the rich blessings Thou hast for me. Help me to submit myself to Christ and realize the power of the unwearied God within me renewing my strength and courage and making me adequate to meet every demand made upon me. Through Jesus, my Lord. *Amen.*

SIDNEY W. POWELL
First Baptist Church, St. Paul, Minn.

LIVING UPSTAIRS

Seek those things which are above.—Col. 3:1

Gilbert Chesterton once observed that in the house of life many people are content to live in the cellar. Nay more, they seem to assume that the cellar is the only room in the house. Chesterton did not go on to specify just what he meant—nor need he. The cellar suggests something below level, a place dim, if not dark, where small dusty windows admit but little sunlight and, to one living there, permit no clear and far-reaching views. Obviously there are many influences by which, if we are not redeemed from them, we are apt to be led to live our mental and spiritual lives in a cellar.

St. Paul does not deny that the cellar is real. He does not even question whether or not a cellar is necessary. What he affirms is that the cellar is not the proper abode for anyone and that to become a Christian is to move upstairs. It means thinking and living on a higher plane. It means finding life's front window and seeing out and up and on. It means seeking and finding those ultimate values of beauty, goodness, truth, and sacrificial love which only clean living and high thinking can bestow.

Prayer is the stairs up which we climb from the cellar to life's true living room. By prayer we reach up to that point at which the Grace of Christ—Divine Love reaching down—takes hold and lifts and redeems. This day, therefore, I shall begin to "seek those things which are above."

ETERNAL FATHER, cleanse my mind that it may be pure enough to know Thee; sweeten my heart that it may be good enough to love Thee; strengthen my will that it may be strong enough to seek Thee; and so discipline my life that it may be fit to serve Thee. This I ask through Him by whose light I see and by whose love I am lifted, even Jesus Christ our Lord. *Amen.*

H. D. McKeehan
The Abbey Church, Evangelical and Reformed, Huntingdon, Pa.

HE SHALL BE LIKE A TREE

He shall be like a tree planted by the rivers of water.—Ps. 1:3

What lovelier figure is there in the immortal Book of Psalms than this? So, says the psalmist, is an upright person, as a well-watered, fruitful tree, embowered with leafy beauty.

Some years ago there stood on a farm in northeastern Indiana a tree famed for miles around. Some called it the "Tree of Mystery," for it was distinctive and stood apart. When the leaves of other trees were withering, the leaves of this mysterious tree were green and flourishing. The mystery tree occupied a conspicuous position upon a hilltop. People came from far to see it. Little children loved to play under its branches.

Now it came to pass that a new highway sealed the mystic tree's fate. The hill had to be leveled and the tree cut down. Workmen appeared on the scene and went to work. It seemed sacrilege, but the grand tree was felled. Then the secret of the mystery tree came out. Deep down in that hill was a never failing spring of clear, cool water. True to the urge of nature, the tree had sent its roots deep in the soil moistened by the never-failing spring.

This is a parable of the people who through faith have deep springs of the Spirit from which to draw. No matter how severe the seasons of the soul, they stand up against the storms. They have tapped an invisible reservoir of strength and comfort. Such people are like trees planted by the rivers of water.

ETERNAL FATHER, strong to save, may it be that we shall grow in grace and knowledge of Thy Son and in the life of the Spirit, even as a tree planted by the rivers of water bringeth forth its fruit in due season. We ask it in the name of Him who as a youth "increased in wisdom and stature, and in favor with God and man." *Amen.*

EDGAR DeWitt Jones
Central Woodward Christian Church, Detroit, Mich.

NOT PROPHETS BUT WITNESSES

And when he had spoken these things, while they beheld, he was taken up.—Acts 1:9

Ponder our Lord's last earthly words—"And when he had spoken these things, while they beheld, he was taken up." What were the words just spoken? They comprised an earnest admonition that the disciples become witnesses rather than prophets. Note what precedes: "They asked of him, saying, Lord, wilt thou at this time restore again the kingdom to Israel? And he said unto them, It is not for you to know the times or the seasons, which the Father hath put in his own power"—I'm not needing prophets; it's not best for you to know times and seasons—"But ye shall receive power, after that the Holy Ghost is come upon you; and ye shall be witnesses unto me, both in Jerusalem, and in all Judea, and in Samaria, and unto the uttermost parts of the earth."

Last words are usually important. Surely the last words of our Lord must be. The people were interested in times and seasons. In other words, they wanted the prophet's role. Our Lord wanted "witnesses."

Are you witnessing for Him? Do you tell the world what He means to you? This testimony on your part will intensify His meaning in your own life, and as you testify you grow a better testimony. Not prophets but witnesses—this was His last plea.

LORD, help us to witness for Thee, always and everywhere; and grant that our witness may turn men and women to Thee and to eternal life. *Amen.*

L. N. D. WELLS
East Dallas Christian Church, Dallas, Tex.

LIVING BY FAITH

I am crucified with Christ: nevertheless I live; yet not I, but Christ liveth in me: and the life which I now live in the flesh, I live by the faith of the Son of God, who loved me, and gave himself for me.—Gal. 2:20

There are three ways we can think about our lives. We may think that as individuals we count for nothing. That is the way of pessimism, which cuts the nerve of effort and leads to weakness and despair.

We may think that we are all-important. That is the way of *egotism*, and leads to a distorted sense of values that prevents harmonious cooperation with other people for ends which are greater than ourselves.

Or we may think of our lives as having meaning in the purposes of God. That is the way of *responsibility*. It does not result in a sense of futility or self-importance, but it does take life seriously. That is the way of the Christian faith.

As humans, we can stand almost anything except the fear that when we have given our best or endured the worst, after all it made no real difference what we did or who we were. Life takes on a new depth and richness when we confront all of life's contingencies with the faith that this adventure of living counts in the purposes of God, and that *we* count.

O GOD, our Help in ages past, our Hope for years to come; we who need Thy help and hope turn to Thee, who hast been the abiding Friend of all people in all times, in all places. Shine Thou within our hearts, giving us the light of the knowledge of Thy glory in the face of Christ. Set our feet in the ways Thou hast chosen for us. Confirm our spirits in the faith which overcomes the world. Teach us to be Christ's disciples, and to find in Him our life and our peace. *Amen.*

MORGAN PHELPS NOYES
Central Presbyterian Church, Montclair, N.J.

DIVINE GUIDANCE IN HUMAN AFFAIRS

In all thy ways acknowledge him, and he shall direct thy paths.
—Prov. 3:6

Does acknowledging God in all one's ways leave any room for the use of common sense or the exercise of personal judgment? Of course it does, for common sense itself suggests that since these mental powers of ours came originally from God, it is well for us to confer with Him concerning all of life's problems and especially life's perplexities.

One of the most serious heresies of the day is the notion that God is not interested in the details of the ordinary human life. The fact is that, having invested in us, in our creation and our redemption, He is concerned with all that legitimately concerns us—business, physical health, friendships, pleasure, as well as the salvation of the soul and the final supremacy of His Kingdom.

But it has to be kept in mind that this promise of divine guidance is vindicated only as fellowship with God is cultivated habitually. Occasional, spasmodic appeals for advice are very likely to prove disappointing. The final argument for the value of prayer in general is based upon the experience of those who make a business of partnership with God. If there were published the story of how individuals have profited by acknowledging God in all their ways, some items would seem very trivial to some, but all in all such testimony would be human enough to attract the attention and confirm the faith of a great many people.

O THOU FATHER OF LIGHTS, with whom is no shadow of turning; accept my thanks for answers to prayers for guidance already given me. May I never so overestimate my own powers of discretion or the value of the opinions of men as to fail to confer with Thee first of all concerning the meaning and conduct of life. In the name of Jesus Christ. *Amen.*

FRED L. DECKER
First Methodist Church, Gloversville, N.Y.

FREEDOM THROUGH TRUTH AND DISCIPLINE

Ye shall know the truth, and the truth shall make you free.—John 8:32

The disciplined mind is as important as the disciplined body; indeed, it is far more important. The mind trained to look through catchwords and slogans is not deceived by half-truths or falsehoods. It seeks the truth, and when the mind gains the truth it is strengthened against most of the shocks that so often break down our inner fortresses of character and faith.

Freedom is one of the watchwords of the struggle of today. It is the right and the power of putting one's personality, one's abilities and talents, into the places where they belong. It is "belonging" to the family of humankind. It is life based on truth. Knowing the truth and accepting its responsibilities disciplines the mind, and a disciplined mind takes charge of the whole life.

The mind that has found the truth—truth about God, about the nature of life, about the supreme values worth living and dying for; truth about Jesus and His mission in setting up the Kingdom of God as the ideal society based on the law of love, love of God and love of neighbors; truth about oneself and what the self is able to be and do—that mind becomes the commanding officer in the whole regiment of life's inner reserves. The truth shall make us free, and nothing else can or will. Nothing else can make us sufficiently strong or bold.

GOD OF ALL TRUTH AND POWER, lead us by Thy light to find truth and by truth to be made free. Grant us freedom from all that oppresses and enslaves life, freedom from tyrants and their false goals for life. Grant us vision to see the truth, will to pursue and defend it, courage to live and die for it. Teach us to know the simple grandeur of the life, the teaching, the death, and the living presence of Jesus Christ our Lord. *Amen.*

RAYMOND A. McCONNELL
First Plymouth Congregational Church, Lincoln, Neb.

JESUS IS PLACED IN THE TOMB

There was a garden, and in the garden a new tomb in which no one had ever been buried. Because of the Jewish Preparation Day they buried Jesus there, for the tomb was close at hand.—John 19:41–42

We have each closed many tombs in our own lives. It can seem like a good solution to take our problems and frustrations, push them into a tomb, and block them off with an immovable stone. That is the way we avoid many of the things in our lives that we can't deal with. But that's not quite the meaning of the tomb in this garden.

For the Christian, the tomb is both an end and a beginning. Where one story ends, another one begins. Mary must have felt great sorrow as the closing of the tomb completed the painful passion of her Son. With the early Christian community, however, she discovered that the life of Jesus continued. Out of emptiness and death came life. From behind that lifeless rock emerged great power.

Like Mary and the early Christian church, we must find the strength to open the tombs we have closed. We must find new life in the parts of our experience we have closed off. We must pray that resurrection occurs in the private graveyards that we have established in our minds.

LORD OF THE RESURRECTION, O God of new life, we have buried our sadness, frustrations, and problems in the tombs of our minds. Heal the wounds of our past. Where we find death, give new life. Open these many tombs and fill them with the power of Your Risen Son. *Amen.*

GERALD HORAN, OSM
President, Servite High School, Anaheim, Calif.

✝

YOU HAVE TO BE PRESENT TO WIN

This is the day that the Lord has made; let us rejoice and be glad in it.
—Ps. 118:24

The sign on the wall at a senior citizen's bingo event read: "You have to be present to win." What is true about a bingo game is also true about our lives: only when we live in the present can we claim the prize of a fulfilling life.

When I was told recently that I had cancer and would need an operation immediately, I got a lesson in living in the present. I concentrated on what was happening to my body at that moment. Simple activities such as sitting up in a chair, walking, taking a shower, and eating solid food took on almost cosmic meaning. Life became so precious that a flower or a word of love brought tears to my eyes. Perhaps I had never been this present to the moment, this conscious of life and its demands and rewards. As I walk the road to recovery, I will take with me gratitude for the intensity of feeling and the deep thanksgiving for life that I was given in those early days of illness.

Being present to win requires letting go of the baggage of the past— the hurts, anger, losses, and grief. Being present to win requires giving up worry and anxiety about the future, and welcoming the gifts and joys, as well as the sorrows and pains, of the moment. That takes every ounce of faith and spiritual discipline developed over a lifetime. It means cherishing every moment of life, loving more unselfishly, listening more compassionately, and spending energy on what is life-giving. Living in the present wins life's greatest gifts.

GRACIOUS GOD, we thank You for this day and the gifts it will bring to our lives. May we receive the joys and sorrows, pleasures and pains of this day as opportunities to grow in love, in wisdom, and in gratitude for life. *Amen.*

CAROLYN HENNINGER OEHLER
Executive Director, Scarritt-Bennett Center, Nashville, Tenn.

✝

FIXING OUR FOCUS

But when he noticed the wind, he became frightened and began to sink . . .
—Matt. 14:30

Mr. Fisher's words kept ringing in my ears, "Keep your eyes on the first telephone pole on the other side of the field." Out of the corner of my eye I saw a rabbit bounding away, but I kept my eyes fixed on that pole a quarter of a mile away. "Concentrate," I told myself, "concentrate."

Although it was my second summer to work on Mr. Fisher's farm, this was my first time to pull the planter behind the big John Deere tractor. I wanted my rows to be as straight as Mr. Fisher's were. The secret, he had told me, was to keep my eyes fixed on an object on the other side of the field. The tractor would follow my eyes.

Although I didn't realize it at the time, Mr. Fisher's words about the importance of a fixed focus have a much broader application. Indeed, they reveal one of the secrets for successful living. In the passage for today, as long as Peter looked at Jesus, all was well. But when he took his eyes off Jesus and looked at the storm-tossed waves, he began to sink.

Nothing is more important than fixing the focus of our lives, for that focus will shape our perceptions, our values, and our decisions. A shifting focus causes life to lack cohesion, purpose, and meaning. The abundant life we desire, a life that weathers the inevitable storms, can be attained if we will fix our focus on God.

GRACIOUS GOD, grant me the resolve to fix my focus on You. When my vision strays, lovingly redirect my eyes to behold Your beauty and goodness. *Amen.*

RONALD L. FARMER
Dean of the Wallace All Faiths Chapel,
Chapman University, Orange, Calif.

KEEPING LIFE FIT

Fear not them which kill the body, but are not able to kill the soul.
—Matt. 10:28

When wild ducks were flying south, one was attracted by the feeding grounds of a farm below. Accordingly, he joined the well-fed domestic ducks, adopting their life and privileges. The next year when the wild ducks went south they called to him. He spread his wings but could not get going. He was unfit to keep company with his own kind. The next year they called, but he could hardly hear them and didn't even try to join them.

Somebody has remarked that our Christian fellowship is "not Christian enough." Was it not the great apostle who said, "I keep my body under"? Byrd, the explorer of both North and South Poles, would certainly join him in keeping his body disciplined so that it could endure the climate at the polar regions. We are being told much about the disciplined life today. When any people give up butter for guns they are to be reckoned with.

The modern world is increasingly demanding disciplined bodies, minds, and spirits. "I keep my body under" means that all of life is to be kept fit for anything.

O GOD OF ALL LIFE, we give Thee thanks for the riches of being, for "in Thee we live and move and have our being." Give us increasingly disciplined powers that we may bring them to bear upon our day and generation with effectiveness. We ask in the name of the Lord of Life, Jesus, the Man of Galilee and strong Son of God. *Amen.*

CLARENCE W. KEMPER
First Baptist Church, Denver, Colo.

WHERE IS GOD?

*For I am persuaded that neither death, nor life, . . . nor things present,
nor things to come, . . . shall be able to separate us from the love of God,
which is in Christ Jesus our Lord.*—Rom. 8:38–39

Where is God *now?*" some people are asking—as if one might believe in God in time of peace but not in the midst of war. But such an idea rests upon two errors: a misreading of history and a wrong conception of God. The history of the human race is not some smooth story in which sweetness and love are always and everywhere triumphant. Human progress has come not only out of education and the persuasions of love. There is, in fact, no sphere of life from which conflict is altogether absent.

Nor is God merely an amiable Being who runs away when the going gets tough. He is a God of love and mercy. But He is also a God of judgment and wrath, whose justice is revealed in the terror of life, as well as in its sweetness. The God who has brought us through all the long centuries of suffering and struggle does not suddenly disappear now that, in this century, we must fight a terrible war. Where is God? He is where He has always been—in the sunshine and in the storm, in the quiet of a peaceful home and in the grim struggle of a battlefield. God is great and compassionate enough to go with us wherever we have to go.

OUR FATHER, through all the long history of our race Thou hast led us. On bright days and on dark, in joy and in pain, we have been upheld by Thy power and love. Therefore, in the stress and strain of our time, we will trust and not be afraid. Through whatever valley we must walk, Thou wilt go with us, even as our Master on a cross of suffering commended Himself to Thy Fatherly care. In His name. *Amen.*

HERMAN F. REISSIG
First Union Congregational Church, Quincy, Ill.

THE POWERHOUSE OF THE ETERNAL

For God hath not given us the spirit of fear; but of power, and of love, and of a sound mind.—2 Tim. 1:7

God's offer is power. Dr. John Baillie of Edinburgh, who was present in the fighting around Dunkirk, tells of that remarkable delivery. Brave men took their little craft and, risking everything, brought their brothers off to safety and to England. Here was power to save organized and used in a remarkable way. Then, a few days later, as some who did not "accept deliverance" made their way southward into France, he tells of meeting a French soldier so gripped with fear that he was no longer a man. Baillie, remembering the French soldiers of the old war, took hold of the man and shook him and called him to be a man again. Fear had destroyed his ability.

There is a story of a man in the early church over which we never cease to marvel. You remember him. Peter was his name, and he seemed to be a bold, daring disciple until the test came; and then he showed himself a coward. He let Christ down that night before a girl's accusation.

A short time later, however, we see this same man as the leader of the little group of Christians in Jerusalem. Now he is unafraid of what others can do unto him. What transformed Peter? It was the power of God. "All power," said Jesus, "is given unto me in heaven and in earth. Go ye therefore, and make disciples." "And, behold, I send the promise of my Father upon you: but tarry ye in the city of Jerusalem, until ye be endued with power from on high." "But ye shall receive power, after that the Holy Spirit is come upon you: and ye shall be witnesses."

NOW UNTO HIM that is able to keep us from falling, and to present us faultless before the presence of His glory with exceeding joy, to the only wise God our Savior, be glory and majesty, dominion and power, both now and ever. *Amen.*

HARRISON RAY ANDERSON
Fourth Presbyterian Church, Chicago, Ill.

WHY WE FIGHT

Sanctify the Lord God in your hearts; and be ready always to give an answer to every man that asketh you a reason of the hope that is in you with meekness and fear.—1 Pet. 3:15

This war is not a holy war; but it is a religious war in that it is a formidable, head-on conflict between two opposing philosophies of life. This is a struggle within the spirit of man where ideas are even more destructive than bullets.

Although a victory for us may not be essential to the preservation of Christianity, which has more than once existed underground, a defeat would menace our every liberty and every institution. It would be a setback to the free exercise of religion for which so many have given their lives in the past.

Our choice is not between black and white; it is not an easy clean-cut decision between good and evil, but that kind of choice most frequent in life. Between two grave alternatives we choose the one which promises most for the future. While there are still a few friendly democracies left to fight beside us, we choose, with our eyes wide open, between the rigors and sacrifices of war, and the defeat of all freedom, the certainty of spiritual slavery. As free men we had to fight.

O GOD OF HOSTS, grant us courage to fight for what seems to us to be the right. Give us the courage to fight to the death for those ideals in which we believe. And we pray that, whether we live or die, the right shall prevail, and that liberty shall not perish from the earth. In the name of Him who laid down His life for us. *Amen.*

GEORGE STEWART
First Presbyterian Church, Stamford, Conn.

LOOK UP

Lift up your eyes, and look on the fields; for they are white already to harvest.—John 4:35

Jesus knew the limitations of His disciples, knew that they were under the heel of Rome and influenced thereby, knew that they were unlearned and had little training. Yet by counseling them to look elsewhere, he cautioned them against looking at the discouraging aspects of their lives. "Lift up your eyes," He said, "and look on the fields." Jesus knew that the upward look helps, and that the downward look hurts. He knew that trials are temporary, that the darkest hour must give way to dawn, that the fiercest storm must blow away, and that weeping may endure for the night and yet joy comes in the morning.

Let us, therefore, look away from loneliness, anxiety, and fatigue. Let us look first to the patriots before us, whose bleeding footprints stretch from the snows of Valley Forge to the sands of Pearl Harbor. Let us, furthermore, gain inspiration by looking at our loved ones back home, for whose very lives and liberties we are now struggling.

Finally, let us, through prayer, look to God, the Father of us all, and hear Him say, "As thy days, so shall thy strength be"; "God is faithful, who will not suffer you to be tempted [tried] above that ye are able"; "Lo, I am with you alway, even unto the end of the world"; and "I am the resurrection, and the life: he that believeth in me, though he were dead, yet shall he live." Do not look down, but look up, and in so doing receive hope, steadfastness, cheer, and life everlasting.

O GOD, our Father, direct our attention away from those things that distract and disturb. Help us to fasten our gaze upon the eternal and unchanging nature of Thy love for us. May we know of Thy abiding presence with us, and be conscious of Thy guidance and support and protecting care. *Amen.*

MURRAY C. JOHNSON
First Friends Church, Kokomo, Ind.

BE STRONG

Thou therefore endure hardness, as a good soldier of Jesus Christ.
—2 Tim. 2:3

During World War I, a boy received orders to report to the Canadian armed forces. His father and mother went down to see his entrain. His mother said: "Jim, I put a New Testament in your bag. Promise me that you will read it when you have opportunity." The boy promised he would as he kissed his mother good-bye. The father went through the gate with his son and, before the "all aboard," said: "Jim, you are the third Jim in our family. Your grandfather came to our part of Montreal when it was out in the sticks. In his home the first religious service was held. He was elected to the municipal council, and you know how he was honored when he died. His name was Jim. I have tried hard to be the best kind of a dad to you. Promise me that you, too, will keep the name clean." Jim said, "I will." And he did.

As I write [in 1942], my boy is waiting to go to Fort Leavenworth. He will measure up to the mental demands to be made of him. But how about the spiritual combat? Will he make it easier for his buddies to take the strain of army life? Will he have courage, prove himself a morale builder?

That depends on his spiritual resources, his trust in God, and his loyalty to Jesus Christ.

MY FATHER AND MY GOD, help me to be conscious of Thy presence and Thy power. Give me the courage, the resolution, the steadfastness, that I may be a good soldier of my country and of Jesus Christ. *Amen.*

W. ERNEST COLLINS
Central Congregational Church, Topeka, Kan.

CHOOSING CHRIST

Choose you this day whom ye will serve.—Josh. 24:15

This is part of Joshua's last charge to the tribes of ancient Israel. It makes all the difference in this world, and in the next, whether we choose Jesus Christ as our Savior, our King, the One who is to rule our lives. There are three things to note:

First, *you* alone can choose for yourself. Others may advise, may pray for you—but only *you* can choose.

Second, *this day*. God's standard of time is now. We have no time but *now*. Tomorrow is too late.

Third, *whom*. You will have a supreme loyalty. Will it be the flesh or the spirit? Will it be Christ or Satan?

Choose ye, now, and choose rightly or else you will go down into utter defeat.

O LORD, help us to make right choices, in every moment and every eventuality of life. Help us to remember that the choice of Jesus means that we have the gift of God, even eternal life. *Amen.*

ROBERT HUGH MORRIS
First Presbyterian Church, Haddonfield, N.J.

REMINISCENCES OF A CHAPLAIN

O magnify the Lord with me, and let us exalt his name together.
—Ps. 34:3

In a pocket Bible I carried through World War I, I had a covenant which I read as follows:

I TAKE

God, the Father, to be my God . . . . 1 Thes. 1:9
Jesus Christ to be my Savior . . . . Acts 5:31
The Holy Spirit to be my Sanctifier . . . . 1 Pet. 1:2
The Word of God to be my Rule . . . . 2 Tim. 3:16–17
The People of God to be my People . . . . .Ruth 1:16

I GIVE

Myself, all I am, and all I have, to the Lord . . . . Rom. 14:7–8
And I do this deliberately . . . . Josh. 21:15
Sincerely . . . . 2 Cor. 1:12
Freely . . . . Ps. 110:3
And forever . . . . Rom. 8:35, 39

O THOU WHO ART LIGHT, and in whom is no darkness at all, let no cloud of our hatred or smoke of hot revenge dim for us the brightness of Thy face. And, in the end, bring us and our enemies together into the beauty of Thy Peace. *Amen.*

SAM J. MATHIESON
Central Christian Church, Denver, Colo.

THANK GOD AND HAVE COURAGE

Let not the wise man glory in his wisdom, neither let the mighty man glory in his might, let not the rich man glory in his riches: but let him . . . glory in this, that he . . . knoweth me.—Jer. 9:23–24

The might of America is not her millions but the quality of her men and women. The power of democracy is our trust. Without it the future would be dark indeed. We have the facilities for giving everyone the good life. Let us thank God and have courage.

Let not the wise glory in wisdom. Our cities need a revival of civic virtue. We should be ashamed of our tragic record of inefficiency and corruption in business and in government.

Let not the mighty nation glory in its might. Instead we must rise up in the power of God to establish the life of this land on righteousness which alone can exalt a nation.

Today the United States is a rich nation composed of many poor folk. Let not the rich nation glory in its riches.

God delights in righteousness. Let us have courage to emphasize our constant need for Christian character. Through the Spirit of God the world may have new life. God at work in our lives will build a world of loving-kindness and righteousness.

ETERNAL GOD, Father of all peoples, in humble penitence for our sins we ask Thy forgiveness. Direct those responsible for our national welfare to take the necessary steps to build a just and peaceful world order. Help this stricken world speedily to set in order the productive forces that satisfy human needs. In the time of prosperity fill our hearts with thankfulness, and in the day of trouble suffer not our trust in Thee to fail. *Amen.*

PHILIP ALLEN SWARTZ
First Congregational Church, Poughkeepsie, N.Y.

OUR SOULS ARE MADE FOR CHEER

In the world ye shall have tribulation; but be of good cheer. I have overcome the world.—John 16:33

We live in a beautiful world. There are far more beautiful spots than ugly spaces. Perhaps there are only enough of the latter to enable our human souls to appreciate the beautiful.

It is a sad world if looked at from some angles, but think of the joy that may be found everywhere—and a good sprinkling of it in every home and in every life. There are tears, to be sure; but really there are far more smiles, and laughter may be heard in connection with almost every situation. Perhaps God made our souls primarily for song and laughter.

This thing we know to be true: hope always outrivals despair, and good cheer will always master tribulation. And is it not better so? Happy are they who come to believe

> That Life is ever lord of Death,
> And Love can never lose its own!

It is well at times to realize how much has been said for the sake of comfort and courage, and how definitely millions of lives have been and are dedicated to the creation of comfort and cheer. If we look about us, we shall find opportunities ourselves to bring happiness to some lonesome soul and cheer some heart that is on the point of breaking.

DEAR GOD, our Father, make us aware that sorrow may ever be turned into joy by those who possess the creative spirit. Give us ever a vital appreciation of the beauty and joy which are ours—as an expression of Thy Divine Love. *Amen.*

GEORGE O. MARSH
Central Christian Church, Glendale, Calif.

THE SOLDIER AND GOD

What shall we do?—Luke 3:14

When the soldiers asked John the Baptist, "What shall we do?" he answered, "Be content with your wages." This virtually meant, "Do not be a malcontent. Do not mutiny. Be loyal and serve without reproach."

Our Lord did not come to condemn the world, but to save the world. God works through us as poor instruments in His hands, and sometimes His saving process sends us to perform tasks that are difficult and disagreeable. We must always contend against the forces of evil. In the war the line is definitely drawn and the objectives definitely fixed—whether God and His free children shall inherit the earth, or become slaves to terrorism.

Believers in God and His righteousness have a right to feel that they are fighting on God's side. Their battle is to keep the ideals of Jesus from perishing from the earth. These ideals are worth fighting for, and we are confident that they shall in the end prevail.

Your life is for the glorification of God, and whether you give it on the battlefield or elsewhere you may have the blessed assurance that He understands and cares for you in this life and in the life to come. "He shall give his angels charge over thee," and you need not fear. It is not the length but the quality of life that counts; and one may exercise his or her faith in the ultimate victory of the Cross over sin, Satan, and death in the service of one's country, as in the quiet pursuits of everyday life at home.

O GOD, look upon the hearty desires of Thy humble servants, and stretch forth the right hand of Thy Majesty to be our defense against all our enemies. Through Jesus Christ our Lord. *Amen.*

GEORGE DAVIDSON
St. John's Episcopal Church, Los Angeles, Calif.

THE GOER-BEFORE

I will go before thee, and make the rough places smooth; I will break in pieces the doors of brass, and cut in sunder the bars of iron.—Isa. 45:2 ARV

It was a man of high faith who caught this message from God in a difficult day. And his strong faith made him a man of dauntless daring.

When God speaks thus to us—and He surely does—what ground of excuse have we left? Can we plead the hardness of our circumstances when He has pledged the sufficiency of His power?

Some people are haunted by fears that come stealing out of the past. Such fears are connected with things that have happened. Other people are more shaken by fears that scowl at them in the future. Such fears, of course, are tied up with things that may happen. God's forgiveness will cover the yesterdays and their failures; the Cross of Christ has no meaning if it does not tell us that. But what of tomorrow? Here is the answer:

I will go before thee.
I will go before thee—and make the rough places smooth!
I will go before thee—and break in pieces the doors of brass!
I will go before thee—and cut in sunder the doors of iron!

For the past—His pardon! For the future—His presence!

Then let us deal with our future by dealing first with Him in the beginning of every day. Let us say it to ourselves with unwavering faith: "He goes before me!"

GOD, I do not ask for courage for the whole of life, but rather for courage to live a moment at a time, and that moment for Thee. For Christ's sake. *Amen.*

PAUL S. REES
Covenant Tabernacle Church, Minneapolis, Minn.

BUILDING GOD'S KINGDOM

The kingdom of God cometh not with observation.—Luke 17:20

Sitting on the sideline will never bring in the kingdom of God. The good world we all desire does not come in that way. Jesus had gone throughout Palestine preaching the coming of the Kingdom of God. The Pharisees sarcastically demanded of Him, "When?" To which He replied, "The kingdom of God cometh not with observation." It takes more than watching to boil the pot; it takes building a fire. Thus is given to the humble and the brave a share in building a better world!

And He added, "Neither shall they say, 'Lo, here! or, lo there!'" They could not think that their land was the only land; nor must we think that our race is the only race. The Kingdom of God was to reach beyond even the "Promised Land" and the "Chosen People." What a privilege to have a share in following the Christ with such conceptions! Thus to all people everywhere an opportunity to help make a better world!

And then He said, "For, behold, the kingdom of God is within you." Narrow and bigoted it may be, or broad and humble and brave. God desires to build His temple within us. "Know ye not that ye are the temple of God, and that the Spirit of God dwelleth in you?" (1 Cor. 3:16). Jesus healed ten lepers, but only the despised Samaritan among them returned to thank the Healer. In him was the true Kingdom, the right spirit, and God's temple.

O GOD, our eternal heavenly Father, we do thank Thee that Thou hast granted unto us the privilege of having a share in Thy divine plan; and we pray for courage, humility, and consecration that we may be worthy to be coworkers with Thee. In Christ's name we pray. *Amen.*

JOHN G. TRUITT
Suffolk Christian Church, Suffolk, Va.

INVISIBLE VICTORIES

He that ruleth his spirit [is better] than he that taketh a city.
—Prov. 16:32

Some of the greatest victories are invisible victories. They are won in our hearts where no person can see the battle that is going on.

A cheerful countenance and a gay spirit may represent an inner victory. They may be the result of a determination not to shed gloom on the spirits of other people. A woman once said that her favorite passage of Scripture was, "Grin and bear it." These words are not in the Bible, but the thought behind them describes many heroes of the faith.

A courageous heart may not be the result of temperament. It may be the result of an inner struggle and ultimate victory. As Jesus stood before Pilate, He seemed to possess the ultimate courage—the courage to go where duty led and to refuse to hate. This was the result, not of the lack of struggle, but of inner victory in the struggle. In Gethsemane He received strength to win out in His own life.

O GOD, who dost call us to a faith that can overcome the world, make us victorious in our inner life. Make us steadfast in the face of temptation, courageous in time of danger, and unwearied in hope. *Amen.*

ROLLAND W. SCHLOERB
Hyde Park Baptist Church, Chicago, Ill.

THE CONTEST OF FAITH

Enter the great contest of faith! Take hold of eternal life.
—1 Tim. 6:12 (GOODSPEED)

Much of life is competitive. It is a struggle. The flesh is in conflict with the spirit, and the spirit with the flesh. Reason and better judgment are often antagonistic to feeling and emotion. Good intentions, and the will to do, are opposed by the desire to conform and the fear of being conspicuous.

Circumstances sometimes thrust us into positions which are not to our liking. But when duty calls—when principles are at stake—we may not consult our own feelings or desires. Perhaps the destiny of a world hangs in the balance. Millions of humans beings may reap the rewards of our heroism, or suffer the results of our failure to do our best. Under the stress of similar forces a great soul once cried out: "But none of these things move me, neither count I my life dear unto myself."

The Christian life calls for the heroic. We are asked to forsake all and follow the Christ. We are enjoined to set for ourselves no lesser standard than perfection. We are reminded that the gate is narrow and the road hard which leads to life. Anything less than our best is unworthy of Him. Watchfulness, effort, and supreme loyalty are among the conditions we must meet. Courage, fortitude, and divine help are necessary to such attainment. St. Paul appeals to his young friend Timothy by means of a challenge. "Enter the great contest of faith! Take hold of eternal life."

MASTER, Thou knowest the world in which we live. Thou art sufficient for every time of need. Give courage for the task which awaits our doing. Let us not lose faith with one another because of it. May we see beyond the present conflict a world at peace, wherein dwelleth righteousness. *Amen.*

BENJAMIN EITELGEORGE
University Park Methodist Church, Denver, Colo.

THE NEW DAY

And I saw a new heaven and a new earth; for the first heaven and the first earth were passed away; and there was no more sea.—Rev. 21:1

How strange are life's ways! How wonderful are God's ways! For it is the darkness that ushers in, with the beauty of the morning light, the new day. One summer Hilaire Belloc, the well-known writer, started out on a walking tour. He took with him an adventurous novice. They set out to cross the Pyrenees, expecting to get over the mountains before dark.

However, overtaken by darkness, they spent the night high up on the mountain. Toward morning a great wind arose. It began to blow with tremendous force, dislodging huge blocks and sending them down over the heads of the men so that they felt in their faces the splinters of the great stones.

The novice, seized with fear, took hold of his companion, who had scarcely stirred in his blanket, and said, "I think it is the end of the world." Mr. Belloc turned to him and said, "Oh no—this is the way that the dawn comes up in the Pyrenees." Such is the story of much of life, and we must understand God's ways in it. There is life's crucifixion. There is God's garden. There is life's darkness. There is God's light. There is life's grave. There is God's resurrection. And be of good cheer, whatever comes; God will not fail His children. He is our refuge and strength. Our trust is in Him. The dawn of His new day is sure to come.

MAY THE LORD bless us and keep us: may the Lord make His face to shine upon us and be gracious unto us: may the Lord lift up His countenance upon us and give to our hearts peace, both now and always. *Amen.*

JOSEPH C. MACDONALD
The Union Church, Waban, Mass.

THE DANGER OF STOPPING TOO SOON

*And the man of God was wroth with him, and said, Thou shouldest
have smitten five or six times, then hadst thou smitten Syria till thou
hadst consumed it.*—2 Kings 13:18–19

The greatest danger which confronts any of us is the danger of stopping too soon, of crying "quits" before the job is completely done, of having faith and courage enough to go so far but not enough to go all the way.

We start out in life with high hopes and lofty ideals, but soon we realize that the road of life is a rocky road and an uphill one. Temptation comes; disillusionment comes. Personally we are not as capable nor as effective as we had thought we were. Nor is the world as friendly to our hopes and ideals as we thought it would be. The result is that we are apt to lose heart and comfort ourselves with the thought that we have at least made an effort. We have shot thrice. But Rome was not built in a day, nor will the Kingdom of God be established in one generation. It is a long, slow business which will never be accomplished by those who grow weary in well doing.

The crown of life, the conquest of evil, the establishment of righteousness among people and nations comes only to those who refuse to stop too soon, to cry "quits" before the job is done.

GRACIOUS GOD, we are weak, but Thou canst make us strong. May Thy Holy Spirit ever strengthen and sustain us in our conflict with evil, our battle for the right. We ask it in the name of Him who overcame the world, even Jesus our Lord and Savior. *Amen.*

THOMAS S. MUTCH
First Presbyterian Church, Morristown, N.J.

THE UPLIFTED LOOK

I will lift up mine eyes unto the hills, from whence cometh my help.
—Ps. 121:1

From the altar window of the little Chapel of the Transfiguration in western Wyoming I see, as I lift my eyes, the three towering, snow-covered peaks of the mighty Tetons. The day was gloomy when I paused in the chapel. But those great mountains spoke of stability, peace, and eternity.

You young men and women who may read these lines are going through many trying experiences even as I did in the First World War. To see you through them you need to cultivate the "uplifted look." You must retain in your own soul those crystal clear moments which reveal, amid chaos, the stability, the peace, the love, and the mercy of the Eternal God, out of which will come for you courage, faith, and hope.

During the bloody Meuse-Argonne battle a comrade said to me with conviction, "This puts the fear of God in a fellow." In the midst of shot and shell he had sensed a window open towards God and utilized the "uplifted look." Such an experience may come to some of you. Yet if you desire, you may have the experience often. Visions of God come more frequently as you commune with Him through meditation, through reading His Word, through prayer, through the fellowship of worship. By these means the "uplifted look" may be a daily experience.

DEAR GOD IN HEAVEN, I thank Thee that Thou hast smiled upon us, that Thou hast taken our hands in Thine to lead us over life's way. I know that with this faith in my heart, all things do somehow work together for good to them that love Thee. Lead me and all my comrades to those high moments where we shall see Thee in all Thine infinite compassion waiting to bless us with faith and courage to find our way through these troublous days. *Amen.*

WALTER A. VOSS
Trinity Lutheran Church, Sioux City, Iowa

THE BASIC BEATITUDE

Blessed is he whose transgression is forgiven, and whose sin is covered. Blessed is the man unto whom the Lord imputeth not iniquity, and in whose spirit there is no guile.—Ps. 32:1–2

A beatitude is a statement wherein blessedness is attributed upon certain conditions. There are a hundred of them in the Bible. Blessedness is more than happiness, for it has to do with the soul. Christ was always blessed, though not always happy. It means success in life at its highest. It is eternal. God is the "blessed" God, and we can be blessed.

The foundation of all blessedness for us, as David found, is knowing that our sins are forgiven. Sin imprisons us, keeps us away from God. When God grants pardon, freedom begins.

Have you had the experience of the forgiveness of sin? It is a very great and very necessary experience. Seek it and obtain it. The way is made plain in Isaiah 55:7: "Let the wicked forsake his way, and the unrighteous man his thoughts: and let him return unto the Lord, and he will have mercy upon him; and to our God, for he will abundantly pardon." We are told the basis of this in 1 Peter 2:23: "[Christ] bore our sins in his own body on the tree, that we, being dead to sins, should live unto righteousness: by whose stripes ye were healed." The great peace of God will come into your heart when you thus have peace with the Eternal. Whether, then, you live or die, you are the Lord's.

COME TO GOD as your Creator, Judge, and Redeemer. Formulate your own prayer, and speak to Him directly in your own words. He is seeking you and will meet you. Be absolutely sincere, for He knows your deepest thoughts. Hold back nothing from Him, that He may give Himself fully to you. *Amen.*

EARLE V. PIERCE
Former President, Northern Baptist Convention, Minneapolis, Minn.

CHRISTIAN GROWTH

Jesus increased in wisdom and stature, and in favor with God and man.—Luke 2:52

The text above is one of the most interesting statements made in the Scriptures concerning the life of Jesus Christ. Jesus grew.

He grew in wisdom. He learned more and more concerning people, their tragedies and triumphs, their weakness and strength. He learned about the way in which God works through nature. His wisdom in itself drew men to Him.

He grew in stature. He was not a weakling. He worked hard and played hard. Size and height are included in this statement, of course. He grew especially in strength and manliness.

He grew in favor with God. God loves all people, but especially those who do His will. Jesus was learning each day to serve God better. Therefore, He was growing in favor with God.

He grew in favor with people. He helped others, trusted in others, was interested in their problems, their sorrows, and their joys. He was always deeply concerned about the welfare of people.

Do you want to be more like Jesus? You will need, then, to grow as He did. Become more helpful to others every day. Let your worship and service of God mean more to you each day. Learn more of wisdom, and practice those things which make for good character.

Seize every opportunity to understand life better. You will become more Christlike in every way. Seek God's help, for that you will need in accomplishing this end.

Begin today!

HEAVENLY FATHER, teach us to grow in Thy ways. May we be like Jesus in wisdom and worship and love. Hear us, in our Savior's name. *Amen.*

VICTOR I. GRUHN
North Austin Evangelical Lutheran Church, Chicago, Ill.

FAITH, HOPE, AND LOVE

But now abideth faith, hope, love, these three: and the greatest of these is love.—1 Cor. 13:13 ARV

Everyone has hopes. Hope is like a sprinkle of water. Just as water bubbles forth from the spring, so thoughts and plans bubble forth from the spring of hope. Usually our hopes are colored by the things that have happened in our lives thus far. If life has inspired us with several noble hopes, we are indeed fortunate. Aside from individual and specialized hopes, there are some general hopes which it is good for all to have. It is good to hope for employment in a congenial occupation, time to cultivate a hobby, pleasant social contacts, an agreeable home life, and a satisfying religious experience.

Faith will help us realize our hopes. Without faith, hopes are mere daydreams. Those who have achieved have been those who sought guidance from beyond. To trust God and to see through the eye of faith the realization of our noble hopes is the tonic that will guide us through the storm. Faith will keep the fires of victory burning in our hearts. Without faith we perish.

Both our hopes and our faith must be permeated with love. Without love we become the most fatigued and unhappy persons imaginable. Love of those things for which we hope, love for God and love for the justice of our cause will carry us through. If we would see the dawn tomorrow, we must be loyal to the obligations of today. Faith, hope, and love are guideposts on the road to true life.

GOD OF OUR FOREFATHERS, and our God; inspire us with noble hope; strengthen our faith; and permit our love for justice and righteousness to grow daily under the guidance of Thy Holy Spirit. *Amen.*

DARWIN X. GASS
Heidelberg Reformed Church, Schwenkville, Pa.

COURAGE FINDS ITS SPRINGS IN GOD

God is our refuge and strength, a very present help in trouble. Therefore will not we fear, though the earth be removed, and though the mountains be carried into the midst of the sea.—Ps. 46:1–2

Once in the days of the Protestant Reformation, when all external circumstances seemed to be going against the reformers, Luther roused himself from gloomy conversation with his friend Philip Melancthon with the exclamation, "Come, Philip, let us sing the Forty-sixth Psalm."

Whenever we are discouraged or despairing, that is a good suggestion to adopt. The whole of the Forty-sixth Psalm is strong medicine for gloomy spirits. But we may well give special study to the four affirmations of faith in the first two verses.

What we really are saying is this: Whatever may be the cause of your discouragement, whether it be failure in personal character, or the sickness of some loved one, or the failure to achieve some ambition, or just gloom because of the awful conditions of the world—whatever may be the cause of your discouragement, bring God into it and see what a vast difference He makes. The Gospel reveals to us through Christ a God who moves us to heroic lives. It was said of Oliver Cromwell's men, "They feared God so greatly that they feared nothing else beside." That is the kind of courage that can sustain us in a day when nations rage and earth changes and mountains are shaken into the sea.

O GOD, who hast set us to live in a time of clouds and thick darkness, Thou art our Light. We bless Thee for all great souls who in dangerous days have put their faith in Thee. Be to us both refuge and strength, that living always in Thy sight, we way be made strong and very courageous to do Thy will, through Jesus Christ, our Leader and Lord. *Amen.*

THOMAS GUTHRIE SPEERS
Brown Memorial Presbyterian Church, Baltimore, Md.

THREE WAYS OF MEETING TROUBLE

Strengthened with power through his Spirit in the inward man.
—Eph. 3:16 ARV

There are always three ways of meeting trouble. The first way is to try to run away from it. I was an Army Y.M.C.A. secretary with the A.E.F. in Siberia in 1919, and I know many of our men would have promptly gone A.W.O.L. had it not been for the Pacific Ocean between them and home!

The second solution is to get mad, see red, and fight back blindly—just wild blows, and plenty of profanity to ease your feelings. But that doesn't get you anywhere, either—and you may hit the wrong fellow!

There is a third and better way. We can face our problems and reorganize our lives to meet them. Here is where religion can help. The teaching and example of Jesus show how to organize life on the highest level. Robert Freeman in France did this and wrote:

> Captain of my soul, lead on;
> I follow Thee come dark or dawn.
> Only vouchsafe three things I crave:
> Where terror stalks, help me be brave!
> Where righteous ones can scarce endure
> The siren call, help me be pure!
> Where vows grow dim, and men dare do
> What once they scorned, help me be true!

O GOD, when I come face to face with trouble, help me to take myself in hand and face it in some constructive way. Give me spiritual power, self-control, and deeper insight, that out of every difficulty I may emerge a better person. *Amen.*

ALBERT W. PALMER
President, Chicago Theological Seminary, Chicago, Ill.

DIVINE GUIDANCE

Thou wilt shew me the path of life.—Ps. 16:11

A real faith in the guiding power of Almighty God can make a vast difference in any person's life. Particularly is this true of soldiers. Problems will arise for them that do not come in private life.

Some of these problems will be small, everyday difficulties which will be solved with a little patience and ordinary common sense. Others will be tremendous problems, much too hard for them to cope with alone. When they meet the inevitable fork in the road of decision, it will not always be easy to make a choice. If their choice is to be a wise one, and a courageous one, they will need the help of the Eternal. But how shall they obtain it?

First of all, they will need to lay the matter squarely before God. When they state the problem, and lay it out before God and themselves, they are able to see the alternatives more clearly.

Second, they will have to trust in God to make the decision and to reveal the Divine Mind. After speaking to God, they will have to wait for God to speak to them. There may be earthquake, wind, and fire, before the still small voice of the Eternal speaks to their hearts.

Daily we face situations demanding decisions. If we accept God's guidance we shall acquire the habit of making right decisions, and more and more His choices will be stamped upon our characters to become our personal decisions.

O GOD, the Protector of all that trust in Thee, without whom nothing is strong, nothing is holy; increase and multiply upon us Thy mercy; that, Thou being our Ruler and Guide, we may so pass through things temporal, that we finally lose not the things eternal. Through Jesus Christ our Lord. *Amen.*

CHARLES J. GUNNELL
Christ Episcopal Church, Waterloo, Iowa

SAFETY IS WITH GOD

Wait on the Lord; be of good courage, and he shall strengthen thine heart: wait, I say, on the Lord.—Ps. 27:14

Many illustrious folk have said, "One with God is a majority." The Bible says the same thing in these words, "If God be for us, who can be against us?" And Paul added, "I can do all things through Christ which strengtheneth me."

David had the same experience, which he revealed in the Twenty-seventh Psalm. He feared no one, because he could say, "The Lord is my light and my salvation." His enemies stumbled and fell before him. Even a host encamping about him could not cause his heart to fear. He could maintain his confidence in the very midst of war.

Well, we can have that same kind of confidence, security, and victory. But there are some conditions to be met. They are mentioned in the text. Here they are:

"Wait on the Lord." We must be in prayer before God. We must trust in Him. General Pershing is said to have remarked on one occasion, "Every day I stand at attention before God." Lift your heart in prayer before the Eternal each day.

"Be of good courage." That is the second condition. All true soldiers of Jesus are of good courage, because they derive their strength from the Lord. All Christians are certain of victory because they know that "we are more than conquerors, through him that loved us."

LORD, help me to take time each day to stand at attention before Thee. Make me a person of courage, so that I may fear no one. Fill my heart with strength, that I may have Thy omnipotent power at my command. Inspire me to be like Jesus, who turned what seemed to be a defeat into a most glorious victory. In His name. *Amen.*

A. T. TOMSHANY
First Presbyterian Church, Kansas City, Kan.

FACE THE EAST

The set of their faces is towards the east.—Hab. 1:9 ARV

One of the weaknesses of a good deal of living is the disposition to look back. Lot's wife tried it, and the result was ruin. Cunningham, the noted college track man, when he was at his best, lost a race. He was running swiftly and strongly in that peculiar way of his which ate up distance and promised victory. Almost unconsciously, in his anxiety to know how far the second man was behind him, he glanced back over his shoulder, lost his stride, and his competitor passed him and won.

Paul was perhaps the greatest man of all Christian history. And the secret of his greatness is, in part, contained in those immortal words which were the motto of his life: "Forgetting those things which are behind, and reaching forth unto those things which are before."

The key to his life were the words of the text, "The set of their faces is towards the east." Get the idea! Create the habit! When the day dies, bury it. Get rid of it, else it may prove to be a burden for your back and shackles for your feet. Be in at the birth of the new day. In it lies the promise of an unspoiled day. A brand new chance to make something new, and fine, and immortal, lies ahead. But remember that those who make life fine are the ones who move forward and upward with their faces fixed on the smiling, glowing east.

O GOD, our Father, the Father of all mankind; let Thy blessing rest upon us as we linger a moment with Thee. Give to us now the consciousness of Thy very presence. Enfold us in Thy love; keep us always near Thee. Glorify Thyself through us, as Thou dost lead us through this tangled maze of life; crown us at the end of it. Through our Lord Jesus Christ. *Amen.*

W. R. HARSHAW
Former Executive Secretary, Presbyterian Synod of Minnesota

EASTER GLORY THROUGH THE YEAR

Call to remembrance the former days, in which, after ye were illuminated, ye endured a great fight of afflictions.—Heb. 10:32

Easter comes. For most of us it is a day of radiant glory, thrilling in memories, imaginations, and aspirations. It brings a sense of life that has the capacity for immortality, and a surge of desire to be fit for a vibrant eternity.

Easter goes. The routine days close in on us. We are apt to feel that we have been but witnesses of a "departing glory." Before the threat of lonely commonplaceness we cry out for that which will maintain the glory.

Easter is our salvation. At the heart of it is the conviction that life is not measured by a cradle and a grave. Life is sustained by the dynamic of an endless life. For those who are willing to take it, the hypothesis of an endless life sustains the glow and glory of our richest experiences.

To act as though life were endless is to find new significance in this day, to enter with other persons into the sense of endless fellowship, to get into proper perspective the irritating disproportions of the moment, to know the chance of love that never fails, and to find the source of an eternal energy that makes possible the best in oneself and an eager desire for the best in others. Those who live with the writer of the Epistle to the Hebrews "after the power of an endless life" see always in their mirrors the shining "human face of the Eternal."

O GOD, grant me the assurance of an endless life, that in the grasp of Thine eternal love I may know the faith, courage, and purpose of those who never die. *Amen.*

THOMAS W. GRAHAM
Dean, Graduate School of Theology, Oberlin College, Oberlin, Ohio

RESOURCES FOR DAILY LIVING

I can do all things.—Phil. 4:13

Christianity is the power of God in the soul of humankind. It ought to provide inner resources of spiritual power for daily living. If it does not do this, we have failed to respond with adequate faith to what God in Christ so freely offers us.

Down the centuries multitudes of people have found through Christian faith resources for triumphant daily living. Beset with difficulty, suffering trial and disaster, tossed hither and yon by life's changing circumstance, they could not be beaten. In every situation they "endured, as seeing him who is invisible." Listen to one of these heroes of the faith: "I have learned, in whatsoever state I am, therein to be content. I know how to be abased, and I know also how to abound: in everything and in all things have I learned the secret both to be filled and to be hungry, both to abound and to be in want. I can do all things in him that strengtheneth me."

So completely had the great apostle learned this secret that at the close of his life, looking back, he could say: "I have fought the good fight, I have finished the course, I have kept the faith."

What Christianity meant for Paul, it can mean for us in increasing measure, if by faith and trust and prayer and communion with Christ we lay hold upon the manifold grace of God.

Oh live in us again, even in us.
Oh clothe Thyself, Thy purpose, yet again in human clay.
Work through our feebleness Thy strength,
Work through our sinfulness Thy nobility,
Work through our helpless poverty of soul
Thy grace, Thy glory, and Thy love. *Amen.*

WILLIAM F. KOSMAN
Salem Evangelical Church, Allentown, Pa.

GOD'S CARE

He careth for you.—1 Pet. 5-7

I wish that I could write something which would help all young people to rise against every temptation, keep their minds from growing hard, give them faith in a good God, and preserve them from fatalism. When I was a very young man I heard a sermon based on the text, "For he careth for you."

I've never been in the armed forces, and I've never faced the perils of the battlefield. But I have faced perils to my character. And the only way I had of overcoming them was the remembrance of that text. "He" means God, and "you" means me. *God cares for me!* And *me* isn't my body, but my soul.

If you come out of this war with a whole body, but with a stained soul, you will be badly off, for "out of the heart are the issues of life." There will be need for you in the world when the war drums are silenced. The world needs your best thinking and your noblest actions. Finding God will be your greatest achievement and will yield the finest decorations.

ALMIGHTY GOD, Thou refuge of all Thy children; grant unto us that we may ever turn to Thy loving-kindness and tender mercy. As the storms of life and the dangers of war menace us, may they never shake our faith that Thou art our Father and that Thou carest for us. *Amen.*

FREDERICK K. STAMM
Clinton Avenue Community Church, Brooklyn, N.Y.

SPIRITUAL FREEDOM

Ye were called for freedom; only use not your freedom for an occasion to the flesh.—Gal. 5:13 ARV

Liberty is the most passionately demanded human blessing and the most dangerous human possession.

Paul, in the great passage Galatians 5:13–6:10, develops the doctrine of true moral freedom. He says in effect: Nobody is to tell me what I am to do. Even the sacred Scriptures are not a set of rules that I must follow. I am to decide freely what is helpful in the Bible practices and suggestions and what in them is out of date and therefore not useful to me. I am a free man, a free son of God, and therefore not to be bound by rules and conventions and the prejudices of the past. I will do what I believe to be right.

This is glorious doctrine but very dangerous. Paul knew it. He therefore insisted that the only ones who should dare to live lives of liberty are those whose central desire is to use their liberty for the highest good.

I may not do what I will unless I will what is good. A libertine is not free. One only is free who is led by that inner Guide, the Spirit that shows us the meaning of life. Such a person brings forth the fruit of the Spirit— "love, joy, peace, longsuffering, kindness, goodness, faithfulness, meekness, self-control."

Let us ask ourselves: Am I fit to be free? Will I produce the works of the flesh or the fruits of the Spirit? If I could do exactly what I pleased, would it be good?

FATHER ETERNAL, whose service is perfect freedom, make us fit to be free. Save us from the slavery of indulgence and from the bondage of selfishness. Purify our hearts and guide our purposes that Thy will may become our will. *Amen.*

THEODORE G. SOARES
Neighborhood Congregational Church, Pasadena, Calif.

✝

HUMBLED BY GRACE

Hope in the Lord from this time on and forevermore.
—Ps. 131:3 NRSV

In a world that applauds accomplishment and celebrity, it is easy to assume that God values us more highly when our ambitions and goals have been fulfilled. Thus, when we fail or are unsuccessful, we not only disappoint ourselves, but we may fear we have disappointed God.

The psalmist reminds us that God desires our trust, not our achievement. When we come before God, our hearts should not be filled with pride, neither should our eyes be lifted up in arrogance. Our deeds cannot possibly compare with the gracious works of the One who fashioned the heavens and the earth, yet who also knows the flight of the solitary sparrow. The proper attitude before God is humility. We are to be like the infant who, without earning it, finds peace, comfort, and assurance in a mother's arms. We should be thankful for God's boundless love that embraces us in victory and in defeat.

GRACIOUS AND MERCIFUL GOD, Your wisdom is beyond our comprehension and Your love is stronger even than death. Enable us so to trust You that even when we fail, we may know that Your care is constant and secure. *Amen.*

KAREN WESTERFIELD TUCKER
Associate Professor, Liturgical Studies,
Duke Divinity School, Duke University, N.C.

LOVE AS GOD LOVES

Be devoted to one another in brotherly love. . . . Be joyful in hope, patient in affection, faithful in prayer. Share with God's people who are in need. Practice hospitality.—Rom. 12:9–13

In a world "gone astray" with much around us which is dictated by the quest for more power, pleasure, recognition, and wealth, we are called to love and honor others above ourselves. I am always amazed at the levels of dogma, hype, and half-truths spoken in the quest of getting what "we" want rather than what God wants. The scriptures are clear! God wants us to love and honor others above ourselves. As Christians, we honor people because they have been created in God's image, because they are our brothers and sisters in Christ, and because they have a unique contribution to make to Christ's church. In a culture that absolutely adores radical individualism, we are called to action in loving and serving others.

How do we do it? Here are some possibilities: Have a committed daily prayer life. God will identify whom we are to serve, if we ask. Attend church regularly to commune faithfully with other believers. Join a small group or Bible study in order to share your life with fellow Christians. Trust the Lord Jesus and the Holy Spirit in giving us the courage, wisdom, and strength to love and honor others above ourselves.

LORD, we thank you for all your blessings and the bounty of what you have created in us. Help us to focus less on ourselves. Help us, Lord, in the strength of your Holy Spirit to love and honor others above ourselves. *Amen.*

GREGORY R. AITKENS
Financial Planner and Director of Christians In Commerce
for Southern California and Arizona,
Mission Viejo, Calif.

LIVING VICTORIOUSLY

If thou faint in the day of adversity, thy strength is small.—Prov. 24: 10

Life hands many a hard situation to us. Some have more difficult problems than others, but we all usually get our share sooner or later. We differ not so much in the number of hard things we meet as in what we do when these come.

Some of us crumple up and faint—the storm comes, the house goes down. Others of us meet trouble stoically; we get hard, even bitter; we strike back at life and try to get even. We don't often get even, but we grow brittle and crack to pieces.

Some of us, when trouble comes, use it as an occasion for finding new resources, so we can meet the situation and live victoriously in spite of it, like Paul, who said, "I take pleasure in infirmities"; "When I am weak, then am I strong." How could this be? It could work that way if our load forced us by exploring to discover some new resource which would give us the use of the power we did not use before. This isn't strange; it is natural. In history, our burdens became heavy; so we explored and found steam and electricity, which hauls our loads and lights our way. Needs meant new power if we took them rightly.

Today we are encountering new dangers, new burdens, new testing. We can quit; we can grow bitter; or like Paul we can seek God, the source of strength; and find that character comes by testing, and even a cross can be a road to victory. The soldier can find a thousand excuses for doing the first two, but many of us will find the glory of doing the third. This is the message of religion, and plenty have discovered that it works.

O GOD, help us to find that "night brings out the stars" and darkness in life is phosphorescent with Thy presence. *Amen.*

ALBERT W. BEAVEN
President, Colgate–Rochester Divinity School, Rochester, N.Y.

CHOSEN PEOPLE

Ye have not chosen me, but I have chosen you.—John 15:16

The Twelve were very much surprised, I am sure, when Jesus said to them, "Ye have not chosen me, but I have chosen you." They had been under the impression that it had come about the other way entirely. They had met Jesus, heard Him talk, been attracted by His personality, and finally decided He was worthy of their loyalty; so they had chosen to follow Him.

Now, from one side, that was a true description of what had happened. But for the moment, at least, Jesus wanted to emphasize the other side. He had put His hand on Andrew and on Simon. To James and John He had said, "Follow me." He had sought out Nathaniel and the rest. Jesus had chosen them.

It is a mistake for us to think that the whole load either of the credit or the blame for what we are or will be is upon us alone. Christian faith in God includes a recognition of our dependence upon Him. To be a Christian is not only to make a choice for Christ; it is also to answer "Yes" to the call God is giving you as you read this page. And if you answer "Yes," you will find that your courage and faith will be strengthened according to your need in any trial; and if it is your good fortune to win victory for Christ, you will be humbled by the knowledge that the good that comes is not yours alone but Christ's who has worked in and through you. So when we realize that it is God who chooses us to serve Him and our fellows, that realization will give us the two things a soldier needs above all, courage and humility.

O GOD, who art ever calling Thy children to Thyself, give me such a sense of Thy presence in this world that all that I am and do shall be to Thy glory. In fear and in struggle, in triumph and in achievement, will Thou be at my side. Through Jesus Christ. *Amen.*

EUGENE CARSON BLAKE
Pasadena Presbyterian Church, Pasadena, Calif.

THE HELPFUL PRESENCE OF GOD

Whither shall I go from thy spirit? Or whither shall I flee from thy presence?—Ps. 139:7 ARV

In these words is revealed a majestic conception in which God transcends space and boundary lines and becomes at home in all the world. It is natural for us to associate God with specific places like a house of worship, or the city in which we grew up, or a holy experience. We need to learn there is no place to which we may go but God is there, there is no experience into which we can come but God's companionship is possible.

There was a time when religious people, in burden and humiliation, were overwhelmed with fear that to be taken away from their holy city and their holy places meant to make God remote and far away. But out of the terrific bondage and discipline in a strange land they came in the confidence that the humble and contrite can find God anywhere.

Tucked away in the book of Deuteronomy is one of the most treasured promises of the Bible. It is found in the farewell address of a great leader. The people for whom he had done great things had come to rely upon him. Then the time for him to leave them was at hand. In that crucial situation the marks of keen insight and strong leadership are shown as Moses, turning their attention to a source of support which would never be withdrawn, said: "The eternal God is thy dwelling place, and underneath are the everlasting arms." Here was One on whom they might rely with no fear of ever being left alone. He was the God of every place and of every time.

OUR FATHER GOD, in the glad confidence that Thou art everywhere and always our friend and helper, make us so sensitive to Thy Presence that wherever we are we may be sure that we are still with Thee. Help us to know that in every day when we wish it so, Thou art still our Guide and Friend. *Amen.*

CHARLES B. TUPPER
First Christian Church, Springfield, Ill.

BRINGERS OF THE DAWN

The dayspring from on high shall visit us.—Luke 1:78 ARV

Luke tells us in poetic language that God promises us the dawn of a more cheerful world. There is a physical dawn, and there is a spiritual dawn. Shakespeare says:

> Night's candles are burnt out, and jocund day
> Stands tiptoe on the misty mountain tops.

A Hebrew prophet foresees that God will win and justice triumph, at the rising of "the sun of righteousness" with healing in its rays.

In gloomy, world-shaking periods, Christians look forward to the dawn of a brighter age. An early Christian leader said of Jesus, "He has changed sunset into sunrise." A man of modern faith affirms, "God's day ends in dawn. It is high time that we recover the assurance of religion that night never speaks the last word and that dawn is irresistible." Civilians and members of the armed forces, through their devotion, courage, and vision, can earn the honored title, "Bringers of the Dawn."

O GOD, who canst change darkness into radiance, grant unto me companionship with Christ and with all the dawn-bringers through the ages. In duty, in danger, in human relationships, and in quiet moments, empower my comrades and myself to see Thy light of truth and goodness. Establish in me sure vision and unfading faith. In the name of Christ, my Leader, the Dawn which comes from Thee. *Amen.*

FRANCIS T. COOKE
First Congregational Church, Bristol, Conn.

THE ESTABLISHED HEART

His heart is fixed, trusting in the Lord. His heart is established. He shall not be afraid.—Ps. 112:7–8

A cool head and steady hand are invaluable assets in troublous times. The psalmist informs us that those who trust in God will be neither disturbed nor dismayed, no matter how numerous or mighty are the assaults against them. Nothing can undermine their stability. Those who trust in God can say of all their enemies, even as Athanasius said of Julian who persecuted him, "He is a mist, and will soon disappear."

The question might be asked, "How may these articulated bones of ours become the formidable force before which both adversity and adversary will be obliged to retire?" The answer to this question is simple, "Let the breath of the eternal God be breathed into us." As a frail wire plus the electric current can do more than massive cables without it, so can those in whom God's Spirit lives do more than they who know not God. The secret of a powerful and efficient life is God.

Shakespeare said, "Conscience doth make cowards of us all." But through faith in God, conscience, mind, and heart are strengthened. Life, then, is marked by calmness, self-possession, and firmness. John Wesley, even as the darkness settled upon his earthly life, fell asleep whispering: "The best of all is—Immanuel—God with us." That is life's most steadying truth, a truth that makes us strong in death and—what is more—strong in life.

O THOU BLESSED CHRIST, our Hiding-Place in the day of tempest, our River of Water in a world scorched with hatred and war, and our Shadow of a Great Rock in a weary land; help me to hide myself in Thy holy fellowship, so that nothing can make me afraid. In Thy precious name I pray. *Amen.*

IVAN H. HAGEDORN
Bethel Evangelical Lutheran Church, Philadelphia, Pa.

ON THY WAY, PILGRIM

Beloved, I beseech you as sojourners and pilgrims.—1 Pet. 2:11 ARV

If someone should say of Jesus that He was as honest as the daylight or that Paul would always be found among the contributors to community betterment, who would say that this would be a fair appraisal of their worth? There was something about these men, and others like them, which could not be limited in any contemporary scene. Their eyes were fixed on some far country which they expected to reach "in God's good time."

The pilgrims of God desire and contend most earnestly for justice among all people; but they are not content when everyone has a parcel of ground and a ration of bread. They are moved by some grander achievement than creature comfort. And they are on the move, not always fast, sometimes painfully slow. Sometimes they move in darkness with only the pressure of God's hand in theirs. But always, unless their courage fails, the light returns and they gird on their traveling pack again. They are never in too great a hurry to pour the oil of healing on some wounded person. No one cries for bread but they respond. They minister as they go to human needs, but the far call of God will not allow them to halt along the way. They make our cities beautiful, but tell us plainly that they seek a city whose builder and maker is God.

We see such pilgrims pass from earthly duties through the portal we call death, moving as they say into a fuller light, a larger life. So you are a pilgrim and a sojourner as all your ancestors were. Wonderful! Let not earth contain your desire.

O GOD, Thou art in the fresh dawning light of each day which brings new opportunities and new duties. Help me to travel with my face uplifted and my spirit assured of Thy strength to meet all my needs if I but trust Thee. *Amen.*

JARVIS M. COTTON
Waverly Presbyterian Church, Pittsburgh, Pa.

A LIFE WITH A SINGLE AIM

Seek ye first the kingdom of God, and his righteousness; and all these things shall be added unto you.—Matt. 6:33

The life of our Lord Jesus Christ had a single aim and purpose, and from the beginning He was intent on doing the will of the Father. He would have us be like Himself in singleness of aim, and so He commands, "Seek ye first the kingdom of God, and his righteousness."

The soldier's life knows singleness of aim. They are called to serve their country, and business and pleasure are cast aside in the one all-consuming purpose. Senator Gillette told in the Senate of the pledge which he found in the diary of a young man from Iowa who gave his life in World War I at Chateau Thierry: "America must win this war. Therefore, I will work, I will save, I will sacrifice, I will endure; I will fight cheerfully and do my utmost, as if the issue of the whole struggle depended upon me alone."

The Lord Jesus wants such determination in the ranks of His followers—men and women so devoted to Him and to His Kingdom that pleasure and business and even home itself will not hold them from complete dedication to Christ. And such followers of Christ would prove a tower of strength for their comrades as they pledge their Lord, "I will work, I will save, I will sacrifice, I will endure, I will do my utmost, as if the issue of that Kingdom depended on me alone."

O GOD, when we look at Thy dear Son, we see the glory of a life with a purpose. Bring my whole life under Thy control; and may my body, mind, and soul be kept for the Master's use, and be wholly Thine. For Jesus' sake. *Amen.*

EARL W. HANEY
Eagle Rock Presbyterian Church, Los Angeles, Calif.

COURAGE FOR THE DAY

Be thou strong and very courageous.—Josh. 1:7

In the first chapter of the Book of Joshua there is the refrain of an old song. Joshua is to assume a heavy responsibility. Moses is dead, and he must carry on in the name of the departed chieftain. But he is weak and trembling. How can he bear the burden of a leadership that needs more than he possesses? The answer is at hand.

"Be thou strong and very courageous," is God's message to Joshua. It comes to him through an old tradition, an inner sense of God's presence, a summons to immediate and challenging duty. The words he repeated, over and over again, in the long watches of the night and in the beat of battle, "Be thou strong," sustained him. His muscles would swell at the use of the words, "Be thou very courageous." His spirit would leap as a war horse at the sound of the trumpet.

Modern psychology and timeless religion agree here. Power wells up out of the depths at the summons to power. God speaks to the listening soul in the great phrases of a nation's life.

Today we need strength as always. In the use of mighty words, words that are winged with the fire of faith, we become strong. God speaks, and the soul knows strength in the marching songs that embody a nation's courage and a divine summons to duty.

GRACIOUS FATHER, give me this day a new insight into life's meaning and a new source of courage. Duty has called me, and I am eager to answer her call. Send me forth from this moment of communion with Thee deepened in faith, firmer in courage, and stronger in spirit. Help me to pray this my prayer in all unselfishness and in eager desire to do my duty as Thy child. *Amen.*

WALTER AMOS MORGAN
Chestnut Street Congregational Church, Worcester, Mass.

TRIUMPHANT TRUST

For I know whom I have believed, and am persuaded that he is able to keep that which I have committed unto him against that day.
—2 Tim. 1:12

The text for today is a statement of triumphant trust. It is your right in Christ. It is Paul making sure and vital those words of Job: "Though he slay me, yet will I trust in him." This trust is a most personal matter. The personal pronoun must be used. No one entering the armed service of this country uses the word *we* in taking the oath of allegiance.

"I know whom I have believed." Belief about God or Christ is not enough. It is between Christ and you. We must know Him, know that "Closer is He than breathing, and nearer than hands and feet." There was a time when Paul believed many things about Christ. Those were the days when he was the persecutor of the Lord.

The moment Paul believed in Christ he became a new creature. Then he could say, "I can do all things in Christ." He was in Christ, and Christ in him. "It is no longer I that live, but Christ liveth in me." Have you ever said, "Well, I trust that if God is God this will happen." You ought to say, "I will trust Him whatever happens." That is the triumph you may have when, like Paul, you can say, "I know whom I have believed."

Did we in our own strength confide,
Our striving would be losing;
Were not the right Man on our side,
The Man of God's own choosing
Dost ask who that may be?
Christ Jesus, it is He;
Lord Sabaoth, His name,
From age to age the same,
And He must win the battle. *Amen.*

HARRY T. SCHERER
Presbyterian Church, Webster Groves, Mo.

WE MUST CHOOSE

Jesus steadfastly set his face to go to Jerusalem.—Luke 9:51
But when the young man heard the saying, he went away sorrowful.
          —Matt. 19:22

I watched a street car as it came to the intersection. The motorman went to a trap door in the street, opened it and threw the lever, then returned to his car and turned on the power. As the car moved on, it turned into the street north. "Life is like that," I said to myself. "Each person has the power—and the responsibility—of choosing as to direction and goals in life."

We are equipped with a device within us which makes it possible for us to throw the switch which changes the direction and determines the goal of life, and then we turn on the power. In other words, we are what we choose to be. A friend used to say, "Character is crystallized choice." We choose not only direction and goal, but companions, habits, attitudes.

Consider these two young men: the one came to the Teacher and asked what he must do to be a man, to "have eternal life" as he put it. In reply Jesus outlined the moral standards of his day. "I have done all this," he replied. Then Jesus prescribed a major operation for this man whose malady, selfishness, was sapping his life. He could not take it; he turned away sorrowful.

The other young man was Jesus. He loved life, but He loved God more than life. He steadfastly set His face for a goal when He saw a cross standing in that road. We love Him today for His choice and His life of love. The other young man's name is not even remembered. How life is altered by the choices we make! We are what we choose to be.

LORD OF MY LIFE, guide me in making the right choice. May both the direction and the goal of my life please Thee, for I want to be your servant. *Amen.*

                          BENJAMIN E. WATSON
               Central Christian Church, Pasadena, Calif.

ON GETTING READY

The house was built with stone finished at the quarry, so that neither hammer nor ax nor any tool of iron was heard in the temple while it was being built.—1 Kings 6:7 NRSV

When King Solomon was building the temple, he ordered that all materials be prepared at a distance. It was not simply the sacredness of the task that concerned Solomon. He knew something of the disappointment to the builders when a stone could not be used because it was not prepared adequately enough before it was brought to the site.

We are engaged in a great undertaking to determine which set of nations shall order and control the world in which we live. We are trying ultimately to build a structure of peace. The essential parts of that "building," whether material or human, must be brought from vast distances, made ready and trained far from the scene of operations.

Often we cannot see the use of the long, hard periods of preparation that we have to go through. But if our united effort is to succeed, as succeed it must, we must see to it that, when the crisis comes for us, we are ready, believing that any hardship is welcome, if only it prepares us quietly and perfectly to fit into our appointed place in the house of Peace that we are building.

> For the want of a nail the shoe was lost,
> For the want of a shoe the horse was lost,
> For the want of a horse the rider was lost,
> For the want of a rider the battle was lost,
> For the want of a battle the kingdom was lost—
> And all for want of a horseshoe-nail.

O GOD, make me ready to face what I must, prepared, trained, unafraid, willing, in the faith that if I do my utmost, my effort will not be lost. *Amen.*

DANIEL BLISS
Second Congregational Church, Greenwich, Conn.

I WILL LIFT UP MINE EYES UNTO THE HILLS

I will lift up mine eyes unto the hills, from whence cometh my help.
—Ps. 121:1

Never was there such a time as this, when men and women of every faith are calling upon God for strength, comfort, and peace. We all feel the desperateness of this hour and the great need of a spiritual empowerment in our lives to meet its demands.

People all over the world are praying as never before. Certainly it is essential to have an intimate communion and fellowship with God. A more thoughtful and better understanding of the Gospel of Redemption and the power of the Holy Spirit to empower and comfort is the daily need of life.

The daily prayer life is as essential to our spiritual living and strength as is our daily food to our physical life. We shall need constantly to keep our faith strong in the divine guidance and helpfulness of God—a faith that can see beyond the darkness and the strife the dawn of the day of the Kingdom of God.

"Sad will be the day for every man when he becomes absolutely contented with the life that he is living, with the thoughts that he is thinking, with the deeds that he is doing, when there is not forever beating at the doors of his soul some great desire to do something larger, which he knows that he was meant and made to do because he is still the child of God" (PHILLIPS BROOKS).

You can give ear to the discords of life, or you can listen to the harmonies of the eternal verities.

HEAVENLY FATHER, in this hour may I be conscious of Thy presence. May I feel the comforting and strengthening power of Thy Spirit. Help me to live nobly and to consecrate my life to Thee that I may do Thy will always. In Christ's name. *Amen.*

JAMES A. LEACH
Wesley Methodist Church, Oklahoma City, Okla.

THE SET OF THE FACE

If any man will come after me, let him deny himself, and take up his cross, and follow me.—Matt. 16:24

Jesus was willing to "set his *face* to go to Jerusalem," because He had already set His *faith* in a cause that made personal sacrifice a secondary consideration.

Jesus did not go around looking for opportunities to suffer. Don't let any sad-faced fanatic tell you differently. Jesus loved life as much as you and I love it. And He taught His disciples to "rejoice, and be exceeding glad." But whenever He found evidences of "inhumanity to man," He "set his face," He gave His all, and He willingly took the consequences.

Someone of self-centered motive could have said, "It is none of my concern." To One who had identified His own interests with the interests and the needs of those around Him, the price of inconvenience and persecution was none too great to pay.

Jesus said, "If any man will come after me, let him deny himself, and take up his cross, and follow me." It may be against the evils of our social order or the selfish temptations of our own lives that we are called upon to take a stand. Wherever and whatever our particular Jerusalem may be, it is our task, as His followers, to set our face and take the consequences. It becomes easier to make the sacrifice after we have sensed the privileges and the responsibilities that come to us as members of the universal family of God.

O GOD, help us to be too tempered to be tempestuous and too big to be worried with the criticisms of little people. But grant us the courage to stand against every evil that denies to our brothers and sisters the right to life, liberty, and the pursuit of happiness. *Amen.*

CECIL F. CHEVERTON
President, Chapman College, Los Angeles, Calif.

PEOPLE OF FAITH

Now faith is the substance of things hoped for, the evidence of things not seen. For by it the elders obtained a good report.—Heb. 11:1–2

The author of the great Epistle to the Hebrew Christians, scattered abroad, wants them to know what faith had accomplished in their history. The eleventh chapter is a roll call of the Hebrew heroes of faith. It begins with a very practical definition of faith in practice. Three words describe it.

First, it is *substance*, the solid foundation of our hopes. Second, it is *proof* of the reality of the unseen. In the laboratory of hard experience these heroes proved that there is nothing so real as the spiritual powers at our disposal. Third, it is adequate and satisfying *knowledge* of God, the Creator and Redeemer. Faith produces that knowledge. It can be found in no other way. "I *know* him whom I have *believed*," Paul wrote. The obedience of faith is "The Organ of Spiritual Knowledge"—so a discerning preacher paraphrases the words of Jesus, "If any man willeth to do the will of God, he shall know . . ."

There is nothing more vitally needed today than men and women of faith. Like the engineering firm which took for its slogan "We Specialize in the Impossible," we should also make that our own motto, remembering that to God, and Godlike people working with Him, "nothing is impossible."

My faith looks up to Thee,
Thou Lamb of Calvary,
Savior divine!
Now hear me while I pray,
Take all my guilt away,
O let me from this day
Be wholly Thine. *Amen.*

A. A. SHAW
Former President, Denison University, Granville, Ohio

THIS IS THE DAY

This is the day which the Lord hath made; we will rejoice and be glad in it.—Ps. 118:24

Psalm 118 opens with the admonition, "O give thanks unto the Lord; for he is good." It closes with the same words. To the writer, God is a God of mercy, of everlasting mercy. God is on his side in the great struggle because he is on God's side. Fear of what people can do to him is gone. Such trust is better than trust in people or confidence in governments. The combined opposition of nations cannot bring defeat. Our enemies may reject the cornerstone of a permanent world structure, but one day that stone will be rightly placed.

In the face of enemies and threats, the psalmist declares, "This is the day which the Lord hath made." We need to become saturated with this belief. We need to shout it above the din of battle. It is God's day!

It is a day for great sacrifices, for Spartan discipline, for heroic thinking and acting. It is a day of shattered confidence in brute force, in human systems, in material values. It is a day for building a new world order. It is a day for "all-out" confidence in God's power and righteousness. It is a day to rebuild our Christian faith, hope, and love. It is a day for prayer.

What we do personally with today will determine largely the tomorrow of all who share it. "This is the day which the Lord hath made."

OUR FATHER WHICH ART IN HEAVEN, hallowed be Thy name. Thy kingdom come. Thy will be done in earth, as it is in heaven. Give us this day our daily bread, and forgive us our debts, as we forgive our debtors. And lead us not into temptation, but deliver us from evil, For Thine is the kingdom, and the power, and the glory, forever. *Amen.*

HARRY G. KNOWLES
First Christian Church, Houston, Tex.

HOPE

Now the God of hope fill you with all joy and peace in believing, that ye may abound in hope, through the power of the Holy Ghost.
—Rom. 15:13

The religion of Jesus is a religion of hope—hope bound with the belief that a good God is working out His will for the world in spite of our indifference, ignorance, and wrongdoing. What are the fondest hopes which we possess as we carry on in every sort of situation in a perplexing life? The hope of peace on earth; the hope that the whole race of humanity will dedicate themselves to our righteous God; the hope that we shall be reunited with loved ones and friends; the hope of a normal life in a community of enterprising citizens; the hope of life beyond the grave; the hope of fulfillment for our deepest and noblest desires; the hope of the vision and blessing of God.

Some of these hopes are as natural as hunger and thirst. Certain of them are especially inspired of God, the fruit of the religious life. We need to cherish every aspect of hope. God will not fail in His promises to accomplish that which is right.

Let us, then, thank God for the hope He has inspired. We must realize that our vocation as Christians is to dedicate our lives to the seeking and attainment of every noble hope that God would instill into our hearts. For to abound in hope through the power of God's indwelling Spirit is to be filled with joy and peace.

"O GOD OF HOPE, fill us, we beseech Thee, with all joy and peace in believing, that we may ever abound in hope by the power of the Holy Spirit, and show forth our thankfulness to Thee in trustful and courageous lives; through Jesus Christ our Lord and Savior. *Amen*"

(From *Prayers, New and Old*).

JAMES C. GILBERT
St. James (Old Swedes) Episcopal Church of Kingessing, Philadelphia, Pa.

A GREAT VICTORY

But Daniel purposed in his heart. . . . —Dan. 1:8

Daniel is one of the most inspiring characters in the Bible. He is a symbolic man who is loyal to his convictions and firm in his resolve to be true to what he believes to be right. There is nothing weak or vacillating about him. He did not fall an easy prey to the temptations by which he was surrounded.

Transported from his home and carried off to a strange land where people's habits and ideals were different from his own, "he purposed in his heart that he would not defile himself." He lived the same clean, honest life in Babylon that he had lived in Jerusalem. He showed courage of a high order. For the highest form of courage is not being brave in a moment of danger but resisting the constant appeals to dishonor.

How was Daniel able to do this? By opening his window toward Jerusalem; by remembering his home, his family, the traditions in which he had been reared; above all, by looking to God for strength in daily prayer that he might be faithful to the end. Daniel won a great victory. May God help each one of us to will a victory like that while we too are away from home.

ALMIGHTY GOD, who sees that we have no power of ourselves to help ourselves, keep us both outwardly in our bodies and inwardly in our souls, that we may be defended from all adversities which may happen to the body and from evil thoughts which may assault and hurt the soul. Through Jesus Christ our Lord. *Amen.*

RAYMOND CALKINS
First Congregational Church, Cambridge, Mass.

THE DO-SOMETHING

This do.—Luke 22:19

Long before those in our day set out to reshape the face of the world
to a "new order," Jesus was urging His own ideas of such things, "the
New Testament," "the New Covenant," His new order. On the eve of His
martyrdom He sups with His followers. In His hands He takes from the
table bread and wine, and He who is about to die salutes the New Order.

In His time He had used lilies, trees, birds, seed, bridges, rocks, houses,
journeys, water, light, salt to illustrate His truth. Now He will illustrate
once more. This man of parables and pictures will use bread and wine—
now the fundamental food. He will make them illustrate His body and
blood—that is to say, Himself.

Himself! What do we do with ourselves? What should we do? He
broke the bread and "*gave unto them.*" He said, "*This do.*" Do what? Why,
give yourselves. There are plenty to do the other things. That's the trouble;
that has been the trouble from the beginning. Jesus always saw that. But
now it's to be the new order. The whole spirit of everything He ever strove
and stood for was always undercut from that old order. "Remember Me,
but not by dreaming, teaching, praising; not only by these; no, they are
never enough, never. You must learn the greater things. This do. Give yourselves for truth and for each other."

O HEAVENLY LIFE, I lay my small life in the bosom of Thy vastness. I
pray that my love for Thee may increase, that my communion with Thee
may increase, that my diligence and service may increase, and that all my
faithfulness to Christ may increase; until of this increase may arise that new
order in the world for which people of faith must endure. *Amen.*

O. W. S. McCall
New First Congregational Church, Chicago, Ill.

THE LEDGER OF LIFE

*Whatsoever things are true, . . . honest, . . . just, . . . pure, . . . lovely,
. . . of good report; if there be any virtue, . . . any praise, think on these
things.*—Phil. 4:8

Out of an average group of a hundred young men twenty-five years of age able to obtain life insurance, fifty-four will be dead broke, thirty-six dead, five weak, four in comfortable circumstances, and one rich, when they reach the age of sixty-five.

These strange facts arise from the balancing up of their account in the Ledger of Life. Every life has its debits and its credits. Our debits are duties, obligations, and responsibilities. Our credits are rights, privileges, and prerogatives. Fulfillment of the debits procures and secures the credits.

A "duty" is that which a person is morally obliged to do, or refrain from doing. An "obligation" is any duty imposed by law, promise, contract, social requirement, or kindness. A "responsibility" is that for which one is held accountable. A "right" is a power to which one has a just or lawful claim. A "privilege" is a right or immunity granted a peculiar advantage or favor. A "prerogative" is a prior or exclusive right or privilege, especially as attached to office or rank.

Any building, in order to endure, must rest upon a foundation fixed upon bedrock. Any life, in order to endure, must rest upon the foundation of "confidence." This, in turn, rests upon the bedrock of "satisfaction," which must be deeply imbedded in the earth of "service." Service, in the sense of usefulness, is the secret of "success," which is the progressive realization of any worthy ideal.

OUR FATHER, today and every day, ere I meet others, let me meet Thee, face to face. Cleanse and strengthen me for my tasks. Pardon my sins, O God, and guide me in thought and deed. I humbly pray through Jesus Christ, my Lord. *Amen.*

EVERETT S. SMITH
First Christian Church, Miami, Fla.

DOES GOD CARE?

Are not five sparrows sold for two pence? and not one of them is forgotten in the sight of God.—Luke 12:6 ARV

Does God care? Does He know my name? Does He love me, or am I lost in the crowd? If this question troubles you, you can be sure that it troubles everyone; but you need not wonder, for God does love you.

The picture that made the deepest impression upon my early life is one that is familiar to you. There is a doctor sitting by the bedside of a little girl, praying, watching, waiting hopefully for the crisis to pass. God is like that; Jesus is the Great Physician. Have you ever seen a shepherd out on the hillside caring for his sheep? He is one who knows, and leads, and guides his own flock. "The Lord is my shepherd; I shall not want."

My father is a pal to me. Some of my earliest recollections are of sitting on my father's knee, listening to his stories, or of walking through the meadows with him, holding his hand. I knew that my father would do anything for me. I knew that he loved and would protect me. God is like the best in our earthly fathers. God is like a mother. "As one whom his mother comforteth, so will I comfort you."

No matter what the world believes or knows about a person, no matter how low one has sunk, a mother will still believe and still find good in him or her. So, when the uncertainties of the world beset us—and they come to us all—let us never forget that short sentence that we learned as little children at our mother's knee: "God is love."

O GOD, help me, that in the midst of all the perplexities and doubts that fill my mind, I may find perfect peace and confidence in the fact that Thou dost love me. In the name of Jesus. *Amen.*

JAMES ROBERT SPEER
Westminster Presbyterian Church, Bloomfield, N.J.

GOD'S INSTRUMENTS

Here am I; send me.—Isa. 6:8

The other evening I attended a meeting of Alcoholics Anonymous. It was a rare experience, for here are redeemed men and women with more real Christianity than you find in some churches. They have rediscovered their faith in God and have put it to work. They have learned anew to pray.

They have a missionary zeal that sends them out, as one chap said, "in every spare minute that I have. As soon as I get home from work I begin my AA work. There are just not enough hours in the day for all that I want to do. This is the greatest thing that I have found." One mother of eight said, "I would like to get on the housetops and shout how much this has meant to me. Since February the children and I have had a new daddy."

Now most of us are glad that we don't have to experience chronic alcoholism to develop faith in God. But the fact is that all too often we get stuck on a plateau halfway between, content in our half-existence. These people at the meeting positively sparkled with their enthusiasm and power. When they quoted Jesus as saying, "I came that they may have life, and may have it abundantly," they knew what they meant.

This movement actually possesses what a lot of churches have only in theory. And yet all churches can have it actually as well. One of the alcoholics said, "We are merely God's instruments, doing work that is effective because He gives us power." Isaiah's vision was no phantasm; it was not an exercise of a diseased imagination; it led to the consecration of life, to the settlement of a divine purpose, to the warming of the heart into sympathetic obedience towards all things Divine, and therefore largely human.

O GOD, consecrate me to Thy purposes, that I may see Thy way and have power to do Thy work. *Amen.*

JAMES M. DAVIS
First Congregational Church, Ravenna, Ohio

THE POWER OF CHEERFULNESS

Be of good cheer.—John 16:33

The prospects for cheer in Jesus' life were far from bright when He spoke the words above. It was midnight. Jesus was to face the betrayal by Judas, the denial by Peter, the desertion by His friends, and the arrest by His enemies. And on the morrow were to come trials, the sentence of death, the bearing of His cross, and the agony of the crucifixion. But He was cheerful and courageous, ready to meet whatever awaited Him.

Jesus was cheerful because He knew that God was with Him, that His Father was pleased with Him, and that He had committed Himself to the will of God. He believed that His heavenly Father, who cared, understood, and loved Him, would not fail Him in His hour of need.

Cheerfulness springs from faith in God and fellowship with Him. Cheerfulness gives strength and courage to trust in His love, wisdom, and power. Cheerfulness deepens sympathies and enlarges visions of obligations and opportunities to tell others. Best of all, cheerfulness is the power which enriches and makes real spiritual comradeship with God.

What the experiences of tomorrow will be is known only to God. But the cheerful individual will make the most of these experiences of life. Out of the power which cheerfulness will give, will emerge a better self, a keener sense of human values, a constructive philosophy of life, and a creative fellowship with others and God.

GOD, our Father, make available to us this cheerfulness and courage. Help us to understand that "all things work together for good to those who love Thee." Enable us, we pray Thee, to take cheerfulness and courage with us into whatever life may bring. Guide our steps and our lives by Thy Spirit of Love, Understanding, and Wisdom. *Amen.*

ELMER D. PALMER
First Methodist Church, Sheldon, Ill.

COURAGE IS NOT ENOUGH

Only be strong and very courageous, to observe to do according to all the law . . . that thou mayest have good success whithersoever thou goest.
—Josh. 1:7 ARV

Courage does not stand alone. It is an end result of other attitudes. Where the word is mentioned in the Bible it is usually linked with something else. Joshua is instructed to be obedient to the law which Moses taught. The psalmist relates it to a hope in God and a waiting for God. At the end of Paul's journey to Rome it is recorded: "Whom [the brethren who welcomed him] when Paul saw, he thanked God, and took courage."

Courage is not to be found in a life that has never faced risks. It is lacking when a life is unrelated to God, or to a cause that is worthy. But when we stand facing some great need, aware that there is a "power not ourselves that makes for righteousness," God works in us, and courage replaces insecurity and fear. Jesus prayed in a time of crisis; and, putting his life in the hands of God, He went out to meet adventure in the highest spirit of courage the world has ever known. We too can have courage if our life has other foundations.

> Courage is armor
> A blind man wears;
> The calloused scar
> Of outlived despairs;
> Courage is Fear
> That has said its prayers.
> —KARLE WILSON BAKER

O GOD OF ALL COURAGEOUS MEN, grant that, being obedient to Thy laws and in harmony with those who seek Thy face, we may walk today in the spirit of courageous faith. *Amen.*

JOSEPH C. CLEVELAND
Community Church, Kansas City, Mo.

LET US THINK ABOUT GOD

In the beginning God. . . . —Gen. 1:1

The quest for God is universal; it is the noblest quest of humanity. Jesus never presented a single argument for the existence of God, His own divinity, or the immortality of the soul; evidently He believed that in our best moments we would accept these.

Many of the stars above are suns with their worlds like our own solar system. These and other heavenly bodies move with orderliness and precision and form a part of a universe so large that its immensity confounds us. You cannot face these facts without thinking about God!

Light moves at the seemingly incredible speed of 186,000 miles per second. What is a "light year"? It is the distance light would travel at the speed of 186,000 miles per second during 365 days! The light which you see from yonder fixed star left that star many light years ago. You cannot face such facts unless you think about God!

No wonder the psalmist said, "The heavens declare the glory of God," or that Kepler looking at the stars exclaimed, "O God, I am thinking Thy thoughts after Thee."

Begin and continue your religious life by thinking about God. Make your concept of God the beginning of your faith and hope and life. Then recognize Jesus Christ as the highest and best revelation and expression of God we can possibly receive. If you would know God, read the gospel story and become acquainted with Jesus.

LORD OF THE UNIVERSE, we praise Thee. We dedicate our lives to Thee; then we wait in quiet meditation and silent introspection until Thou hast consecrated that which we have dedicated. Reveal Thyself to us, we pray, through Thy Son and our Savior, Jesus Christ. *Amen.*

MYRON L. PONTIUS
Former Pastor, Central Christian Church, Jacksonville, Ill.

MAKING OUR DREAMS COME TRUE

Your old men shall dream dreams, your young men shall see visions.
—Joel 2:28

Christy Matteson dreamed of being a great baseball pitcher. He traded all the kids out of their baseballs until he had a whole pail full. He cut a hole in the shed on the back of the lot—as wide as the home plate, as far from the ground as a man's knee, as high as an average man's shoulders. Then he stepped off the distance to the pitcher's plate and out to work. He kept at it until he could throw all those balls through that opening in the side of the shed. With string he divided the opening into three sections representing a ball shoulder high, right over the center, and around the knees. After being able to put a straight ball just where he wanted it he began curving the balls. No wonder he became one of the great pitchers of all time.

God has made us creatures who naturally look up. High aspirations stir in our souls. Great hopes surge deep within us. Worthy ambitions lure and urge us on. Dreams put meaning into many a dark hour. So today let us deeply resolve to be true to our dream; it is the best thing that we have. Let us pray that every worthy dream may come true. Let us resolve that no experience will ever take from us the vision splendid.

He whom a dream hath possessed treads the impalpable marches,
From the dust of a day's long road he leaps to a laughing star.
—SHAEMAS O'SHEEL

O THOU who hast made us capable of dwelling in the world that is and in the world that ought to be, grant us such a genuine consciousness of Thyself in Jesus Christ our Lord that we will more and more love Thee and serve Thee. Increase our faith, deepen our hope, purify our love, that we may more perfectly love Thee and worthily magnify Thy Holy name. *Amen.*

REW WALZ
First Presbyterian Church, Rapid City, S.Dak.

BECAUSE OF YOU

And for their sakes I sanctify myself, that they also might be sanctified through the truth.—John 17:19

Everything has a cause behind it. Things just don't come to pass without reason. Happiness has a cause; so also has hopelessness. Order rules, or chaos reigns, not as a matter of chance, but as a matter of cause. Sings the lover at the marriage altar, "A wider world of hope and joy I see, because you come to me." We are what we are, and our world is what it is, because—

Because means "by a cause." How we need to look to our causes! Are they petty or great? worthy or unworthy? the kind that make or unmake a person? Happy are those who know their cause is right and so can give themselves to it wholeheartedly. When they say, "I do this because—" their voice has a ring that we like to hear, and their eyes look straight forward.

"For their sakes," said One greater than any of us, "I sanctify myself." He had a cause which made Him happy to give all He had for others. If the best the world has ever known gave Himself, can we do less?

As soldiers you fight, not alone to defend your native land, but for all that we count dear—for life, liberty, and the pursuit of happiness; for the building of a new and better world order; for the Kingdom of God on earth. And because of you "a wider world of hope and joy we see."

FATHER, we thank Thee for the new day. May we face it with courage and cheer. We pray not for an easy life, but for a useful one. Give us wisdom to make right choices and confidence and faith to meet the unexpected. Cleanse our hearts from evil thoughts and hard feelings. Make us strong for what we have to suffer, and brave for what we have to dare. In the name of our great Helper and Friend. *Amen.*

OLIN BERRY TRACY
First Congregational Church, Melrose, Mass.

SPIRITUAL PEACE

Thou will keep him in perfect peace, whose mind is stayed on thee: because he trusteth in thee.—Isa. 26:3

This is one of the great promises of the Bible. It was written by the prophet during a period of confusion and chaos, when dependence upon external conditions produced a sense of futility and fear. It points the way to a sense of peace which depends not upon environment but rather upon God.

Experience in time of crisis confirms this statement of the prophet. There is a peace which can be realized in human hearts. This perfect peace comes when God's will and God's purposes are made central in life, when our minds are stayed on Him.

The realization of this inner peace is made possible by trust between the individual and God. Most of life's personal values come from the presence of this quality. Distrust erects a barrier; trust breaks this barrier. Values flow from life to life. So is it when we trust in God.

This trust in God, this willingness to rest our weary hearts in Him, brings into life a faith that cannot be destroyed, a courage that can never falter, a hope that gives light to the future, a love that will never let us go. When these qualities focus in a human heart, perfect peace is realized in the midst of a turbulent, trying world. Here is attained a serene and certain confidence, adequate for all of the experiences that life may bring.

ETERNAL GOD, whom Jesus taught us to know as our Father, help me to trust Thee in all of life's experiences. Help me to live in thought and deed in accordance with Thy will for my life. May I have the consciousness of Thy presence wherever my duty may take me. May that peace which comes alone from Thee be always in my heart. *Amen.*

L. WENDELL FIFIELD
Plymouth Church of the Pilgrims, Brooklyn, N.Y.

A THREAD OF PURPOSE

If God so clothe the grass of the field, . . . shall he not much more clothe you, O ye of little faith?—Matt. 6:30

"Life in such days as these," says one of our religious leaders, "is like a great terminal switchyard at night, with its intricate network containing hundreds of tracks and its bewildering confusion of lights merging off into the darkness. You and I are the engineer on the incoming express. It seems utterly impossible that we should be able to find our way in and out of that maze to the station platform where we are awaited. But through it all a track has been prepared for us. Everything has been thought out in advance by the dispatcher high up in the signal tower. All we have to do is to hold our hand on the throttle, and to keep moving forward at a proper speed, and we shall arrive safely at our journey's end." Is that a true picture of life? Does God have a plan for each of us? Does He think out in advance our course through the years? Paul believed so. Even chained in a Roman dungeon his voice rang out confidently, "Forgetting the things which are behind, I press on." Jesus believed it. He said to His anxious companions, "The very hairs of your head are all numbered." So endorsed, so accepted, such a conviction cannot be unreasonable. Moreover, there are thousands of happy, successful men and women ready to testify today that believing this, living this, makes them "more than conquerors" in these days that try the stoutest hearts.

O GOD, I am in Thy hands. My life is in Thy keeping. Help me this day and all other days to make Thy will my will, and to walk forward confidently, sure that what Thou hast planned for me is better than anything I can plan for myself. Through Jesus Christ our Lord. *Amen.*

CARL H. ELMORE
First Presbyterian Church, Englewood, N.J.

POWER FOR YOUR LIFE

I can do all things through Christ which strengtheneth me.—Phil. 4:13

This was Oliver Cromwell's text. He said, "The world needs a man, a good, great, strong man." And the divine mandate came to him, "Thou art the man." Again and again this text of Paul's became a great comfort and strength to him. When Paul wrote it he was face to face with conditions even more challenging than today. Three-fourths of the people were slaves; he himself was a prisoner in Rome. And yet he thinks, speaks, and acts like a conqueror.

He expresses absolute confidence: "I can do all things." How superb is his dauntless faith and courage. It reminds us of Emerson's essay, "Self-Reliance": "They can conquer who believe they can." Said Napoleon: "Obstacles? If that is all, let us go forward." And William Carey, the humble shoemaker who made history in India pioneering for Christ, gave us this slogan: "Expect great things from God; attempt great things for God."

The source of power is supernatural: "Through Christ which strengtheneth me." When explorers first discovered the Amazon River, the world's largest, one said to the other, "Only a great island could produce such a river." But another replied, "An island! It takes a continent to produce such a river." Exactly! And the stream of Christian living can flow only from the continent of God Himself. When Paul was asked the secret of his hopefulness and strength, he would say, "Christ lives in me."

Lord, what a change within us one short hour
Spent in Thy presence will avail to make!
We kneel how weak; we rise how full of power! *Amen.*

R. Kells Swenerton
First Methodist Church, Redlands, Calif.

MEMORIALS AND THEIR MEANING

This day shall be unto you for a memorial.—Exod. 12:14

The memorial idea has prevailed among all kinds of people from the earliest times. The Old Testament contains the record of many memorials. The greatest of these was the day set apart to commemorate the safety of the people of Israel from the destroying angel and their deliverance from bondage to the oppressor. Year by year, generation by generation, this occasion was ordered set apart as a time of joyous gratitude to God.

We too have a Memorial Day. We as a people are also summoned to remember. Ours is not primarily a religious institution, yet it has for us a profound spiritual significance. While we separate the functions of church and state, we do not separate religion from the total life of the nation. As a people we have reason to be profoundly grateful to the Father of nations because we have been delivered from fear and oppression and been given opportunity for the freest life any citizens have ever known.

Now we are engaged once again in a struggle to set our planet free from bondage to an order of life intolerable to free spirits. Once again the making of history is upon us. Under God and with faith in the ultimate triumph of righteousness we can make the days to come memorable beyond all comparison; for our aim is not the release of a single people, but of the whole race of humankind. For such a cause we need the full devotion of the entire nation and full trust in God who has made and kept us a nation.

FATHER OF ETERNITY, we come to Thee in Thy greatness; we look to Thee for strength in this time of overwhelming need. Grant us the power to accept and to stand up to all our tasks. Give us wisdom to plan with clear mind and understanding heart. Beyond our sense of power may we have the spirit of righteousness and love. We ask it in Christ's name. *Amen.*

WILLIAM EVERETT ROBERTS
Community Presbyterian Church, Beverly Hills, Calif.

CONFIDENCE IN GOD

The lifter up of mine head.—Ps. 3:3b

An army camp is near the church I serve. One Sunday afternoon a corporal knocked on my study door, and when he entered I saw the most homesick fellow within a hundred miles. But his problem wasn't just homesickness; he wanted help for something much more serious. In an effort to forget his plight he had been drinking; and suddenly his foolish attempt to retreat from his problem had rebounded, and he was kicking himself for his attempted escape.

"I came over here to ask you to write to my folks and tell them that I'm a heel, and that now I'm going to try to do right," were the first words that poured from his lips. On and on he went, recounting his life.

To make a long story short, the letter was written; but I didn't write it. He did!

After he had signed his name, he looked over the desk to me and smiled. "Well," said he, "I feel better. This sorta helped me to lift up my head again. The folks will know that I won a battle!"

There's something in such a victory! The greatest enemy we have is ourselves. When we trim that adversary we've used some fine God-given resources. When we use the inner spiritual resources of our lives to establish, or re-establish, our character, we can thank God, "the lifter up of mine head."

God speaks in the still small voice of educated conscience. He doesn't always depend upon earthquakes to awaken us to the presence of evil.

O GOD, grant me the voice of Thy will for my life. Enable me to put my trust in Thee and in Thy ways. May Thy will be done in me, that I may be clean and free from stain. *Amen.*

RUSSELL WHARTON LAMBERT
Centennial Methodist Church, Rockford, Ill.

GIVE THANKS FOR MEMORIES

In my Father's house are many rooms . . . I am going there to prepare a place for you. And . . . I will come back and take you to be with me that you also may be where I am.—John 14:1–3

My wife and I often walk with our dog, Samson, through the narrow, tree-lined roadways of a cemetery near our home which circle a small, still pond. One particular evening, the day before Memorial Day, we noticed people among the gravestones of loved ones arranging flowers, clearing away weeds, making ready for Memorial Day. I noticed one particular man standing before a gravestone in respectful silence with head bowed. Though I did not speak to him, I had no doubt he was reflecting upon life—life with the deceased loved one or loved ones.

Such memories stir a longing and sadness within the heart. Such moments also bring us face to face with our mortality and finiteness, for we too will one day pass from this earth; it is the way of all flesh. Christ said, "I am going to prepare a place for you . . . that you may be where I am." In these words our Lord gives us a meaning and hope for life that extends beyond the few years on this earth unto eternity.

As we left the cemetery that evening, I came to better appreciate the significance of Memorial Day. In giving our respect and honor to the dead, our appreciation for life on earth is strengthened, and our hearts are refreshed by the goodness of God in whom we trust to prepare a place for us to abide with Him forever.

O GOD OF THE PAST, PRESENT, AND FUTURE, thank You for life on this earth. Thank You for the good memories of loved ones who have modeled the Way of Life to me. Strengthen, I pray, my trust in You. Refresh my hope. Prepare me here on earth for eternal habitation with You. *Amen.*

MIKE MOYER
Campus Minister, William Penn University, Oskaloosa, Iowa

Read 1 Sam. 7:9–12

†

HERE I RAISE MY EBENEZER

Then Samuel took a stone and set it up between Mizpah and Jeshanah, and named it Ebenezer; for, he said, "Thus far the Lord has helped us."—1 Samuel 7:12

What is this "Ebenezer" business, anyway? An Ebenezer was a standing stone or stones set up by the Israelite leader Samuel to commemorate God's intervention in history to save His fragile confederation of tribes from certain annihilation by the powerful army of the Philistines.

The lyricist who penned the hymn "Come Thou Fount of Every Blessing" wrote, "Here I raise mine Ebenezer; hither by Thy help I've come." An Ebenezer—not a name and not really just a stone—is something much more relevant and precious to each of us. It is a concrete reminder of God at work in our lives and in the lives of those around us.

Do you have Ebenezers? Many of us do. Often they're shared within families or even passed down across generations. They're not piles of rocks, of course, but memories kept close to our hearts. They may be born of joy: God's presence which has brought a special blessing. They may be born of sorrow: God's presence which has taken us through times of difficulty.

An Ebenezer may be represented by a place, a person, or an event which reminds us that God is not distant, but an active presence in our lives. They represent not just memories but also promises. Have you raised an Ebenezer? Do you know of others who have? If so, you will have a special confidence that God is at work with and through you.

LORD, ours is a faith with a memory. Because we have seen Your activity in our lives in the past, we are confident of Your activity in our lives in the future. Help us to never forget Your presence. Encourage us as we raise up Ebenezers that remind us of Your goodness behind us and offer promises of Your goodness before us. *Amen.*

D. T. Knobel
President, Denison University, Granville, Ohio

FAITH IS . . . REGROUPING

Do not remember the former things, nor consider the things of old. Behold, I will do a new thing. . . . I will even make a road in the wilderness.—Isa. 43:18–19

Regrouping may mean little to you, but it is a very meaningful term in military strategy. When the enemy lines collide and the battle (not the war) is over, the side which suffered the apparent defeat does not contemplate surrender, it speaks about "regrouping." They analyze why they lost, calculate the weak spot in the enemy's lines, and develop a new strategy for effective counterattack.

The regrouping strategy is of course mostly known in sports, especially football. The opposing teams are allowed to huddle and regroup to discuss a game plan they hope will surprise and beat their opponent.

Businesses do this when they go through periods of recession. They may permanently discontinue some unprofitable lines they carried at a loss. They may cut overhead, trim their personnel, and regroup their resources.

Regrouping is an act of dynamic faith!

It is possibility thinking in action.

Do not dwell on old mistakes; concentrate on new ideas.

What do you do when you've had a nonproductive day? A streak of ill luck? A poor semester in the classroom? A stagnant relationship?

When you face setbacks, don't send up the white flag. Don't throw in the towel. Instead get your best thoughts together. Reorganize, retool, or regroup! Then go back at it again with vengeance!

That's faith, and it moves mountains.

LORD GOD, give me the strength and the insight to regroup "when the going gets tough." Bring people of faith to my side, that we might "huddle" and adopt a strategy that will encourage and lift us to new levels of success through dynamic faith in a God who makes all things possible! *Amen.*

ROBERT H. SCHULLER
Pastor, Crystal Cathedral, Garden Grove, Calif.

A CHILD OF GOD

Thou wilt shew me the path of life: in thy presence is fullness of joy;
at thy right hand there are pleasures for evermore.—Ps. 16:11

Every Christian man or woman who had to learn the catechism as a child will remember how in baptism he or she "was made a member of Christ, the child of God and an inheritor of the kingdom of heaven." Today let us dwell on one portion of this:

I. "The child of God": not a child—just any one among many without any special mark or distinction—but the child—a definite, particular child—a son or daughter with a name. God looks upon me not as a man, a woman, a child, but a particular child. I am known to Him as an individual. I have a name, and He knows it. He knows me by it.

II. And not only am I "the child of God," but I am the beloved child of God. Our Lord Jesus Christ has brought to me this precious truth. Nothing else compares in importance with this. If God knows me and loves me, I need fear nothing.

III. How few of us have lived in the confidence and strength of this. Think of what would happen to our worries and fears if we once got hold of this truth! Think of all the inferiority complexes that would vanish away.

Can I live by this truth today? Can I face the days ahead with my head high and my heart strong and joyful because I believe it more deeply? I walk before Him not as one lost in a great common herd; but He calleth His own by name, and He loves me. I am His Beloved Child!

O GOD, who hast prepared for those who love Thee such good things as pass our understanding; pour into our hearts such love toward Thee, that we, loving Thee above all things, may obtain Thy promises, which exceed all that we can desire. Through Jesus Christ our Lord. *Amen.*

WALLACE E. CONKLING
Bishop of Chicago, Episcopal, Chicago, Ill.

MORAL COURAGE

Whosoever therefore shall confess me before men, him will I confess also before my Father which is in heaven.—Matt. 10:32

The little lad Tom Brown had gone away to school and was getting ready for bed in the big dormitory with all the other boys around him. It had come time to say his prayers. Should he kneel down there and pray before everybody? He knew that they would hoot and laugh and throw things at him. Would it not be wiser just to crawl into bed and say his prayers to himself? That would have been the easy thing to do.

"What difference," he might have said, "whether I pray kneeling down by my cot where everybody can see me, or in bed with the covers over my head?" He knew that it did make a difference. Those boys who mocked him would never have thought quite so much of him again if they had seen him lower his colors under fire. He would have found it easier the next time to have played the craven's part. All life would have been changed for him if he had not been true that night.

Yes, it does make a difference. Have you ever noted on a railroad how extremely thin is the rail of a switch where it joins the main track? It is not much thicker at first than a knife blade, but it is sufficient to turn the train off the main line into the siding. Life itself often turns upon very small events which in themselves are trivial enough. That is why every action in life that is bound up with moral and spiritual life is so supremely important.

HEAVENLY FATHER, help us to be steadfast and unafraid as we face the perils that lie ahead; and bring us to a new day of peace, a world in which Jesus Christ is King of kings and Lord of lords. We pray in the name of Jesus Christ. *Amen.*

STUART NYE HUTCHISON
East Liberty Presbyterian Church
Moderator, Presbyterian General Assembly, Pittsburgh, Pa.

SPIRITUAL RESOURCES FOR DARK DAYS

When ye shall hear of wars and tumults, be not terrified. . . . In your patience ye shall win your souls.—Luke 21:9, 19 ARV

Dark days are upon us. We are beset by tensions, conflicts, and devastating fears—for ourselves and our children, for America's democracy, for our civilization, for Christianity.

In the midst of these fears we turn to the Gospels to find the guidance of Jesus. He helps now to build a faith that conquers fear, a faith in God. Jesus bids us turn from fear of what human anger, hate, and destruction can do, to the forces that are timeless and that cannot change.

Jesus urges His disciples to exercise a patient endurance during dark days. This means a control over the intellectual life, a determination to keep a calm mind and to develop wisdom and good judgment. It means emotional control when our feelings of love and hate, of prejudice and fears, are deeply stirred. It means spiritual control which helps in mental and emotional control. The sources of this spiritual mastery lie in prayer, the reading and study of the Bible, and in worship.

In these dark days Jesus calls us to a new faith in Him and His way of life, to a creative patience that keeps active a spiritual vision and a spiritual power, which in God's own time will make permanent a world of love and peace.

O GOD, we pray that in life's dark days we may have the light of Thy wisdom and the warmth of Thy love to guide and bless us. May we realize that we are never alone, but that Thy almighty strength is always available to us. Deepen our faith and empower our spirits to live and work for Thee and for the triumph of Thy Kingdom of love and unity over all the world. *Amen.*

WILFRID A. ROWELL
Hinsdale Union Church, Hinsdale, Ill.

GOD'S REWARD

He hath said, I will never leave thee, nor forsake thee. So that we may boldly say, The Lord is my helper, and I will not fear.—Heb. 13:5–6

In battle a good offense is the best defense. This is also true in facing the temptation of life. Let us not look for shelter or an "easy" place in which to maintain our faith; but let us dare to stand for honesty, purity, and truth in difficult and pagan areas.

The Master has a Distinguished Service Cross which He wants to pin on you. His "Well done, thou good and faithful servant" is of greater worth than the medals of all nations. Strive for it.

Here are a few suggestions: Hold on to God—He is always near. Cultivate a wholesome sense of humor. "A cheerful heart is a good medicine." Keep your speech clean and your mind centered on wholesome thinking. Be quick to help others. Remember the folks at home. Develop a rugged piety, a goodness which is attractive but unbreakable. Remember you are a child of God; you belong to Him, and He will never forsake you. Pray regularly; God is listening.

HEAVENLY FATHER, make me a follower of Christ. If I stumble into sin and fail to follow Thee, bring me to my senses. Lift me up and set me on the way which leadeth to life eternal. Make me a true friend, a loyal citizen, and a faithful follower of Jesus. Speak to me, God, in my lonely, weak hours, and with Thy grace, comfort and strengthen me so that I shall live up to the highest I know. In Jesus' name. *Amen.*

E. S. HJORTLAND
Ascension Lutheran Church, Milwaukee, Wis.

MORE THAN DUTY

Jesus said unto him, Thou shalt love the Lord thy God with all thy heart, and with all thy soul, and with all thy mind.—Matt. 22:37

Have you been doing more than your duty lately? Do you realize how great an area of experience lies beyond the boundary line that ordinary duty and obligation draw in our lives? Beyond that line are many of the finest things a life has to offer. Whether it be an individual, or a family, or a nation, the highest and best is reached only when we do more than can actually be demanded. Fulfilling the conventional obligations of religion is necessary. But if we stop there, we remain on a kind of subsistence level of religious living—enough perhaps to sustain life, but offering little in the way of continued growth.

While "religion begins in commandments," it is also true that "it ends in freedom and spiritual comradeship." When we say: "The eternal God is my dwelling place," "There shall thy hand lead me, and thy right hand shall hold me," "I will fear no evil; for thou art with me," then our religion becomes no longer the fulfillment of mere obligation. It is transformed into an attempt to live in companionship with the Great Friend of humankind. In that companionship ordinary duties and obligations are easier of fulfillment, but beyond that we discover that we are now twice as ready to live well as life is to compel us!

O THOU to whom we owe the obedience of our lives, we would render unto Thee no scant measure of devotion, but rather the complete loving service of ready hearts. Help us, that our consciousness of Thy nearness and care may increase from day to day, so that we may live constantly in the sense of Thy companionship finding the richness and strength of life that is for all those who love Thee and follow Thee with a full measure of their lives' devotion. *Amen.*

FREDERICK M. MEEK
All Souls' Church, Bangor, Me.

GOD'S PRESENCE

My Father shall give you another Comforter . . . even the Spirit of truth. . . . know him; for he dwelleth with you, and shall be in you.
—John 14:16–17

God's presence is not merely a thought, but a reality. God does not exist for you and me as Christians merely as a Supreme Being or an Eternal Reality, or as a cosmic Force. God is not merely the "Wholly Other"—a transcendent God—but God dwells in you and me by His Holy Spirit. This is not only the promise of our Divine Lord as recorded in the Scripture but the experience of countless hundreds who have found it to be a fact.

God's Spirit is in you and me by our faith and trust in Jesus Christ our Lord. This presence of God does not come to us as some sixth sense, adding something to our intellect, to our feeling, or to our wills; but it comes to us in our whole mind, dwelling there and making it vital and powerful. We are the dwelling place of the Spirit of God; we are His temple.

Our personalities are His means of expression so that God in His presence dwells within us each day. The presence of God does some very vital things for us. He gives us power for every day, power to do the things that we should do, and power to build our characters as they should be built. In this the Spirit of God becomes our Teacher, our Guide, and our Comforter. So God comes to you and me, not as some power outside of us, but as a Divine Power within us for everyday life.

Spirit of God, descend upon my heart;
Wean it from earth; through all its pulses move;
Stoop to my weakness, mighty as Thou art,
And make me love Thee as I ought to love. *Amen.*

ARTHUR J. McCLUNG
First and Calvary Presbyterian Church, Springfield, Mo.

SCORING

And Terah died in Haran.—Gen. 11:32

Nowhere have I encountered a more consummate tragedy than that described in the five words of the text. The tragedy lies not in the fact that Terah died, but that he "died in Haran." He had started for the Land of Promise, had succeeded in getting three-fourths of the way there, and then—he died in Haran. Within scoring distance, he failed.

In the game of baseball, no one scores by getting on first base or even by getting clear around to third. He scores only when he crosses the home plate. So too in the great game of life, no one scores when he gets on first base (physical), or on second (mental), or even on third (moral and social). He scores only when, having touched the other three bases, he crosses the home plate (spiritual).

Terah was a good man, but he failed to score; he died on third, and there can be no greater tragedy than that! To have a strong, clean body puts a person on first base; to win a well-disciplined mind gets one around to second; to play a game fairly, to live in favor with others, and to keep oneself morally straight advances him or her to third. What a tragedy if one dies there! To score, we must cross one more base, the spiritual; for without God at the center of it, we cannot live a satisfying life.

FATHER OF ALL, grant as I play the game of life that I may play it on the square, that I may keep my body healthy, my mind clean and alert. May I live in splendid comradeship with others and in harmony with Thee. Spare me Terah's tragedy; do not let me die on third; but grant that I, like Jesus, may score in the game of life. *Amen.*

DONALD H. TIPPETT
First Methodist Church, Los Angeles, Calif.

DAILY STRENGTH

Thy shoes shall be iron and brass; and as thy days, so shall thy strength be.—Deut. 33:25

The cross is not greater than His grace. The storms cannot hide His blessed face. . . ." Here, in our text, is God's just adjustment. There will never be too much strength; nor will there ever be too little. It's "tailor-made" help. It fits the individual need at the moment of the greatest need. It is help held in reserve. I cannot draw on it ahead of time; it will be given only as I need it. It is apportioned, fitting, and sufficient. As the need arises, so comes the help. The burden cannot be put on me suddenly and unawares. God's grace will fill my heart before the burden falls upon my shoulders.

I have no way of knowing or forecasting the trouble or the affliction. I do not know what the day will bring, but I do know that with the burden of the day will come His strength. Before the sorrow of tomorrow can strike me, it must pass God. He stands before my life as a sentinel. I cannot, in a certain sense, prepare myself for the morrow; God must prepare me for it. I wait for the days to come; I know that with their burden will come the needed strength, with their perplexity will be provided the needed guidance, with their sorrow will be given sufficient comfort. The day will not be too long, the path too steep or difficult, or the burden too heavy. "As thy days, so shall thy strength be."

DEAR GOD, let us gratefully keep in mind Thy promise of strength in accordance with our needs. May we meet each day's trials with high courage and confidence born of unquestioning faith. *Amen.*

CLINTON C. COX
Drexel Park Presbyterian Church, Chicago, Ill.

SLAVERY OF THE SOUL

Be not afraid of them that kill the body. . . . Fear him, who after he hath killed hath power to cast into hell.—Luke 12:4–5

Increasingly, in the world in which we live, the amount of physical security available to us is lessened. Human life today is cheap. For those who are basely selfish this is a tragedy—for those who live the life of love and service, it is relatively unimportant. Even prison and persecution will not daunt the Christian, because Christians live for One who is supreme over all earthly rulers and powers.

More important than personal happiness and safety, more important than freedom from the slavery to an enemy, is the soul freedom which no one can take from us. Of what value is political, religious, and economic freedom if we have subscribed to a slavery to sin which holds us in the bondage of evil habits and ideals? Our nation and the world must learn that material things are valueless, even dangerous, if we have not achieved a spiritual and moral freedom that transcends in value all earthly powers and riches. Yes, better to be a Christian, a slave to a conqueror, than to be politically free, yet bound by the bonds of sin and selfishness to a way of living which is morally and spiritually degrading.

The Christian life issues in a victory that no amount of force or power can shatter. Cherish, then, those values which are more important than life itself.

ALMIGHTY GOD, Thou who didst create and dost sustain us now, we earnestly pray that we may never become slaves to sin. We seek to serve Thee and Thee only as long as we shall live. Through Jesus Christ our Lord. *Amen.*

CECIL E. HINSHAW
Friends University, Wichita, Kan.

PUT YOUR MIND ON GOD

He that hath seen me hath seen the Father.—John 14:9

When we have made up our minds to succeed in anything, we begin to do a lot of thinking about it. "We put our minds on it," as we say. Since you came into the Army, Navy, Air Force, or Marine Corps, you have put a lot of thought on your new job—handling a rifle, servicing a plane, driving a tank or truck, aiming a gun.

The more you have studied your work, the better you have understood it. It is all real and vital. But when we talk about God, things become foggy. We grope in the mist. God realized this difficulty, and so He sent us a Man like ourselves who went through life meeting all the knocks and temptations, dangers, and disappointments that strike us, but who understood and trusted God so well that He could say that anyone who knew His life and character would really understand what God is like. So your job is to study the life of Jesus the way you study your rifle or your airplane day after day.

You will discover how He liked people—all sorts of them—how He hated anyone's being unjust or hard, or even being crabby. You will also see that He was forever getting help and courage from His Father. Go ahead and discover for yourself just what kind of person Jesus really was. Then you will know His Father and yours. You will find all about Jesus in the four short biographies His friends wrote about Him, the first books of the New Testament.

ALMIGHTY GOD, my Father, who knowest my heart, my needs, and my hopes, help me to know Thy Son, Jesus Christ, that, knowing Him, I may know Thee also. Help me to understand the people about me and to be a friend to some of them. Unite me in the moments of this prayer with those I love who are far away. In the Spirit of Christ. *Amen.*

MURRAY SHIPLEY HOWLAND
First Presbyterian Church, Binghamton, N.Y.

THE WHITE LINE

I determined not to know any thing among you, save Jesus Christ, and him crucified.—1 Cor. 2:2

The fog was terrible. We had to creep along at five miles an hour and less—but we arrived home safe and sound, thanks to the white line!" This from a personal letter reminds us that from time to time we have occasion to thank God and the Highway Commission for the white line running down the middle of the road. Just so wide, just so white, and in the exact center, this line must be. The traveling public has learned to depend on it. It must be maintained as near perfect as possible.

Our faith ought to be a white line both for ourselves and for others. "Let your light so shine," said Jesus, and, "Ye are the light of the world." Will others arrive safe and sound if they follow our leading? Can those who are nearest to us depend on the honesty and integrity of our "white line"? In the fogs of fear and uncertainty which often envelop life's highway, can others find guidance and confidence in us?

Every one of us in the service, both of our country and of our God, are offered the unequaled opportunity to make clearer and brighter the white line of personal religious certainty. Through self-denial to self-expression; through devotional services to devoted service; through the defeat of the cross to the Victory of the Crucified—shall we not make this our road, the road of the white line?

OUR FATHER IN HEAVEN, help us to stay close to the white line of service, the white line of sacrifice, the white line of love, the white line of Christ. Our feeble lamps illumine it but a short way beyond us, but we can see enough of it to know that we are safe. Help us to keep to the safety of Him who is Way, Truth, and Life. In His blessed name. *Amen.*

GLENN RANDALL PHILLIPS
First Hollywood Methodist Church, Los Angeles, Calif.

SOWING AND REAPING

Be not deceived; God is not mocked: for whatsoever a man soweth, that shall he also reap.—Gal. 6:7

This is not a threat; it is more than a promise; it is a statement of a principle.

This war will not last forever. We hope it will not last for long. But, long or short, most of the people who are in the armed forces of America will presently be back in civilian life. The world will reap the harvest of the war; the individual will reap the harvest of his or her own thoughts, words, deeds, aspirations, attitudes, failures, and successes during the war.

There will be constantly recurring temptations to lose faith in God and people, to surrender ambitions and principles, to abandon religion and morals. But one of the things that makes us better than the beasts is our ability to look ahead and to determine our conduct today on the basis of what is to be tomorrow, next week, next year, a thousand years from now.

Think of yourself in the years that are to be. Cling to your faith as you will wish in a later time that you had done. Resist temptation today in such a way that you can rejoice in your victories ten years from now. Keep yourself as clean as you would like to be when you look into the eyes of a pure spouse in a better day than this. Be true to your after-self. By your life today do not curse but bless the person you are to be when the war is over.

O GOD, my Father, keep me strong and clean during these days when temptation and danger surround me. Help me to fight against evil without and within, with faith in Thee, the Eternal Goodness. Bring me through this war with nothing to be ashamed of. In the name of Jesus Christ. *Amen.*

LEVI T. PENNINGTON
Pacific College, Newberg, Ore.

RESOURCES FOR WINNING

Act on the Word, instead of merely listening to it and deluding yourselves.—Jas. 1:22 (MOFFATT)

What we want out of religion is an assurance that God is available for all the necessities of life. One of the liabilities that we face in this matter of religion is that we just take it for granted and do not pay any serious attention to it as a discipline of life.

The ancient psalmist once lifted the prayer: "Keep back thy servant also from presumptuous sins." It is one of the strangest of human habits that in the realm of the delicate and intangible we presume on the constant presence of that Spirit that will give us power and poise for living. If we want to be a musician or an artist, we do not so presume on the laws of music or art. If we are to be good soldiers, we dare not presume upon our position or our defenses. But in the realm of successful and effective living, we constantly presume upon the laws of spiritual living. We actually presume upon God and take as a matter of course His continued interest in and care for us.

There is no rare strengthening and emancipating idea to be found anywhere than that on which Jesus laid such constant stress—that this universe that we are a part of is God's world, that its forces are not foes but friends of His sons and daughters, that we can use every one of them for our advantage. Paul summed up Jesus' teaching by saying: "All things are yours; . . . the world, or life, or death, or things present, or things to come; all are yours."

O GOD, our eternal Father, equip us with that faith and fortitude that we need to will the victory most worth winning. Grant us a release from the tensions of time, that we may have an experience of the quality of living that is eternal. Through Jesus Christ our Lord. *Amen.*

OSCAR THOMAS OLSON
Epworth-Euclid Methodist Church, Cleveland, Ohio

THE THINGS THAT LAST

Thus "faith and hope and love last on, these three," but the greatest of all is love.—1 Cor. 13:13 (MOFFATT)

The dizzy pace of current events can upset us tremendously. Things are happening around us and to us so rapidly that some of us have begun to think that nothing will last. Would it not be wise for us, then, to snatch whatever satisfaction the present moment offers? Why let any thought of yesterday or tomorrow affect our conduct now? Why not lay aside all scruples, bid conscience cease to speak, and discard religion altogether? If Edgar Allan Poe were right in saying that life is a tragedy whose hero is "the conqueror Worm," then life would be futile and morality foolish.

But this philosophy of life is a lie. There are enduring values. As Paul puts it, "faith and hope and love last on." Yes, even in wartime these things last on. Because they are permanent realities they are worth giving ourselves to. Because Christianity is based upon these abiding things it is now more necessary for us than ever before. It alone gives meaning to all of life.

Dostoevski tells of a thief and a harlot waiting together for the end in a dark room. By the light of their last candle they read a tattered Gospel someone has left behind. They come to the story of Lazarus, and they begin to say to each other: "He raised Lazarus from the dead; He can raise us." That's it; "faith and hope and love last on," and even death cannot entomb them.

O GOD, grant that I may give myself not to the things which are passing but to the eternal. Help me to keep my faith in humanity and God. Let not hope die within me. May I, remembering that Thou dost love me, never lose my capacity for loving others and loving Thee. Abide with me through life's changes. Through Jesus Christ our Lord. *Amen.*

TALMAGE C. JOHNSON
First Baptist Church, Kinston, N.C.

DIMES OR DIAMONDS?

Seek, and ye shall find.—Matt. 7:7

Thomas L. Masson tells us that out of a number of years of endeavoring to meet the wants of vagabonds and beggars, he came to the conclusion that they were all "one-dime" people. Beggars, he declares, are looking for dimes. Yes, and they will get them, for there is a very real sense in which people receive from life just what they demand of it.

Therefore, as we confront this strange destiny which seems to bestow lavishly upon some and to withhold to the point of penury from others, what is our asking? Are we seeking dimes or diamonds? Will we be content with bread, or shall we cry out for the Bread of Life? Have we the courage to seek out the heights of self-sacrifice which can be scaled only at cost of bruised souls and bleeding hearts? Jesus asked for a cup and a cross—dare we?

O GOD, forgive us our petty askings. Rebuke us in our willingness to be content with any second best. Give us the courage to ask for life and the readiness to pay its price, e'en though it be a cross. In Jesus' name. *Amen.*

RAYMOND V. KEARNS
First Presbyterian Church, Salina, Kan.

ANXIOUS IN NOTHING

Men ought always to pray, and not to faint.—Luke 18:1

To be "anxious in nothing" (Phil. 4:6–7) is not saying, "I don't care." The one who says, "I don't care" is sowing tares which will bring a terrible harvest. "Anxious in nothing" means that the peace of God has crowded out earthly care. What is the secret? It is not found in the philosophy of the stoics who set their teeth and determine to master the ills of life, but rather in "letting your requests be made known unto God."

Paul, as a prisoner awaiting trial in Rome, looked steadfastly into the face of death. Everything in the future was absolutely dark and uncertain. Then it was that he wrote his brethren in Philippi and cheerfully bade them, "In nothing be anxious; but in everything by prayer and supplication with thanksgiving let your requests be made known unto God."

We are too often guilty of that evil habit, worry, that should play no part in a believer's life. Worry is to be banished. It accomplishes nothing and narrows the spiritual horizons. Worry turns out the bright light of God.

God has by no means nor in any event promised to do everything for us; there are some things we must do for ourselves. He has promised never to leave nor forsake His own. He has promised to save unto the uttermost all who come unto Him through Christ Jesus. He has promised that all things shall work together for good to them that love Him.

Paul gives us his recipe for the cure of care—prayer.

O GOD, in this day which I can see not a hand's breadth before me, guide me in the way I take. Help me that I may keep ever before me the righteousness of Thy cause. Give me strength of body, mind, and spirit to tender the best service within my power for God and home and native land. This I pray in the name of Christ Jesus, my great Captain. *Amen.*

JOHN BUNYAN SMITH
First Baptist Church, San Diego, Calif.

WEAPONS OF THE SOUL

Put on the whole armor of God.—Eph. 6:11

Paul, writing about Christian soldiers, lists their weapons: First, the *belt*, which bound their garments so that there would be nothing loose as they went into battle. The belt was to brace them for action and keep them tense and firm. The belt stands for truth. A braced body symbolizes a mind alert and ready.

Second, the *breastplate* protected the vital organs. It stands for righteousness, an attitude of complete sincerity, a life of unquestionable moral integrity. No one can serve family or community or nation unless his or her purpose is honest.

Third, the *shoes*. For the Roman, as for the modern soldier, shoes were an important item. They must stand a lot of wear and must not hamper swift movement over rough ground. They stand for a zeal which can endure through the war and help in building peace.

Fourth, the *shield*, shaped like a small door and covered with thick leather, was especially useful in warding off flaming arrows. The shield stands for faith, by which today a soldier wards off temptation.

Fifth, the *helmet*, stands for the protection of a constant relationship with God.

Sixth, the *sword* is a symbol of the power of a spiritually dedicated life.

Finally, an invisible weapon, the weapon of *prayer*, refers to the mood of expectancy at the hands of God which should characterize the Christian at all times.

ALMIGHTY GOD, keep us strong in our faith and eager in our desire to magnify Thy name. Through Jesus Christ. *Amen.*

Frank Fitt
Grosse Pointe Memorial Church
Presbyterian, Grosse Pointe Farms, Mich.

THE QUEST FOR GOD

Seek ye the Lord while he may be found, call ye upon him while he is near.—Isa. 55:6

Trouble teaches us to pray. Our extremity becomes God's opportunity. In darkness we seek light.

Today there is a new thirst for God. We are crying with Job of old, "Oh that I knew where I might find him!" Like Job, we too can find traces of God in fossilized rocks, in the plan and precision of the stars, in the evolutionary history of fishes, birds, and beasts.

Job studied the ostrich and saw responsibility evaded, as a female bird ran away from her nest of eggs, leaving them to destruction in the sand and winds. He studied the horse as it went fearlessly into battle, but he decided that this was meaningless because the horse did not know the meaning of his action.

It is in humanity that Job discovers an ethical counterpart to God which makes communion between the two possible and hence revelation of God to us. So God spoke to Job out of the wind and said, "Gird up now thy loins like a man." And Job said, "Now mine eye seeth thee," and he repented.

Centuries later, Jesus of Nazareth came preaching, saying, "He that loveth his life, shall lose it: but he that loseth his life for my sake, shall find it." Then He walked the way of the cross and was crucified. A Roman soldier, standing beneath that cross, looked up and said, "Certainly this was a righteous man." He was more. He was the Son of God and He was God. Hear Him speak: "Before Abraham was, I am." "I and my Father are one." "Repent: for the kingdom of heaven is at hand."

Jesus, I live to Thee,
The loveliest and best;
My life in Thee, Thy life in me,
In Thy blest love I rest. *Amen.*

HAROLD E. DITZLER
First Reformed Church, Los Angeles, Calif.

OUR RECORD

We are compassed about with so great a cloud of witnesses.—Heb. 12:1

I once heard Branch Rickey tell of his first game of professional baseball. It was in Philadelphia. After the game the team rode to their hotel in an old-style omnibus. As it turned into Chestnut Street, Mr. Rickey saw a great crowd down the street. Evidently there was a fight, or a fire, or an accident. The curiosity of youth had to be satisfied, and so he jumped off the bus and ran on ahead.

He discovered that the crowd was composed of ball fans reading the details of the afternoon's game from a bulletin board. A hasty glance at the record showed one thing above all else: there was his name and after it a record of the kind of a game he played—both runs and errors. Branch Rickey testified that he never had such a sobering experience before. He realized right from the start of his career that what he did, and how he did it, was of the utmost interest to thousands of baseball devotees.

Soldier, sailor, pilot, marine, all eyes are on you. God sees the very core of your heart. A world awaits. Be clean, be loyal, be efficient. The future is with you. That's why our gaze is fixed upon you with breathless expectancy.

O GOD, save us by Thy sacrifice; keep us by Thy Spirit. May we be as clean in the dark as we are in the light. Make us an honor to God, an example to our brothers and sisters. May it be that others, seeing our good works, may want to glorify our God. *Amen.*

GEORGE W. KNEPPER
Former Pastor, High Street Church of Christ, Akron, Ohio

GOD CARES FOR YOU

He careth for you.—1 Pet. 5:7

"He careth for you." These words were written by the apostle Peter to comfort the Christians in days of persecution and suffering, when many were tempted to ask themselves, "Does God care?" even as we are assailed by doubt when the world is ravaged by war.

Does God care? Does anybody care? The bitterness without may at times creep into soldiers' thoughts, until they remember dear ones at home who never cease to think of them and pray for them, because they love them. To remember them and with them, though many miles apart, will keep the home fires burning in their hearts. And, so long as somebody truly cares for us, we have no right to be careless. So long as somebody has faith in us, we have no right to be faithless.

And God cares! There is a hell of hatred in the world today, but there is also a great love in the universe which will prove to be the solvent for all our ills. And that Love cares for you and me. God will win. To think that wrong will win is a contradiction in itself. Have faith in God! If you are willing to belong to Him with all your heart, He will take care of you.

OUR HEAVENLY FATHER, we seek the stillness of our souls to come to ourselves as we come to Thee. We want to commune with Thee and rest in Thee so that we may be able to face the hardships that await us with the calm and deep assurance that we are in God's care whatever may happen to us. Take out of our hearts everything that is not in harmony with Thee so that we may draw power from omnipotence as we pray to Thee and walk with Thee. Bless our loved ones at home; and help us to believe that they and we, though far apart, are united in Thy love. *Amen.*

ARTHUR B. RHINOW
First Presbyterian Church, Ridgewood, N.Y.

WHAT DOES GOD MEAN TO ME?

The Lord is my shepherd.—Ps. 23:1

What does God mean to you? Perhaps the psalmist was asked that question, and the picture of the shepherd caring for his sheep, even to the point of risking his life, came first to his mind. God was all of that, certainly, but that was not enough for the psalmist. God was also a guide who with His rod and staff guided one down through the valley of the shadow of death; and how we do need guides! Even so, the psalmist was not yet satisfied. God was a friend, a true friend, who took one into His home and provided food and shelter and protection, even against enemies, and filled one's cup of joy full and overflowing.

To us Jesus comes into this picture as the Shepherd who gave His life for us and so has become the Way, the Truth, and the Life. He tells us that God is a father—"Our Father."

O GOD, be to me this day my Shepherd, my Guide, my Friend and my Father. Help me so to live through the hours of this day that Thou canst use me to further the Way, the Truth, and the Life. *Amen.*

MURRAY S. KENWORTHY
First Friends Church, Carthage, Ind.

GOD'S LOVE

God so loved the world, that he gave his only begotten Son, that whosoever believeth in him should not perish, but have everlasting life.—John 3:16

In the midst of a world that seems to have been abandoned by God, there is a shining light, glowing with an inescapable truth—namely, what seems to be the greatest tragedy in our history, the crucifixion of Jesus, the Son of God. Although that terrible scene does show forth the stupidity and sin of humanity, preeminently it is the standing witness to the infinite love of God.

Surely if God could so give His Son to make the one true and complete sacrifice, that we might look upon Him and find salvation, nothing that could happen on the face of the earth can make us doubt that God is indeed love and that it is His will for all to find their way to peace and joy.

Surely, also, if God in the person of His blessed Son learned the meaning of human suffering, temptation, and fear, we who know so little of the wholeness of God's plan for the world can with great assurance turn to Him when we are tempted, when we suffer, when we fear; for we know that He will give Himself to us to be our strength, because of His great love for us.

This little life that we live here is but the beginning of an eternity of blessed growth towards that perfection which will bring to us the security and serenity which we all truly seek. We may therefore, by keeping our faith in Him and holding close to Him, find a refuge in time of stress, courage in the face of danger, and strength in time of temptation.

O GOD, who hast prepared for those who love Thee such good things as pass our understanding, pour into our hearts such love toward Thee that we, loving Thee above all things, may obtain Thy gracious promises. *Amen.*

DON FRANK FENN
Church of St. Michael and All Angels, Baltimore, Md.

WALKING WITH JESUS

Jesus . . . went with them.—Luke 24:15

Walking is almost a lost art, but there are wonderful fellowships with a walking companion. Let us put ourselves in step with the walking Jesus. Through the poetess He would say:

> But as we meet and touch each day
> The many travelers on our way,
> Let every such brief contact be
> A glorious, helpful ministry.
> —SUSAN COOLIDGE

Jesus walked with many a willing person on the road. He still walks with willing, though tired and hungry, souls.

Scott, the South Pole explorer, with his fellows, devout men, trudged the snow and ice, apparently alone. When at length they rested, each reported, "I thought somebody else was with us." Jesus was with them, but they almost did not see Him and hence somewhat doubted His presence.

What wonders are missed because eyes are not focused to see! With eyes closed by blatant selfishness, dimmed by the dust of despair and doubts, blinded by false or foolish notions, shut by the pressure of conflicting ideals, we limp along, failing to see who it is that burns our hearts as we walk. Scott's men who walked with Jesus had sorrow which does not need to be repeated. We may walk with Him and know Him.

O FATHER IN HEAVEN, open Thou my eyes. So much I have not seen. Let me now see. Help me always to remember that the pure in heart see God. Purify me that I may see Jesus, who is willing to walk with me. In His name. *Amen.*

E. H. STRANAHAN
William Penn College, Oskaloosa, Iowa

HOW TO FOLLOW JESUS

He said to them all, If any man will come after me, let him deny himself, and take up his cross daily, and follow me.—Luke 9:23

In this, one of Jesus' most penetrating sayings, we find His standard of discipleship. Jesus is here giving us three tests.

First of all, *self-denial*. Jesus was interested in the self-disciplines that spring from an inner compulsion of the spirit. "Let him deny himself!" This has been the familiar climate in which the great souls of history have customarily lived. Only through the habit of humble, daily, toiling attention are worthwhile accomplishments ever achieved. There can be no self-development apart from self-denial; it is the law of growth.

Second, *self-expenditure*. "Let him . . . take up his cross daily," said our Lord; let us give ourselves to some high endeavor that is larger and finer than we are. Voluntary assumption of some of the burdens of this suffering world is the touchstone of a person's religious sincerity. True Christians always care, care enough to make their faith result in facts.

Third, *self-dedication*. Jesus ended his description of Christian character by saying, "Follow me." That is, "Dedicate your life to the eternal principles for which I have lived!" The more evil the day, the more important it is to incarnate those values which alone will redeem the day. The sins of our generation are too deep to be changed by anything less than complete self-bestowal. Dedicate yourself, therefore, to the unremitting service of Christ, and you will discover a release of spirit and a happiness of mind that you had not dreamed possible.

O GOD, enable me to keep myself dedicated to Thee. Grant me the power to deny myself that I may develop myself for Thee and expend myself daily in Thy service. *Amen.*

WILLIAM H. HUDNUT JR.
First Presbyterian Church, Springfield, Ill.

ONE GOLDEN DAY

My grace is sufficient for thee: for my strength is made perfect in weakness. Most gladly therefore will I rather glory in my infirmities, that the power of Christ may rest upon me.—2 Cor. 12:9

Returning from France on a transport at the close of the First World War, I came across these lines:

> Dark skies must clear, and when the clouds are past,
> One golden day redeems a weary year,
> Patient I listen, sure that sweet at last
> Will sound His voice of cheer.

A year in France as a buck private in the army had brought its full measure of dark skies, but all of that was past now. It was literally true that "one golden day redeems a weary year."

Through all the succeeding years I have never ceased to be thankful that I listened for "His voice of cheer" and looked forward to the golden day when my face would be turned homeward. Listening for His voice I found strength for every need.

The temptations that come to young people away from home and loved ones are more than they can withstand unless their lives are open to a power greater than their own. That very need opens the way for a closer and dearer companionship with the great Companion of the Way. Wherever you are, you can have the blessed experience of His Presence walking beside you.

O THOU GREAT COMPANION OF THE WAY, open my mind and heart to Thy redeeming presence until every unclean thought and every unworthy purpose shall be consumed in the white heat of Thy perfect love. *Amen.*

CLINTON E. OSTRANDER
University Congregational Church, Seattle, Wash.

CONQUERING THE SHARKS

I can do all things through Christ which strengtheneth me.
　　　　　　　　　　　　　　　　　　　—Phil. 4:13

A few years ago we were driving leisurely over the Royal Palm Bridge at Palm Beach, when suddenly two cars whizzed by. Upon arriving at the pier we discovered that they were expecting the arrival of a swimmer from Bimini. He was picked up two miles off the coast, having failed to swim the entire distance because he was finally conquered by exhaustion. In fact, it was only with the assistance of those in an accompanying boat who beat off the sharks that he had gone as far as he did. Lying in the hospital that night, through swollen face, lips, and tongue, he was heard to say, "I had rather died, than have failed."

His failure was due to lack of strength. Physical strength is important in undergoing physical hardships, and to face physical difficulties, one must be physically fit. But enemies just as great face us from within—enemies which are not seen but only felt, enemies which sap our spiritual vitality and weaken us for the finer and better things of life. We need not fail in our battle against temptation and sin. There is always One at hand to beat off the "sharks" which attack the soul. We know we have One "who was in all points tempted like as we are, yet without sin." And we can say, "I can do all things through Christ which strengtheneth me." We cannot fail if we have Him.

O LORD CHRIST, grant unto me the necessary strength which Thou only canst supply, that I, like Thee, may face life's temptations with the calm assurance that I cannot fail because Thou art my strength. In Thy name I ask. *Amen.*

WALTER LOWRIE RITTER
First Presbyterian Church, Altoona, Pa.

LIVING TOWARD OUR IDEALS

I punish my body and enslave it, so that after proclaiming to others I myself should not be disqualified.—1 Cor. 9:27 NRSV

How many young men have I not hailed at the commencement of their career, glowing with enthusiasm and full of the poetry of great enterprises, whom I see today precocious old men, with the wrinkles of cold calculation on their brow; calling themselves free from illusion when they are only disheartened; and practical when they are only commonplace."

—MAZZINI

Jesus was a young man but little more than thirty years old when He was crucified. His inner circle of followers were young men, most of them younger than Himself. In choosing them He realized the value of the devotion and clear-sightedness of youth; and at the last He entrusted to this group of young men the high task of carrying on the work He had begun.

In our own day, as in His, He is the leader of young people, young men and women alive with that idealism that is in youth the only realism, the realism of Christ. The crude selfishness and cynicism of life too often dampen the enthusiasm of our earlier years. Young people may wisely "gamble on the future, belonging to Christ" and jealously cultivate and nourish the ideals that He has aroused in them. His words, to His most impetuous disciple, come to us through the centuries and under whatsoever conditions may exist. "What is that to thee? *Follow thou me.*"

O GOOD JESUS, enlighten me with the brightness of internal light, and cast out all darkness from the dwelling of my heart. Restrain my wandering thoughts and crush the temptations which violently assail me. Join me to Thyself with the inseparable bond of love. *Amen.*

EDWIN P. RYLAND
Evangelist, Los Angeles, Calif.

GOOD CHEER

*In the world ye shall have tribulation: but be of good cheer: I have
overcome the world.*—John 16:33

These are days when we are liable to become discouraged. In such a
state we lose confidence in ourselves and in others and God seems far
off. We need to hear Jesus' message of encouragement, "Be of good cheer."
Our mood of depression may be due to thinking too much about ourselves
and the conditions in the world today. It has been said, "When the outlook
is dark, try the uplook."

In the Bible we find two cures for discouragement. First, we are to lift
our thoughts and prayers toward God. We will gain faith in His wisdom,
power, and purpose. This is the victory which gives us the power to overcome the world and all its evil forces. When we open our hearts to God's
Son, He brings us cheer amid our doubts and discouragements. We realize
that after His apparent defeat on the cross, He won a glorious victory on
Easter Day.

The second cure is in finding something worthwhile to do. When Paul
was discouraged in his cell in Jerusalem, God said, "Be of good cheer," and
sent him to Rome for a new mission. In the upper room Jesus told His
disciples to be of good cheer because He had overcome the world, and
then sent them forth to win new victories for Him in the world. Our faith
in Christ who conquered sin, death, and all the evil forces of the world
gives us the victory over our world. Abiding in Christ gives us life, joy, and
peace. As a result we become people of good cheer.

HEAVENLY FATHER, may the Spirit of Christ give us courage for today,
strength for our burdens, and such faith in Thee that we may have good
cheer in our hearts and victory over all the forces of this world. We pray in
Jesus' name. *Amen.*

WALLACE H. CARVER
First Presbyterian Church, Arlington, N.J.

CHRISTIAN STRENGTH

I have written unto you, young man, because ye are strong.
—1 John 2:14

Heroic seems the expression of strength. You watch a Native American athlete, well stripped, with billowy muscles, ponderous chest, heavy shoulders, a long stick looped at the end, and two thongs across. In this loop he catches up a ball. Then, swinging it, he shoots the ball skyward as a released arrow, out of sight. Now that's strength!

We admire mental and spiritual power as well. How accurately some people think. They give much to civilization. They build spiritual resistance; their "No," spoken at the right moment, is positive. They never surrender to evil. Cromwell's soldier, refusing the enemy's command to capitulate, exclaimed, "Surrender? Never! I am a soldier of Cromwell." The world needs characters in critical times who say to enemies of His Kingdom, "Surrender? Never! I am a soldier of Jesus Christ."

My father and mother were sticklers for integrity of life and language, and for spiritual development. They knew what was needed. I wanted to be strong physically; and they, by pure living and clean habits, helped me. I needed to develop mentally, and they made possible advances in intellect. I needed to be spiritually right, to know God and His Son, and to acquire the strength that overcomes evil; and they taught me. For their sakes, and for their Christ—and mine—I would be strong, have the word of God abiding, and overcome the wicked one.

ALMIGHTY GOD, Source of all strength; strengthen me now that I may be brave in the hour of danger, pure in the face of temptation, and true in the circumstances that would call me from the faith of loved ones and of Thee. May I ever be a good soldier of Jesus Christ. *Amen.*

EDWIN McGREW
President, William Penn College, Oskaloosa, Iowa

THE SECRET OF PATIENCE

Let us run with patience the race that is set before us, looking unto Jesus the author and finisher of our faith.—Heb. 12:1–2

We are not willing to admit many of our spiritual weaknesses, but most of us will admit that we are impatient—with our friends, the Government, even God Himself! We would like to possess our souls in patience, but how, in heaven's name, can we? Is there a secret of patience? The writer of the epistle to the Hebrews replies that the secret is to concentrate upon One who is Patience incarnate.

Tertullian once said that the Pharisees should have recognized who Christ was by His patience. In His temptations He refused the short cut to fame and power; in His dealings with His apostles He had constant disappointments but never lost faith and hope; upon the cross He was patient even with those who crucified Him, and prayed for them. His was an active patience. Patience does not mean passivity. It means doing our best in the confidence that God will use our best and the right results will follow.

We are not to "sit" with patience but to "run" with patience. Anyone who has learned a new language or how to play a musical instrument knows what active patience is—how much work has to be done in faith, in order that results may follow. Jesus could run with patience the course that was set before Him, with all its hardships, because of His faith that God would use His life—that out of apparent defeat would come victory.

O GOD, help me to run with patience the race that is set before me. May I find strength by looking unto Jesus, the author and finisher of my faith. May I share His quiet confidence in the eternal victory of Truth and Beauty and Goodness. *Amen.*

EVERETT H. JONES
St. Mark's Episcopal Church, San Antonio, Tex.

LISTENING TO GOD'S VOICE

Everyone who cares for truth, who has any feeling for the truth, recognizes my voice.—John 18:37c (THE MESSAGE)

I first began to learn the discipline of listening when I became a short-wave radio listener. Each year I entered the Boy Scouts of America short-wave radio listening contest. Awards were given to the Boy Scouts who listened to the largest number of short-wave broadcast stations in various categories within a specified period of time. Participants had to exercise diligence, flexibility, and patience. In the midst of long periods of silence on the short-wave radio, one might hear the sound of a station not previously heard before.

Every good amateur radio operator listens before speaking. The purpose of listening is to determine if someone else is already transmitting on a desired frequency. Is another person saying something that you want to hear? Is there a conversation already in progress that one might wish to join? There are times when I simply listen because it is so informative to hear what other people are saying.

As a disciple of Jesus Christ, I find that I must shrink from my busyness. There are times when I need to be silent and wait for the voice of God to speak in the silence of my life. I ask God daily to teach me the discipline of listening. In the silence of our quiet times, we will hear the voice of Jesus. As we seek the truth we will recognize Jesus as the voice of truth.

LORD, teach us how to wait and to listen. In our waiting, surround us with patience. Move us beyond our fascination with doing. Tame our hearts, minds, and souls with the awesome power of sheer silence. Grant us the gift of listening. *Amen.*

ERNEST S. LYGHT
Resident Bishop, New York Area, The United Methodist Church

"BUT IF NOT . . ."

> *. . . Our God . . . will deliver us out of thine hand, O king. But if not, be it known unto thee, O king, that we will not serve thy gods, nor worship the golden image which thou hast set up.*—Dan. 3:17–18

Shadrach, Meshach, and Abednego never compromised their total commitment to obey God and worship Him as He commanded. And when their faithfulness threatened their very lives, their confidence in God did not diminish but in fact increased.

George Will has told a story about a telegraph message which a commander in the British Royal Air Force sent to his superiors during the Second World War. His airmen were under siege from a relentless attack in the South Pacific. The British officer cabled the following words: "Supplies are low. Munitions are running out. Can't last much longer. Please send reinforcements. But if not—" And the cable ended.

When this officer wrote, "But if not—" he was making an intentional allusion to the faith and perseverance of Shadrach, Meshach, and Abednego and making a promise to follow their faithful example. His message would have been recognized by all those to whom the cable was addressed.

The Good News for those whose faith and hope is in the Only Son of God is that we ultimately have no need to say, "But if not . . ."—our eternity with God is secure and untouchable. But our confidence in that future grace gives us the hope and courage to do whatever the glory of God and the good of humanity demand of us, no matter what the cost right now.

HEAVENLY FATHER, I place my trust in You and in the certainty of the salvation You have given to me in Jesus Christ. I am confident that You are able to deliver me from any difficulty in life—but I trust Your goodness and trust that whatever happens to me, You work for my good and Your glory. You are the Source of true Life, true Liberty, and true Happiness. I acknowledge You as God, no matter what I face today. *Amen.*

ROBERT B. SLOAN JR.
President, Baylor University, Waco, Tex.

DIVINE POSSIBILITIES

> *As Pharaoh drew near, the Israelites looked back, and there were the*
> *Egyptians advancing on them. In great fear the Israelites cried out to*
> *the Lord.*—Exod. 14:10

Fear is an intense emotion that can overwhelm you and cause you to be afraid to risk, step out, go forward, take charge, make a change, confront a challenge, and trust that God will be there to help you. This story tells of the Israelites' summons to a deeper level of faith and belief in the power of God. After they marched out of Egypt, all Pharaoh's horses, chariots, horsemen and troops pursued them from behind. Mountains were on the east and the west and the 1,050 mile long Red Sea flowed in front of them. As the Israelites were camped by the Red Sea, they believed that they were in an impossible situation.

We too find ourselves in impossible situations. We see no way out and feel trapped, hemmed in, and paralyzed. The walls begin to close in and darkness pervades because we allow our human fears to overwhelm our divine faith. Fear stifles. Faith liberates. Fear holds back. Faith moves forward. Fear terrifies. Faith comforts. Fear despairs but faith brings hope.

In the midst of your uncertainties, ambiguities and doubt, you must have faith in divine possibilities. When confronting your Red Sea, that passage of water that separates you from achieving your potential, don't give up or turn back. Lean not upon your own understanding but acknowledge God in all your ways and He will direct your path. Stand firm on the foundation of your faith and you will see the power of God transform your fear into faith. Moses' faith in an almighty and powerful God allowed him to raise his staff and stretch out his hand over the sea, and through faithful and obedient action, God parted the Red Sea and the Israelites walked through on dry land.

DEAR GOD, help my unbelief. Allow me to trust You in the little things and in the big things, for with you, all things are possible. *Amen.*

LISA D. RHODES
Dean of the Chapel, Spelman College, Atlanta, Ga.

IT'S ALWAYS TOO SOON TO QUIT

My soul, wait silently for God alone. For my expectation is from Him. He only is my rock and my salvation; He is my defense; I shall not be moved.—Ps. 62:5–6

An inspirational message by an unknown author inspires me to always be the best I can be:

"The Best Day of My Life"

Today, when I awoke, I suddenly realized that this is the best day of my life—ever! There were times I wondered if I would make it to today—but I did. And because I did, I'm going to celebrate what an unbelievable life I have had so far! Today, I will share my excitement for life with other people; I'll make someone smile, perform an unexpected act of kindness for a stranger, tell a child how special he is, and tell someone I love how much they mean to me.

Today is the day I quit worrying about what I don't have and start being grateful for all the wonderful things God has already given me. And tonight I'll thank God for the best day of my life and with childlike expectation know that tomorrow is going to be another "best day of my life—ever!"

DEAR LORD, bless the men and women who choose to serve their country. Help them to have their "best day ever" every day. Fill their hearts with dreams and help them stay on track by surrounding them with people who will encourage them. Give them the strength to move closer to their dream, hope to continue along their journey, and wisdom to not allow the words of others to hold them back. Help them to do their personal best each day and be the best person they can be. *Amen.*

RUDY RUETTIGER
The "real" Rudy from the TriStar Movie "Rudy"
Motivational Speaker, Las Vegas, Nev.

SPIRITUAL ROOTAGE

The Father that dwelleth in me, he doeth the works.—John 14:10

The life of a plant depends primarily upon its rootage. Humans live superficially unless their taproots reach spiritual reality. Overwhelming days such as these test the rootage of everyone, and only those who are adequately rooted withstand the manifold pressures satisfactorily.

Jesus' rootage enabled Him to be in the storm but not of it. He radiated that power which came from the Infinite, through His rootage. "The Father that dwelleth in me, he doeth the works." Here is the secret of those whose spiritual house stands when the rains descend, the winds blow, and the floods beat. Rootage is available to all who will adjust their personal attitudes.

Prayer produces power and inner peace. Meditation gives a sense of oneness with the cosmic purposes and processes of God. Regular participation in common worship gives a sense of social undergirding and spiritual fellowship of the Way.

Destiny is not a secondary or surface determination. It lies in the area of primary causes. Power which is not created cannot be transmitted. We cannot share what we do not possess. Without the sense of God indwelling, the Father worketh not in and through us. In respect to the door which leads to divine power, we need to remember that the handle is on the inside. To open it is to discover the Way which leads to inner peace—and world peace with justice.

ETERNAL GOD, grant us the adequate, inner resource; and reveal to us the conditions for laying hold upon it as made manifest by Thy Son Jesus Christ. We pray for freedom from spiritual blindness, indifference, and error. In the name of Him whose name is above all names. *Amen.*

J. W. FIFIELD JR.
First Congregational Church, Los Angeles, Calif.

AS FOR ME

But as for me and my house, we will serve the Lord.—Josh. 24:15

That "as for me" brings us up standing! Nothing is more needed in our makeup than the ability to say it.

It was comparatively easy for one of the crowd to join in the general response after Joshua had taken his stand. It was not so easy for Joshua to take his stand regardless of what anyone else would do. That took courage. That took the stuff that leaders are made of. No wonder the crowd followed Joshua! They would follow him today.

In all important issues the crowd is divided. For the crowd is only a cross section of humanity. The hero is there, and the coward; the wise person, and the fool; the evil-hearted, and the good; the weak, and the strong. And the undecided are there—a host of them—waiting for confident leadership, for the one who can say, "As for me!"

If you have a conviction, and a word to say, stand up and say it. The world needs those who "dare to stand alone."

This story of Joshua suggests the most important and most far-reaching decision we are ever called upon to make: whether to serve God—or not. With Joshua it was a choice between the living God and dead idols. With us it is a choice between the living God and our own selfish desires.

Stand up and be counted!

O LORD, whatever others may do, help me to choose and to serve Thee, in sincerity and in truth. Give me the courage to do the right even though all around me are doing wrong. Keep me humble, but keep me true. Help me so to speak and so to act that others may also be led to follow Thee. In Jesus' name. *Amen.*

ASA J. FERRY
First Presbyterian Church, Wichita, Kan.

NOT ALONE

And yet I am not alone, because the Father is with me.—John 16:32

Never alone! The walls of circumstance can shut us out from many things, but it is well to remember that they only shut us in with God: Divine Love pursues us to the far reaches of the earth and ceases never to care for us. There is no separation from this love, except the closed door of our inner sanctuary. In the darkest hour, Heaven gives Light; in the perilous hour there is Strength; in the loneliest hour there is Presence. Nothing can "separate us from the love of God, which is in Christ Jesus our Lord," since Christ is God's and we are Christ's.

But this is the deep experience of individuals. It is not something to be taken for granted. Rather it is something to be expected and experienced as the deep within us responds to the Deep without, and the Deep without becomes the Deep within. This abides! This is Eternity at our hearts.

Of late the thought keeps coming into our mind that God is the God of individuals. He will save the individual out of the clutches of any mass situation; He will hear us above the noise of strife; He will single us out, as He does all people everywhere, and be our Companion, and then draw us back together in His love.

It is this faith that sustains us at home and you who are in service. For this reason we can pray and you can pray, knowing that He breaks through the limitations to bless the seeker.

DEAR FATHER, Thou Companion of our souls, we welcome Thy abiding Presence in this quiet moment. Fill all our moments with Thy love. Help us as we go forth this day to remember the love of family and friends that reaches across the distance. In the name of Christ. *Amen.*

CHARLES F. THOMAS
First Friends Meeting, Des Moines, Iowa

THE CHALLENGE OF PATRIOTISM

If I forget thee, O Jerusalem, let my right hand forget her cunning.
—Ps. 137:5

The Fourth of July is no time for a shallow celebration. Patriotism is too sacred for that. The man who said, "If I forget thee, O Jerusalem, let my right hand forget her cunning," was far from home and in a strange land. The uppermost thought in his mind was his own country, his city, his home. He had been asked to sing a song of his native land while in captivity, and he had refused on the grounds that it might appear that he was forgetting his own dear city. This man of Bible times was willing to consecrate his all—whatever it might be—for love of his country.

We remember this day the values that are included in true patriotism—all those things which have made our country the greatest on earth, those things for which we should be willing to die. There is something almost divine in true love for one's country. Religion and patriotism are woven together. Love to God means love for those high things which He has created. Those words were spoken together with a prayer. Let us pray.

O ETERNAL GOD, in Thee do we trust. May we keep sacred the heritage from our fathers and mothers. Bless, we pray Thee, those who keep the home fires burning, and those who defend our land.

> God bless our native land!
> Firm may she ever stand,
> Through storm and night:
> When the wild tempests rave,
> Ruler of wind and wave,
> Do Thou our country save
> By Thy great might! *Amen.*

E. P. ANDERSON
Calvary Methodist Church, Nashville, Tenn.

BEAT YOUR BEST

We beseech you, brethren, . . . that as ye have received of us how ye ought to walk and to please God, so ye would abound more and more.—1 Thess. 4:1

At the Northfield Student Conference, the West Point delegation was holding a little group meeting in a dimly lighted tent. "What is Christianity?" was one of the perplexing questions that was asked. There was a moment's silence; then from a dark corner came an inspired answer, "Christianity? Why, Christianity is Oscar Westover." How one would like to have known him—a West Point cadet whose life had so commended his religion to his mates that in his absence he should be offered by one of them and accepted by the rest as a working definition of the living embodiment of the Christian religion.

It is not for me to tell you what your spiritual dare should be. You know your own life. There is just one big thing I dare you to do: beat your best. Spiritual investments are repaid a thousandfold. Don't worry about your few little loaves. Invest what you have. The returns will be far more than you realize. Catch some great challenge of service. We do great deeds under a "Magnificent Obsession."

Don't be discouraged if you fail in your first efforts. Coach Meehan of New York University says, "We learn practically nothing from a victory. All our information comes from a defeat. A winner forgets most of his mistakes."

DEAR GOD, our Father, Thou knowest that I am but one. Thou knowest that my little share in a world struggle can count for but little. Thou knowest that I am not strong. Help me yet to remember that I am one. Let me never forget that what I do counts. So help me to live always at my best, and teach me to go beyond my best for my country and for Thee. *Amen.*

WILLIAM H. DANFORTH
Chairman of the Board, Ralston Purina Co., St. Louis, Mo.

EYES TO SEE

Having eyes, see ye not? and having ears, hear ye not? and do ye not remember?—Mark 8:18

If you have eyes to see, you will find the great truths hidden in the common things of life. They do not lie on the surface—God has hidden them as He hid the gold and the jewels. Only those who dig shall find them; for there is healing and blessing in the digging and in the finding.

When you rise early and see the dawn break after the night, God is saying, "I will always bring light out of darkness. In the creation of the World, out of the black void I brought light; and the glory of earth came out of darkness and my love for you." No matter how dark the night is now, joy cometh in the morning. A new day for you, new friends, new adventures and joy. The day will dawn; the lark will sing; and God will bring you new joy. Have faith in God!

If under the winter snow you see the flowers growing, you know that spring is coming. You will live in the fragrance of the flowers that will bloom tomorrow. "Memory was given that we might have roses in December." Remember the happy times God gave you. He is preparing happier times for you tomorrow. Have faith in God!

After the storm comes the rainbow. It is the bow of the promise of God. God put it there Himself and said, "It is my promise to you." A storm may drive you from your native shores and away from home and friends; but if you have eyes to see, you will discover the rainbow, and joy will come after the storm. Have faith in God!

FATHER, I thank Thee that when my spirits droop and my heart is fearful, Thou dost always drape Thy rainbow around the threatening clouds. Forgive my sins, and grant to me that conquering faith without which no one can win in life. *Amen.*

R. Wilbur Babcock
Temple Baptist Church, Minneapolis, Minn.

THE MYSTERY OF THE ATONEMENT

My God, my God, why hast thou forsaken me?—Mark 15:34

In this day when the right seems pressed back along so many lines of conquest, we are face to face with the noninterference of God—the perplexing problem of theism! The fact that a loving God will stand back in the shadows when He might help and deliver! The feeling that there are hours in our lives when God will not stand between our souls and pain, sorrow, catastrophe!

We know the answer although we cannot fully comprehend it. This separation, this noninterference of God at Calvary, is a part of the mystery of the Atonement. The bearing of our transgressions made this separation of His soul from God necessary. That was death. For the first time in all history Christ was alone! That spiritual death, separation from God, brought about Christ's physical death—He died of a broken heart.

Because this happened, no believing soul in this universe need ever feel alone. He was separated that we might forever walk with God; He was forsaken that we might know God's fellowship; God left Christ for an hour that He might stay with us forever! May there never be an hour in our lives when any doubt can cry to us in the shadows, "Where is thy God?"

FATHER IN HEAVEN, knowing the Cross as we do, make us sure that nothing can separate us from Thee. Teach us that Thou art in the shadows as well as in the sunlight, that there is a prize in pain. May we allow Thee with perfect trust, as the Maestro of life's symphony, to play upon the lower strings of sorrow and trial, and, as the Great Artist, to splash some shadows upon the canvas of our lives, that Thou mayest increase the beauty withal. Help us to trust Thee, Thou great Artist of our souls. Through Jesus Christ, our Lord. *Amen.*

LOUIS H. EVANS
Hollywood First Presbyterian Church, Hollywood, Calif.

LOOK BEYOND THE HILLS

I will lift up mine eyes unto the hills, from whence cometh my help. My help cometh from the Lord.—Ps. 121:1–2

The writer of the Hundred and Twenty-first Psalm was in exile far from home. Though he was living in Babylon, the most gorgeous city of antiquity, the hills of home were calling to him. Those hills were deep dyed with memory, and it wasn't only the memory of home, but the memory of God and all that made His people great. And so, from exile, he wrote: "I will lift up mine eyes unto the hills, from whence cometh my help." And then as he thought of those hills, he looked beyond them and remembered that his help came from God.

The God who made the hills is greater than the hills He made. The author of Isaiah says: "O Zion, that bringest good tidings, get thee up into the high mountain." From that high point the messenger could see how the battle went and bring tidings to those who awaited them.

A traveler once made arrangements with a guide to take him to the top of a high mountain to see the sunrise. They had not climbed long when there arose a terrible thunderstorm. "It's no use to go on," the gentleman said. "We cannot see the sunrise in the midst of this fearful storm." "Oh, sir," said the guide, "we will soon get above the storm." They kept climbing, and soon they could see the lightnings playing about the mountains and beneath it was very dark, but when they passed up above the clouds all was light.

We must look beyond even the hills of strength. We must remember that our help comes from God, who is above the hills. If we climb high enough and get close enough to Him, we shall be able to bring tidings of peace.

GOD OF THE ETERNAL HILLS, in Thee do I put my trust this day. Keep me from harm and sin. Help me to serve my God and my country faithfully, that I may be a messenger of peace. *Amen.*

ARTHUR W. RATZ
Fort Street Presbyterian Church, Detroit, Mich.

FAITH

Be strong and of a good courage; for the Lord thy God is with thee whithersoever thou goest.—Josh. 1:9

These words were spoken by God to the young man who was being commissioned as the leader of God's people. They indicate that strength and courage depend on the faith that the moral law of the universe is the moral will of the Living God. The God and Father of our Lord Jesus Christ is the Creator and Redeemer of the world. When we work with Him we are committed to a cause that is greater than any person or nation, and that cause cannot fail. People grow old and die, nations perish, and civilizations decay. But God is Alpha and Omega, the first and the last, the one who was, and is, and will be forever the Eternal and living God. His purposes are the framework of the universe, and they cannot perish. To understand what God is doing in the world, to love what He loves, to want what He wants for ourselves and for all people, and to work with Him in the great task of overcoming evil and putting good in its place—to do these things is to find everlasting salvation and the way of eternal life. Faith in God makes it possible for us to go all out in service of the good and to know that only in so doing can we really live.

O THOU ETERNAL AND LIVING GOD, upon whose holy will rests the moral law of the universe; gradually Thou hast spoken to us through teachers and prophets and saints in all ages and among all peoples, and at last Thou hast revealed Thy character and love fully in the person of Thy Son, our Lord and Savior, Jesus Christ, the center of history and the light of the world. Refresh us now with the benediction of Thy Holy Spirit, and fill us with faith in Thy creative and redeeming love for all humanity. This we ask in the name of Jesus Christ. *Amen.*

JOHN K. BENTON
Dean, School of Religion, Vanderbilt University, Nashville, Tenn.

FAITH THAT SURPRISES

*Stand fast therefore in the liberty wherewith Christ hath made us free,
and be not entangled again with the yoke of bondage.*—Gal. 5:1

Some people plod along and we always know what to expect of them.
They never rise above or sink below that same dependable way of
living. These are very useful people, and the world needs them badly. But
many of us are different. We never have much influence, or many important decisions to make; so we never show the stuff we are made of. Then,
all of a sudden, we face a tremendous problem. Some people find, at such
a time, a "faith that surprises." It surprises in one of two ways. Sometimes
we are surprised because people did less than we had expected. Even more
often we are surprised because their inner faith and courage produced
greater results at the decisive moment than we had dreamed possible.

When Jesus taught, the Pharisees, religious leaders of His day, listened
to Him, but they didn't catch His spirit as the simple fishermen did. Their
faith surprises us, because it was less than we should have expected. When
present-day leaders face Christ's teaching of freedom, some interpret it as
freedom to devour and crush other people and nations for their own
purposes. Others of us think He meant freedom for all people to do what
they ought to do, not freedom for one to enslave another. Such people,
with such a faith, will surprise even tyrants with their answer to the
problem of freedom for all humanity.

O LORD, may the knowledge of Thee which I gained long since become
an active faith now, such as will keep me true, throughout all the unknown
days that lie ahead. *Amen.*

HOWARD ELMO SHORT
First Christian Church, Cuyahoga Falls, Ohio

THE MINISTRY OF A CHRISTIAN

Thanks be unto God, which always causeth us to triumph in Christ, and maketh manifest the savour of his knowledge by us in every place.—2 Cor. 2:14

In the reading suggested above, Paul says in substance that when we become Christians we deliver a sixfold ministry.

First, we are dynamic. We release a power for righteousness and lead other people into the same sort of living. We find truth. We commend our way of living to people and to God.

Second, we live dangerously. We are not afraid to live expansively. We are unafraid of any sort of opposition as we proceed with our tasks.

Third, we live optimistically. We are convinced that the Christian way of living is the highest and best way of living. Into this way of living, by our lives, we invite our brothers and sisters.

Fourth, we have definite goals toward which we direct our energies. We are convinced that the great purpose of living is to build humankind into one great family with God as Father.

Fifth, we know and we demonstrate that this kind of life can be lived because Paul, St. Francis, and thousands of other people have lived it. We, too, can and do measurably live it.

Sixth, we demonstrate that this way of living is satisfying and glorious. We belong to the group of people who in every generation give praise to the Lord with our thoughts, words, and deeds.

OUR FATHER IN HEAVEN, we ask Thee to enable us to live creatively and redemptively. We ask Thee to help us to show by word and deed that the ministry of a Christian is always and in every place and circumstance a thing of power. Keep us, we pray Thee, true to our Savior in every life situation. This we ask for Christ's sake. *Amen.*

THOMAS W. CURRIE
President, Austin Presbyterian Theological Seminary, Austin, Tex.

OVERCOMING TEMPTATION

Blessed is the man that endureth temptation; for when he hath been approved, he shall receive the crown of life, which the Lord promised to them that love him.—Jas. 1:12 ARV

A temptation is a desire to do what we know we ought not to do. We pray, "Lead us not into temptation." God doesn't lead us into temptation, but He does permit us to be tempted. For temptations are useful in aiding us to become strong in life and character—provided we overcome those temptations.

The question arises, "How shall we overcome our temptations?" First, we should train our moral powers upon the enemy. There are doubtless many reasons for the fall of Singapore. We do know one reason. The big eighteen-inch guns of Singapore were not trained upon the jungles of Malaya. They were trained upon the sea. The enemy did not approach by way of the sea but by way of the jungle. We have moral powers which can overcome any evil habit. Let us use those moral powers upon the enemies of our souls.

Second, we should develop the habit of faith. Faith is the mainspring of all activity. If we didn't have faith in our abilities we would never attempt to do anything. Jesus taught His disciples to have faith in God. You and I must have faith in God and in ourselves if we would overcome our evil desires.

Third, we must profit by the experiences of others. The fact that others have overcome their temptations should serve as an inspiration to us in being absolute masters of our own will to do good—to overcome evil with good.

OUR FATHER, we are thankful that Thou hast given us a place in Thy Kingdom. May we labor in Thy service, being led by the Spirit of God, that we shall be more than conquerors in the struggles of life. Through His name. *Amen.*

R. B. Hawkins
First Methodist Church, Tallapoosa, Ga.

WORSHIP IS MY OPPORTUNITY

I was glad when they said unto me, Let us go into the house of the Lord.—Ps. 122:1

Benjamin Franklin said: "If the world is so bad with religion, what would it be without it?" Abraham Lincoln said: "Take all of the Bible that you can on reason and the rest by faith and you will live and die a better man." Theodore Roosevelt said: "I need my church to feed my soul and refresh my spirit. I go once a week for my own sake and for the influence of my example." He was a soldier and found that soldiers live better and fight better if they take hold of God and let God take hold of them.

Most of our great Americans have been churchgoing people and not ashamed of it. If I were a soldier I would regard the opening door of a neighboring church, or the post chapel, or the place where the chaplain had set up the altar in the field, as an invitation from my Maker to go in and meet Him there. Don't give up church attendance because you are away from home and home customs. Your mother and father are praying for you; and your friends are praying for you, more than you think. They want you to come out of this clean and with your faith unshaken. Church worship will help you, as will nothing else.

Remember, the war will end, but your life will not end with the war. Your country will expect you to come home and take your place as a citizen with clean morals, broad religious faith, and honest-to-goodness patriotism. You need the church, and the church needs you! You both "make good" together, and your country will lose or gain by the kind of a person that you are.

HEAVENLY FATHER, help me to believe that I cannot live by bread alone or by the things outside of me only. I have a mind and soul to keep. Help me to enrich my inward self by going where that inner self is fed— the church of Jesus Christ. *Amen.*

HENRY R. ROSE
Church of the Divine Paternity, New York, N.Y.

WHAT DO THEY GET YOU?

Fight the good fight of faith.—1 Tim. 6:12

We are talking all the time about good Christian values including faith, hope, and love. What, really, in this hard-bitten world do they get us? In what coin do they pay off? Do courage and good faith make a contribution to any cause?

The answer is that no cause can succeed without them. The answer is that there is no satisfaction afterward without them. Before, during, and afterward, these are the essentials. They nerve the arm for the undertaking; they strengthen the will during the fray; they give satisfaction at the conclusion of the battle.

We must believe in our way of life; we must have the courage to stand for it; the afterglow will recompense us.

What memories belong to those who have fought the good fight! We take these shining experiences and play them like records, and their music is glorious!

ALMIGHTY GOD, grant to us confidence in the power of spiritual values. Help us to feel at all times that Thy mercies endure forever and that Thou art forever turned towards us in love. May we accept not only Thee but Thy way of life. May we gird ourselves, arm, mind and spirit, for the conflict by putting on the whole armor of God. Through Jesus Christ our Lord. *Amen.*

FLOYD A. POE
City Temple, Baptist, Dallas, Tex.

CREATIVE LIVING

Thou upholdest me in mine integrity.—Ps. 41:12

Creative courage and creative endurance lead us into creative fellowship and service. It is a wonderful thing to know that you are brave and strong, with a mind and body unfettered by harboring wrong. In a world filled with wrongs, hatreds, and injustices that would smash our world, it takes a lot of courage to be really Christian and help build a better world.

In emergencies every part of us needs to be genuine, for hypocritical parts will not stand the test. When we have God's presence we forget petty personal troubles and worries, for with Christians there is that companionship of Someone bigger and stronger than we ourselves will ever be. Christians gather strength and keep the faith. By so doing they continue to gain confidence because God upholds them in this assurance.

> Help the weak if you are strong;
> Love the old if you are young.

God's plans are not provisional—they are fully guaranteed forever. What a thought! We can be active, selfless coworkers with God! "In all thy ways acknowledge him, and he will direct thy paths."

DEAR HEAVENLY FATHER, teach us when we are in doubt to go into silence and think Thy thoughts along with Thee in prayer, so that we may find the solution to all our problems. *Amen.*

WILLIAM J. SAYERS
Friends Memorial Church, Muncie, Ind.

MAKING THE PERSON

Ye are the salt of the earth: but if the salt have lost his savour, wherewith shall it be salted?—Matt 5:13

Bad people in airplanes, or good people on mules—which is more important? Which is more needed? For years we've been working on airplanes and paying very little attention to people. We made a mistake. We would have been wiser to have worked with people and to have neglected the planes. Then we'd have had good people on mules instead of bad people in planes. Wouldn't that have been better?

A New Englander named Thoreau warned us that we were heading for hell because we were "making improved means for unimproved ends." We were making the tools with which to do whatever we wanted to, without realizing that the tools would be every bit as effective for evil as for good. The same chemistry, the same machinery, the same cleverness and equipment, can help achieve either heaven or hell. The other day a soldier, badly wounded, remarked, "We'd be better off if we'd learned less about chemistry and more about Christ." That impresses me as intelligent and sound.

Better to have good people on mules than bad people in planes! Think it over. We used to talk about it when I was flying for the Navy in 1918 and 1919. But we didn't realize how important it was. If we had, you wouldn't be where you are now. If you will realize how important it is and govern yourselves accordingly, during and after the war, there needn't be another war in the next generation. God be with you!

OUR FATHER GOD, as we wait on Thee in prayer, deliver us from the evil of wanting to enlist Thy help in carrying out our own desires. Help us sincerely and earnestly to want to understand and do Thy will. We ask it in the name of Christ. *Amen.*

EMORY W. LUCCOCK
First Presbyterian Church, Evanston, Ill.

DEGREES OF DEDICATION

I indeed baptize you with water unto repentance: but he that cometh after me is mightier than I, . . . he shall baptize you with the Holy Spirit, and with fire.—Matt. 3:11

Jesus not only demonstrated the degrees of dedication set forth in the foregoing text, but attained with power and goodwill the highest degree of all. In this present world conflict, it will be necessary for us to attain that degree if we are to win the peace as well as the war.

John's baptism by water was a preparation for God's call to service. It was a dedication of the individual to the will and purpose of God, cost what it may and lead where it would.

The baptism by fire is the test of service. Jesus met this test in the fires of persecution, sacrifice, and death on the cross. He proved that He could take it, as many individuals and nations are doing today. And, as we pass through the fires, it is a help to know that He also endured and is with us.

Many go this far and no further. But Jesus went to the third degree of dedication; He received the baptism of the Holy Spirit. In spite of the worst the world could do to Him, He maintained the spirit of forgiveness and intelligent goodwill toward friend and foe alike. Even in His death He said, "Father, forgive them; for they know not what they do."

Only those who attain this degree of dedication go far enough to share in Christ's redemptive powers for humankind. That He expected us to do so is indicated by the question He put to His disciples just before leaving them: "Are ye able to drink of the cup that I shall drink of?" Their reply was, "We are able."

ALMIGHTY GOD, enable us to establish right relationship with Thee and others in order that we may have the assurance of Thy guidance and that through us Thy Spirit may enter victoriously into our world. *Amen.*

SAMUEL N. OLIVER
First Congregational Church, Muskegon, Mich.

CARRY YOUR MOTHER IN YOUR HEART

Who can find a virtuous woman? for her price is far above rubies.
—Prov. 31:10

It's because of my damned mother. I can't have any fun." The speaker was a soldier on furlough. The audience was Chaplain Jesse Halsey. The two weeks' furlough was about ended. Soon the veteran would be back in the front lines. He had set out at night to find whiskey and a woman. But memories of his mother kept him from whiskey and harlots. Though he used a soldier's strong language to describe her, he was actually proud of her and could not let her down. Knowing his mother was noble, he was held back from treating other women ignobly.

Isn't that the kind of control that strong people want—inner power for self-control? There's no doubt about one thing. Every normal person has to fight temptation. But there is a way to win. It is fairly easy to think straight and to do right when in church or at home. But service men and women can't duck into a church or run home every time temptation assails them. We must learn how to carry our church and home inside our hearts. Our defenses have to be within our own lives. The silliness of trusting outer strongholds alone is shown by the tragedies of Singapore and Maginot Line. Their big guns were pointing the wrong way when the crisis struck. And they had depended upon strong outer fortifications to save them. John said, "Greater is he that is in you, than he that is in the world." Let the Spirit that raised up Jesus from the dead dwell in you!

HEAVENLY FATHER, Thou art my refuge and strength. I know I am not able to beat down temptation if I have to do it alone. I want the irresistible Spirit that raised Jesus from the dead to dwell in my heart. Come in, Spirit of God, to my heart and take control. Grant me spiritual power, for Jesus' sake. *Amen.*

FLOYD ALLAN BASH
Central Christian Church, San Antonio, Tex.

GIFTS OF THE MASTER

Peace, be still . . . And there was a great calm.—Mark 4:39

The narrative of the stilling of the storm is an effective description of one of the valuable gifts of Jesus to a world that has steadfastly turned to Him for help. When He was awakened by the frightened disciples, He was not so much concerned with the treacherous waves He saw as He was with the storm of fear which had taken possession of His formerly calm companions. He stilled the storm of fear in the hearts of the disciples. He gave them a sense of security in the midst of great danger. He bestowed upon them a feeling of certainty together with a recognition of the adventure in which they were sharing.

Another gift of Jesus is that of inner rest. True followers normally do not sit comfortably in the shade all the time meditating upon the eternal verities. Normally, they are active people, conscious of the tremendous load of responsibility which is theirs. There is something about Christian discipleship that pulls one into unresting activity. Yet with all this unresting activity, the disciple of the Master has the gift of inner rest.

In these days of great crisis and in times of chaos in individual lives, it is necessary, if the boat in which we ride is not to be swamped, that we receive from Jesus these two gifts.

ALMIGHTY GOD, Father of the Prince of Peace, we beseech Thee that Thou wilt give us peace this day. Be pleased to erase from every heart all hate and vindictiveness, and fill us with the spirit of understanding. May all the powers of evil be put down, and the legions of righteousness come to reign in all lands. Grant that we may company with Thee this day, that we may be strong in the security that comes to those who seek Thee out. We pray for Christ's sake. *Amen.*

FRED HOSKINS
The United Church, Bridgeport, Conn.

RULERS AND THE RULER

The government shall be upon his shoulder. . . . Of the increase of his government and peace there shall be no end.—Isa. 9:6, 7

We are thinking in terms of government today as never before in our lives. We are appreciating government as never before. We see the necessity for it, because its structure is threatened and must be defended with every ounce of our energy and every penny of our income. We will do this because, as we see it, our ideals are the highest and our motives the purest of all the peoples of earth.

So many changes have come so quickly that we are dazed by them. But in our amazement and excitement our hearts are comforted by God's promise of an ultimate worthwhile government which will never fail and will be for all the peoples of earth. Greater than our government—much as we believe in it—is the government of our Lord Jesus Christ. We have a Ruler who conquered death in His resurrection and ascension. And before He left this earth He promised to return and set up a kingdom—beneficent, stable, permanent, prosperous, and peaceful. This shall come to pass: God has decreed it; the battered world needs it; and all creation anticipates it.

If we can remember that sunshine comes after shadows, light after darkness, and the day after the night, we shall carry on until the task is finished.

OUR HEAVENLY FATHER, we are grateful that Thou hast inspired the hope within us that makes it possible for us to look beyond the crumbling of the present to the permanence of the future. We are grateful for our spiritual Commander-in-Chief, Jesus Christ, and by Thy help we will follow Him until the kingdoms of this world become the Kingdom of our Lord Jesus Christ. *Amen.*

L. G. Gates
First Baptist Church, Laurel, Miss.

A RELIGION FOR A REAL MAN

Play the man.—1 Cor. 16:13 (MOFFATT)

"Play the man." The writer paid a heavy price for his faith. He was bitterly hated, persecuted, driven from place to place. Never was there a more daring pioneer. He launched three great missionary journeys, covering large portions of what are now known as the Near East and Europe. He was brought before magistrates, cruelly scourged, imprisoned, tortured, shipwrecked three times, stoned by the mob, finally condemned and beheaded by order of the Roman Emperor. Barring Jesus of Nazareth, he was the greatest man of the first century. His name was Paul.

"God doesn't want jellyfish; He wants men!" said a rugged, old Christian sea captain, in the midst of a terrible tempest, to his first mate who was showing signs of cowardice and disloyalty.

It is written of Christ that when the crisis hour of His life came, "He steadfastly set his face to go to Jerusalem." He refused to quit or to retreat.

Just before Paul said, "Play the man!" he said, "Stand firm in the faith!" Real faith in God makes real men. To believe something wholeheartedly is to achieve something worthwhile. God give us clean, strong, dependable men in this tremendous day.

MY FATHER GOD, present out yonder in the spaces that no one can measure, and here with me in this place, I offer Thee the adoration and love of my heart. Forgive me, cleanse me, empower me. Help me to be loyal, faithful, efficient today; and when the night comes may I not be afraid to look the Master in the face. Hear my prayer for victories of justice and righteousness, and for peace that shall endure, Christ's peace for people and nations. In His name I pray. *Amen.*

W. E. McCULLOCH
Superintendent of Missions, United Presbyterian Synod of Calif.

BE TRUE

But Daniel purposed in his heart that he would not defile himself.
—Dan. 1:8

The other evening I sat with a young couple, married for eighteen months, who were facing a major life change. They had built themselves a new home. They had dreams of a family, of friends, of a place of service in church and community. Now it was all changed. The husband had been called by his draft board to report for his physical examination. He knew he would have to leave. As we faced the breaking up of their home, the delay of their plans, and the possible loss of their property, the young man said, "What I want to know is this: What will we be like when we come out of this war; will our morals and our dreams and our hopes have been shattered?"

No one can answer that question for him now. It will have to be answered differently for different people. The answer depends upon whether he and the others of you are true to the best you know. Some young people will doubtless come out of this war with shattered dreams, impoverished morals, and a lost faith. Others will reinforce themselves daily from the great Source of high living. The memory of loved ones, their treasure house of Scripture, and their own religious faith will keep them on the high road. They will be able to say, "I have fought a good fight, I have finished my course, I have kept the faith." That is the prayer of all your Christian friends back home for you.

> I would be true, for there are those who trust me;
> I would be pure, for there are those who care;
> I would be strong, for there is much to suffer;
> I would be brave, for there is much to dare. *Amen.*
> —HOWARD ARNOLD WALTER

CECIL E. HAWORTH
Central Friends Church, High Point, N.C.

TAKE HEED

Take heed unto thyself, and unto the doctrine.—1 Tim. 4:16

Paul wrote to Timothy to "take heed unto thyself, and unto the doctrine." Timothy was a preacher, and it was essential that he preach the pure gospel. Doctrine is important, for doctrine is teaching. In other words, Paul meant this: "Take heed unto thyself, and unto the gospel which you preach." In this brief narrative, let us look at the first part of Paul's admonition, "Take heed unto thyself." This does not mean that one is to omit the doctrine, but the doctrine and one's character form the chief concern of Paul in this case. "Take heed unto thyself," as to what you think. "As he thinketh in his heart, so is he." One's thinking has much to do with the appearance of his or her countenance, and we're told it helps to shape one's head.

Take heed unto thy speech. It still remains true that "thy speech betrayeth thee." Impressions are made by one's words and deeds.

Take heed unto thy conduct, remembering that people look on the outer appearance, but God looks on the heart.

Take heed unto thy prayer life. "More things are wrought by prayer than this world dreams of." "Prayer changes things." "Pray without ceasing." "The effectual fervent prayer of a righteous man availeth much."

O GOD OUR FATHER, hear our petition. We are dependent upon Thee. Thy gifts come as gently as the dew from heaven. We would be more like our Elder Brother, Thine only-begotten Son. Show us the way through Thy Word. Help all our infirmities. In Christ's name. *Amen.*

P. H. Welshimer
First Christian Church, Canton, Ohio

I AM THINKING

I will be with thee: I will not fail thee, nor forsake thee. Be strong and of a good courage.—Josh. 1:5, 6a

I am thinking of the need of my soul for Light, and Faith, and Strength, and Thee, O Lord. If I could find Thy dwelling place, could come unto Thy seat of power, I should be safer than alone—both safe and sure. But it is not safety that I seek, Lord. I want Thy strength and courage and graciousness, Lord Jesus. I want Thy peace in my soul, that I may praise Thee first, and then be a source of strength to others, a friend in need on land, in the air, or on the sea; in life, Lord, or in death, never failing a pal, or a stranger—following Thee."

After this fashion I prayed; and there came the memory of a sweet companionship felt one morning, the fellowship of One who does not criticize, but consoles instead. Consoles and gives one heart. One who loves me and mine better than I know to love another, and besides can do for all whom I love what my heart craves to do for them, and they for me. One who is too close to overlook us. Too strong to lose us. Too loving to think of Himself before us when danger strikes. Too altogether wonderful to disappoint us if we should see Him suddenly, face to face; or, as Stephen saw Him, waiting beside the throne for His first Christian soldier to follow Him all the way to the throne.

Our Father,
Thy Love and Strength and Mercy give,
To souls for whom Thy servants pray:
Grant unto all who seek to live
According to Thy Word and Way
The splendor of Thy presence, Lord,
Thy wonder of Companionship. *Amen.*

ARTHUR DRIVER GEE
Baptist Church, Chestnut Hill, Pa.

ACHIEVING PERSONAL ADEQUACY

In Him who strengthens me, I am able for anything.
—Phil. 4:13 (MOFFATT)

Ο̲ne day some years ago I watched the sandy-haired son of one of my seminary professors wrestling with a larger boy. The struggle went on with some anger until the little fellow was on his back, his opponent perched triumphantly on top. A few moments later, as the irritated small boy started for home he remarked, "I'm going home to eat something that will make me strong."

There is a certain wisdom here, a resolution to do something about apparent weakness, a determination to seek new sources of strength which is suggestive for all of us. There are hours when we are thrown by our fears, knocked off our feet by grim despair, and pinned down by our disillusionment. It may be, however, that such hours turn out to be the beginning of our salvation if they send us in search of the spiritual resources that can make us strong.

As Carl Sandburg suggests, when we reach out for "lights beyond the prison of the five senses, for keepsakes lasting beyond hunger and death," we add something to our personal adequacy and discover, as St. Paul did, that "in Him who strengthens me, I am able for anything." That discovery is life's ultimate wisdom, the source of unfailing strength and courage.

GRACIOUS GOD OUR FATHER, Thou hast been our strength through the days of our years, our fortress through periods of peril. Make us able now with courage, faith, and immortal hope. Sustain us in darkness and lead us into light. Through days of confusion, be Thou as a mighty rock within a weary land, and guide us in the end to Thy Kingdom, through Jesus Christ our Lord. *Amen.*

HAROLD BLAKE WALKER
First Presbyterian Church, Utica, N.Y.

IMMORTALITY

Though, after my skin, worms destroy this body, yet in my flesh shall I see God.—Job 19:26

If we grow skeptical about immortality, let us ponder the cheery certainty that life has both a changing and an unchanging side. The physical tenement which we inhabit is in a constant state of change. As our cells regenerate and replenish themselves, we acquire the equivalent of a brand-new body every seven years, and some parts of us are replaced more frequently than that. New blood is supplied each passing day, and "we get new skin oftener than we get new suits of clothes." Such are our changing bodies!

But there is an unchanging side to us, whose quality of continuity is apparent even now. Suppose that two decades ago you committed some sin. Physically you have had three selves since then and are not now the person who did the erstwhile deed. But conscience and society say that you are the identical person and accountable for it all. Such are our unchanging spirits! When finally these bodies are laid away they will continue to change as they always have done; but the spirit, which is unchanging here, will continue unchanging yonder.

O LORD, we rejoice in the personal perseverance of the soul beyond the grave. Help us not to use immortality as an escape from the present life or responsibility. May we rather employ it to put wider horizons around our earthly days. In the name of the Risen Lord Christ we pray. *Amen.*

E. MARCELLUS NESBITT
First United Presbyterian Church, Beaver, Pa.

ONE SOLITARY LIFE

In the world ye shall have tribulation: but be of good cheer: I have overcome the world.—John 16:33

I am sharing with you a contribution of another which has meant much to me. I do not know the author. To him I give full credit and my own personal appreciation also.

"Here is a Man who was born in an obscure village, the child of a peasant woman. He grew up in another obscure village. He worked in a carpenter shop until He was thirty, and then for three years He was an itinerant preacher. He never owned a home. He never had a family of his own. He never went to college. He never traveled two hundred miles from the place where He was born. He never did a single one of the things that usually accompany greatness. He had no credentials but Himself. He had nothing to do with this world except through the naked power of His divine manhood.

"While still a young man, the tide of public opinion turned against Him. His friends ran away. One of them betrayed Him. He was turned over to his enemies. He went through the mockery of a trial. He was nailed upon a cross between two thieves. His executioners gambled for the only piece of property He had on earth while He was dying, and that was His coat. When He was dead, He was taken down and laid in a borrowed tomb through the pity of a friend. . . .

"I am far within the mark when I say that all the armies that ever marched, and all the navies that were ever built, and all the parliaments that ever sat, and all the kings that ever reigned, put together, have not affected the life of man upon this earth as powerfully as has that One Solitary Life."

ETERNAL FATHER, Thou who dost hear and heed every sincere prayer, help me to have such confidence in Thy Son that I may follow in His way. *Amen.*

THOMAS A. WILLIAMS
First Methodist Church, Wichita, Kan.

THE BEST THINGS

*Remember now thy Creator in the days of thy youth, while the evil
days come not, nor the years draw nigh, when thou shalt say, I have no
pleasure in them.*—Eccles. 12:1

It always pays to give up the *good* things for the *best*. My mother was
right—she knew what she was doing—when she inscribed the verse
quoted above on the flyleaf of my first Bible. We work, strive, reason, strain
every human faculty. We pull and tug with might and main—to attain
happiness, contentment, peace, joy, and satisfaction. We die hard, but in the
end we are forced so many times to the conclusion that all is vanity and
vexation of spirit. That is the message of Ecclesiastes. Pleasure does not
satisfy. And we cannot attain in our own strength to a high degree of righteousness and goodness. So, pray God, may very many of us do a very
sensible thing. Let's let go, and let God. Why try to be the captain, first
mate, crew, and all on this journey through time and into eternity?

To sum it all up, God must be remembered! Preferably, and best of all,
before weakness and old age overtakes us. When whatever we have of
goodness is set aside in favor of the best—His best—we find ourselves
possessed of a wonderful supply of "inside information," God-given
through the medium of His Word, the Bible. With Jesus Christ as our
personal Savior, knowing where we came from, where we are, and where
we are going, with the knowledge that our sins have been forgiven, we
travel along through life with a spring in our step and unbounded joy in
our heart. We travel through trust in Him.

OUR FATHER, we thank Thee from the bottom of our hearts for that
day when, by Thy matchless grace, we stopped "trying" and started
"trusting." Help us to be workers of whom Thou wilt not have to be
ashamed. In Jesus' precious name. *Amen.*

ARNOLD GRUNIGEN JR.
Investment Banker, Vice-Chairman
Christian Business Men's International, San Francisco, Calif.

THE CROSS

The preaching of the cross is to them that perish foolishness; but unto us which are saved it is the power of God.—1 Cor. 1:18

The cross has for everyone three aspects. It is an object, a term, and an experience in the Christian life. In order to profit from our frequent reference to it we should strive to understand it better.

The cross was an experience in the life of Jesus. Down through the ages the story has been told of One who, bearing His own cross, marched out to Calvary's hill to be crucified. The act showed His willingness to go all the way through His love for others. There was genuine truth in the statement of His tormentors, "He saved others; himself he cannot save," for His heart of compassion led Him to die to save others, but His spirit of self-sacrifice prevented Him from saving Himself.

The cross represents a quality in the total life of Jesus. It cannot be considered alone as the few hours' experience at the close of His life. He deliberately chose the cross, the sacrificial way of life, at every turn in His career. The good was not good enough for Him. He chose only the best. The cross represents that spirit of self-denial and His acceptance of the difficult way throughout His life.

Again, the cross is the way of salvation. It is also the necessary way of life for us. "If any man will come after me, let him deny himself, . . . and follow me." This means that we must accept the way of hardship and sacrifice as good soldiers of Christ in helping Him to establish His Kingdom upon the earth.

OUR FATHER, help us to understand the suffering that Jesus endured upon the cross, the sacrificial way which He chose throughout His life, the power in the cross to save us; and help us to have the courage to make sacrifices for high ideals. *Amen.*

JOSEPH S. FAULCONER
First Christian Church, Ashland, Ky.

THE FINAL GOOD

We know that all things work together for good to them that love God,
to them who are the called according to his purpose.—Rom. 8:28

Paul once said, "And we know that all things work together for good to them that love God." During days of stress and trial many people become discouraged and feel that all is lost. It is then that it is well to bear in mind that God's people will never be forsaken. History has proved this time and time again. Every great gift has come through sacrifice. The children of Israel had their Sinai before they could see the Promised Land. David had to suffer trials of grief and a broken heart before he could sing. Christ went to Calvary with a cross to redeem a world. And the disciples had to endure suffering and even persecution, before the Church could grow.

Today we are again faced with formidable trials. Although we may not readily understand why this world chaos must be, we do know that the Church of Christ, built upon the foundation of sacrifice, will be the comfort of the world. In due time the words that Paul spoke so long ago will once more be fulfilled, and we shall truly know again that "all things work together for good to them that love God."

O LORD, who careth for and watcheth over Thy people, it is to Thee that we turn in the hours of trial and need as well as in the hours of joy and happiness, in order that we may at all times feel the closeness of Thy Spirit guiding us in the pathways of our destinies. Give us grace to love, eagerness to serve, and power to accomplish, so that we may be a part of Thy program to bring about ultimate peace and happiness for all humankind. Help us to have the vision to understand that through our Master "all things work together for good to them that love God." *Amen.*

CHARLES PAUL CARLSON
Captain, 22nd Infantry (Motorized), Camp Gordon, Ga.

ON BEING CONTENT IN A WORLD LIKE THIS

I have learned, in whatsoever state I am, therewith to be content.
—Phil. 4:11

Like it or not, we live in precisely this kind of world. We can—and must—of course, adjust ourselves to make it possible to live in this world. We can drift and be worldly, rebel and be bitter, jump out the window and quit, or adjust ourselves to our environment and be content.

A world like this is not designed for weaklings. Its inflexible natural laws and its maladjusted social order are severely testing our abilities to find the proper relationship to the sum total of things—a relationship designed for peace and contentment.

To be content to live in a world like this, we must build ourselves a world within a world, an inner temple of peace and harmony, a sanctuary where communion can be had with the Most High God and an understanding of the meaning of our relationship can be reached in the light of God's far-off design for a world out of joint.

This world-within-a-world is a haven for us in our despairing moments where we can retreat for renewed understanding and strength. Here we fall asleep at nightfall, and from thence we go out to meet the world in the morning. Within this sanctuary we live with what is easy to believe until we can easily accept what we have once doubted. Here we can find the lovely and the beautiful until we can see the loveliness of a crude world without. Here we can come to know the Father and, for knowing Him, can better appreciate His children.

O GOD, in the secret of Thy tabernacle within me do I worship Thee. Speak Thy will unto me that I may understand Thy way, and lead me out among Thy people in the spirit of joyful service. Give unto me, according to Thy promise, the peace of goodwill. Make me calm within. *Amen.*

S. O. KIMBROUGH
First Methodist Church, Anniston, Ala.

A GOD OF ALL COMFORT

Praise be to the God and Father of our Lord Jesus Christ, the Father of compassion and the God of all comfort.—2 Cor. 1:3

Paul was a powerful witness to God's comfort in the face of great stress and despair. The apostle wrote to the church at Corinth about his sufferings because he wanted them to understand that God's grace is all-sufficient and that through our human frailty we allow Him to demonstrate His power to care for even us in the midst of hardships (vs. 8–9).

It's not apparent what the particular struggles were that challenged Paul. Yet his situation was severe enough that he was ready to give up, his self-reliance completely gone. At this point God delivered him from the "deadly peril." Through this experience the apostle's faith was strengthened as he came to a greater understanding of God as both comforter and ultimate provider.

Paul's sole reliance was on the heavenly Father, "who comforts us in all our troubles" (v. 4). This comfort can't be found in the encouragement of a friend or in our own ability to solve problems. It is best described as an ever-present conviction that whatever the outcome of a situation, we are safely held in God's hand. Sharing this comfort with others not only gives hope, but also permits them to experience the power of faith.

GOD OF ALL COMFORT, Creator of all that is good, grant to me understanding for the precious suffering that befriends me and others in the world today. Help me to stand firm in my faith that others might see You in me. May the Holy Spirit that lives in me bathe me in Your perfect peace as I face this day. *Amen.*

J. GREG POPE
Executive Director, Saint Thomas Foundation, Nashville, Tenn.

THE MIRACLE OF FAITH

Love is patient, love is kind; love is not envious or boastful or arrogant or rude. . . . It bears all things, believes all things, hopes all things, endures all things. Love never ends.—1 Cor. 13:4–8

Help him! He's drowning!" I looked over to see my best friend Nick struggling in shallow water. I ran into the ocean and pulled him out with the help of a bystander. I was relieved when I saw his lungs fill with air. "He must have just hit his head," I thought.

As the emergency crew examined him, Nick was able to give his vital statistics, his name, and his address. But we all stood there speechless as the lifeguard asked him to move his toes . . . and he tried, but could not.

Nick was a star athlete, and the doctors were saying that the diving accident had left him a quadriplegic—he could not move at all below the shoulders. When I went to visit Nick that night in the hospital, I didn't know what to expect or what to say. But he was strong, and his faith was remarkable. He comforted me. He also moved his bicep that night, something his doctors never expected. He said it was faith.

Nick was in the hospital for six months, a metal halo in his skull. Everything had changed, without a moment's notice . . . everything but Nick's smile, and his love for God. Every day Nick inspired me with his perseverance and his trust in God's goodness. He was not irritable or resentful, but instead he was patient and kind. He continues to bear all things, believe all things, hope all things, and endure all things, ever trusting in Jesus Christ our Lord. Now, almost five years later, Nick is at USC pursuing a business degree and getting stronger each and every day.

O BLESSED GOD, let us all be instruments of Your peace and love. Let us seek truth in this world, and hope and trust in Your everlasting care. Please help us to be patient, kind, and forgiving, in the name of Jesus Christ, our Lord. *Amen.*

BROOKE E. NORTON
Student Body President 2001–02, University of Notre Dame, Ind.

WHEN IT IS HARD TO BELIEVE ANYMORE

*Then he said to Thomas, "Put your finger here and see my hands.
Reach out your hand and put it in my side. Do not doubt but believe."*
—John 20:27 NRSV

Most, if not all, of us doubt—some of us often and some seldom. What is there to be said about the phenomenon of doubt among those of us who try to be faithful?

First, doubt is forgiven before it happens. We do not have to be right to be Christian. God and God alone makes that judgment, and it has already been made in Jesus Christ. We are children of God. That is irrevocable. Doubt, even the dark night of the soul, is forgiven—not one time, not seven times, but seventy times seven, and it is forgiven before the doubt comes.

Second, and even more important, doubt is essential to dynamic faith. Israel understood that God is on the move, and the people of Israel symbolized the dynamism of their faith by the movement of the Ark of the Covenant to new places at new times. Faith is a journey of doubt and belief. We only arrive at certainty to move on to uncertainty and back again. And that movement itself is rooted in freedom, the freedom of God to be who God wills to be in any place at any time.

So the beauty of the story of doubting Thomas and his friends is this: those closest and most devoted to Jesus had doubts just as we do, but Jesus came again and again to them in forgiveness and grace. We can never doubt too often or too much. We can never persist in unbelief too long, for the love of God endures forever, and the spirit of Christ is always among us to surprise us and help us see through to the heart of the matter.

LOVING FATHER, I thank You for Your abundant grace that meets me in my times of doubt. I pray that You will send Your Holy Spirit to light my way in moments of unbelief, that I might dwell in Your kingdom of faith forever. In Jesus' name I pray. *Amen.*

JOSEPH HOUGH
President, Union Theological Seminary, New York City, N.Y.

THE ULTIMATE FAITH

If God be for us, who can be against us?—Rom. 8:31

In the darkest days of the Civil War, when, for a time, it appeared that the cause of the Union might be lost, a speaker was addressing an assemblage. As he spoke of the foreboding days that lay ahead, his words cast a deepening gloom over the audience. Suddenly, from among a crowd in the rear of the group, a little old wrinkled lady named Sojourner Truth arose, and in her quavering voice interrupted the speaker with this challenging question, "Is God dead?"

The days in which we live are dark. Terrific forces of evil seem to be in control. An enemy smashes at the ideals that we hold dear and for which we would gladly give our lives. If, however, in the midst of the rush and roar and devastation of things we can say over and over again, "God is not dead! God is not dead!" we shall find a new faith, and a new hope, that will give us courage to go on.

Let us say with Paul: "If God be for us, who can be against us? . . . I am persuaded that neither death, nor life, nor angels, nor principalities, nor powers, nor things present, nor things to come, nor height, nor depth, nor any other creature, shall be able to separate us from the love of God, which is in Christ Jesus our Lord."

DEAR GOD, our everlasting, ever loving Father, give us, we pray, that sense of Thy presence, and that confidence in the ultimate triumph of Right, that we shall be enabled to stand strong in our faith. *Amen.*

HUBERT W. HODGENS
Florence Avenue United Presbyterian Church, Los Angeles, Calif.

ANOTHER CHANCE AT LIFE

So he made it again.—Jer. 18:4

Roy Regals, the young man who ran in the wrong direction at the Annual Rose Bowl Football classic, took a new grip on life when his coach sent him from the shower room where he was suffering in the agony of his terrible blunder, with the words, "Roy, get up! You are going out on the field to play again. The game isn't over."

God takes the clay of our lives and places it on the wheel of life. The whirl is our response. If we make the right choice, the right decisions, and become pliable in the hand of the Master Potter, He makes us again.

The prodigal, returning from failure and defeat, said to his father, "Make me."

Jacob was not a good player. But God appeared one day and said, "My son, I built this ladder from earth to heaven. I want you to climb back to the heights from whence thou art fallen and I have brought my angels to help you up again."

God, too, says, "Get up. You can go out and play again. The game isn't over."

How are you playing the game? If you have fumbled the ball, remember there is still another chance.

> Though I forget Him and wander away,
> Still He doth love me wherever I stray.
> Have Thine own way, Lord! Have Thine own way!
> Thou art the Potter; I am the clay.
> Mold me and make me after Thy will,
> While I am waiting, yielded and still. *Amen.*
> —ADELAIDE A. POLLARD

DON H. HOUSEHOLDER
Trinity Methodist Church, Los Angeles, Calif.

FOLLOW THROUGH

I have fought a good fight, I have finished my course, I have kept the faith.—2 Tim. 4:7

O ur neighbor on the farm had a flock of sheep. The male member of that sheep family was none too friendly. One day the boy at that farm wanted to show his country schoolmates some fun. He had us all climb up on the rail fence to watch the event. The sheep were in the barnyard through which ran a ditch which was then half full of mud and water. This boy approached the flock, and Mr. Ram came out to meet him. Soon the boy was running with the ram in full pursuit. He jumped the ditch while Mr. Ram went in head first. The ram sulkily climbed out over the bank with his wet wool and took his place again in the flock. The boy recrossed the ditch, and the same event was repeated. It happened four times. That old ram didn't seem to learn his lesson. However, by the time of the fifth trial, the bank had become so slippery from the ram's wet wool that when the boy began to jump his feet went back from under him, and on his knees he was exactly right for the ram. This time it was he who went head first into the ditch instead of the ram, and the ram seemed to be satisfied.

That old ram taught me a good lesson. Do not quit when you get your wool wet, or at the first rebuff. Keep right after your worthy goal until you get it. We have a big job to do now, but by all working together we can win and help establish a just and lasting peace. Let us keep the faith and finish our course!

O GOD, help us to open our minds to the inflow of the power of Thy spirit, that we may make our lives channels through which Thy love and goodwill may flow into this torn world. *Amen.*

EDWARD ARCHIBALD THOMPSON
First (Park) Congregational Church, Grand Rapids, Mich.

THE STRENGTH OF A PEOPLE

Run ye to and fro through the streets of Jerusalem, and see now, . . .
if there be any that executeth judgment, that seeketh the truth; and I
will pardon it.—Jer. 5:1

As the Hebrew prophets saw it, the greatest danger which confronted their people was not the military might of the great enemy empires, real as that danger was. Their greatest peril lay in their own interior rottenness. History is full of examples, including modern ones, which bear out the prophet's contention.

But the Hebrew prophets did not stop there. The hope of the nation lies in its people who love justice and seek the truth. So great is their power for good that the prophet says that if one such be found he shall be enough to save the city of Jerusalem. While we may not take this statement literally, we must take it seriously. The chief bulwark of any nation—without which all other bulwarks fail—is the character of its people, men and women who love justice so much they practice it, who love truth so much that they believe it in preference to lies, although these be what they want to believe.

Nor dare we escape the personal reference of these words of Jeremiah. They march right up to you and me and ask us what we are going to do about it. A majority isn't needed—just a few. A start can be made with you alone. The king of Israel called Elisha "the chariot of Israel, and the horsemen." So everyone is that "executeth judgment, that seeketh the truth."

FATHER OF ALL HUMANKIND, we pray for our country that it may be strong. Deliver it from the evils which eat like a cancer from within. Let justice mark all its dealings, and let truth be cherished. We pray also for ourselves. Lead us in paths of righteousness for Thy name's sake. Grant us to see the truth as Thou dost set it before us in this our day. *Amen.*

WARNER L. HALL
First Presbyterian Church, Tuscaloosa, Ala.

PEACE ON THE INSIDE

Peace I leave with you, my peace I give unto you: not as the world giveth, give I unto you. Let not your heart be troubled, neither let it be afraid.—John 14:27

The above are strange words to read at such an hour as this. Yet I believe that Christ would have us enjoy peace in our hearts even though the outward conditions may be chaotic. Christ comes to bring quietness to the troubled soul. As oil upon the ocean's waves will calm the turbulent sea, so the inner dwelling with Christ will be a soothing balm to the troubled heart. We are called to experience many things in this life, yet through them all there is the promise of Christ to be with us. How many go to bed each night with troubled hearts! How many face each morning's light with disturbed minds! Hear the challenge of Christ to us. "Let not your heart be troubled, neither let it be afraid." How could Christ make such strong and positive statements? Simply because He would go with us through all of these experiences. He says, "Do not be afraid; I will be there to help and to guide."

It may be in the valley, where countless dangers hide;
It may be in the sunshine that I, in peace, abide,
But this one thing I know—if it be dark or fair,
If Jesus is with me, I'll go anywhere!
—C. AUSTIN MILES

Let us begin this day with a prayer to Christ to be our guide.

O LORD, keep my heart in perfect quietness this day. Be Thou my guide; lead me as Thou wouldst have me go. My life I yield to Thee; whatever Thou wouldst have me do, whatever Thou wouldst have me be, I would do and become through Thee. Wilt Thou radiate the glow of Christ through my heart. *Amen.*

WESLEY J. DRUMMOND
Immanuel Baptist Church, Elgin, Ill.

FEAR OR FAITH?

Fear not: for, behold, I bring you good tidings of great joy, which shall be to all people.—Luke 2:10

Franklin Roosevelt once said: "The only thing we have to fear is fear itself." The most destructive influence in an individual, or nation, is fear. The most effective weapon used by the enemy is fear. By it their own people are held in subjection. By spreading fear they have accomplished more than by their military might or strategy.

Christianity was born in an age of the world's cruelest dictators. In spite of persecution and martyrdom this valiant small company, witnessing day by day, spread Christianity until in two hundred years they had constructed a church in every city from Alexandria to Rome. In three hundred fifty years they had rocked the mighty Roman Empire until it crumbled.

A person is never defeated if faith lives on in his or her heart. Jesus said: "Upon this rock [this faith] I will build my church; and the gates of hell shall not prevail against it." An individual, a church, or a nation established on the rock of faith cannot be shaken by an individual or nations. After four years in a concentration camp with Dr. Niemoller, a person bears this testimony: "Only those of strong religious faith survive."

The Christian message we must keep singing in our hearts is this: "Joy to the world! the Lord is come." This is our witness: "Be of good cheer: I have overcome the world."

OUR FATHER, we hear Thee say to us, "O ye of little faith," as we remember our fears. May we know in Thee that we have perfect security for our spirits. Thus we pray, "Lord, increase our faith." May we truly know that with Thee all things are possible, and without Thee we can do nothing. Undergird us by Thy strength and give us courage to follow Christ. *Amen.*

CARL O. OLSON
First Presbyterian Church, Stillwater, Minn.

HOW DOES GOD HELP US?

He shall call upon me, and I will answer him.—Ps. 91:15

An American boy once studied theology at the University of Berlin. Having learned that the external world is governed by immutable laws, he had tried in vain to solve the riddle of divine aid: How can God help us? Then one November afternoon the wisdom he had been seeking flashed into his mind. That moment of illumination was one of the great moments in his life. If he closes his eyes today he can still see in clear memory that little Berlin street—a fruit store, a tailor shop, a shoemaker's window, and at the end of the street a purple and white sign above a subway station.

Those surroundings—and into the boy's mind flashed this wisdom: "God helps us, not by changing our external situation, but by changing our inner life. He leaves our external situation just as it is, makes no effort to perform a miracle there. But into our mind He thrusts new wisdom; within our heart He rouses new courage. This is God's help. It is a change, not in the world without, but in the world within." Gradually that new wisdom became the core of that boy's religious faith. For his entire life that faith has been to him a source of unfailing strength. He is now trying to share that faith with you. For he knows that to you as well as to him it can be "the victory that overcomes the world."

Teach us, O God,
To serve Thee as Thou deservest—
To give and not count the cost,
To fight and not lick the wounds,
To toil and not ask for rest,
To labor and not seek for any reward
Save that of knowing we have done Thy will. *Amen.*

JAMES GORDON GILKEY
South Congregational Church, Springfield, Mass.

THE CERTAINTY OF OUR HOPE

And so all Israel shall be saved. . . . There shall come out of Zion the Deliverer, and shall turn away ungodliness from Jacob.—Rom. 11:26

A little boy led in prayer last night in our midweek meeting. These were his words: "O God, we will win this war because You are with us and that makes us right."

There is no doubt about the eventual outcome of the struggle in which the nations of the world are involved. The only unknown factor is the length of time it takes our sufferings to waken us spiritually. "All Israel shall be saved"—of that we may rest certain. God has said it.

And of this, too, we may be sure—whatever means are necessary to "turn away ungodliness from Jacob" He will take. His love hasn't accomplished that. His abundant blessings have not. The presence in our homes of our fine children has not. The depression did not. Perhaps this war alone will bring it to pass. This terrible homicide—as the last plague—will continue until such time as America recognizes the Great Deliverer already "come out of Zion."

OUR FATHER, break our hearts quickly with the burden of our sins. If it be Thy will, may this catastrophe not find us stubborn and unyielding to Thy voice. Give us wisdom to seek out Thy forgiveness. Give us judgment; make up our lack of devotion to Thee quickly. For Christ's sake. *Amen.*

WILL W. ORR
Westminster United Presbyterian Church, Des Moines, Iowa

THE IMPORTANCE OF FAITH

But without faith it is impossible.—Heb. 11:6

The first century was difficult for the Hebrew Christians. Persecution strained their newly formed loyalty to Christ. Some had deserted, and others were losing their enthusiasm. Something had to be done quickly. The writer of the Book of Hebrews recognized this, and he did it. He reminded those discouraged people of the importance of faith. He recalled a catalogue of the great notables of their national history and pointed out convincingly that they were great, not because of their possessions or material security, but because of their faith.

The writer of old had caught the gleam of a great truth. The big things of life have always been accomplished on the basis of faith. The story of faith is one of magnificent recklessness on the part of faithful people who burned their boats on the beaches and ventured into the unknown.

Today we need to remind ourselves of this great truth. Discouraging things have happened, and perhaps more discouraging things are ahead. We must maintain our balance by the stabilizing force of an unshakable faith—faith in our country, faith in our God.

Strong Son of God, immortal Love,
Whom we, that have not seen Thy face,
By faith, and faith alone, embrace,
Believing where we cannot prove,

Thou wilt not leave us in the dust:
Thou madest man, he knows not why;
He thinks he was not made to die;
And Thou hast made him: Thou art just. *Amen.*

G. Roy Bragg
St. John's Methodist Church, Newburgh, N.Y.

THE KNOWN AND THE UNKNOWN

The secret things belong unto the Lord our God: but those things which are revealed belong unto us, and to our children forever, that we may do all the words of this law.—Deut. 29:29

If God would only reveal Himself! If He would only make plain His will and show me my path! Why does He permit the horror of war and wholesale destruction? What is the meaning of tremendous changes that are turning the world upside down? Thus we complain in the quiet of our own thinking. The lack of ability to see the whole picture and the ultimate purpose of all events tends to make us rebellious.

Then it is that we need to learn the lesson of our text. There are some things secret. They do not belong to us. We are not able or ready to know them as yet, and we must not let our speculation or consternation regarding the unknown cause us to neglect the things that are revealed. For they belong to us. They are ours to do, and only by doing the things that are revealed shall we ever come to know the things that are secret. We walk by faith—not by sight.

So we must live by the known till we find the unknown. Let it be our everyday habit to inquire of God regarding our plain and well-known duties. Let us listen to Him in the morning, and then live according to His plain commands during the day.

O LORD GOD, Thou art the Ruler of the world, and in Thy wisdom Thou hast done all things well. Teach us to trust in Thy power to govern the world. Take away from us all impatience and self-will, and give us grace to serve Thee faithfully under all circumstances, and to find our rest and security in doing Thy gracious will. Reveal unto us more and more of the mysteries of the unknown through our faithful performance of our known duties. Through Jesus Christ. *Amen.*

OTTO H. BOSTROM
Church of Gustavus Adolphus, New York, N.Y.

AS YOU WILL, YOUNG MAN

I am the way, and the truth, and the life: no man cometh unto the Father, but by me.—John 14:6

A wise old man who lived alone in a cabin in the hills was so gifted with wisdom that people came to him with problems and questions, to which he always gave excellent counsel and the right answers.

One day a giant youth thought he would catch the old man off guard; he had a little sparrow in his big hand, and he was going to ask the old man this question: "Is this bird dead or alive?" If the wise man said, "Alive," he would crush the bird and prove him wrong; and if he said, "Dead," he would open his hand and let it fly away. So this youth approached the brilliant old sage with a twinkle in his eye and put forth his question. The wise old man, without any hesitancy, and with a smile, said slowly, "As you will, young man, as you will."

Is it not true that unlimited power of choice is given to everyone? Day after day, to every question in life the answer of time is, "As you will." Even God has given us a free choice in life, and as we stand in the forks in the road, there is always a right and a wrong way for us. Pilate's question is still our question: "What shall I do then with Jesus which is called Christ?" God the Father answers, "As you will."

Good friend, believe and trust in Christ as your Savior, and you will always have God's mighty arm to hide you in this life and to keep you for His eternal glory. "As you will."

"CREATE IN ME a clean heart, O God; and renew a right spirit within me. Cast me not away from thy presence; and take not thy holy spirit from me. Restore unto me the joy of thy salvation; and uphold me with thy free spirit." *Amen.*

W. H. MURK
Temple Baptist Church, St. Paul, Minn.

THE VOICE THAT WINS OVER FEAR

Be of good cheer; it is I; be not afraid.—Matt. 14:27

Popularity has its drawbacks, and our Lord found this out after He had fed the multitudes. Realizing it would take a master hand to restore order, Jesus sent His disciples away, telling them to take ship for the other side of Lake Galilee. They obeyed, but the trip was terrible. Fear gripped their hearts, and in that hour Christ came to them with relief.

It may be that you have obeyed the command of your Lord, and yet things have been going rather badly with you since you entered the service. You expected decency to be regarded with respect, but sneers and jeers are your portion. The routine of life in the service is not what you expected it to be—at least in its results. Hindrances, rather than helps to your faith, crush heart and mind. It is at the height of such storms that He comes.

Often we fail to realize His approach and are frightened even when relief is at hand. Some duties have fearful faces and scare us as did ghost stories when we were children. Yet at such times Christ draws near with His words of cheer. Or it may be that you have been challenged concerning your faith. You are afraid of the laughter which may be raised at your efforts to reply. Forget your fears. Obey His urge, and in such a time He will arrive with strengthening powers.

ALMIGHTY GOD, hear us this day as we draw near in spirit and in truth. Grant to us the assurance of pardon already prepared and incline us to accept it on Thy terms. May every hour be improved by loving service and every mile traveled witness loyalty to nation and God. Above all, speed the coming of a lasting peace. In Christ's name. *Amen.*

REGINALD COLEMAN
Central Presbyterian Church, Austin, Minn.

THESE THINGS WILL NOT GO

Strengthen the things which remain.—Rev. 3:2

Many of the securities which we thought were solid are crumbling in these critical times. But there are eternal things that cannot go and will not go. They are the timeless, everlasting, sustaining values of God. During the first century, when the world was going to pieces, John wrote a message of cheer to the church at Sardis: "Strengthen the things which remain." What are these realities that will not go?

First, God's love. "I am persuaded, that neither death, nor life, nor angels, nor principalities, nor powers, nor things present, nor things to come, nor height, nor depth, nor any other creature, shall be able to separate us from the love of God, which is in Christ Jesus." No matter what happens, take refuge in the golden pledge that the love of God remains constant as a magnificent stabilizer for courageous living.

Second, the power of prayer. Someone asked Blake, the artist: "What do you do when you lose vision?" He turned to his wife for the answer. "We kneel down and pray," she replied. The mightiest power in the world, which can conquer anything, is the power of prayer.

Third, Jesus Christ. He is "the same yesterday, and today, and for ever." His truth remains; His divinity remains. His deathless message of salvation from Calvary's cross remains; No force on this earth is powerful enough to overthrow Him. Long after the sun has set in the skies forevermore, His Person, His work, and everything for which He stands will remain.

O CHRIST, Thou art from everlasting to everlasting. When all things go, Thou wilt not leave us nor forsake us. We believe in Thee and Thy eternity. Help Thou our unbelief. *Amen.*

HENRY V. KAHLENBERG
Trinity Lutheran Church, St. Petersburg, Fla.

THE PRESENCE OF GOD

*God is a Spirit: and they that worship him must worship him in spirit
and in truth.*—John 4:24

Real religion is what happens when men become aware of the presence of God." But how may we become aware of the presence of God? Only by thinking of Him as a Spirit. But what does it mean to think of God as a Spirit? Are we to think of Him as a kind of "Ghost"? To many such thoughts are uncanny and unreal. Jesus taught us to think of God as Father in heaven. By His life and teaching Jesus helps us to think of God in terms of His purpose for us and for others, His plan for the world, His love of humanity, His coming rule "in earth as it is in heaven."

It is helpful to think of an earthly father and mother. Though we may not see them or touch them because they are separated from us in space or even by death, we may know their presence with us as we think of their hopes for us, their plans for us, their pride in us, their love for us, all enduring long past their physical presence with us. We may not "feel" them near us, but they are spiritually present in our memories, our hopes, and our love.

Right across the centuries, people have known the presence of God as a healing, strengthening, empowering reality, meeting them in their plans, their purposes, their temptations, and their victories. The Spirit of God was made real in Jesus. "God is a Spirit: and they that worship him must worship him in spirit and in truth."

O GOD, who hast revealed Thyself in Jesus Christ, grant us grace that we may worship Thee in spirit and in truth. Thou art closer to us than breathing and nearer than hands and feet. Help us to be true to Thee and to live in the strength of Thy presence. *Amen.*

ALEXANDER C. PURDY
Hartford Seminary, Hartford, Conn.

A GOD THAT CANNOT BE STOLEN

Ye have taken away my gods which I made, and the priest, and ye are gone away: and what have I more?—Judg. 18:24

This story of Micah of Ephraim introduces us to a time when God was worshiped through idols. Micah felt secure in his religious life. He had hired a priest and owned the images of his faith. He said, "Now know I that the Lord will do me good, seeing I have a Levite as my priest." He was well content.

Now the tribe of Danites, who were looking for suitable land in which to dwell, passed by Micah's home. They stole the images and induced the priest to come with them. Then it was that Micah was aroused from his complacency. In desperation he implores them: "Ye have taken away my gods . . . what have I more?" But the Danites laugh and go on their way.

Sometimes we bow to gods in our day which are capable of being stolen. We worship money and the things it can buy and neglect much that is finer than gold. We worship work by keeping our "noses to the grindstone," and thereby lose time for love and culture in the home and community. We worship pleasures and conveniences and forget those things that help the soul.

The Christian faith invites you to know the Father of our Lord and Master, Jesus Christ. For here is a God who cannot be stolen. Here is a God who loves us and can be loved by us. We can turn the words of Micah about, and speak in confidence instead of despair, and say, "You have taken away many things which I have made, and have gone away; but I have much more, a God that cannot be stolen."

O GOD OUR FATHER, thou canst give to us a faith steadfast and sure, for Thou art a God who cannot be stolen. Send us, we pray, strength and guidance during these days of stress. In Jesus' name. *Amen.*

LAWRENCE E. TENHOPEN
First Congregational Church, South Haven, Mich.

THE POWER OF MINORITIES

For God so loved the world, that he gave his only begotten Son, that whosoever believeth in him should not perish, but have everlasting life.—John 3:16

Dr. James Stewart says in his wonderful book, *The Strong Name:* "No one can look at the world today and observe the tragic disillusionments and rampant degradations without being driven to the conclusion that something in the organism of the human race has gone mysteriously and terribly wrong.... It is the glory and the doom of man to have been made for fellowship with God. Of all the faculties and capacities which he possesses, incomparably the greatest is his capacity for God. . . . Reconciliation with God is, therefore, the cardinal issue, far and away the most crucial problem confronting the soul of man today."

These are staggering truths, particularly when one faces them in the light of the fact that our God is the person or thing to whom or to which we give our first allegiance. Yet why should we be overwhelmed when we realize that God has not only created us to have fellowship with Himself but given us in the Living Christ a power to make ourselves new creatures?

My, what a challenge to realize that the normal life is the life that has fellowship with God! The abnormal life is the life that is separated from Him.

ALMIGHTY GOD, my heavenly Father, help me now wholly and unreservedly to surrender my will to Thee. May my faith in Thee never waver, and may I give Thee always the maximum opportunity to work through me to bring in the day when Thy Kingdom shall be on earth even as it is in heaven. *Amen.*

A. J. ("DAD") ELLIOTT
Famous World War I "Y" Secretary
Secretary, Christian Evangelism Among Youth, Chicago, Ill.

WHAT SHALL BE MY BURDEN TODAY?

*Take my yoke upon you and learn from me; for I am gentle and lowly
in heart, and you shall find rest for your souls. For my yoke is easy,
and my burden is light.*—Matt. 11:28–30 (WEYMOUTH)

Only God could make an invitation like that and have it stand through
the centuries. We have burdens that we should be free from; we have
burdens we'll have to bear; and there are some burdens Jesus Christ would
have us share with Him.

Christ is the Lamb of God that taketh away the sin of the world. There
is one burden you need not bear. That burden is the burden of sin. There
is only One who can remove it.

Life has its burdens too of which Christ does not promise to relieve us;
rather He promises us His help to bear them. Such hectic days as these
brings burdens of infirmities, the blasting of hopes and ambitions, and the
heartaches of loneliness and sorrow. No Christian need expect to be
immune from them. But in each of these burdens we can invite the great
Burden-bearer to share with us and make up to us our losses and our lacks.

"Take my yoke." In comparison with the load of sin which He would
remove, this is a light one. There is something we can do for Him and in
His name. It may not be much—perhaps a cup of water—but it will not
go unnoticed. Let Him take away your sin, share your legitimate load; and
in return you give Him a lift.

FATHER IN HEAVEN, I accept this invitation and challenge today. What
I cannot do for myself I humbly entrust to Thee. Take away my sin and
guilt. What I can do for Thy Kingdom I will seek to do well. Grant me the
help promised to those who trust Thee. I pray in Jesus' name. *Amen.*

CLYDE W. MEREDITH
Dean, Divinity School, Marion College, Marion, Ind.

SEEING CLEARLY

Moreover the word of the Lord came unto me, saying, Jeremiah, what seest thou? And I said, I see a rod of an almond tree. Then said the Lord unto me, Thou hast well seen.—Jer. 1:11–12

The world is in need today of persons who can see clearly. In the midst of strife we are prone to look at life from a narrow viewpoint and with dulled vision. We need to climb to a mountaintop where we can get a better perspective and see the world as a whole. If we cannot actually climb to a high point we may have the experience in our imagination. Let us try to shut out all unpleasant facts of life and forget all sordid details. Let us recall the most beautiful landscape that we have enjoyed in the past. As we think of the details that blended together to make it a perfect whole, what thought of God comes to us?

In nature we see a perfect blending of colors. There is nothing to mar the harmony and the beauty of the scene. In order to have the same harmony in our relations with others that we find in nature, what changes would be necessary? Jesus gave a full statement of our relations when He said, "Thou shalt love the Lord thy God with all thy heart, and with all thy soul, and with all thy mind, and with all thy strength. . . . Thou shalt love thy neighbor as thyself."

Strife and trouble come when we violate this truth. We need spiritual vision in order to see clearly the way ahead to victory in the present crisis and in the future as well.

OUR FATHER, with our faces to the future and with confidence in the final outcome of this crisis, we look to Thee for strength to face whatever the day brings. Help us to see life clearly and see it whole. Give us a proper perspective, that we may live rightly with others. In Jesus' name. *Amen.*

JAMES ALEXANDER BAYS
Church Street Methodist Church, Knoxville, Tenn.

MY BODY A LIVING SACRIFICE

I beseech you therefore, brethren, by the mercies of God, that ye present your bodies a living sacrifice, holy, acceptable unto God, which is your reasonable service.—Rom. 12:1

Paul has set a difficult task—the presentation of our bodies as living sacrifices. There is an implied contrast. The Romans offered sacrifices in the same manner as did the Jews, the sacrifices of animals which had been killed within the precincts of their temples. Paul invites the Roman Christians to be themselves sacrifices.

Many of them became, in truth, living sacrifices, giving themselves in the Colosseum to the death, singing hymns of praise to God as they did so, and bringing the effective witness of fearlessness, forgiveness, and love. Acceptance of Christ as their Savior, their Way of Life, and living by and through Him became in itself sacrificial living.

But for many this was a new religion. It involved not the sacrifice of earthly possessions, of beasts of the field, but a living, vitalized sacrifice of body, mind, and experience. That is still involved in the Christian faith. It may be my opportunity through this war, to be a living sacrifice, holy, acceptable unto God, my spiritual service.

MY FATHER GOD, hear Thou, and hearing, understand, I pray Thee, my needs wherever I may be, on the high seas, on a continent distant from my home, in the air above, or in the waters beneath the sea. In the heavens above and throughout the earth Thou art near. I shall hear Thy voice and obey Thy commands. Thou wilt keep me as in the hollow of Thy hand. For all this I thank Thee and magnify Thee, world without end. *Amen.*

FRANK E. MOSSMAN
President, Southwestern College, Winfield, Kan.

ENDS AND MEANS

They spake the word of God with boldness.—Acts 4:31

In that great classic war epic, Homer's *Iliad*, the victory of Greece over Troy is postponed for eighteen books out of twenty-two, because two army generals of the Greeks quarrel over the very same issue that brought the war between the two countries. Isn't this an example of our human inconsistencies? How easy, sometimes, to see Truth in the ideal and miss it in the real. Many a Sir Launfal travels afar in search for the Holy Grail, only to find that he passed it by over his own threshold. It was Hogarth, the artist, who pictured a man in stocks for a private debt working on paper a scheme to pay the national debt. It is not growth when we lack power to control our power.

Yours is a great mission. Nothing short of a universal standard of conduct; of the recovery of sacred human rights; of regard for persons as persons, and not for sex, color, or caste; and of the protection and preservation of life has taken you from the restraining influences of home and loved ones. God give us all integrity that we shall not practice any means that will cancel such noble ends.

By His supreme sacrifice our Savior showed that there were values greater than mere existence. Most people die *of* something; he died *for* something, and all who have His spirit share a dedication for the kind of world He believed in, and for which He gave us a blood transfusion. He has overcome death, but we must keep Him alive.

O THOU SOURCE OF LIFE and Goal of all endeavor, give us, we pray Thee, inward integrity. Grant us freedom, not to do as we like, but to like to do as we ought. Take our little quota of service and use it until the day dawns and the shadows flee away. Through Jesus Christ our Lord. *Amen.*

WILLIAM P. LEMON
First Presbyterian Church, Ann Arbor, Mich.

BEGIN THE DAY WITH GOD

And in the morning, rising up a great while before day, he went out, and departed into a solitary place, and there prayed.—Mark 1:35

A friend whose watch was not keeping accurate time took it to a jeweler. "When do you wind your watch?" asked the jeweler.

"At night, of course, just as everybody does."

"No," replied the jeweler, "not everybody. Most people wind their watches at night, but not jewelers; for one who knows the mechanism of a watch knows that it is best to *begin* the day on a full spring."

If we would keep in step with God we shall do well to tune our hearts to the eternal drumbeat by *beginning* each day with prayer.

This was the Master's custom, and it has been the secret of the power of countless others who moved amid the discords and confusions of their time with a constancy and a courage that awakened the wonder of all who knew them. So valuable did Jesus find this practice that He used to arise while His disciples were still asleep and steal away to a quiet spot for his "morning watch."

> Still, still with Thee, when purple morning breaketh,
> When the bird waketh, and the shadows flee;
> Fairer than morning, lovelier than the daylight,
> Dawns the sweet consciousness, I am with Thee.
> —HARRIET BEECHER STOWE

OUR FATHER, help us to begin each day with Thee, and to bring our wills into tune with Thy will. May the sense of Thy presence be with us to strengthen us and give us courage for whatever experiences may come to us. *Amen.*

JAMES D. MORRISON
Colgate-Rochester Divinity School, Rochester, N.Y.

COWORKERS WITH GOD

I planted, Apollos watered; but God gave the increase. . . . We are God's fellow-workers.—1 Cor. 3:6, 9 ARV

How many of us need to achieve in these days the happy combination of *dependence on God* with *energetic work in His Spirit!* This is a sound principle of the New Testament—eternally true of our religious and our total practical workaday life. Too many of us have never realized that God works in our world according to absolute physical, social, and moral laws. We wait, too much of the time, for God to do *for* us what He will do only *through* us. God could stop a worldwide war! God could end the spread of cancer and venereal disease! But God has made you and me rational men and women, and He expects us to use our freedom for good or for ill. He could, but He will not violate this freedom.

Are we prepared—wherever we are at this moment, whatever tasks and duties we face—to let ourselves be used as instruments of God's goodwill? This will not be any drab, dull dependence on God. It will be the most thrilling life in the world, because in this type of life we shall share in the vital, triumphant, joyous life of our Creator! Such dependence upon God will not mean sitting around and doing nothing but counting prayers. It will mean making our lives prayerful in attitude so that the "orders of the day" will express God's will. Then we shall know that we are cooperating with God's eternal purposes. There is nothing more challenging than this kind of life!

ETERNAL GOD AND FATHER, whom we know supremely in the person and life of Jesus Christ, grant us this day such a fresh and clear vision for our lives that our thoughts, words, and deeds may be in harmony with Thy holy will and partake of Thy triumphant purposes both in this world and in Thine eternal Kingdom. Through our Master we pray. *Amen.*

CHARLES W. KEGLEY
St. Paul's Lutheran Church, Evanston, Ill.

BUILDING PEOPLE WHILE WE BUILD MACHINES

I will give thee two thousand horses, if thou be able on thy part to set riders upon them.—2 Kings 18:23 ARV

The ability of America to build machines has been demonstrated in these days in a manner to surprise the most optimistic. Planes, ships, guns, motors—every type of equipment is rolling off our plants by thousands. When schedules were first announced, the nation was doubtful whether they could be met, but this question mark has been removed.

While all America rejoices to see the mechanical part of our nation's defense making such marvelous strides, it is well for us to study again one of history's most often repeated lessons. The shores of human history are lined with the wreckage of nations who have developed the power to build *things* and have fallen short in the far more important task of building *people*. Little of permanent good or permanent strength will come to us if we have "two thousand horses" and lack the riders to set upon them.

Beginning with George Washington, our greatest patriots have realized the importance of religion in its relation to national permanence. Christianity and democracy are inseparable. Both grow in a common soil, and neither can thrive without the presence of the other. Spiritual character is as necessary to America today as planes and battleships.

GOD OF OUR FATHERS, we bow in gratitude before Thee for the gifts of iron and steel and material things, and for the ability of our people to weld these into the implements we need in defense of our nation. Grant us to see that without without spiritual power and character these will not suffice to make us and keep us free. Help us in our daily life to remember that "blessed is the nation whose God is the Lord." We ask in Christ's name. *Amen.*

J. O. J. TAYLOR
Central Methodist Church, Fitzgerald, Ga.

QUEST AND DISCOVERY

O wretched man that I am! who shall deliver me from the body of this death?—Rom. 7:24

Our great difficulty has been the discovery of a master key to the stronghold of righteous living. Paul's voice sounds almost frantic in this cry. He had reason for his outburst. He had made at least two false starts.

When Paul first asked, "How can I be good?" he adopted the traditions of his Jewish forebears. They stressed obedience to law. Now law is essential to a moral society, but it does not make people good. It merely forces them to act as if they were good. Paul felt the tendency to evil still rampant in his soul.

His second attempted solution was akin to the Greek teaching of his day which stressed the power of man's wisdom to keep him honorable. In other words, follow the dictates of your conscience; do the best that you know how. But that was just Paul's problem. He found that his nobler instincts were too easily subdued. There must be a better way. And there was!

Paul discovered that commitment to Christ brought the only sense of moral security that he had ever known, and he left this magic sentence for every struggling, tempted soul: "The love of Christ constraineth us." Notice Paul says "constraineth," not "restraineth." The secret is to be so dominated by Christ and so positively aggressive in Christian performance that corrupt desires are forgotten. This is the one positive answer to the problem of the good life: that Christ should live again in me.

GRACIOUS GOD, help me to share the moral achievements of great Christ-conquered souls, to know the vitality of Christian character, to capture the thrill of consistent goodness. Inspire in me those noble thoughts which lead to noble action, and find in me those pure desires which reflect the very presence of the Christ whom I love. *Amen.*

W. PAUL LUDWIG
Second Presbyterian Church, Washington, Pa.

THE INSEPARABLE LOVE OF GOD

Neither death, nor life, nor angels, nor principalities, nor powers, nor things present, nor things to come . . . shall be able to separate us from the love of God, which is in Christ Jesus our Lord.—Rom. 8:38–39

She was a pastor's wife, a refugee from Germany, who told the tale of separation: how her husband had been torn from his people and his work; how the boys had been scattered, one in concentration, one in Australia, one in America. To be separated from those you love most and the things you cherish is like ripping a man's skin from his flesh. No pain cuts deeper.

Paul understood this when he wrote the words above. Was he not an exile from his own Jewish people? Had he not turned his back on the profession for which he had trained? Had he not given up a home and family? All for the sake of proclaiming the one eternal satisfaction that a human being can ever know—the inseparable love of God.

You do not have to be in prison or shipwrecked or mobbed, as Paul had been, in order to be lonesome. You can feel desperately deserted even when companions and acquaintances are all around. In such moments the certainty of Paul's affirmation spreads its warmth through your whole being, and you can face anything, knowing that you will never be really lonely again.

O GOD, who followest me beyond the heights, below the depths, how can I thank Thee for Thy love to me? Only let me know that Christ, who knew the deepest loneliness, is my Companion. Then can I do all things through Him. Then shall I do all things for Him, and nothing shall be loss. *Amen.*

EDWIN A. GOLDSWORTHY
First Baptist Church, Rahway, N.J.

THIS THING I DO

Be strong and of a good courage.—Josh. 1:9

When the body of Captain Robert Scott was found near the South Pole there was discovered a letter he had written to his friend, Sir James M. Barrie.

In that letter Captain Scott tried to tell how cold it was and how hopeless it was and said, "But it would do you good to hear our songs and our cheery conversation."

Think of that! The last word that was written was long drawn out, and it spelled "courage." The letter was brought back and given to Sir James, and he kept it in a little casket in his home. He carried it once to St. Andrews University, and its contents found their way into that classical address which he called "Courage."

Perhaps life has lost its zest; and you, with your back to the wall are not even strong enough to fight. Across the centuries there comes not only the example of our Lord, but His challenge. On His last night, facing the cross, alone in the upper room with eleven disciples whose courage would fail them in a few hours, He said, "Be of good cheer; I have overcome the world."

Be strong!
We are not here to play—to dream, to drift.
We have hard work to do and loads to lift.
Shun not the struggle—face it; 'tis God's gift.
Be strong!

O GOD OF PEACE, who hast taught us that in returning and rest we shall be saved, in quietness and in confidence shall be our strength; by the might of Thy Spirit lift us, we pray Thee, to Thy presence, where we may be still and know that Thou art God, through Jesus Christ our Lord. *Amen.*

HUGH THOMSON KERR
Shadyside Presbyterian Church, Pittsburgh, Pa.

BUILDING THE GOOD LIFE

He that findeth his life, shall lose it: and he that loseth his life for my sake, shall find it.—Matt. 10:39

A true life is one which has been worked out through difficulties, dangers, struggles, and suffering. Self-indulgence leads to degeneracy and decay. Self-denial is the pathway of usefulness, nobility, and happiness.

Those who have enriched the world have fought and struggled and braved hardship and danger. Those who have lived in ease and luxury have seldom made any valuable contribution to the progress and happiness of humanity.

Struggle and hardship build character. The ore must pass under the hammer and through the fire before the pure gold is extracted from it. God's aim is not merely to make us comfortable. He is trying to make Christians, real Christians, of us.

The people who are struggling and enduring for the sake of others are the truly happy people. There is no real joy in living in ease and self-indulgence. The dissatisfied, pessimistic, cynical people today are the ones who are living in ease and indolence. The downward way is broad and easy; the upward way is narrow and difficult.

He who did most for this world suffered most. He walked the way of loneliness, hardship, abuse, self-denial, suffering, and—the cross.

OUR FATHER, Thou hast been good to us in the days gone by, and we thank Thee. In the days before us, help us to meet duty, hardship, and danger as ones who would serve Thee and our fellow people. Help us to walk in the steps of Him who "came not to be ministered unto, but to minister, and to give his life a ransom for many." Save us from the guilt, the penalty, and the power of sin, through Jesus Christ. *Amen.*

WM. E. SWEENEY
Broadway Christian Church, Lexington, Ky.

LOOK TO THE STARS

That phrase, once again, denotes the removal of what is shaken (as no more than created), to leave only what stands unshaken.
—Heb. 12:27 (MOFFATT)

There is an interesting story of two adventurers who were crossing one of our great deserts. In their notebooks they had very carefully written descriptions of the landmarks which would show them their way. But a mighty storm arose which drove them into a cave. When they dared to come out they found that trees had been uprooted, rocks cleft, and even the course of the streams changed. One of the men immediately went into a panic. "Now we shall die in the desert," he complained. But the second one was quiet and calm. When evening came he mounted his surveyor's transit and pointed it to the heavens. In a minute he turned to his frantic companion and smiled. "Everything is all right. The stars are still there."

These two men represent two attitudes which may be taken toward the crises of life. One may become panicky and declare that there is nothing of permanency in the universe. Or one may have the other attitude, that of looking toward the stars. There are abiding values in God's moral and spiritual universe. There is truth, and beauty, and love. There is a law-abiding universe; goodness is the supreme value; right and not might will ultimately prevail. We can be as sure of these things as we are of the stars. That is what the author of Hebrews meant when he wrote the verse above.

DEAR LORD AND FATHER OF US ALL, grant us wisdom, grant us courage for the living of these days. Give us clean hands and a pure heart so that we may stand in Thy presence unashamed. Give us the faith that makes us more than conquerors through Him who hath loved us. *Amen.*

W. L. CROWDING
Waynesboro Methodist Church, Waynesboro, Pa.

WHAT WILL YOU DO WITH IT?

It is not what goes into the mouth that defiles a person, but it is what comes out of the mouth that defiles.—Matt. 15:11 NRSV

The issue of ceremonialism may seem dead. It is alive in more subtle fashion in the question: What will you do with what comes to you? We join the Pharisees as we offer our stock excuses concocted of modern psychological jargon. We insist that our irritable conduct is the result of our miserable breakfast. We do an evil thing and lay the blame on heredity—we are just made that way! Thomas Carlyle's philosophy is explained in terms of his dyspepsia, and the economics of a whole region can be understood by means of the composition of the soil. So we reverse Jesus' emphasis: that which goeth into the mouth is important—it defileth us!

A person's experience is important but not of primary importance, else we could make first-rate philosophers by increasing dyspepsia and courageous soldiers with a shot in the arm.

Take the emphasis to everyday life. Criticism comes to us. The criticism is not of first importance. What we do with the criticism is the main consideration. One can become upset or ignore it, or one can use it to smooth the rough edges of inefficiency. Trouble can evoke a response of better understanding of the issues of life or an excuse for not having done more. The war can produce moral looseness or a sense of fellowship with a yearning humanity which longs for freedom to live in fullness of life. What comes to a person is not of primary importance. It is what he or she does with what comes that counts in God's sight.

OUR FATHER, in every experience may we find Thy hand and mind, and trust Thy love to work all things together for our good. In this day, may we take every experience and use it by Thy grace to shape our lives in the likeness of Christ. *Amen.*

THOMAS C. BARR
First Presbyterian Church, Nashville, Tenn.

COME OVER AND HELP US

Come over into Macedonia.—Acts 16:9

Mephistopheles in Goethe's *Faust* observes, "It was to give room for roaming that the world was made so wide." The apostle Paul recognized this fact and became one of the greatest roamers in history. He believed that we all belong to God and to one another. The Gospel of Jesus is for universal appropriation. We are God's miracle, and there is glory in the humblest soul. Thus Christ crossed from Asia to Europe, and later to the American continent from Canada to Brazil and the Golden Gate. What a night that was for the world! Here was an influence at last that put humanity before nations.

There was no leavening lump to be found anywhere in heathendom. Slavery ran rampant, and fear was written on the faces of the people. It was a zero hour in the world's history, with two nations sinking like stars to ruin. Everywhere men and women were crying out, "Come over and help us!" Then, in a great moment of despair, God sent His Son to the world and Christian unity was born.

Again we hear the sound of pain and tumult. Nations have gone wrong, and leaders have lost vision. The world has slipped back! The spirit of hate fills the earth! Greed paralyzes progress! Provincialism threatens the unity of the world order. The cry is heard in a thousand places, "Come over and help us!" This cry does not come from the heads of nations. It rises from the common people, who, sick of poverty and war, long for peace and happiness. We must answer their call in the Spirit of the courageous Jesus.

O GOD, Fountain of life and truth, give us wisdom, charity, and understanding, that the glorious message of Thy Son may be welcomed as the promise of the better age to be. *Amen.*

WILLIAM E. DUDLEY
Flatbush Congregational Church, Brooklyn, N.Y.

IN GOD'S COMPANY

Surely the Lord is in this place; and I knew it not.—Gen. 28:16.
I will go down with thee into Egypt.—Gen. 46:4

Jacob needed to be reminded that no matter where he went, God was always near at hand. Every one of us must discover, sooner or later, that religion is never a matter of locality, but of a personal, intimate consciousness of the constant presence of God.

Life had been rather hard for Jacob. He had been expelled from his own home by his brother's wrath, to find a new life in a remote country. In the darkness of that first night, as he slept alone under the stars, with a stone for a pillow, he made his first discovery: "The Lord is in this place." Long years afterwards, hungry, and faced with a severe famine, he found himself compelled to go down into Egypt, where there was food. But he was afraid of the journey. God spoke to him, bringing that needed confidence, "I will go down with thee into Egypt."

Wherever you are—right now—close your eyes, shut out the noise of the world, and there, deep within your heart, realize God is near. Repeat to yourself slowly that psalm you learned when you were young. It begins, "The Lord is my shepherd." And as you come to those glorious words of confidence, make them your own: He is walking with me; I am in God's company; wherever I go, He is by my side; I will trust in Him.

MY FATHER, I thank Thee that Thou hast never deserted Thy children. Help me to realize Thy presence as I go out to live my life. May I be truer, stronger, more faithful, more courageous, because Thou art with me. May I be purer and kinder and more devoted to the cause of righteousness because I feel Thy companionship. Keep me, and all of my comrades, and all of my loved ones, and all of Thy children everywhere, in Thy company. In Jesus' name. *Amen.*

HAROLD NASH GEISTWEIT
First Baptist Church, Elmira, N.Y.

HIS PRESENCE IS THE GOOD NEWS

Keep on doing the things that you have learned and received and heard and seen in me, and the God of peace will be with you.—Phil. 4:9

I had traveled further in twenty-four hours than at any time in my life. I was twelve time zones away from my home in East Texas, in the middle of Siberia, literally on the other side of the world. I was staying with a Russian family who had opened their small apartment and hearts to a stranger visiting to set up future mission trips to work with children with special needs. The woman of the home spoke excellent English and enjoyed seeing the pictures of my home, family, and church. Her generation was prohibited from church, and she had many questions about how our church functioned. "Can you pray directly to God and to Jesus?" she asked. "Do you pray only at church or can you pray anywhere?" I told her that I had prayed since I had arrived in her home; prayers for her and her family, thanksgiving for safe travel, for guidance in the work ahead. I told her that in our faith, Jesus was always with us, closer than our best friend. After some thought she said, "I don't deserve a friend like that." I smiled and said, "Neither do I, but that is the Good News of the Gospel; He is with us and is our Friend and Savior even though we don't deserve Him."

It doesn't matter where you are, you are not far from God. Paul writes, asking the church to continue to do what they have learned, and that in that doing, "the God of Peace will be with you." In your life, you have been taught and are growing in God. Turn those lessons into acts of love and mercy and each time that God of Peace will make His presence known.

HEAVENLY FATHER, I give You thanks for the Good News of Your redeeming love that You showed to me in Your Son, Jesus. I pray that You will fill me with Your perfect peace that I might grow in love and understanding of You. All this I ask in Jesus' name. *Amen.*

GILBERT C. HANKE
National President, United Methodist Men, Nacogdoches, Tex.

†

THE ENDS OF THE EARTH

Sing to the Lord a new song, his praise from the ends of the earth.
—Isa. 42:10–11

After the parting of the Red Sea, Moses' sister Miriam sang in praise of God's great and victorious deed. But now, says the prophet Isaiah, a new song is to be sung from one end of the earth to the other. "Let the sea roar and all that fills it, the coastlands and their inhabitants. Let the desert and its cities lift up their voice, the villages that Kedar inhabits, let the inhabitants of Sela sing for joy, let them shout from the top of the mountains."

Kedar and Sela were remote, isolated places in Isaiah's world. Have you ever found yourself serving in some remote place? I serve a church that is back in the woods, with only a dirt road leading to the site. We have no running water and no electricity, and yet every Sunday our church is filled with God's praise. Sing praise to God wherever you are: on board a ship in the middle of an ocean, stationed in a far away land, serving in a large metropolitan area, visiting your small hometown. Sing praise to God in the skies, on top of a mountain, on the water, on the beach, in the middle of the desert. Isaiah tells us that God is doing a new thing, and that new thing is that God has planned a future for you. That is why we can praise Him all over the world.

O GOD, I am thankful that You care for me and that You have a plan for my life. Help me to sing Your praises wherever I am. Thank You for being with me today to bless and comfort me. *Amen.*

CAROLYN BEHRENDT
Minister, Lima Presbyterian Church,
Stillwater, Ohio

OUR SOURCE OF HELP

I will lift up mine eyes unto the hills, from whence cometh my help.
—Ps. 121:1

When the King James translators interpreted this psalm, they should have put a question mark after the word help. "From whence cometh my help," is not a statement but a question that David answers in the next verse. "My help comes from the Lord who made the heavens and earth." God has revealed Himself to humans in nature. We are told that the heavens declare the glory of God and the earth shows His handiwork; every day they speak to us, every night they declare to us, in a universal language, the glory and greatness of God. The next time you find yourself in the need of help or strength, just look around at God's creation, listen for His voice, just know that if He is big enough to create this universe, He certainly is big enough to help you in your hour of need.

OUR FATHER, we thank You for the exceeding greatness of Your power that You have made available to us when we call upon You. Thank You for inviting us to call in our day of trouble and Your promise that You would hear us, and answer us, and show us great and mighty things. Give us eyes to see Your glory, and ears to hear Your voice as You speak to us today through Your creation and through Your Son. We ask these favors in the name of Jesus our Lord. *Amen.*

CHUCK SMITH
Pastor, Calvary Chapel of Costa Mesa, Santa Ana, Calif.

I AM NOT ALONE

I am not alone, because the Father is with me.—John 16:32

Everyone dreads to be isolated. We intuitively know it is not good for us. Each of us tends to think our sorrow or difficulty is unique and separates us from more fortunate individuals. But the facts break this illusion. We are forever united by the common basic problem we must meet, and grow by overcoming. Discipline, courage, endurance are required of us all. We are not alone.

But human companionship is insufficient for the ultimate tests. Our extremity is God's opportunity. Our power, confidence, endurance, and courage are multiplied when we accept the faith that this is God's world. God is never defeated, never at a loss. He turns the wrath of humanity and makes it do His bidding. Nothing is going to be permanently lost; every sacrifice and self-giving will count. We can learn from this disaster, if we will listen to God, so it never need be endured again. Christ comes to us as God's witness, God's proof of His intimate fatherly care and love. Christ is this moment fulfilling His promise. "Lo, I am with you always, even unto the end of the world."

Whenever lonely or low in spirit, the great affirmation, "I am not alone, because the Father is with me. Christ is my constant companion. God is understanding, guiding, empowering me. I am not alone," can strengthen and hold me steady if I repeat it several times each day.

HEAVENLY FATHER, amid so many changes which confuse, I am grateful that Thou art the same yesterday, today, and forever. I thank Thee that I am not alone, that Thou art closer than breathing and nearer than hands and feet. *Amen.*

RICHARD C. RAINES
Hennepin Avenue Methodist Church, Minneapolis, Minn.

FORMULA FOR A SOLDIER'S SUCCESS

Have not I commanded thee? Be strong and of a good courage; be not . . . dismayed: for the Lord thy God is with thee whithersoever thou goest.—Josh. 1:9

One of the greatest words of encouragement and advice ever given in a time of emergency is found in the ninth verse of the first chapter of Joshua. It is the word of Jehovah spoken to Joshua, who had suddenly found himself in charge of an expedition involving the ultimate conquest of a savage and powerful nation.

Three things were important to him as he accepted this difficult commission: to be strong, to be of good courage, and to be undismayed. Here was the demand for physical fitness—his task was too great for a weakling: here was the demand for moral fitness—his job could not be carried out by a coward; here was the demand for intellectual fitness—his expedition was doomed to failure if he was not sufficiently intelligent to estimate its dangers and surmount the dismay that a realization of peril is likely to cause.

But the reason for these clear words is summed up in the last line of the famous text: "for Jehovah thy God is with thee whithersoever thou goest." This formula for physical, emotional, and intellectual stamina has not been surpassed by any later statement, and it is as necessary today as it ever was.

ETERNAL GOD, who hast ordained the laws by which we must live, and who hast not changed in thy love for your children; give us wisdom, courage, and strength to do Thy will as each day reveals it. Through Jesus Christ our Lord. *Amen.*

EDWIN MCNEILL POTEAT
Euclid Avenue Baptist Church, Cleveland, Ohio

THE WORDS WE LIVE WITH

By thy words thou shalt be justified, and by thy words thou shalt be condemned.—Matt. 12:37

What words do we live with? What we say and think we tend to become. If our words are ignoble, they pull us down. If our words are depressing, they weaken us. We need noble and challenging words which can enlarge the horizons of our minds. Do we live with the word *courage*? Courage—not fear—will be our best protection. If our knees shake, let's kneel on them.

In times of testing we can live with the word *God*. Prophets of the Bible believed that the crises of history were God's judgment. We too believe that life is inescapably moral. We feel that the chaos of our civilization is due to the moral collapse of our lives. When we make material progress or armed might our god, we get into trouble.

A famous story, "The Lost Word," tells of a young man who crowded God out of his life. He lived happily for a time, but when things began to crash he was afraid and tried to pray. He could not speak the word *God* and therefore could not formulate his prayer. In desperation he discovered that he could not live without regaining the "lost word." Has God been lacking in our conversation? Have we been giving way to fear, to cynicism, and to despair? We will be strong if we bow oftener in God's presence. He can help us find the words we should live with.

O GOD, our Eternal Father, grant us the courage to carry on when the sky is dark and our work is hard. Be with us when we are weary, when fear torments us, when doubts assail our minds. Keep us conscious day by day that we live in Thy presence and that nothing can separate us from Thy love. May we carry on as builders of Thy Kingdom of freedom and peace. *Amen.*

ROBERT MERRILL BARTLETT
Longmeadow Community Church, Springfield, Mass.

LOVE AND HATE

There is no fear in love.—1 John 4:18

A well-known psychologist who answers questions in a newspaper once stated that love does not bind people together in a common cause. It takes hate to do this—so he said.

We must acknowledge, if we are not afraid to face facts as they are, that this seems to be true in the world today. With diabolical efficiency some of the rulers of the world are successfully welding their people and resources into a great unit with a single purpose and are doing it with the fires of hate.

It is our faith as Christians, abundantly proved by history, that hate as a unifying force lasts only a short time. In the end it destroys, not those against whom it is directed, but those in whom it is generated.

Love, a continual and undiminished flow of goodwill toward all men, is the only force which lasts and the only power which prevails. It was love which prompted God to send His Son into the world. It was love which caused Jesus to give up His divine prerogatives and endure humiliation and death. It was love which carried the Gospel down the stream of the years, and it was love which made the Church the mightiest influence in the world. There is power in love—wonder-working power—which will one day fill the earth with peace, for God is Love.

OUR FATHER, we praise and bless Thee for Thine unspeakable gifts to Thy wayward children. As we approach Thee in worship, we pray that we may be lifted up above the low plain of our sinful lives into realms of spiritual communion with Thee. There may our troubled spirits be quiet-ed, our sinful hearts be cleansed, and our selfish wills be transformed into glad submission to Thy perfect will. We ask for Jesus' sake. *Amen.*

STUART R. OGLESBY
Central Presbyterian Church, Atlanta, Ga.

AN OLD CAMP STORY

God forbid it me, that I should do this.—1 Chron. 11:19

A very human story of camp life is told in the scripture noted above. David and his men were fighting as guerillas. Life was hard. Water was bad. In a moment of homesickness, David, not thinking anyone would take him seriously, said he longed for water from the hometown well, which was then in enemy hands. Three brave warriors slipped out. At the risk of their lives they got by the enemy and brought back water from the well by Bethlehem's gate. Of course David was pleased. Who wouldn't be? But he was sobered, too; these men had risked their lives for a selfish whim of his. He could not drink such water. So he poured it out to God. It was too precious for any selfish use.

So with our lives. They are ours in trust. Parents, schools, churches, and a great heritage have made us what we are. We must not use life selfishly. Only as we pour it out for God in unselfish service is it worthy. God forbid that I should use my life for mean ends, for selfish indulgence, or even that I should throw it away foolishly. Rather let it be poured out for God and for others in noble service, for the great cause of justice and righteousness.

O GOD, who hast given us life and hast breathed into our bodies the Divine Spirit, forbid that I should waste my life in folly or in shame. Rather let all my powers be for the blessing of others, and let my strength be poured out in noble service for God and humanity in the Spirit of Jesus. *Amen.*

CASS ARTHUR REED
Pilgrim Congregational Church, Pomona, Calif.

VISIONS OF YOUTH

Whereupon, O king Agrippa, I was not disobedient unto the heavenly visit.—Acts 26:19

Before his judge Paul explains his Christian career as obedience to the call from the highest in his young manhood out on the Damascus road. He describes it as a "heavenly vision," and he did not overstate his experience. It is for every young person. The prophet Joel proclaimed such promise of God: "Your young men shall see visions." Isaiah's vision of the Lord one day in church is but another illustration of how the static always becomes dynamic before the unveiled Throne.

All life is conditioned by vision. Sight is a gift, but seeing is the finest art in the world. Life depends on how we see things, for the measure of a person is the measure of his or her vision. It is the difference between the stonemason and the sculptor, the carpenter and the architect, the housepainter and the artist. It leads the race ever onward.

Life is constructed along lines of vision. The vision of the mind is knowledge. The vision of the conscience is duty. The vision of the heart is love. The vision of the soul is faith. These are the four great cornerstones of character and consecration and incomparable career. And life is consecrated only in obedience to the highest vision. Paul's explanation of his life is the secret of every great life—to find God's will and to do it.

OUR FATHER, we thank Thee for the vision of youth, even the heavenly vision. Help us so obediently to follow in the footsteps of Him, the Light of the World, that someday we shall be with Him on those peaks on which no shadow falls. In His name. *Amen.*

W. F. POWELL
First Baptist Church, Nashville, Tenn.

COME

Ye will not come to me, that ye might have life.—John 5:40

If you should be in Scotland and some friends were to invite you into their house, they would likely open the door and say, "Come awa', come awa'." Rather strange, isn't it? We say, "Come in." If your Scottish friends wished to make their invitation unusually warm, they would say, "Come awa' by."

Are not all of these meanings to be found in God's gracious invitation to us in Christ—"Come"? First, "Come away!"—away from sin, away from darkness, away from worry. But also, "Come in!"—into purity, into light, into peace; away from the life you have been living into that which you may live in and through me. Better still, "Come by!"—by me in truest fellowship and communion. "Come" is a little word, but so full of meaning. "Come away! Come in! Come by!"

HEAVENLY FATHER, I thank Thee that Thy gracious invitation means even me. Help me to give it the full, unreserved response which it deserves. "When thou saidst, Seek ye my face; my heart said unto thee, Thy face, Jehovah, will I seek." In Jesus' name. *Amen.*

J. CALVIN REID
First Presbyterian Church, Columbus, Ga.

THE ONLY ALTERNATIVE

I say unto you, Love your enemies, bless them that curse you, do good to them that hate you, and pray for them which despitefully use you, and persecute you.—Matt. 5:44

Many young Muslims were seated in our evangelistic room. One of them brought up the oft-repeated assertion that the principles laid down by Christ in the Sermon on the Mount are neither possible nor practical with human nature as it is. We might have admitted that human nature must be changed by the One who alone can give such a new heart, and we did this later, but at the time it was not necessary for us to answer.

A thoughtful young man in the group replied to the assertion somewhat as follows: "I see that this suggestion of Christ may seem too idealistic; but if the world is to have peace, what alternative is there to the spirit of love for our enemies? For example, if a man throws a stone at me and I toss one back at him, where can the thing end until one of us lies with a broken head? But if I answer to the stone by inviting him into the tea house to have a glass of tea while we talk the matter over, we might come out friends with both our heads whole and no blood flowing from wounds on our bodies. In addition it would be a lot safer for the spectators if no stones were flying around."

He had brought before us a parable such as Jesus loved to use. How to get the spirit of the Golden Rule and the admonition to love our enemies working in the hearts of individuals and the councils of nations is the greatest problem before our present world.

O LORD, daily we ask Thy forgiveness in the prayer that Thy Son taught us. Daily we ask that that forgiveness may be according to the measure of our forgiveness of others. Help that we shall learn to forgive until seventy times seven; help that we shall discover how to walk the second mile. In Jesus' name. *Amen.*

J. CHRISTY WILSON
Missionary, Tabiz, Iran

DIFFICULTY AND DANGER

I have fought a good fight, I have finished my course, I have kept the faith.—2 Tim. 4:7

During the dark hours of late summer 1940, Winston Churchill said to his people: "Let us brace ourselves to our duty and so bear ourselves that if the British Commonwealth and Empire lasts for a thousand years, people will still say, 'This was their finest hour!'"

It is human nature to see difficulty and danger as altogether bad. But it is often the case that the finest and noblest things we know come from situations which are so hard and perilous that no one would deliberately want them. They do, indeed, destroy some people; but some people are cleansed and strengthened and made so heroic by them that the world is lifted a little nearer to God because of them.

It was so with St. Paul. His life was packed full of difficulty and hardship. Beaten, stoned, shipwrecked, imprisoned, deserted by friends, persecuted by enemies, bearing always "a thorn in the flesh," he was still not broken. These only served to increase the stature of his mind and heart. For through them all he "fought a good fight . . . kept the faith." And he would say to us in the difficult days which are a part of our life's portion, "Fight a good fight, keep the faith; for there is laid up for you"—and for those who will be inspired by you—"a crown of righteousness."

GRACIOUS GOD, whom to know and serve is life eternal, we thank Thee that in the hard hours of life Thou art our Companion and our Friend. We praise Thy name that Thou art near to hear our call. Add to our strength and courage; keep us faithful to our faith and steadfast in our fight for righteousness. We trust Thee. We commit ourselves to Thee. Thou canst sustain us, and Thou wilt. Through Jesus Christ. *Amen.*

RUFUS WICKER
First Methodist Church, Jacksonville, Fla.

WINGS

And I said, Oh that I had wings like a dove! for then would I fly away and be at rest.—Ps. 55:6

How human was this troubled psalmist. He had lost temporarily his song and wanted to get away from everything. Trouble had caught him off guard, and he sought an escape through fearful prayer. It was right for him to pray in the time of trouble, but it was wrong to ask for wings to get him away from it. We must be brave enough to face life's hard realities. Wherever we are and whatever happens, we must make the best of things as they are. We have no better opportunity to witness for God than when trouble invades the soul.

Spiritual readiness is essential to life's successful defense. The Caesars were not dethroned with the Christian religion at ease. When early Christianity stood up to life's brutal facts, the crowns of empire were buried in the dust of the centuries. Our warring world is not too much for God to handle. But we must experience more the power and presence of Almighty God and the salvation of His Holy Son. We must keep in our history that religious experience which "hath made and preserved us a nation."

We used wings to lift us up. "They that wait upon the Lord. . . . shall mount up with wings as eagles." Let us in Him be lifted into the confidence and strength of redeemed character. Confidence in the triumph of righteousness! Strength of purpose that a new Christianity shall be born from this travail!

GOD OF THE PSALMIST, we thank Thee that Thy servant recovered his happy song and the courage of prayer. Let not our faith in life depart from us and uphold us by the unfailing strength of Thy Everlasting Arms. Keep us loyal to our best selves, our high callings, and unto Thee and Thy Christ. *Amen.*

ROY L. TAWES
Washington Methodist Church, Hurlock, Md.

CHOSEN TO SUFFER

They therefore departed from the presence of the council, rejoicing that they were counted worthy to suffer dishonor for the name.
                                                                —Acts 5:41 ARV

All of us are called upon to suffer in one way or another. Much of our suffering goes to waste because it is not geared up with an all-compelling purpose. A great cause, such as liberty, chooses those who are big enough to suffer, who "can take it." It chooses people who have the stuff in them to endure hardships; who can laugh at privations; who are willing to give up privileges, comforts, and ease. It chooses people like the apostles who, after being treated in a most shameful way and cruelly flogged, came from that experience rejoicing that they were counted worthy to suffer for the name of Christ.

Great causes have a way of choosing people who are worthy to suffer. And it is through those who suffer that great causes come to victory. The highest blessings that we enjoy today came in this way. Christ on the cross, Washington at Valley Forge, Lincoln baited by newspapers and even by his cabinet members, are a few among many who were chosen to suffer for great purposes and were found worthy—bringing victory to the cause that chose them.

In these days the great cause of liberty is again choosing people to suffer for its sake. Shall we who are chosen be found worthy?

OUR FATHER, we are being called upon to suffer for the sake of all people everywhere. The great cause of liberty, with all that it means, is calling for people who are worthy. Wilt Thou make us worthy in every way. Keep the high purpose of freedom uppermost in our hearts and cleanse us from all selfishness. Dedicate us anew to the high cause of world unity and give us the victory of an enduring peace. And so shall our suffering be not in vain. In the Spirit of Christ we pray. *Amen.*

DOVERT WALTON MCELROY
First Christian Church, El Paso, Tex.

IT MEANS SOMETHING TO LIVE

Even from everlasting to everlasting, thou art God.—Ps. 90:2

Everything has some kind of a "big idea." This is true of our lives. They mean something. Your life gets its meaning from God. My life also gets its meaning from God. When our faith in God is strong, we can see beyond the present confusion. We can realize that our lives are related to something permanent. Just now we are destroying bridges, ships, and every kind of equipment which the enemy might use against us. But it will not be long before we go to building. God will see to that. He will make something of this present struggle in which we are engaged. He will help us as we work out a new world.

We are not working and sacrificing in vain. We have faith that God will make the whole thing mean something. Such a faith helps us to discover the "big idea" behind life today. God thinks that everyone of us has great value. He will not let what we do be lost. "I believe in God, the Father Almighty, Maker of heaven and earth." These familiar words mean something.

O LORD, "from everlasting to everlasting, thou art God." We would hold this fact clearly before us today. Help us to see what it really means and to live accordingly. *Amen.*

C. A. BOWEN
Editor of Church School Publications
The Methodist Church, Nashville, Tenn.

A TRUST THAT TRIUMPHS

Blessed are they that have not seen, and yet have believed.—John 20:29

The enemies of Jesus spoke a profound truth when they said, "He trusted in God." That trust did not prevent his dying upon the cross, but it did release the power of God to perform the miracle of the resurrection on Easter. We modern Christians sometimes demand that our trust in God shall guarantee us health, riches, and wisdom. That cannot be, but our trust will release the power of God in our lives to enable us to be victorious over whatever circumstances may surround. If you have not surrendered to God in a way that enables His power to come into your life, don't hesitate. Do so now.

Paul, with the power of Christ in his life, was able to say, "I can do all things through Christ which strengtheneth me." You will find that the burdens of life can be carried when you have this power. The temptation which led to sin will now be rejected, and you will experience the joy of being bigger than the temptation because Jesus dwells in your heart. With Paul you will say, "It is no longer I that live, but Christ liveth in me."

OUR FATHER, we do not understand how Thy power can come into the lives of individuals, but we have seen it happen, and we have opened our hearts to Thee that Thy power may come into us through Jesus Christ. *Amen.*

FRANKLIN MINCK
High Street Church of Christ, Akron, Ohio

FAITH AMID PERPLEXITY

Perplexed, yet not unto despair.—2 Cor. 4:8b ARV

How true is this phrase of many today! Surely this is a time of bewilderment. It is a time of great material progress and moral and spiritual decay. When the inventions and discoveries of individuals might be used in added joys, they are being used to bring deepest miseries to millions; when they might be the means of providing a more abundant way of life, they have become instruments of horrible death to multitudes.

The one unfailing antidote for despair is faith—faith that, beyond our power to understand, God's purpose is being worked out. Though the universe collapse, the person of faith will be undismayed beneath its ruins. "I had fainted, unless I had believed to see the goodness of the Lord in the land of the living." Faith does not save us from being perplexed, but it does save us from slipping into the abyss of despair. In life's most soul-searching experiences the people of faith will go on. They will also be able to give back the encouraging word to others as did Bunyan's pilgrim in crossing the river of death, "Be of good cheer, my brother, for I feel the bottom and it is sound."

O GOD, our Father, Thou art the One alone to whom we can go for the strength and the grace sufficient for our souls. Thou dost break the power of choking doubt and free us to breathe again the pure air of faith. In the midst of experiences which we cannot explain, give us strength and patience to wait on Thee. Help us to know that we shall never be forsaken of Thee nor left alone to face the issues of life. Guide us that we may love Thee more and joyfully obey Thee. May we ever hear our Master saying to us, "I am with you alway, even unto the end of the world." And may the peace which the world can neither give nor take away guard our hearts and our thoughts in Christ Jesus. *Amen.*

CLYDE V. HICKERSON
Baptist Temple, San Antonio, Tex.

YOU BELONG TO GOD

Ye are not your own. For ye are bought with a price: therefore glorify God in your body, and in your spirit, which are God's.—1 Cor. 6:19–20

From a town out on Long Island, not far from New York City, a young lad was leaving home to enter college. His good mother, very solicitous for her boy, made all sorts of preparations and gave the young man much good advice. The father said very little; but when the day came for the departure, he went with his son over to New York to see him off. When the time came for the boy to board the train, the father took the lad's hand in his, gave it a hearty squeeze, and said simply, "Now, lad, don't forget whose son you are."

What a glory to remember who they are that are depending upon us, and those to whom we truly belong! In the highest reaches of that thought, we stand face to face with our Lord.

Don't forget whose child you are.

O MASTER OF MY LIFE, help me to live this day mindful of the highest claims that are upon me. If temptation comes for me to be weak, to betray any trust, to be less than my better self, may I see the faces of those who love and trust me rising before me, and bidding me remember whose I am. I give thanks today for the strong yet gentle Christ. May my spirit find strength in His strength. May my will be strengthened and enforced by devotion to His will. In His name. *Amen.*

WARREN C. TAYLOR
Forest Avenue Baptist Church, Des Moines, Iowa

FAITH OF OUR FATHERS, LIVING STILL

These four were born to the giant in Gath, and fell by the hand of David, and by the hand of his servants.—2 Sam. 21:22

Our attention has been so fixed upon the story of David and Goliath that we are apt to forget that the giant had sons and relatives who later rose up to threaten Israel's peace and David's life. Goliath was slain, but four other giants took his place; and David himself towards the end of his life had to reckon with them, and David's followers had to engage them in battle.

If David's followers had merely indulged in emotional talk about the brave days of old, instead of reproducing his spirit in their own age, they would have dishonored the aged veteran and darkened the future of their children, for Goliath's sons were seeking to subdue the earth.

Our text has an application to our personal life. We each know our civil danger. For one like Peter it is a tendency to succumb to environment. For another like Nicodemus it is ingrained prejudice. For another like John it is hot temper. For another like Augustine it is sensuality. For another like Gehazi it is covetousness. But whatever the giant that threatens us, ultimate triumph awaits the one who perseveres.

The crowning confidence of David as he faced Goliath was his faith in God. "The Lord," he had declared to Saul, "will deliver me out of the hand of this Philistine." And we may be sure that was the confidence also of David's followers as they battled with Goliath's sons. They were imitators of David's deeds because they were sharers of David's faith.

ETERNAL GOD, our ancestors looked to Thee and not in vain. Thou didst safely conduct them. Make us worthy of the good and true who have gone before us and of all our hopes as disciples of Jesus Christ, in whose name we pray. *Amen.*

ROBERT B. WHYTE
The Old Stone Church, Cleveland, Ohio

KEEP THE LIGHT

The light is still shining in the darkness, for the darkness has never put it out.—John 1:5 (GOODSPEED)

One can imagine the struggle of a tiny candle flame to survive the currents of air in a dark and drafty house. Likewise, we can imagine the light of hope and faith and goodness fighting to survive the fierce rushing darkness which has swept against it during the centuries. But the light still shines! And today, that light in which we have put our faith is exposed to the black clouds and engulfing currents of war, of bitterness, of hate, cruelty, and death. Will the light be extinguished? We are convinced that it will not be. We will not let it be put out. Though we must fight and do devilish things, yet we will keep the light. We will keep it guarded in our minds, in our hearts, in our faith and hope and determination. Yes, by our deeds and, if necessary, by our lives we will help to keep it. For it is the light that counts. It is the light that makes us children of God. It is the light that gives promise to the future. God is in that light.

O GOD, we are truly glad that we have been permitted to perceive and to appreciate the light—the light of life, the light of better things which may be, the light of hope, of faith, of love, of new worlds to be made, of a new and true way, of a redeeming Christ, of Thy Kingdom on earth. Grant that we may never lose the vision or the faith of that light. And no matter what comes, or what we must do, help us, O God, to keep the light burning. For Jesus' sake. *Amen.*

E. C. FARNHAM
Executive Secretary, Church Federation of Los Angeles, Calif.

HOPE

It is good that a man should both hope and quietly wait for the salvation of the Lord.—Lam. 3:26

Hope sustains when everything else fails; through hope we renew the struggle when all seems to be lost. A forlorn hope is far better than no hope. There is hope that "maketh ashamed." I recall clients who thought they had invented a new oil burner which would make them immensely wealthy. The thing was a total failure; afterward they could not think of it without being ashamed.

You see it depends on whether our hope is well founded. If we hope in the promises of God we have a hope which "maketh not ashamed"—a hope which will not be deferred until it "maketh the heart sick"—a hope which is based on God's promises, will take us through life, give us strength for every test and duty. But true hope goes further. It is "an anchor of the soul . . . which entereth into that within the veil."

Many anchors drag in the storm and the ships they were holding drift onto the rocks. Hope anchored in the promises of God will hold. It goes beyond this life.

Our hope is based on a Person, a great Friend, and more than a friend, One whose love surpasses even the love of a brother or a mother. He gave His life for our sins. Since He has loved so much, should we not trust Him?

FATHER IN HEAVEN, I can hope in You, not because I claim to be perfect. I know I have fallen short again and again and still am below the standard of goodness which You must require, but I hope in Your love and mercy because You have made it plain that You love the weak and sinful, and that Christ has died for my sins. Give me the help I need today that I may be strong against temptation and faithful in every duty. Help me to be a good soldier of Jesus Christ. *Amen.*

PAUL B. FISCHER
Attorney, Chicago, Ill.

BEYOND TRAGEDY IS TRIUMPH

Thou art my hope in the day of evil.—Jer. 17:17

There are two points of view: pessimism and optimism, cowardice and courage, defeat and victory. On the one hand there is lack of hope and faith in God, in people, and in the future of goodness. On the other hand there is confidence in the Eternal Goodness, in the divinity in human beings, and in the ultimate triumph of the right. The reason why Christians can believe in the ultimate triumph of righteousness is because their hope is in God—in a God who created a good world, though the world is not now good; in a good God powerful enough, with the help of some of His children, finally to destroy evil in the world.

This is the thought that should grip us in these days—beyond tragedy is triumph. No matter how dark and depressing things may be at a particular moment, they will get better. They must get better if our creed is true that "God is infinite in wisdom, goodness, and love." A Canadian woman once said, "There's only one thing to do, keep on doing what we think is right. God will make things come out right in the end."

With God's help we can take the next step, and then the next step, lending a helping hand to a distressed person beaten and broken by the wayside, and clearing the Jerusalem-Jericho highways of life of all cutthroats and robbers. And we can look up and trust in God.

MY GOD, Thou art my hope in the day of evil. I need Your help. I have followed the ways of the world. I knew better. I ask You to forgive me. And I ask You for strength and love to be better and to do better. Give me courage to be true to truth and to be loyal to Jesus Christ. I make now, the full and glad surrender of my life, all I am and all I have, to You. Use me in Your service. I ask in Jesus' name. *Amen.*

GORDON C. SPEER
First Congregational Church, Ypsilanti, Mich.

HUMAN FRIENDSHIP

There is a friend that sticketh closer than a brother. —Prov. 18:24

In that rare and wonderful book, *The Snow Goose*, by Paul Gallico, there is the story of a lonely man. His body was warped, but his heart was filled with love for wild things. He was ugly to look upon, but he created great beauty. He was a hunchback, and his left arm was crippled. Paul Gallico in speaking of him says that while he had mastered his handicap the thing that drove him into seclusion was his failure to find anywhere a return of the warmth that flowed from him.

That last sentence haunts me. The thing that drove him into seclusion was his failure to find anywhere the return for the warmth that he felt for others. How many people about us have that terrible experience! They feel love; they want friendship; but day after day as warmth flows out from their hearts they feel nothing come back. They are entirely and miserably alone. They are ever seeking what they cannot find. They are ever striving to find something which they can't experience. True, they can find something in an intimate fellowship with God, but no matter how vital is their relationship with God they need also a sense of intimacy with at least one human person.

It is hard for the heart to reach up farther than it reaches out. May it never be said of us that others are driven into seclusion because they failed to find from us a return of the warmth that flowed from them to us.

OUR FATHER, we do thank Thee with all our hearts for the power of human fellowship. We do thank Thee, O God, that one heart has the capacity to save another and to provide for its fulfillment and its completion. Lead us from day to day to find that fulfillment in other hearts, and help other hearts to find it in us, that together we may find it in Thee. *Amen.*

ROY A. BURKHART
First Community Church, Columbus, Ohio

REMEMBER McGREGGOR

Gird up the loins of your mind, be sober, and hope to the end.
                                                    —1 Pet. 1:13

Once I attended an important committee meeting, of which the chairman was named McGreggor. Before the meeting he had given orders not to be disturbed. Yet the telephone rang. Because of its insistent ringing, he finally answered it. Almost immediately he fell on the floor in a dead faint, crying, "My daughter has been killed!" We called an ambulance and got him to a hospital—and the committee adjourned.

Imagine our surprise and joy when his secretary telephoned each of us later and said, "It wasn't Mr. McGreggor's daughter—it was his dog!" From that day to this, when anything looks bad to a member of that committee, he remarks, "Cheer up! Remember McGreggor." It has even become a common saying with people who never knew the man.

Recently I have been wondering about starting a slogan, "Remember Psalm 37." When someone comes to you upset and worried about something, why not say to him or her, "Remember Psalm 37"? This could not only be a great help to the individual but be doing real missionary work for Christ and His Church.

God as revealed in the Bible is an inexhaustible source of power and wisdom. There are strength and comfort for those who will use this mine of resources. Don't we owe it to God, to ourselves, and to our friends to shake off our inferiority complex and tell the world? This would be a simple and practical way of doing so.

O GOD, give us faith in what Thou canst do for us. May we each day use the help which is ours for the asking. May we stand firm, keep cool, and not fret, remembering that all things work together for good to those who love Thee. *Amen.*

ROGER W. BABSON
Statistician and Business Analyst, Babson Park, Mass.

THE FAITH THAT DOES NOT FAIL

I have prayed for thee, that thy faith fail not.—Luke 22:32

What a wonderful promise Jesus makes Peter. He had just instituted the sacrament of the Lord's Supper before leaving the upper room for the Garden of Gethsemane; and the disciples, Peter among them, were declaring their loyalty to Him, come what might. But Jesus turned and said to Peter: "Simon, behold, Satan hath desired to have you, that he may sift you as wheat: but I have prayed for thee, that thy faith fail not." There was danger not only that Peter would go down, but that he would be submerged beneath the flood.

Jesus' promise was fulfilled. Within a few hours, swept off his feet by the hostile atmosphere of the judgment hall and the pert words of the maid, Peter denied the Master with oaths and curses. Peter, however, did not lose his faith as Judas did; for Judas hanged himself, but Peter went out and wept bitterly—that is, he repented, and as a result was forgiven and restored to his discipleship. Neither did Peter's faith fail in the years which followed, but he was faithful unto death. Jesus' prayer for him was answered.

So in your hour of testing, whether it be in the hour of temptation, or danger, or death, remember that Jesus is praying for you, not that you have no trials, but that your faith fail not.

O LORD JESUS, help us to remember that as Thou didst pray for Peter, so wilt Thou pray for us that our faith fail not, but that we may meet bravely whatever may come. If, perchance, we do stumble and fail, may we also remember that Thou art waiting to forgive and to take us back into Thy fellowship. Help us to help others. So be Thou our Friend and Companion. *Amen.*

ALFRED J. SADLER
First Presbyterian Church, Jersey City, N.J.

THE REALITY OF GOD

My soul thirsteth for God, for the living God.—Ps. 42:2

One of the deepest needs of our day is to know God, for this is life. "Oh that I knew where I might find Him!" expresses the longing of all human hearts. How we long to know God, to grasp His reality!

When in some significant moment we come to stand amid the silence of eternity, when in our inmost being we have an awareness of life's abiding values, when in our thinking we have penetrated beyond speculations of theology, when in the purity of our hearts we have felt a freedom from selfish strife, then it is that we stand before God. Then we realize how trivial are our possessions, how insignificant are our speculations, how fruitless are our questions; for above all is God in all His majesty yet humility, in all His greatness yet simplicity, in all His Power yet tenderness. Only then can a we see life as it ought to be seen for we have caught a glimpse of the Eternal. In such a moment we cry out not, "What is God?" but, "Such knowledge is too wonderful for me; . . . I cannot attain unto it."

We find God in life. Moses found God in leading Israel out of bondage. Isaiah found God in serving his nation through one of its most critical periods. Jeremiah found God in the social, the political, the religious struggles of his day. Jesus found God as he sought "to heal the brokenhearted, to preach deliverance to the captives, and . . . to set at liberty them that are bruised." So to us God will become a reality as we seek to live His Spirit in life.

ETERNAL GOD, while all about us is change and decay, be Thou the abiding reality of life. Come to us in the moments of the deep silence of our soul and reveal Thy ways unto us. Lead us into the paths of loving service that we too like Jesus may build into our life the things that death can never destroy. *Amen.*

W. B. MATHEWS
Boulevard Congregational Church, Detroit, Mich.

COURAGE FROM FELLOWSHIP

Not forsaking the assembling of ourselves together.—Heb. 10:25

There are often times when we feel as though we were alone in our struggle to uphold the clean life. Elijah once thought that he only was serving God. All others had deserted to Baal. He wanted, as we might, to quit and die.

There is a sure cure for this despondency: seek out others who possess like purposes. The first Christians did this, assembling regularly, with one accord in one place. The first missionaries did not go into the pagan world alone. On the first mission went Barnabas, Paul, and Mark; on the second, Paul, Silas, and Timothy. Even Jesus dared not attempt the heroic life alone. He soon had His disciples about Him. Their presence was an actual aid to His divine living. Some experiences of healing, the Transfiguration and Gethsemane, He could not face alone. He must have at least Peter, James, and John with Him.

When I left home, my father's best advice was: "Seek out some church at once. There you will find those best able to uphold you in the Master's way." That can always be done. High-souled people are always accessible. Not too far off is a really live church of friendly believers in the Way, the Truth, and the Life. Within reach are the chaplain and other Christian soldiers, who are bravely holding fast that which is good. You need never strive alone. So Elijah learned; so Paul experienced; and so may you find if you are in earnest.

GRACIOUS MASTER, we thank Thee for those companions close about us whose clean lives and loyal faith strengthen ours. We praise Thee that Thou dost never leave us nor forsake us. Make us worthy of these our true companions who uplift us and believe in us. Hold Thou us fast that we may never fail them, ourselves, or Thee. *Amen.*

CHESTER WARREN QUIMBY
Methodist Church, Mifflinburg, Pa.

WORRY IS SIN

In nothing be anxious; but in everything . . . let your requests be made known unto God.—Phil. 4:6 ARV

Worry is fear of imaginary future ills. The scripture word for "worry" is "anxiety" in the Revised Version. Worry is definitely forbidden. "Be not anxious," said Jesus. "In nothing be anxious," said Paul. Jesus gave us two reasons why we should not worry. First, it is the practice of the heathen, who know no heavenly Father. Second, it is not only pagan; it is unnecessary, for your heavenly Father already knows what things you need. He can see down the future farther than you. He also knows the present better than you, including all inventory of the very hairs of your head. You see, worry for a Christian is foolish.

What then? What substitute? Prayer is the substitute. Here is something positive, something that expels fear, makes room for faith and peace to enter the heart. Never worry about anything, says Paul. Instead, in all crises and fears, pray to God, thanking Him in advance for His help to come. Then peace will spring to attention and stand guard at the heart's door.

Paul, although facing physical tortures and impending death, and suffering from a bodily defect, although troubled by thirty years' hostility of his Jewish compatriots, by constant backslidings among his converts, by the occasional desertion of trusted coworkers, by misunderstanding among prominent Christians, never had a nervous breakdown. He had the secret. He often said so. He was content in any situation, because he took all his troubles to his Lord, and thus found release from inner fears.

O FATHER, may our sin of worry be forgiven, for we have doubted Thy power and Thy goodness. We acknowledge Thee as greater than our fears, and we ask Thee to help us get the victory over today's foes as we seek to obey Thy will. *Amen.*

PAUL L. GROVE
Fairmount Avenue Methodist Church, St. Paul, Minn.

THOU SHALT

Ye have heard that it was said by them of old time, . . . but I say unto you.—Matt 5:21–22

Jesus was never merely negative. The Sermon on the Mount is the greatest sermon ever delivered because of that fact. Again and again, Jesus substituted some positive demand for an old restriction.

Jesus insisted that the old law was unalterably true, but He changed the emphasis from negative to positive. To accept Jesus' interpretation would just about make over the conception of the religious life for most of us. Instead of, "Thou shalt not kill," we have, "Thou shalt reverence life." The import of that is tremendous. Almost every relationship we have is included in it. Instead of, "Thou shalt not bear false witness against thy neighbor," Jesus says, "You not only don't talk about them; you do something for them." "Thou shalt not commit adultery," becomes, "Thou shalt think and act purity always." Negatives always limit, but the implications of positive conduct reach out in limitless ways.

The last thing Jesus was trying to do was to make religion too easy. He challenged us to live by His inner spirit, not by any code that could be narrowed into words. The thing that must happen in us is a change of spirit, of disposition, and an inner sensitiveness to the voice and touch of God upon our hearts. The truth of Christ must go down deep in us until it gets under every thought and purpose.

O LORD, to whom shall we go? Thou hast the words for both time and eternity. Forgive us our casual acceptance of Thy truth when Thou hast given it to us as the very soul of our life. May we hear Thy voice and value Thy truth as timeless and final. And may we heed it for our own life and for every relationship with others. In Christ's name. *Amen.*

PETER H. PLEUNE
Highland Presbyterian Church, Louisville, Ky.

KEEPING LIFE IN FOCUS

*The law of the Lord is perfect, converting the soul: the testimony of the
Lord is sure, making wise the simple.*—Ps. 19:7

Probably our greatest need in these days and under present circumstances is to see life in true focus. Reading the Nineteenth Psalm
suggests three ways in which we can gain an insight into this focus:

First, the eloquent words about the reliability of the outer world
remind us that conformity to God's laws should be kept steadily in mind.
The words themselves are so familiar that they need no commentary.

Second, the magnificent declaration of the moral uniformity of God's
orderly world needs to be repeated again and again. There is a justice in the
processes of nature and the processes of all human and spiritual relationships. We may trust God and His judgment and wait patiently in that trust.

Third, there is the world of the inner self. It is a part of nature and of
the moral order, but it has its ways of vexing us.

This inner world begins in doubt; it is hard to understand ourselves.
Hidden faults, sins of pride, mislead us. How Freud and recent psychology
underscore the Christian view about our sinfulness, our need of God's grace!

Yet this inner world finds fulfillment in disciplined aspiration, that
spoken words and hidden aspirations might be acceptable.

The whole psalm witnesses to the power which we find when we keep
life in steady focus.

GOD OF THE CONSTANT VISION, we turn to Thee for insights
which will abide. Help us to see life clearly and to see it whole! So may we
worship and serve Thee in spirit and in truth. In Christ's name we pray. *Amen.*

DAVID NELSON BEACH
Plymouth Congregational Church, Minneapolis, Minn.

GOD WITH US

What shall we then say to these things? If God be for us, who can be against us?—Rom. 8:31

In these days of anxiety and distress, the believing heart turns from human assurance to the divine revelation of protection.

In the eighth chapter of the epistle to the Romans the apostle Paul names the forces of evil arrayed against him. He tells how mighty they seem to be. Then he reveals how weak and ineffective these alarming powers really are, how the power which earnest, believing Christians possess makes them infinitely stronger than the marshaled might of evil. In the twenty-eighth and thirty-first verses he rings out his sublime message of trust: "We know that all things work together for good to them that love God. . . . What shall we then say to these things? If God be for us, who can be against us?"

This is a message that is greatly needed today. Not for generations have the embattled forces of evil been unleashed to do their worst for the world, as today. Things are not going well for many in the armed forces and in the homes today. There have been losses, disappointments, bereavements, sufferings. But to the one who really believes, whose faith rests upon a sure foundation, there comes this assuring thought: "This I know; for God is for me."

David, a hunted fugitive, in danger and in trouble, tells in the Fifty-sixth Psalm of the persecution by his enemies. But he declares, "What time I am afraid, I will trust in thee . . . in God I have put my trust . . . For God is for me."

ALMIGHTY GOD, we trust in Thee. Thou art our refuge. Thou dost help us in all times of need. Thou dost never fail us. Keep us true to Thee, through Jesus Christ our Lord. *Amen.*

HARRY NOBLE WILSON
Pastor Emeritus, Central Presbyterian Church, St. Paul, Minn.

THE STRONG SOLDIER

Thou therefore endure hardness, as a good soldier of Jesus Christ.
—2 Tim. 2:3

A Christian is sometimes compared to a soldier, sometimes to an athlete. Both symbols suggest vigor and strength. So St. Paul warns us that we must "wrestle," "run the straight race," "put on the whole armor of God," "fight the good fight of faith," "stand fast," "endure hardness, as a good soldier of Jesus Christ."

Sometimes nothing is harder in life than just to endure. There are two types of strength. There is the strength of the wind that sways the mighty oak, and there is the strength of the oak that withstands the power of the wind. There is the strength of the locomotive that pulls the heavy train across the bridge, and there is the strength of the bridge that holds up the weight of the train. One is active strength, the other is passive strength; one is the power to keep going, the other is the power to keep still; one the strength by which we overcome, the other is the strength by which we endure.

We sometimes say of others, "They can take it." The ability to "take it," to endure, must be an essential part of our equipment these days. To be able to take bad news without pessimism and reverses without losing our morale, to make sacrifices without self-pity, is essential. It appears that the struggle in which we are involved will be quite largely an endurance test. It will be decided not only by the strength of our material equipment but also by the adequacy of the armor which fortifies our spirits.

ETERNAL GOD, who hast promised that those who wait upon Thee shall renew their strength, arm us with might by Thy Spirit in our hearts. Keep our spirits clean, awake, resolute. We pray in the Spirit of Him who so endured that in the moment of seeming defeat He won His greatest victory. *Amen.*

HAROLD COOKE PHILLIPS
First Baptist Church, Cleveland, Ohio

WHERE OUR LIBERTY ENDS

Let no man seek his own, but every man another's wealth.
—1 Cor. 10:24

"We should not look after our own advantage but after that of our neighbor," is a better translation of the text noted above. A man was arrested. The judge said, "Why did you hit your neighbor on the nose?" "I was exercising on my lawn," the man replied. "My neighbor came along and as I swung my arms up and down and sideways, I hit him on the nose. Haven't I the liberty, your honor, to exercise on my own lawn?" "Yes," answered the judge. "But remember, your liberty ends where the other's nose begins."

Christians have the utmost freedom. But we exercise restraint for the sake of others. "All things are lawful unto me, but all things are not expedient." For example, it is not wrong to be kind to an unbeliever. But to be seen coming out of a tavern with one may be offensive to a weaker Christian, or may give a misleading view of our character to the world. So, while we have the freedom to come and go, it is restricted to what is good and salutary for others. Watch your conduct. It is not a question of personal advantage, but one of thoughtfulness for others, even as our blessed Lord came not to be ministered unto, but to minister, and to give His life a ransom for many.

MERCIFUL GOD, who hast made us free from the bondage of sin, fill us with the love of Thy dear Son that we may not use our freedom as a stumbling block to others. Rather teach us the way of self-denial, that others may see our good works, and glorify our Father which is in heaven. Through Jesus Christ. *Amen.*

W. P. CHRISTY
Lake of the Isles Church, Minneapolis, Minn.

Read Ps. 16:7–8, 11

✝

DIRECTION AT NIGHT

I praise you, Lord, for being my guide. Even in the darkest night, your teachings fill my mind. I will always look to you, as you stand beside me and protect me from fear . . . —Ps. 16:7–8

Driving at night is more difficult than driving during the daylight hours because it's more difficult to see what is ahead. Driving at night without lights is usually impossible. King David, who wrote this psalm, was a military person. He understood the need for good light at night. He understood that he needed protection from being afraid. As God's teachings filled his mind he could "see" even in the darkest night, and with God to protect him from fear, he had direction for life.

When it seems like you live in a continual "night," find the voice and the presence of God. God is available to you through His words in the Bible. At times He speaks through others, and sometimes the Holy Spirit can be heard. When we need direction at night, it's best to look where the light is shining. Follow God's voice to see the path that leads to joy.

O GOD, my Father, it seems dark, even during the daylight. Turn me always in the direction of the true light that comes from You. Help me to hear You speak and provide guidance that meets my needs today. Give me the ability to know truth and to act in ways that are just and right. Fill my life with joy—joy that comes from being at Your side. I pray in the name of Jesus. *Amen.*

H. DAVID BRANDT
President, George Fox University, Newberg, Ore.

A CITY UNDER SIEGE

Blessed be the Lord, for God has wondrously shown steadfast love to me when I was beset as a city under siege.—Ps. 31:21

A prayer for deliverance from enemies, Psalm 31, brought great comfort to me on September 11, 2001. Like so many of the psalms, it is brutally honest with God. The writer pulls no punches in affirming the feelings of both fear and trust. We human beings are complex, and it is possible to be afraid of the situation we are in and at the same time to trust God to see us through.

On September 11, we gathered as a community in the afternoon to lift to God our prayers for the victims, rescue workers, leaders, and others. The images of devastation in New York City loomed before us as we read the psalmist's words, ". . . for God has wondrously shown steadfast love to me when I was beset as a city under siege." As you face fearful situations, I encourage you to share your feelings with God, knowing that God hears your cries for help. "Be strong, and let your heart take courage, all you who wait for the Lord" (Ps. 31:24).

GOD OF THE MOUNTAINTOP AND OF THE TRENCHES, God of the sanctuary and the city, when I am afraid, be my Rock. May I find in You a fortress which is not a barrier to loving others, but a stronghold from which to act. May my trust in You be stronger than my fear. Knowing that You are closer to me than my own breath, I pray. *Amen.*

LAURA S. SUGG
Chaplain and Assistant Professor, Agnes Scott College, Decatur, Ga.

THE UPWARD REACH

Be still, and know that I am God.—Ps. 46:10

Close proximity to great historical events may make it impossible to appraise them. Two men died at thirty-three: Alexander, having conquered the world; Jesus Christ, having been condemned to the death of the cross. Long-range vision alone would enable anyone to see that the cross would outlast the throne by countless generations.

History teaches that dictators, conquerors, oppressors never have the final word; that belongs to God. Our chief concern ought to be to remain in harmony with the will and purpose of God. Therefore it is highly important that we keep in constant touch with God so that His guidance, the inspiration of His leadership, may never be lost to us.

> Thou hast put the upward reach
> In the heart of man.

Nor will we ever be satisfied until we are where God wants us to be— doing His will. And this is possible only if we go on believing that in the end God will have the final word. Take the long look with God and you cannot make a mistake.

OUR HEAVENLY FATHER, help us to remember Thy Son Jesus Christ, our Lord. Give us His strength, His wisdom, His Spirit, His winsomeness. Keep our faces ever toward the light and our feet from forbidden paths, that we may not forge a chain by our misdeeds. Walk with us today; be our Guide, our Counselor, and Friend, that nothing we say or do may dishonor Thee or need undoing. Give us a sense of obligation in our work, and may we do it as in Thy presence. *Amen.*

B. JOHNSON REEMTSMA
"The Tall Philosopher"
Well-known Radio Commentator and Former Chaplain, U.S.A.

CHRIST IS THE VICTORY

Thanks be to God, which giveth us the victory through our Lord Jesus Christ.—1 Cor. 15:57

We do not have sufficient strength in ourselves with which to meet life, and our contemporary world situation is reemphasizing this fact in a most painful way. Our hope is that we shall gain courage enough to face whatever life can bring. We must acquire the spirit of heroism.

Emerson once said that a hero is no braver than anyone else; he or she is only brave five minutes longer. The daring of Christ still astounds us. He shared our bitter lot even to despair, but He was able to carry on, not merely for five minutes longer but continuously. He had unconquerable power in His soul.

His victory is for us. Spiritual fellowship is fundamental—by relying on His presence we are able to triumph.

> Once it was my working,
> His it hence shall be.
> Once I tried to use Him,
> Now He uses me.

Christianity guarantees that the Divine Spirit can work in us and through us. This is the victory of Christ!

OUR FATHER, we are happy to have the opportunity of living triumphantly and gloriously, even though we face so many adverse circumstances. We realize, however, that only as we trust in Thee can we be sure of victory. It is for this reason that we seek the personal presence of Thine own powerful personality for our hearts and lives. May Thy Spirit triumph in us and through us. We ask it in His name. *Amen.*

G. RAY JORDAN
First Methodist Church, Charlotte, N.C.

PROVIDENCE AND THE INDIVIDUAL

We know that to them that love God all things work together for good,
even to them that are called according to his purpose.
                                                    —Rom. 8:28 ARV

We do *not* know that to them that love God all things work together for physical security and comfort. On the contrary, we know that servants of God are likely to get hurt, for the business in which they are engaged is dangerous business. They are called to be spokespersons of God and His purpose in history, and not merely the voice of a public opinion rooted in ignorance or fear or greed. They are called to devote their lives to the welfare of others, the underprivileged, the dispossessed, the exploited. They are called to work for a society which, being organized on the basis of justice and cooperation for the good of all, will make for peace and not for war. They are called to a task which ever has been costly and is likely to be costly for a long time to come.

The wonderful thing we know is that to them that love God, all things work together for moral victory and spiritual triumph. They are not given immunity from the common lot, which, indeed, they would scorn to ask for. They are given wisdom and strength adequate to the task to which they are called. They are given the secret for all conditions of living, so that nothing is able to down them. They are given the victory over sin and suffering and the fear of death. They are lifted into a fellowship with God through which they are able to stand anything that can happen to them on earth and from which neither life nor death can separate them.

O GOD OUR FATHER, who art ever with us, be Thou our light when the day is dark; be Thou our courage when we feel afraid; be Thou our strength when the flesh is weak; be Thou our hope when our own hopes fail; be Thou at all times our help and our salvation. Through Jesus Christ our Lord. *Amen.*

                                                    ERNEST F. TITTLE
                                        First Methodist Church, Evanston, Ill.

MANPOWER

Not by might, nor by power, but by my spirit, saith the Lord.
— Zech. 4:6

"Manpower" is a familiar word. The ebb and flow of fortunes in war are explained by manpower for fighting or for the production of implements of war. But this is more than a physical term. One cannot measure manpower by counting troops or laborers in the factory or the members on a church roll. Statistics can't record all of the resources. Scripture says that under certain conditions one shall "chase a thousand, and two put ten thousand to flight." It may not always be wise to insist upon these proportions. But the principle is everlastingly valid. The physical strength of a person must always be added to the strength of his or her soul and power for marshaling the resources of truth, righteousness, and love.

The universe is synchronized with the moral realities of God. It ultimately defeats hate, dishonesty, and unrighteousness. Because it is a moral universe, it works together with love, truth, and righteousness. When armed with these, we find ourselves working together with God and time, regardless of the mere manpower operating to the contrary. Conscious of these reinforcements, we all have a faith, a courage, and a determination that makes us superior to physical power alone.

A pure heart, a righteous cause, and a faith in a Divine Presence provide a strength sufficient to every task, however difficult.

"O GOD, our help in ages past, our hope for years to come," sustain us for every task with the consciousness of Thy Presence, Truth, and Love. Grant that our inner power may never fail, however strong the temptations or fierce the conflicts. Help us to know that "with Thee we can do all things needful." Prepare our hearts for this day's tasks, we pray. *Amen.*

J. RICHARD SPANN
Laurel Heights Methodist Church, San Antonio, Tex.

WINGS

> *But they that wait upon the Lord shall renew their strength; they shall mount up with wings as eagles.*—Isa. 40:31

The resources of a faith in God are very great. Victor Hugo's lines express the trust people have when they know God has given them the means of deliverance from circumstances of danger and defeat:

> Let us be like a bird, for a moment perched
> On a frail branch while he sings.
> He feels it bend, but he sings his song,
> For he knows that he has wings.

The Christian faith is rooted in reality. Nothing can shake its axioms, and no changes in human society can outmode its truths. God remains the greatest personality in the vast universe, and humanity continues to be the supreme concern of God's creative and redemptive operations. A world in the flames of war is still the footstool of the Eternal and even its "wrath shall praise Him." And beyond the wreckage of such a world, that lonely, lovely Figure of the centuries, the Carpenter of Nazareth, will build the world anew.

ETERNAL FATHER, grant us such impressions of Thy Holy Presence as will be needful for us this day. May the beauty we see and the evidences of kindness and love we behold in the lives of those we chance to meet reassure our faith in the final triumph of the spiritual laws of the Kingdom of Thy Son, our Lord and Savior. *Amen.*

ADIEL J. MONCRIEF
Walmer Road Baptist Church, Toronto, Ont.

PILGRIMS AND STRANGERS

They were strangers and pilgrims on the earth.—Heb. 11:13

There is a sense of exile in all our hearts. There comes to most of us, now and then, the sense that the earth is an alien shore. Some theologians say that this sense of exile is due to "the fall from grace." By our sin humanity has broken the original harmony and is as lost to the environment for which we were created as a bird with a broken pinion.

The poet says that this sense of exile is in us because God is our home and, like water seeking its own level, we are seeking the ocean from which we have come. It is our glory that we yearn for heights beyond our reach, that we go searching for something lost behind the ranges, and that we seek a completeness and self-realization for which our earthly environment is too limited.

When all has been said of this sense of exile and hunger, we have said nothing save that we are hungry for God and for righteousness. To me, the most precious promise of Jesus is that they who hunger and thirst after righteousness shall be satisfied. That promise, of course, makes necessary an afterlife, for no soul is ever satisfied in this world. The ancient Persians said that at death a soul is met by an angel who says, "I am the image of your interrupted ideals and unfulfilled strivings; I am your true self. All that you tried to be, wanted to be, but failed to be, I am. Now we shall merge into one being and as one we shall go on into life."

WE GIVE THEE THANKS, our heavenly Father, that Thou dost haunt us with Thy love and with visions of what Thou dost intend that we shall be. We pray Thee to keep the vision glowing lest we lose our way in the dark. Show us the shame of the second best, and let Thy beauty be upon us. *Amen.*

MARSHALL WINGFIELD
First Congregational Church, Memphis, Tenn.

KEEPING THE TENSION TIGHT

And being in an agony, he prayed more earnestly.—Luke 22:44

Exactly when does a person lose his or her soul? Many of King David's deeds were foul, but because he was often in agony over them, he didn't lose his soul. There was always tension in him between right and wrong. For such a person there is always hope.

Our souls are really lost only on that day when within us there is no longer any tension between good and evil. We are somewhat like violin strings; tension produces music. But let the thumbscrew get loose in inattention, and the violin is worthless until it is tightened again. So long as there is a fight taking place within us between right and wrong, the beautiful and the ugly, the ideal and the present horror, our souls are alive.

Jesus knew this and spent forty days pondering it in the wilderness. All His ministry the struggle continued. So great was His agony of final decision in the Garden, as He faced all the pent-up deviltry of humanity, that He sweat blood.

When within our souls there is a wrestling match like that depicted in the statue of the two wrestlers in the Metropolitan Museum as they struggle in the death grapple, the face of one leering and evil, that of the other strong, clean, and confident, then we are never without hope. But beware of the slum area of the soul where all colors look the same.

O THOU who art "closer than breathing, and nearer than hands and feet," I thank Thee for the church, the school, and the home which planted in my heart high ideals. I pray that I may, by Thy strength, and their memories, keep myself sensitive to the highest within me, in spite of all the forces that tear down. Keep me ever in that presence whereby "I can do all things through Christ which strengtheneth me." *Amen.*

FRANK CLEVELAND MARTICK
First Presbyterian Church, Cloquet, Minn.

THE GREAT CONTEST

Enter the great contest of faith!—1 Tim. 6:12 (Goodspeed)

The great contest of faith draws us from life's sidelines. This contest is a great and universal struggle on behalf of "the substance of things hoped for, the evidence of things not seen." It is born of an inner belief in life's integrity whereby we dare to invest our personalities in the cause of right.

Each one of us is to be a contestant. Some contests are not for us, but this is like a relay race in which we all must share. This activity may be the defense of an intellectual position; it may be some generous attitude of moral judgment. The scene of the contest is simply the place where duty calls. The action is a program of faithful living.

The great contest of faith is at once a risk and a release. We were safe on the sidelines, where we could make no mistakes; now we are in the game. We may fall openly, and we may receive the brickbats hurled by critics. We will be ridiculed, but we will not be ignored. This much is certain. We are no longer victims of cheap unworthy repressions, nor are we bound by cowardly acquiescence in evil. We have gone all out for truth.

Looking back on his career, St. Paul affirmed, "I have kept the faith." Faith for him had been a living, vital path to life, not a prisonlike creed. Our Christian calling is a constant invitation to enter that contest of faith in which there is daily obedience to the heavenly vision. It is our supreme privilege to keep the faith day by day.

SPIRIT OF THE LIVING GOD, help us to enter the great contest of faith and to bring our highest loyalty to our Christian vocation. Teach us to pray by the very attitude of our living. In the quiet of night and amid the busy roar of toil give us the heart of the true learner, whereby we may say, "Speak, Lord; for thy servant heareth." Through Jesus Christ. *Amen.*

PAUL F. SWARTHOUT
First Baptist Church, Hamilton, N.Y.

THE GATES OF VICTORY

The Lord has disciplined me severely. . . . Open for me the gates of victory, that I may enter through them to give thanks to the Lord.—Ps. 118:18–19 (SMITH-GOODSPEED)

Discipline has been emphasized in our day by the severe training of the men and women in the armed forces. Life itself, with its varying experiences of prosperity and adversity, brings a continuous discipline. "Blood, sweat, and tears" are the price for the highest achievement.

Discipline implies that we must first gain absolute control and victory over ourselves. Naturally we rebel against the severities which God has sent to us. We would prefer ease to hardship. David's life had much of misfortune and tragedy, but he confessed that it was good for him. Paul observed that only the disciplined runner reached the goal and captured the prize. When individuals—or nations—have first won the victory over themselves, they have had that experience and power to have a large part in gaining a signal victory for others.

Such a severely disciplined individual enters the gates of victory. It is a proud day when Kreisler has so gained the mastery over the violin that he can enrapture a great audience, or when a cadet flier has by hard, patient toil won his or her wings. God believes in our ability to achieve. Even the Christ was made perfect only by suffering. So with the disciplined follower of Christ. While our hearts are glad, our spirits are humble. We know the price we have paid and know the meaning of victory. We enter the gates of victory and offer sincere thanks to our Lord.

ETERNAL FATHER, give us grace to accept the disciplines however severe that are imposed upon us. May they purify our hearts, give us skill and strength, and increase our usefulness. May we know that this is Thy way of enriching and enlarging our lives. Give us endurance to attain the victory over ourselves. *Amen.*

RALPH D. KEARNS
First Presbyterian Church, Flint, Mich.

ANGELS CARRY FLAMING SWORDS

*And he placed at the east of the garden of Eden, cherubims, and a
flaming sword which turned every way, to keep the way of the tree of
life.*—Gen. 3:24

Here is an arresting picture: angels and a flaming sword! The sword is
the symbol of bloodshed, punishment, death; the angel is a symbol of
love, joy, and happiness. In the Garden of Eden one would expect to find
angels, but why the sword?

The truth here so vividly pictured is that the angel forces of life, when
violated and misused, lash the violator with biting fury. Holy precincts
must not be trod by impious feet. Those things which give life its nobility
and grandeur are the very sources of life's deepest pains and hurts.

> For sweetest things turn sourest by their deeds;
> Lilies that fester smell far worse than weeds.

Think of the home, for instance—a veritable Eden, where angels are to
be found, if anywhere. But if jealousy, selfishness, infidelity, lack of confidence are allowed to enter the home, then it will be seen that angels carry
flaming swords.

There is a Garden of Eden for every person and every nation.
Humanity may enter this Eden, but on God's terms. Violated sanctities are
the sources of the world's running sores. A sense of the sacred is the source
of the world's welling springs of joy.

O GOD, Source of all good, whose judgments are like the great deep;
cleanse our hearts by the inspiration of Thy Holy Spirit, that we may enter
into the gates of righteousness and peace, through Jesus Christ. *Amen.*

A. W. BEASLEY
First Methodist Church, Columbia, Tenn.

PUT TO THE TEST

Think it not strange concerning the fiery trial which is to try you.
—1 Pet. 4:12

Life would be stranger if we did not have some fiery trials to test us. How could there be courage if there were no danger? Or tenderness if there were no pain? Or sympathy and compassion if there were no hardship? How could there be hope if there were no hours of doubt? It is hard climbing that makes the mountaineer strong.

In a furnace the dross burns away, but the gold endures. When the tidal waves beat on the coastal cliffs, the shale and slime "can't take it" and dissolve in defeat, but the granite rock stands undaunted and unyielding. On the threshing floor the chaff goes with the wind, but the wheat abides to become "seed to the sower, and bread to the eater."

The Christians to whom Peter was writing the letter from which the above text was taken faced trials which we will never see. Read Hebrews, the eleventh chapter: "They were stoned, they were sawn asunder, were tempted, were slain with the sword: they wandered about in sheepskins and goatskins; being destitute, afflicted, tormented."

Undoubtedly some couldn't take it. Their faith failed. Their courage dissolved. They failed to be numbered with the victors. Others "endured, as seeing him who is invisible." They were tried as in a fiery furnace and came out gold. The tidal waves of cruel lashings left them unshaken. They were wheat rather than chaff. What others have done I can do!

O LORD AND MASTER OF US ALL, who wast Thyself misjudged, tested, tried, maltreated, and betrayed, and yet triumphed without bitterness, but with victorious love; lend me strength for my hard tasks, valor for my hours of temptation, courage to endure all, and the joy of victory in Thy name. *Amen.*

CLAUDE ALLEN McKAY
First Congregational Church, Binghamton, N.Y.

THE DIVINE DIFFERENCE

My peace I give unto you: not as the world giveth, give I unto you.
—John 14:27

As you go to the wars, "go in peace," as we say when you leave the altars of Holy Communion. The world has been looking for a social order which is just and for a permanent peace which is political. This ideal is high and right, but relatively it is low and temporal. If achieved, it would only be like the fulfillment of the Jew's ideal of a temporal Messiah. Nothing is real which is not eternal.

What we have forgotten is that the absence of war has nothing whatever to do with peace—never did have anything to do with peace. Political peace might girdle the globe while hearts are full of worry and anger and fear. But in the midst of war to the death, the humblest comrade of Jesus Christ may have the peace of God which passeth all understanding. Not as the world giveth, He gives. Go, therefore, to the wars; but go in peace, and the peace of God go with you.

ALMIGHTY GOD, our heavenly Father, we are helpless and troubled without Thee. Protect us by Thy might, and though sometimes we forget Thee, oh remember us in Thy mercy, and forgive us our sins. Fill our souls with the peace of believing in Thy perfect love. Watch over the beloved of our hearts who are absent from us, and keep our homes from evil. God bless our homeland, bring victory to the right, and peace to all the world. Let Thy holy will be done in our hearts; abide with us in never-broken companionship; and bring us to everlasting life through Jesus Christ our Lord. *Amen.*

ARTHUR WENTWORTH HEWITT
The Methodist Church, Northfield, Vt.

THE MIRACLE OF DUNKIRK

We are labourers together with God. . . . And the fire shall try every
man's work of what sort it is.—1 Cor. 3:9, 13

Studdert-Kennedy tells of a cockney from a slum-clearance area, transported to the suburbs, to a bungalow back of which was a patch of ground filled with bricks, tin cans, and broken bottles. He cleaned it up and planted a garden. Every spare moment he toiled in it and finally came to have an inordinate pride in his vegetables and flowers. The rector, passing by one evening, stopped long enough to say, "It is amazing what the Almighty can do with a small patch of ground." "Well, you should have seen it," the cockney replied, "when the Almighty had it all to His-Self."

> Christ has no hands but our hands
> To do His work today:
> He has no feet but our feet
> To lead men in His way.
> —ANNIE JOHNSON FLINT

Mr. Churchill speaks of the miraculous deliverance of Dunkirk, but we must remember that it was only when every English citizen along the coast laid hold of anything that could sail the seas—fishing smacks, freighters, motorboats, yachts—and put forth superhuman efforts, and put themselves utterly at the disposal of God and country, that the miracle was wrought.

Miracles do happen, but only through limitless cooperation between us and God.

O GOD, make us very certain that when we surrender our wills into Thy hands, Thou wilt multiply our powers and make us more than conquerors. And then people, seeing our good works, will glorify our wonder-working God. *Amen.*

F. W. KERR
St. Andrew's Church, Montreal, P.Q., Canada

JESUS' GREATEST MIRACLE

And he took the five loaves and the two fishes, and looking up to heaven, he blessed, and brake; and gave . . .—Matt. 14:19

If we dare deal in superlatives about the miracles of our Lord, it would seem that the feeding of the five thousand surpasses all others; yet its symbolism is in many ways even greater than the deed itself. These people stand for the great masses of humanity and constitute the problem of the world. He says that they "were as sheep not having a shepherd." That is always true of the masses, and that fact is the soil for dictatorships.

Coming to His own symbolism, He is the "Living Bread"—the staff of eternal life. To have bread, the wheat must be buried and rise again and be ground and put into a furnace, all of which is so true of Himself. And concerning this bread, there is absolutely no substitute. Ignorance offers a stone; culture offers things; while infidelity declares, "We are not hungry." But the need is still there, and Christ is the answer.

In a very real sense, also, we ourselves are the bread. Just as when Jesus says, "I am the light of the world," and then turns to us and says, "Ye are the light of the world," so He means that we are in this world what He is. He took the loaves and blessed and broke them. When we let Him take us and bless and break us in His service, then we become disciples and dispensers of the Hidden Manna. I heard a Christian convert from India say, "I want to go back to my people and share their poverty." That is Christianity, and that meets the need of the world.

FATHER, grant that we shall remember the words of our Master. "Greater works than these shall he do; because I go unto my Father." Help us in His name to do that which we can by His power. May our askings be great that what we do for Thee may also be great. In the name of our Blessed Christ Jesus. *Amen.*

GEORGE W. ARMS
Bedford Presbyterian Church, Brooklyn, N.Y.

OUR COMPENSATION IN GOD

The eternal God is thy refuge, and underneath are the everlasting arms.—Deut. 33:27

No matter what happens, those words are true. For centuries they have received the hammer blows of circumstance, the tempests of passion and despair, the sudden, sharp announcement of catastrophe. The words still stand like a great rock in the swollen stream of the years to give us courage and security in the moment of the most awful need and desolation.

They mean that God is the compensation for every misfortune that may come upon us. As individuals we may be surrounded, damaged, and even destroyed by the selfish forces of evil; but as individuals we will also be saved by an eternal God.

Likewise they mean that our cause will go on. We may lose a battle, but at length we shall win the war. This is because the universe is pitched in the direction of truth, justice, cooperation, and the freedom of the human spirit—great goals and goods that are denied by the fascist dictators. They cannot win, for God and all His stars are working against them.

These words also mean that nothing can ever really hurt those whose lives rest in God. They may have to walk through the valley of the shadow of death and leave the earth as they render faithful service to their people, but God will give them the gift of immortality. The really vital part of themselves, their personalities, will confidently live to cooperate eternally with God for the same old thrilling cause of freedom and abundant life.

ETERNAL GOD, may the knowledge of Thy Presence give us physical strength, steady nerves, a sense of saving humor, a deep passion for the freedom of the human spirit, quiet peace and poise, and a knowledge that the welfare of humankind shall be established. Through Jesus Christ our Lord. *Amen.*

CLARENCE SEIDENSPINNER
First Methodist Church, Racine, Wis.

TRY THE NEW TESTAMENT

Study to shew thyself approved unto God, a workman that needeth not to be ashamed, rightly dividing the word of truth.—2 Tim. 2:15

The president of a great technological school was asked what traits or abilities ranked as most important in the success of their graduates. He said: "Even in so technical a field as engineering, personality ranks about eighty percent, engineering skill twenty percent."

Then he went on to say that this was no appeal for shoddily prepared engineers, but that the ability to get along with people was always a greater factor in success than mere skill, memory, high grades, or even genuine ability.

Christians who haven't learned how to get along with people have missed part of the meaning of the Gospel. If they are full of little resentments, small quarrels, misunderstandings, they are human, but they need more of the spirit and technique of Christ. What that is can be found from a systematic study of the New Testament. Try it! It is the answer to success in life as well as eternal life. God offers a saved life as well as a saved soul.

O THOU ETERNAL FATHER, we thank Thee that Thou dost permit us to enroll in Thy service, weak and fallible though we may be. As we train our bodies to respond to command, help that our spirits may be trained to hear Thy commands. Make us coworkers with Thee in building a new liberty upon the earth. Through Christ Jesus our Lord. *Amen.*

RALPH WALKER
First Baptist Church, Portland, Ore.

THE ROCK THAT IS HIGHER

Lead me to the rock that is higher than I.—Ps. 61:2 ARV

Since many lives are lost in the lowlands of confusion, our primary need is for spiritual altitude. The verse above is a good prayer for any one.

> There is a trail within your life
> Where you can climb above the crowd,
> Where you can rise above the earth,
> And look far down on haze and cloud.
>
> There is a trail within your soul
> Where you can climb right up to God,
> And know the source whence blessings flow
> To quicken life in seed and sod.
>
> There is a trail that calls to you,
> "Come, climb, and conquer heights unscaled,
> That you may see with vision true,
> And find life's goal where others failed."
>
> There is a trail that you can climb,
> What though death come on mountain peak!
> The vision comes to those who climb!
> Christ's mantle falls on those who seek!
> —F. S. B.

O GOD, whose mountains tower high above the plains and alleys, teach me to set my spirit on upward trail. Help me in all my climbing to feel the presence of Him who climbed the hills of Nazareth, Gethsemane, and Calvary. *Amen.*

FRED S. BUSCHMEYER
Mount Pleasant Congregational Church, Washington, D.C.

ALWAYS LOOK UP

Set your affection on things above, not on things on the earth.
—Col. 3:2

Up and down are words which we use every day. Usually good is up and bad is down; for we say "he is an upright fellow," "it was a low-down trick." When the apostle Paul spoke of "things above," he was thinking of the noble qualities of character such as kindness, courage, fortitude. When he spoke of "things on the earth," he was referring to the lesser qualities of human character.

Of course we are involved with things on earth. We cannot escape the fact that we live on earth. The task we tackle, the battle we fight, the victory for which we strive—all are concerned with earthly things. But there is a power which gives us strength to do our earthly tasks that comes from above. The ideals for which we strive are divine not human.

When we set our minds on things above, we do what the psalmist suggests: "I will lift up mine eyes unto the hills, from whence cometh my help." We look up to the Man of Galilee and see a vision of the time when evil will be destroyed and we will live in peace and unity. We can look beyond this worldly life to the everlasting glories.

> Christ of the Upward Way, my Guide Divine,
> Where Thou hast set Thy feet may I set mine;
> And move and march wherever Thou hast trod,
> Keeping face forward up the hill of God.
> —WALTER J. MATHAMS

ALMIGHTY GOD, help us to set our minds on those things that cannot be destroyed. Sustain in us the right spirit of love and kindness, of courage and trust. Keep our loved ones within Thy care and grant us a blessing for this day. *Amen.*

GARNER S. ODELL
South Presbyterian Church, Rochester, N.Y.

QUISLINGS AND SABOTEURS

No man can serve two masters: for either he will hate the one, and love the other; or else he will hold to the one, and despise the other. Ye cannot serve God and mammon.—Matt. 6:24

The Norwegians who transferred their loyalty from their own government to that of the puppet regime set up by Hitler were called, after the name of their leader, "Quislings." Those who willfully injure property, or interfere with the activity of the government in time of emergency, or restrict production, are called saboteurs. In an all-out war we must guard against those who might become Quislings or saboteurs.

So, in the Christian life, we must guard against giving comfort to the enemy. We must be on the alert lest by careless action or by doing nothing we slow up the work of Christ. If we love America so greatly that we would sacrifice, serve, and—if need be—die, even so for the Christ who died for us we should be willing to give our last full measure of devotion.

As soldiers of the cross, following Christ, the Captain of our salvation, we should be proud of our Leader, proud to wear His uniform. And, just as we are ready to fight our country's battles, we should be prepared to gird ourselves to fight His battles.

Finally, we must remember that we cannot give a divided allegiance, being faithful to God and mammon, anymore than a Quisling could be loyal to Norway and Germany. As we must choose between terrorism or freedom, so must we divide between the claims of Christ and the lure of mammon.

O GOD OUR FATHER, enable us to be active in Thy cause as soldiers. Keep us from being treasonable to Thee—as we would not commit treason against the cause of our country. Bless us and make us a blessing to others, we ask in Jesus' name. *Amen.*

JAMES HENRY HUTCHINS
Lake Avenue Congregational Church, Pasadena, Calif.

FOR YOUR OWN SOUL'S SAKE

*Yet a man is risen to pursue thee, and to seek thy soul: but the soul
of my lord shall be bound in the bundle of life with the Lord thy
God.*—1 Sam. 25:29

David and four hundred men were living in the hills. The wealthy Nabal
had many flocks of sheep which David's men protected. One day David
sent to Nabal to ask for food, but Nabal curtly refused. Impetuous David
ordered his men to buckle on their swords and follow. He vowed to take
what he wanted and then destroy every living soul in Nabal's household.

When Abigail, sweet and beautiful young wife of old Nabal, heard what
David was up to, she loaded a donkey with food and slipped quietly down
the mountainside to meet the angry young man. This is, in effect, what she
told him: "Nabal is all you say he is, a stingy son of the devil. But you,
young man, have a great future if you will control yourself now. You cannot
afford to kill a lot of unarmed and defenseless people in our household, not
only because it is wrong, but because of the effect that action will have
upon your own soul. Remember you are 'bound in the bundle of life with
the Lord thy God.' Nabal is old and will soon die anyway. Then, remember
thine handmaid."

David thanked Abigail for her advice, and he followed her suggestion.
And later he married Abigail! Young men and women in the armed services
of their country frequently find themselves far away from parental control
and restraint for the first time in their lives. Temptations are many. But no
young person can possibly afford to weaken before such onslaughts
because of the effect that action would surely have upon their souls.

ETERNAL FATHER, if I am tempted to go astray this day, help me to
remember that I am tied in the bundle of life with Thee, and that I cannot
afford to do it because of its effect upon the condition of my immortal
soul. *Amen.*

L. L. DUNNINGTON
First Methodist Church, Iowa City, Iowa

YOUR BIBLE WAITS

Jesus saith unto them, Did ye never read in the scriptures?—Matt. 21:42

It is a devastating thought of how little is left of greatness when all that our Bible has inspired vanishes. The most thrilling part of any spiritual enterprise is never statistical, and yet I find myself attracted in passing to look upon the labor which someone has undertaken to tell us about the Bible. The Sacred Writ contains 3,566,480 letters, 773,692 words, 31,173 verses, 1,189 chapters, and 66 books. The middle verse, he says, is Psalm 118:18. The longest verse is Esther 8:9, the shortest John 11:35.

In a busy day like ours, we would find a set of statistics showing us how we could read these great truths to be of much more value than their technical aspects. Here is one method, not necessarily the best, but at least one set of statistics showing how a busy person can gain a knowledge of the Bible.

There are 929 chapters in the Old Testament and 260 chapters in the New Testament. This makes our previous accounted total of 1,189 chapters in the entire Bible. If we will read three chapters every day and five chapters each Sunday, we can finish reading the entire Bible in just one year. Or, if we desire to read the New Testament alone, and read two chapters a day, we can finish it in less than twenty weeks. If we read only on Sunday, completing five New Testament chapters each Sunday, he will finish it on the fifty-second Sunday. In one afternoon we can begin with Luke's Gospel and at one sitting read the remainder of the New Testament to be thrilled forever with its moving story of power.

O GOD, Thou who art the Father of lights, illumine, we pray Thee, our minds with those flashes of divine insight which are ever near unto us and which are ours only for time to make their discovery. *Amen.*

J. RICHARD SNEED
First Methodist Church, Shenandoah, Iowa

THE YOUNG MAN WHOM JESUS LOVED

Then Jesus beholding him, loved him.—Mark 10:21

Jesus loved John in spite of his faults. He loved him because of his possibilities. Jesus still desires—has desired through the centuries—to enlist in His cause young people of possibilities. Unfortunately the Master is not the only bidder for the life and service of the young people. The devil is just as active in his endeavors to win them as the Lord is.

One of the first lessons that young people must learn is that they are shining marks for the evil one to shoot at. The devil makes capital of the young people's lack of experience. They have not had time to organize their defenses against attack. Is it too much to believe that Jesus loves every young person as He did the one in the story? Is not the fact of the Master's love a call to everyone to use everything at their command to live the life that is the Master's? He has given us wisdom, common sense, memory, affection, and appreciation upon which to call in the fight of life. With His help victory is secure.

WE THANK THEE, Lord, that Thou art the Friend of young people. We thank Thee for that love which passeth all understanding and which impelled Thee to leave Thy home above to come to the rescue of the world. And now we pray for our comrades, young people who have left their homes and all they hold dear to come to the rescue of our grief-stricken world. Fill them with the spirit of unity, and make them joy in the privilege of giving their all that the world may be a fit place for our Lord to come and reign. Through Jesus Christ. *Amen.*

THOMAS F. GALLAHER
Oak Cliff Presbyterian Church, Dallas, Tex.

WHAT PEOPLE THINK OF THEMSELVES

Beloved, now are we the sons of God.—1 John 3:2

In our present situation we face a task which is deeply spiritual in its nature, because it is a life-and-death struggle between two opposing ways of life. In contemplating this it is easier to consider the large, general aspects than it is to consider oneself. But what we think of ourselves will largely determine our service toward the victory for which we strive and pray to God.

John says we are children of God. Back in the beginning of time, when we were created, God breathed within Adam, and he became a living soul. Jesus called us children of God, for He taught us to pray, saying, "Our Father." No higher thought of humankind is possible than this.

When we think of ourselves as a form of animal, with the bestial nature asserting itself, we will live and act as animals. When we think of ourselves merely as the servant of a higher earthly power, be it state or anything else, we become slaves and are drawn away from our God-given heritage.

But we Christians know that we are children of God, heirs of Christ, yea, joint heirs with Him of God. When Jesus said, "Be ye therefore perfect, even as your Father which is in heaven is perfect," He set the standard for our attainment. Humankind is supreme, and is to have liberty, freedom, and all the good things of life. Here, indeed, is the vital thing concerning what people should think of themselves. "Made in the image of my God"—that is it. We are coworkers with God; and God is always with us, to give us strength, courage, and His Spirit.

OUR FATHER, Thou hast indeed made us in Thine own image. Help us to keep that image of Thyself untarnished. Help us to live as Thy children, as free people, as heirs of Christ. Be Thou always at our side. Let Thy light be our light, Thy way our way, and Thy Spirit our ever present help and guide. *Amen.*

W. R. SIEGART
St. Matthew's Lutheran Church, Reading, Pa.

EVEN IN SAVAGE BOSOMS

He hath set the world in their heart.—Eccles. 3:11

For Abraham, stars and sands were the symbols of the world of which he dreamed. For Moses, a flaming bush was the symbol of a Promised Land. Gideon had a vision of a whole country reclaimed for a whole people. From Antioch in Syria, Paul's imagination leaped to Cyprus, to Troas, to Macedonia, to Rome, to Spain. The total world of his time lay in his heart. Columbus, LaSalle, Livingstone, Grenfell, John Wesley were men in whose hearts the world was set as the object of devotion. Geography has superseded astronomy. The breaking up of our systems of "power politics" has brought a close-up view of the world to the person in the street. "Know your geography" is the new challenge to the cultured provincial in London or New York.

"Know your neighbor"—the columnist reiterates the challenge. Ah, the world is not merely space and places! It is people. It is Malayans, Burmese, Filipinos, Japanese. The alluring mystery of rubber and oil, or spices and pearls, is eclipsed by the menacing mystery of human beings awake and thirsting for freedom.

God hath set the world in their hearts as well as in ours. And they will not be denied. The world in their hearts is the same as the world in our hearts. Shall we share it, or fight over it?

FATHER OF HUMANKIND, shake our souls this day with the power of the world that is coming to be. In the contemplation of its awesome magnitudes, let our spirits grow in stature and in power. In the grip of its outreaching forces, may we be lifted to new heights of understanding and devotion. Help us to practice such citizenship now as will prepare the way for the gathering of all nations into the Family of God. *Amen.*

J. MARVIN CULBRETH
University Methodist Church, Chapel Hill, N.C.

THINK ON THESE THINGS

Finally, brethren, whatsoever things are true, . . . honest, . . . just, . . . pure, . . . lovely, . . . of good report, if there be any virtue, . . . any praise, think on these things.—Phil. 4:8

The greatest of Christians speaks to you across the centuries. He makes for you a list of things on which you are to think; things which are "honest," things which are "just," things which are "pure," things which are "lovely," things which are "of good report." He closes: "If there be any virtue, and if there be any praise, think on these things." Take a brief moment in your busy day, close your eyes, think on "these things." Think of your home and of your loved ones. They, you may be sure, are thinking of you.

Breathe a prayer for them, as they so often breathe a prayer for you. Think of the church to which you have been wont to turn for worship and instruction. That church, you may be sure, does not forget you. Think of your country, to which you give yourself and your service. Offer a prayer that your country may be guided and blessed in these days of peril.

You must know that you become like the things that you think. Think courage and you will be courageous. Think strength and you will be strong. Think high thoughts and your thoughts will lift you high.

"THINK UPON ME, my God, for good." *Amen.* (Neh. 5:19)

P. E. BURROUGHS
Secretary, Southern Baptist Sunday School Board, Nashville, Tenn.

FACES OF FLINT

*For the Lord God will help me; therefore shall I not be confounded:
therefore have I set my face like a flint, and I know that I shall not be
ashamed.*—Isa. 50:7

The faces of four outstanding presidents are immortalized on a granite
cliff in South Dakota. Washington represents the conception, Jefferson
the construction, Lincoln the preservation, and Roosevelt the development
of our country. These faces, now deeply carved in hard granite, represent
keen insight, magnificent strength, and conquering courage.

The Lord Jesus had a hard road to travel. The way of truth and purity
and honor has always been difficult. When Jesus sensed the growing opposition, He told the disciples of His inevitable death on the cross. They didn't
understand nor did they sympathize with Him. Jesus rebuked them. In
spite of all this, "He steadfastly set his face to go to Jerusalem."

Two college presidents were riding together on a streamliner. They
were sharing many common problems. It was during the bitter depression
days of the thirties. Finally the older said to the other, "Whenever the way
seems impossible, I think of that verse from Isaiah, 'The Lord God will help
me; therefore shall I not be confounded: therefore have I set my face like
flint, and I know that I shall not be ashamed.'"

ETERNAL GOD, Thou art our Light and our Salvation. As dark days
come upon us help us to keep our lives open to that abiding ray of Light
from above. Help us to set our faces toward the highest and the best we
know. We wait upon Thee to lay hold of that precious promise of strength
and good courage. May Thy love and care, which is ever present, be our
guide and comfort. In Jesus' name. *Amen.*

BERNARD N. KING
College Hill Church of the Brethren, McPherson, Kan.

WHEREVER YOU ARE

Whither shall I go from thy Spirit?—Ps. 139:7

Do you remember the ancient story of Theseus and Ariadne in classic mythology? Theseus had to go down through a dark labyrinth, sword in hand, to do battle with a horrible man-eating monster. Before he went, Ariadne tied a silken thread about his ankle and told him that whenever he felt a pull on that thread he might know that she was thinking of him. Theseus went through that terrifying combat upheld by constant reminders that Ariadne was with him in thought and heart.

Our silken cord is our Christian faith. It brings us constant reminders that when, as followers of Christ, we have to face any terrifying experience, we are upheld by the presence and love of One who understands.

"Whither shall I go from thy spirit?" asked the psalmist, "or whither shall I flee from thy presence?" You may go through heaven and hell itself, he says, but God is still there. You may "take the wings of the morning, and dwell in the uttermost parts of the sea," but even there God will lead you and bear you up. The same God you knew at home is with you now. The same God to whom your loved ones are praying hears your prayers. You can trust Him because He is like Christ. The tragedies and griefs of the world break His heart as they broke Christ's, but He will not let you down. You can never go beyond His love and care.

GREAT GOD, I thank Thee that Thou art here in the midst of all our struggles—here with me at this moment. I thank Thee that I can draw on Thy life to refresh my own, and that even now Thou art giving me strength and courage and peace. *Amen.*

GEORGE E. GILCHRIST
Bethany Congregational Church, Quincy, Mass.

THE PRIORITY RIGHTS OF RELIGION

Seek ye first the kingdom of God, and his righteousness.—Matt. 6:33

There is a scale of values that determines our loyalties. Under certain circumstances some things must be given first place in our lives, even if there are others that we hold very dear. We are in a war because we think that there are certain questions of human right and freedom which must be settled, even at tremendous cost, in order that we may achieve our God-given place in life and destiny. That means that priority must be given to the persons and materials necessary to win.

In the making of human character, religion—our relationship to God—is of primary importance. Our attitude to God determines and conditions all our attitudes. Hence the "priority" of religion. We must give God and His Kingdom first place in the whole scheme of our lives. Only in this way shall we be able to add those other things that will enrich and enlarge our being. The priority of religion makes concern about truth, justice, love, honor and duty more important than what we shall eat, wear, or drink.

It makes the will of God of more value than our short-sighted plans. What would it mean if those of us who call ourselves Christian were to take a few moments each day to think through, in the light of the will of God, the things that we do and the attitudes we have toward others! That might give a real priority to things that are of most genuine importance.

O GOD, give me the insight and understanding to know Thy will for me this day. And give me courage and strength to put it first in my life. Help me never to put my own selfish desires above Thy will for the good of all. *Amen.*

WALTER R. CREMEANS
Westminster Presbyterian Church, Springfield, Ill.

THE GREATEST BATTLE

He was in all points tempted like as we are, yet without sin.
—Heb. 4:15

The most memorable conflict in all history was fought between Christ and the Devil. There is only one which compares in importance. It is the battle you are fighting against the enemies of your soul. The first attack was in the sphere of bodily appetite. Our Lord was hungry. The desire for food was innocent, but He refused to take the Devil's way of gratifying this natural desire. He was fortified by a trust in God to supply His need and, in His Father's own way and time, to meet His craving for food. No appetite should make us follow the Devil's advice!

The second temptation of Christ was to put Himself in a place of peril and then expect God to rescue Him by working a miracle. He was urged to cast Himself from the high wall of the temple just to see whether angels would be sent to keep Him from being dashed to pieces in the valley below; but Christ refused to make such a rash test of the power of God. In the path of duty we can trust God to keep us from falling, but if, to satisfy our curiosity, or in rash self-confidence, we put ourselves in places of moral peril, we need not expect God to rescue us.

The third temptation was to compromise with evil, to worship the Devil, only once, and thus to become the ruler of the whole world. To resist the Devil will mean deadly conflict, even a cross, but the issue will be victory and a throne.

BLESSED SAVIOR, help us to watch and pray, to fight bravely, and to trust in Thee, that we may win for Thee the battle and win from Thee the crown. We ask this in Thy name. *Amen.*

CHARLES R. ERDMAN
Princeton Theological Seminary, Princeton, N.J.
Former Moderator, Presbyterian General Assembly

POWER

For I am not ashamed of the gospel of Christ: for it is the power of God unto salvation, to every one that believeth; to the Jew first, and also to the Greek.—Rom. 1:16

Too many people have the idea that Christianity is a weak, anemic sort of thing. They believe it is good for women and children, but that a normal, strong man does not have any need for it. Most people think of it as being like a little "one-lung" motorcycle which I bought when I was a boy on the farm. I had to save my nickels to get it, and when it came all crated up I took my first lesson in mechanics by trying to put it together.

I finally got it going and took a test run. I found that it was fine while we were on the level; but when we came to a hill it didn't quite have enough power to take me over, and I had to get off and run, and push, and shove to get over the top. A lot of folks think Christianity is like that little motorcycle. If you work and shove and push, and your wind lasts long enough, someday you will get to heaven.

No, that isn't the kind of Christianity Paul was talking about when he said that the Gospel of Christ is the power of God unto salvation. If it were like that and we had to depend upon our own efforts, we would never make the grade; for it is "not by works of righteousness which we have done, but according to his mercy he saved us." It is the power of Christ which saves us, and His is the only power sufficient to lift our lives from the sin and degradation which is our natural state and make us "new creatures in Christ Jesus."

O LORD, help us to yield our lives to be channels of Thy power. Cleanse from our lives anything which would hinder Thy power from being manifest through us. Give us a vision of Thyself so that we will not fear to let Thee have complete control. *Amen.*

R. G. LETOURNEAU
President, Letourneau Co. of Georgia, Toccoa, Ga.

THINK OF THE OTHER PERSON

Therefore all things whatsoever ye would that men should do to you, do ye even so to them.—Matt. 7:12

The function of the Golden Rule is to turn the eyes of the soul outward as well as inward. We are always looking inward, calculating our own rights. We must cultivate the habit of looking outward too, thinking of the rights of others. When I was a little fellow, the big boys liked to play a trick on us. They would line us up, and one would throw down a coin. In less time than it takes to tell, it was covered with a squirming, squealing, kicking mass of boyhood. When it was all over some were crying and others were fighting.

The source of that trouble was that every boy was thinking of two things, and only two. He was thinking of the coin and of his own desire to get it. Nobody was thinking of the other person. The big world is just like that. Business, politics, society, and industry are a mass of squirming, shouting, kicking, gouging human beings, all trying to get life's prizes for themselves, with little or no thought for the rights of the other person.

The prizes we seek in life are big enough for all. There is food enough and warmth enough and clothing enough and happiness for every person in the world—if we were only good enough to think of each other and share life's benefits in a spirit of fairness and unity. In the mind of the great God every human being has exactly the same right to the good things of life that I have. "Therefore all things whatsoever ye would that men should do to you, do ye even so to them."

O GOD, help me to think of my comrades. Grant that the spirit of fellowship, the desire to see others advance, the goodwill that thinks of everyone's advantage, may possess me that I may do Thy will in the loving Spirit of Jesus. *Amen.*

JESSE H. BAIRD
President, San Francisco Theological Seminary, San Anselmo, Calif.

✝ *Read John 3:1–21*

GOD'S GIFTS

And God said, "Let us make human beings in our image and likeness; male and female God created them."—Gen. 1:26–28

As Christians, we readily accept the wonderful truth that "God so loved the world that God sent Jesus into the world as a gift!" And we believe the words of Paul, who proclaimed, "Jesus is the image of the invisible God." For Jesus Himself said, "Philip, those who know me, know God the Father."

But in our chaotic, noisy lives, the fact that we also are mirrors of God's presence rarely breaks in on our consciousness. We muddle along and wonder what life is all about. Yet, on each of our tombstones could be placed the words, "God so loved the world that God sent (our personal name) into the world as a gift." Each of us in our extraordinary uniqueness has been created to give to the world something about God's presence which would never be known if we had not been born. Something of God's goodness, love, and mercy would be lost if we did not exist!

We are all potential channels of God's presence. Our smiles to strangers and friends, our listening to someone's pain, our helping hands, our sharing of the sorrows and joys of others, our responsible use of the talents God has given us—all of these ordinary activities are ways we give God a human form—just as Jesus did. Accept the challenge to be what you are called to be, for remember: God so loved the world that God sent you into the world as a gift!

LOVING GOD, our Creator, You have created us in Your image; You have called us by name. We belong to You. Help us in our daily lives to believe in this truth and to spend our lives loving all people as You call us to love. Empower us to live our lives, conscious that You created us as Your special gift to the world. May we give You praise every day by living in the mystery of that giftedness. *Amen.*

NORMA ROCKLAGE, OSF
Vice President for Mission Effectiveness,
Marian College, Indianapolis, Ind.

✝

KEEP IT SIMPLE

And what does the Lord require of you? To act justly and love mercy and to walk humbly with your God.—Mic. 6:8

It's not complicated knowing what is the right thing to do in many situations. It's really pretty simple. At the very base is just knowing right from wrong. For many people it can actually be felt in the gut, a reminder of something we learned as children. Values of being trustworthy, loyal, helpful, friendly, courteous, kind, obedient, cheerful, thrifty, brave, clean, and reverent have helped over one hundred million Scouts know right from wrong.

Knowing what is the right thing to do in a given situation and having a simple set of instructions makes life easier. Knowledge alone is not enough, however, and won't make much difference by itself.

We can only do what we can do. We can't do what we can't do. But we can do something: doing a good turn daily, being prepared, helping other people at all times requires action. The words Micah uses are action verbs: Act . . . Love . . . Walk.

It's not complicated. First we need to know what to do. Second, we have to act upon those simple truths.

DEAR GOD, in a world of complexity, remind me of simple truths. Help me to be physically strong, mentally awake, and morally straight. Give me the strength to act justly, love mercy, and walk humbly with You. *Amen.*

RON SCHOENMEHL
Boy Scouts of America, San Diego, Calif.

✝   *Read Ps. 87*

EVERYONE WAS BORN IN HER

Indeed, of Zion it will be said, "This one and that one were born in her, and the Most High himself will establish her."—Ps. 87:5

Psalm Eighty-seven is a 2,800-year-old song of unity and peace. Many scholars believe the psalm was written and first performed by those responsible for conducting worship in the temple in Jerusalem. "Everyone was born in her . . . All my fresh springs are in you." All creation draws its life and inspiration from the city of peace.

And yet we have turned "the city of our God" into a city of death. Over the centuries Jews, Christians, and Muslims have slaughtered one another prosecuting their claims to the holy mountain. Jesus Christ Himself calls Jerusalem "the place where prophets are killed" (Luke 13:33). What better evidence is there of our failure to live up to our promise as children of God than that we despoil the place God loves the most?

Hear what God is saying: "You Jew, you Christian, you Muslim, you Buddhist, you Hindu; you white, black, brown, yellow; you man, woman, child—all of you did I create from the dust of the narrow streets of my city, the city of peace. You are, all of you, neighbors. Start acting like it!"

DEAR GOD, who gave the Son You love to die in the place You cherish, help us to see that so often our actions are the mirror image of Your hopes for us. Help us to know that when You say peace, You do not mean war; when You say love, You do not mean hate. Build Your glorious city anew in each of our hearts. Keep us strong to do Your will. *Amen.*

JOHN H. TAYLOR
Executive Director, Richard Nixon Library & Birthplace Foundation,
Yorba Linda, Calif.

WHEN GOD COMMANDS

Whatsoever is commanded by the God of heaven, let it be diligently done.—Ezra 7:23

When in the service of our armed forces, we learn to take commands and fulfill them to the best of our ability. In the doing of this we learn to be sincere. Our heavenly Father has commanded certain things to be done by His children. From the Book Divine we learn what God has commanded. The aim of all should be sincere fidelity to that Word.

One of the common failings of all is to become a little careless, indifferent, and discouraged. Now the prophet tells us to be diligent, which means we must be everlastingly doing what God desires. This calls for a daily renewal of our zeal for God and the right, and for our country. "Let us not be weary in welldoing: for in due season we shall reap, if we faint not."

To obey the commands of God and to be diligent in observing them when the outlook is so discouraging, when all seem to have forsaken God—this calls for strength and courage, especially when clouds of doubt arise. But we may always remember that we are not alone. "Lo, I am with you always, even unto the end of the world." God's Son Jesus Christ has promised that His grace will be sufficient. They who trust God need have no fear.

ALMIGHTY GOD, in Thee alone we put our trust. Thy power none can resist. To Thee we come for strength to do Thy will. Forgive our feeble efforts to obey Thy commands. Protect the helpless; give Thy healing help to the wounded and liberty to the captives; restore the sick; help those who suffer for their faith; grant to conquered and enslaved peoples a final deliverance. Help us to be patient in welldoing, that in due time peace and unity may come, and all peoples everywhere may acknowledge God as Lord of the earth, and Thy dear Son Jesus Christ as King of kings. *Amen.*

IRWIN W. GERNERT
First Lutheran Church, Nashville, Tenn.

WE BELIEVE IN GOD

The fool hath said in his heart, There is no God.—Ps. 14:1

Sometimes we meet people who think it a sign of superior intelligence to question the reality of God. I have heard men boast of their skepticism. They say that religion is the invention of priests, that it is an "opiate of the people," that it is the wishful thinking of dreamers. The Bible speaks plainly and bluntly of all such persons.

Look upon the wonders of the world and all the marvels of the sky. Unfailing law controls all creation in every part, from tiny leaf to giant oak, from drop of water to ocean currents, from falling pebble to the movements of the stars. Can such order come by chance? That does not make sense. When we see a watch or an automobile we know that someone planned and made it. And when we look upon the marvelous order of the universe every sensible man knows that a master Mind must plan and control it all. That master Mind is God!

Look at the world within you. Can it be that your powers to think and achieve, the love that binds you to home and dear ones, the voice of conscience, the sense of honor, your hope of immortality—do all these gifts that every sensible man values more than life come from nothing? That does not make sense. Gifts like these do not come by chance. They can come from none other than God. They are His gifts to us. Therefore we believe in His wisdom, and we trust His goodness.

ALMIGHTY GOD, dispose our hearts to believe in Thee, that being fully persuaded in Thy faithfulness we may trust Thee to do for us more abundantly than we are able to ask or think; through Jesus Christ our Lord. *Amen.*

COSTEN J. HARRELL
West End Methodist Church, Nashville, Tenn.

SOUL REST

I will give you rest. . . . And ye shall find rest unto your souls.
—Matt. 11:28–29

When Jesus sent the man back home and assured him that his son was healed, He gave soul rest. When the disciples were in the storm at sea and Jesus quieted their fears, He gave soul rest. When Martha wept for Lazarus and Jesus restored him, He gave soul rest.

When the soul is alarmed and dismayed by "fightings without and fears within," and the soul learns to hear Jesus say, "I and my Father are one," He gives soul rest. When the soul, like a fluttering bird in the storm, is beaten and buffeted and we hear, "He careth for you," He gives soul rest. When the soul, dizzy with the swirl of the universe, beaten under with its material insecurities, looks upon the great ship called the Church, and feels that it is slapped with its own wet sails of futility, and yet over against all these stacks the power of His resurrection, the mounting witness of the centuries, the paramountness of the place of Jesus in the world of the best; when the beset soul can hear Him firmly and in ringing tones declare, "The gates of hell shall not prevail," yea, when the soul hears Him say, "Not even a sparrow falleth," He gives soul rest.

When the soul quakes and is baffled at what lies beyond the gateway of the deep red sunset of our mortal sojourn and hears again, "I go to prepare a place," He gives, and I find, soul rest.

O THOU WHO ART ETERNAL—the Spirit of all—may we see in our time of need the overbrooding shadow of Thy nearer presence. Here and now, despite the willfulness of our ways, we commit unto Thy unfailing love ourselves and all we hold dear. Lift us up, strong Son of God, that we may see and know the true and eternal horizons of life. For Thy name's sake. *Amen.*

JAMES E. WAERY
First Congregational Church, Iowa City, Iowa

THE GOD OF NATURE

The heavens declare the glory of God; and the firmament sheweth his handywork.—Ps. 19:1

Our family had been camping along the shore of Lake Okoboji. The scenery was beautiful; the swimming and the blue water of the lake was delightful. We had had an unusual amount of joy together. And one evening we decided to hike along the lake shore to watch the water in the moonlight. As my four-year-old daughter, holding my hand, walked along with me, we both seemed to feel the rare splendor of the scenery. In a spontaneous expression I said, "Marjorie, isn't that a beautiful new moon?" After a moment's pause she inquired in response, "Daddy, where do they get the new moon?"

The four year old's question is the question of life itself. We face a mystery. But is there a better interpretation than that in the psalm, "The heavens declare the glory of God; and the firmament sheweth his handywork." Despite humankind's destructive doings it is still true that nature is a revelation of the Eternal God. As Dean Brown says, "Can a stream rise higher than its source?" From the majesty of the mountains we think to the Creator of the mountains.

CREATIVE SPIRIT, we would be alert to see and to hear and to respond with appreciation and enjoyment to all that is good and true and beautiful. *Amen.*

C. CLIFFORD BACON
First Methodist Church, Des Moines, Iowa

THE POWER OF PRAYER

I can do all things through Christ which strengtheneth me.—Phil. 4:13

Dr. Alexis Carrel, distinguished scientist, says that he has known many who were cured of depression and other diseases by prayer. He tells this story: A man remained in church after the congregation had departed. When the minister found him gazing at a carving of Jesus on the cross and asked, "What are you doing?" he answered, "I am looking at Him, and He is looking at me." This is one of the meanings of prayer—Spirit with spirit meets. We are in the presence of reality.

Our Lord said, "I came not to judge the world, but to save the world." When He looks at us, we see ourselves as we are. All our excuses and shams fall away before His eyes, but this is not all. He shows us our sin and our weakness in order to show us His mercy. We see the sin of our souls and are cast down. He bids us look to Him through whom life can be redeemed, making us a redeeming power in the world. He shows us what we are in order to show us what we may become. He sees the broken life, and then He sees the life made whole. We look at ourselves and sometimes give up hope. He looks at us and says, "Be of good courage." We look at the difficult situation in which we find ourselves. He says: "Be of good cheer; I have overcome the world."

Prayer brings us to the Source of Power greater than ourselves. In our need and helplessness we find strength. Life takes on new meaning. We are not alone. God is our refuge and strength.

O THOU SEARCHER OF ALL HEARTS, we look unto Thee from whence our help cometh. In Thy power is our courage. In Thy light we would follow. Take us, O Lord, as we are, and make us by Thy grace what we ought to be. *Amen.*

ROGER T. NOOE
Vine Street Christian Church, Nashville, Tenn.

AN AID TO PEACE OF MIND

Is anything too hard for Jehovah?—Gen. 18:14 ARV

God had made a promise to Abraham which seemed to be contrary to nature and therefore impossible of fulfillment. Abraham took this promise in the mighty stride of his truly great faith and had no trouble with it. Experience had taught him that God is dependable. His promises might seem impossible, but they were reliable and came true.

Sarah, Abraham's wife, did not share his assurance. Abraham looked to Almighty God and said: "He can do it, and He will." Sarah looked upon the human agencies where the promise was to be fulfilled, and she said: "It cannot be." She laughed at the promise of God. And God said: "Why did Sarah laugh? Is anything too hard for Jehovah?"

This question contains a thought good for constant use, especially in times of trouble. Let us pause and ponder it. Is anything too hard for Jehovah? Every instrument which advances science brings new evidence of the wisdom and power of God revealed in our universe. The Bible is a history of God's powerful intervention in the lives of His people. Can anything be too hard for Him?

Jesus gave the definite answer to this question when He said: "With God nothing shall be impossible!" Let us firmly believe that, and apply it to all situations of life.

OUR GOD AND FATHER, we know that our doubts and fears are not justified by any lack or failure in Thee, but came as a result of our slowness of heart. We often face problems and tasks beyond our power. Make us very sure that they are not beyond Thy power and that Thou wilt rightly care for everything that we give into Thy keeping. In this assurance let us find courage and strength, peace and rest. We pray in Jesus' name. *Amen.*

OTTO G. A. EYRICH
St. John's Evangelical and Reformed Church, Lincoln, Neb.

LIFE IS WHAT YOU MAKE IT

I have played the fool.—1 Sam. 26:21
I have kept the faith.—2 Tim. 4:7

These were the epitaphs of two gifted men of long ago, each bearing the name of Saul.

"I have played the fool," was the solemn finding of Saul, the first king of Israel. To him had come the high honor of being the man to rule over Israel. God had richly endowed him with the gifts and talents becoming a great king—a magnificent physique, a jovial personality, unbounded physical courage—and the attributes of a born leader. Yet because of his inability to conquer himself, his was one of the greatest failures in history. Looking back over wasted opportunities and ungoverned impulses, he faces the bitter realization, "I have played the fool."

"I have kept the faith," were among the last words of Saul of Tarsus, apostle to the Gentiles, "chief of sinners, saved by grace." Looking through the bars of his Roman dungeon, he reviews a life filled with sacrifices and awaits death with the calm assurance that always comes to those who keep faith with God and with themselves.

These epitaphs taken from the biographies of two prominent men of long ago are sobering reminders that life is largely what we make it— either a tragic failure by the misuse of God-given talents, or a glorious success by keeping faith with God and one's own self.

OUR FATHER, realizing our weakness and our limitations, we implore Thy help and guidance that we may worthily live as becometh sons and daughters of God. Forgive us all that is past and grant that we may more satisfactorily do Thy will during these days of crisis. Protect our loved ones by Thy might and grant to us courage and strength to do our duty. *Amen.*

JOHN L. FERGUSON
Belmont Methodist Church, Nashville, Tenn.

KEEP ON

The good man lasts and lives as he is faithful.
—Hab. 2:4b (MOFFATT)

Habakkuk was speaking in a day much like our own. The Babylonians were the Axis powers of his world. Having defeated Egypt and Assyria, they were knocking at the gates of Jerusalem. They were ruthless, cruel, defiant, boastful, and were succeeding everywhere. Evil seemed triumphant. Habakkuk agonized to discover why God permitted this to happen. Then God spoke. He assured him that evil would not have the final word. God, in his own good time, would act.

Then God said in effect, "Keep on! Don't lose faith in righteousness; go right on living by your ideals." In the long march of history the individuals and nations that trust in their own power and resources and defy morality are doomed. But the righteous live. They live in the light and consciousness of God's favor.

Surely this is a word for us. Keep on keeping on! Go on doing the things you know are right. Knowing that you are with God will give you strength. Though others and nations deliberately resort to lies, dishonor treaties, deify the state, and devalue humanity, you keep spotless your honor, hold fast to the truth, exalt God to the supreme place in life that is His by right, and remember that in God's plan we are but a little lower than the angels. God says, "Keep on living by the standards that you know are right!"

ALMIGHTY GOD, who art righteous, just, and holy, we are sure that Thou art still in command of our world. In this conviction we commit ourselves to Thee and are resolved to follow the things we know to be true, honorable, just, pure, and lovely in Thy sight. Deliver us from temptation and strengthen our purpose to be true to Thee by the power of the Holy Spirit working in us. *Amen.*

GEORGE W. KIEHL
First Presbyterian Church, Newell, W.Va.

COURAGE FOR DIFFICULT DAYS

Have not I commanded thee? Be strong and of a good courage.
—Josh. 1:9

Thomas Carlyle said that life's ultimate question to every individual was, "Wilt thou be a coward or a hero?" Courage is not an instinct. Fear is an instinct. Courage is something that you acquire. It is a basic virtue like honesty and is indispensable for a Christian. Courage to face life comes from religion.

We must have courage to face life's inevitables: pain, suffering, and sorrow. When trouble comes, the coward says, "Run away." The hero says, "Stay and master it." Midnight and the rain are no respecter of persons. Some people know how to handle their rainy days better than others. Robert Louis Stevenson, when he was dying of tuberculosis on the island of Samoa, said, "I was made for contest, and the powers have willed that my battlefield should be this dingy, inglorious bed."

We must have courage to fight for a better world. Sir Norman Angel in *The Great Illusion* says that the reason that nobody in Europe was able to stop Hitler was that no nation was willing to fight, except for itself. We must be willing to fight for the oppressed of the world.

God cannot use a coward or a discouraged individual. Four times God tells Joshua, "Be . . . of a good courage." Remember Elijah's courage on top of Mount Carmel. Remember Peter's courage after Pentecost. Remember the courage of Daniel. We must have courage to face difficult days—but God gives those who ask Him that courage.

MOST GRACIOUS GOD, our heavenly Father, we do thank Thee that the Son of God, Jesus our Savior, was a fearless Man and had the courage to face the difficult days confronting Him. Give us courage to live and fight for a better world. *Amen.*

JAMES MILTON MCKNIGHT
Armstrong Memorial Presbyterian Church, Norfolk, Va.

FAITH IS THE ANSWER

Alleluia; for the Lord God omnipotent reigneth.—Rev. 19:6

True faith in God does not imply that we anticipate an easy future or believe that God will intervene to crown our righteous cause with an early victory. Faith is not confidence in God's willingness to serve those who seek His support. Faith is surrender to the will of God, even though that will may include the dark night of Gethsemane or the anguish of Calvary. Faith is serene trust in God's ability to use all human forces and passions for the fulfillment of His eternal purposes. It is a divinely inspired conviction that God's plans cannot be frustrated, that even the wrath of humankind can be made to praise Him.

People of faith read both their Bibles and the book of history. They behold there the eternal unity of God's message and method. They see clearly the guiding hand of God in all the movement of the centuries and the changing fortunes of individuals and nations. Yes, "the Lord God omnipotent reigneth." He is still Lord of His own creation.

There have been many dark nights in the world's history, but the Sun of Righteousness has always risen to gild again the eastern hills with entrancing dawn of a new day of peace and progress. The God who is "the same yesterday, and today, and forever" still controls His own universe. "God's tomorrow will be brighter than today!"

O THOU SUPREME COMMANDER OF THE UNIVERSE, grant unto us the quiet certainty, that over all our ways brood Thy wisdom and Thy love. Breathe over our minds the benediction of Thy grace and speak to us the assurance of Thy forgiveness. Give us courage sufficient for the daily task and lead us from temptation to victory and peace. For Thine is the Kingdom and the Power and the Glory forever. *Amen.*

W. W. McKinney
First Presbyterian Church, Ambridge, Pa.

WHEN THE GUNS STOP

They shall beat their swords into plowshares, and their spears into pruninghooks.—Mic. 4:3

To most in the armed forces, the time visualized by Micah seems a long way off. Even the end of the present war seems very distant. Yet it will come, and it's good to prepare spiritually for the letdown that the armistice will bring.

I was in France about eight kilometers behind the front lines when World War I stopped. My brother and I took a walk out into the countryside in the Argonne Forest. We came upon a bonfire about two miles out of town, there being no further need for a blackout. The boys around the fire were singing hymns. The chaplain led in prayer and then gave a short message telling the soldiers what peace could mean. We left that scene of peace and good fellowship with "Blest be the tie that binds" ringing in our ears.

Back in town, the cafes were full, and drunken soldiers were spewed out on the sidewalk. We saw one man with his head cut open—not by an enemy bullet, but by a beer bottle in the hands of an inebriated friend. Perhaps the pattern for the ensuing peace was from the fabric of that celebration.

When peace comes it will be either a prayer-meeting peace or a drunken peace. It will either have in it the elements of goodwill and understanding of the needs of all people, or be stupid and bestial. The latter will result in a brief armistice; the former may result in a world wherein dwelleth righteousness.

OUR FATHER, although now we be people at war Thou knowest that we would rather be people of peace. Help us to learn those principles upon which a lasting peace may be built. Help us to learn to love one another. Help us to walk in the footsteps of our unity-loving Prince of Peace. In His name. *Amen.*

NORMAN E. NYGAARD
Chaplain, Lockheed Overseas

SUBMISSION AND CONSECRATION

Not every one that saith unto me, Lord, Lord, . . . but he that doeth the will of my Father.—Matt. 7:21

"Thy will be done." Twice Jesus used these words. On that last night when He prayed alone in Gethsemane, He saw ahead the scorn, the suffering, and the inevitable death. To be sure, He had followed courageously the road that led to this very hour. But now in the final moment of testing, it seemed too much. There was still an opportunity to slip out and escape. But this would be a cowardly denial of all He had lived for, and with unwavering confidence in the goodness and wisdom and ultimate triumph of God He cried, "Nevertheless not my will, but thine, be done." And He set for us the supreme example of submission to God's will.

But life is not merely passive submission. When He gave His disciples the model prayer, Jesus taught them to say, "Thy kingdom come. Thy will be done in earth, as it is in heaven." How often we have repeated the familiar words. Yet if we would pray them right, they call for self-dedication to a glorious task. The Kingdom comes on earth when we learn to devote ourselves without reserve to the cause of justice and mercy, of uprightness and goodwill, of unity and love. An impossible ideal? Jesus did not think so. He showed the way Himself in tireless effort to bring in that Kingdom and challenged all the faith in us to follow Him in doing God's will.

HOLY GOD, we have seen the matchless courage of Jesus, who, seemingly alone, faced the impossible task of bringing Thy Kingdom to an evil world, believing that with Thee all things are possible. Today across the ages His challenge comes to us in a troubled hour, bidding us follow Him. Lord, make us strong to do Thy will when we see it, and patient to wait on Thy will where yet we cannot see. In His name. *Amen.*

FREDERICK W. STEWART
Denison University, Granville, Ohio

A FAITH TO FIGHT FOR

This is the victory that overcometh the world, even our faith.
—1 John 5:4

Y ou in the armed forces have the difficult task of keeping "chins up" when you know that separation from friends and loved ones, dangers of sea, land, and air, and death itself must be faced. In a way, though, the difference between this new life of yours and the old is only one of degree, not of kind; and successful service anywhere requires faith. Robert Browning, regarded by some as England's greatest poet, expressed it as follows:

If I stoop
Into a dark tremendous sea of cloud,
It is but for a time; I press God's lamp
Close to my breast; its splendor, soon or late,
Will pierce the gloom: I shall emerge one day.

"God's Lamp" is the profound conviction that your life and mine, if directed by the sincere desire to cooperate in His purposes and plans, count for time and eternity.

This faith is yours for the taking if you want it—an *assurance* that out of this war, world peace will be brought nearer; a *conviction* of the reality of God, working out His purposes in spite of humans and through each humble believer, even though the time needed includes centuries as well as days.

O GOD, help us to believe in Thy indwelling Presence in spite of dark clouds. We thank Thee for the brave souls who all down through the ages have been victors over suffering and sorrow because of their faith in Thee. Give us brave hearts, and help us to hold fast to our trust in Thee and to our faith in Thy Son Jesus Christ, our Master, Savior, Lord, and Friend. *Amen.*

ELAM J. ANDERSON
President, University of Redlands, Redlands, Calif.

UNFINISHED JOURNEYS

Whensoever I take my journey into Spain.—Rom. 15:24

Paul was intensely interested in his chosen work. He began in the city of Antioch, then journeyed through the provinces of Asia Minor, and next entered Europe. As he went from place to place his vision grew, his horizon widened; he took the world as his field of labor. He wrote to the Christians in distant Rome that he would visit them when he made his "journey into Spain." Undoubtedly he looked forward to it with longing.

Meanwhile he kept busy with his daily tasks and also proceeded to gather funds for the needy in Jerusalem. He expected to deliver those monies and then set out on that projected journey. All this was upset by his arrest and trial. In place of going to Spain he reached a Roman prison. His plans were ruined and his liberty lost, but he did not get discouraged nor become embittered and pessimistic. In place of complaining, he accepted the true pattern of life, as shown in his letter to the Philippians, in which he said, "I have learned, in whatsoever state I am, therewith to be content."

We all have "unfinished journeys." Our true worth is shown by the manner in which we meet those disappointments. Paul kept cheerful and planned for the future although there was as yet no promise of release.

OUR FATHER, in times of stress and disappointment we call upon Thee to reveal to us the comfort of Thy presence, even amid the clouds that envelop us. Teach us to know Thy will, and show us how to follow it. Help us to plan our "journeys." Strengthen us for the daily task, and may the peace that passeth understanding be ours even though the journey may remain incomplete. *Amen.*

WILLIAM E. VANDERBILT
Washington and Jefferson College, Washington, Pa.

THEY THAT SHALL BE OF THEE

They that shall be of thee shall build the old waste places . . . and thou shalt be called, The repairer of the breach, The restorer of paths to dwell in.—Isa. 58:12

That is a fine word of bold optimistic anticipation. One of the most refreshing feelings that ever thrills the human soul is that of becoming comfortably confident that the ideals it has held and loved and labored for will be secure in those who come after. One of the bitterest disappointments death is ever made to reveal to the soul is that the cause it has given so much of its time and affection to must now be committed to those who come after and yet care nothing about it, and by whom the withering effect of neglect will surely soon be made evident.

To you, young men and women arising now to power, we throw the torch! We have tried honestly to build nobly; we have tried to shape well the things of lasting value. We cannot bear to think of being buried out of all this if you fail to catch and hold high the great Christian ideals. It isn't death we fear. We dread only to be buried away from these great ideals of faith we have held so immeasurably dear all our lives, if you who come along allow them to wither.

But we gather courage, for we do believe in you. We have calm confidence that you are those who are, in true faith in God, to build the waste places and keep in repair the paths of God's ways among humanity.

> Faith of our fathers! living still
> In spite of dungeon, fire, and sword,
> O how our hearts beat high with joy
> When e'er we hear that glorious word!
> Faith of our fathers, holy faith!
> We will be true to thee till death. *Amen.*
> —FREDERICK W. FABER

MERTON S. RICE
Metropolitan Methodist Church, Detroit, Mich.

MAKING FRIENDS WITH GOD

Those that seek me early shall find me.—Prov. 8:17

It is saddening to note how many people turn to God only as a last resort. So long as things are going well with them and they have the material comforts they wish, the health they desire, and their friends about them, no thought of God or their relationship with Him enters the vestibule of their minds. It is only when something tragic happens to them that they turn to religion. You recall what the tavern hostess said of Sir John Falstaff: "He cried out, 'God, God, God!' three or four times. Now I, to comfort him, bid him not to think of God; I hoped there was no need to trouble himself with such thoughts yet."

The pathos of all this is of course that we do not and cannot get from God the help we need in a crisis unless we have made God's acquaintance before. When we are in trouble, we do not expect help from strangers; we expect it from friends and we are not disappointed. Our friends have shared our joys; they help bear our sorrows. He who calls to God only in emergencies does not always find Him even then. We cannot borrow character in a crisis. We cannot fix up a friendship with God, and expect it to mean very much, on our deathbed. Since, therefore, faith and character and inner spiritual resources will someday be indispensable, we should seek them now. Since someday we shall have to cry to the gods of our choice, we should find now One who will not fail us.

O GOD, our Father, whose love can save to the uttermost, we thank Thee that no life is too marred that Thou canst not redeem it when penitence doth admit Thy grace. But save us from basely presuming upon Thy mercy. Instead of offering to Thee but the dregs of life, help us to give our best to Thee, who hast given Thine all for us. Through Jesus Christ our Lord. *Amen.*

THOMAS N. CARRUTHERS
Christ Church, Episcopal, Nashville, Tenn.

ORDINARY ANDREW

One of the two which . . . followed him, was Andrew.—John 1:40

One of the mysteries of Christian history is the power by which individuals of ordinary gifts have achieved extraordinary things. The New Testament is the greatest of books and the Church the greatest of institutions, but the men who wrote the one and founded the other were for the most part ordinary men. The man called Andrew, first among those who "left all and followed" Jesus, is an example of the extraordinary use of ordinary gifts. His name is an encouragement and a challenge to us all.

Jesus once told a story about a man whose employer had given him a sum of money to invest. It was a small sum. Others had been given more. And he did nothing with it. When time came for an accounting he had made no profit, and his master blamed him with bitter words.

Jesus was not a businessman, however, and His interest was not in cash, but in character. The five-talent man and the two-talent man invested their trust funds shrewdly and courageously. The one-talent man thought that, being poorly endowed, he need not take a risk or make an effort.

The point of the story is the responsibility of ordinary people. In the pressing business of the times we must depend on one-talent people. Not on them who have much, not on them who have nothing, but on them who have a little does the welfare of the nation and the world depend. Great ability, heroism, and work may do much, but they can do nothing without the help of ordinary men and women.

O GOD, we are ordinary people, but we have an extraordinary Savior. Help us to mirror His life, to use our ordinary talents for Him, and to see them become extraordinary. *Amen.*

ALVIN E. MAGARY
Lafayette Avenue Presbyterian Church, Brooklyn, N.Y.

WINNING FULL CITIZENSHIP

We are unprofitable servants: we have done that which was our duty to do.—Luke 17:10

Christianity is a religion of doing "more than is expected." The goal of ordinary citizenship is the fulfillment of duty. And a remarkable community would exist where most of the people accepted their civic responsibilities. But Christians who would win full citizenship will go beyond duty. They will go the second mile; they will give their cloaks as well as their coats. They will exceed the established limits of personal obligation.

Daily let us strive to do more than is expected of us. Let us do so, not for reward or praise, but for the inner satisfaction of knowing that such a life fulfills the requirements of Christian citizenship. Wherever you are—and Americans today are all around the world representing the United States before all nations; whoever you're with—and Americans are thrown shoulder to shoulder with all kinds of races and peoples; whatever is done—and Americans are seeing life at its worst and its best; be the best that you can be, and do the best that you can do!

We can do no more than we are capable of doing. We can be no more than we have a capacity to be. But very few individuals ever make their lives complete. There is so much unused energy, so many unused brain cells, so much of the spirit that never gets expressed. What a goal to serve and reach when we touch the limits of our own qualifications and capacities. Go beyond all former limits and goals. This growth and progress in character and service is the way of winning full citizenship.

"LORD, increase our faith!" Help me to have confidence in the gifts which thou hast bestowed upon me, and send me out to serve in the will to be and do the best of which I am capable. May Jesus inspire and help me. *Amen.*

CARLETON BROOKS MILLER
First Congregational Church, Battle Creek, Mich.

LITTLE VICTORIES

Behold, the hour cometh, yea, is now come, that ye shall be scattered, every man to his own. . . . But be of good cheer: I have overcome the world.—John 16:32–33

There seemed small cause for cheer. Jesus was about to go on trial for His life, to be condemned, and finally to be executed on a cross. And confronting that prospect, He said, "Be of good cheer: I have overcome the world." Had He?

We know that He had only a few followers. And they were to scatter while He was being tried. Yet, looking back across the centuries, we know that these words are profoundly true. He had conquered the world within Himself. "Not my will, but thine, be done." That was His prayer, and that was the basis of His triumph. Whenever we conquer ourselves, we have made the first conquest. Greater is "he that ruleth his spirit than he that taketh a city." Jesus had overcome the world within Himself. But He had also conquered another world.

A few people had caught His vision. And on the lives of those believers He would build the greatest institution on earth, the Christian Church. It was a little victory that had overcome the world. And it is possible for us to be winning such little victories all of the time, in our places of responsibility, within our own minds, and in all our relationships with others. And one day, by virtue of these little victories, the Kingdom of righteousness and peace will be established throughout the world. Little victories that overcome the world!

ETERNAL GOD, show us, we pray Thee, that out of small things Thou canst create that which is of great moment. Give us the strength we need this day to overcome the world and so take our place by the side of those who are building for a fairer tomorrow. In the name of Him who overcame His world. *Amen.*

LEE FLETCHER
First Congregational Church, Albany, N.Y.

RESOURCES FOR VICTORIOUS LIVING

Be still, and know that I am God.—Ps. 46:10

No wonder there is a growing consciousness of need, a wistful yearning for spirituality, a crying out for quality and strength of life among increasing numbers of people young and old. Walter Lippmann remarks on the way in which modern life goes forward "in a bath of noise," so that, he reminds us, if we are to think at all, we must, for part of the day, create about ourselves "a pool of silence." Spiritual sanity and balance demand that we go below the surface. Blake understood life in saying:

> Great things are done when men and mountains meet;
> This is not done by jostling in the street.

Professor Pupin of Columbia, who has published his fascinating autobiography under the title *From Immigrant to Inventor*, perfected the telephone for general use. He says that his great problem was to eliminate the sounds of the earth. At first these earth sounds made themselves heard over the telephone and confused the sounds of the human voice, and the problem was to tune the telephone so that it would be dead to the earth's sounds and respond only to the others. What a parable this is of the problem which this generation faces if it is to develop the dynamics of mind and heart and will, which taken together form a dynamic effective personality, set in the midst of opportunities, privileges and tasks of this modern day.

O GOD, our Father, help us to tune out the static of our day and tune in Thy voice and the voice of Thy Son Jesus Christ. Grant Thy blessing upon us, in the Master's name. *Amen.*

JAMES C. BAKER
Bishop, Los Angeles Area, Methodist

A GOODLY HERITAGE

The Spirit itself beareth witness with our spirit, that we are the children
of God: and if children, then heirs.—Rom. 8:16–17

Recently I read a biography of a long line of noble ancestry of the Daniel family, who all received as heritage the Great Hollow Farms handed down from ancestors for generations. The biographer tells us it was common to see the elder Daniel walking over vast acreage daily with a faithful collie at his side. Instead of a cane he carried a weeder. When he lifted a weed he could be heard to say to the collie: "There it is, Jack. You know, we must pass these farms on to the youngsters cleaner, greener, and better than when we received them." What a parable of life for every man and woman! We must hand our acreage back to God more cleansed than when we received it.

It is not true that I came into this life empty-handed. I brought with me the best and the worst my ancestors had to give me. But I also brought something of the blue of the skies; I brought with me something of the holiness of God, of purity of angels, a life fresh and pure—a flower fresh and pure from the paradise of God. And one of these mornings, when I stand at the judgment bar of God, I am expected to hand back that heritage to God used in the service of my Lord and His blessed Kingdom, but purer and more sanctified than when I received it. There is no problem concerning my duty. That is clear. The only problem after all is how best to develop my life for the Lord.

FATHER, we thank Thee for the manifold gifts which we have received of Thee. We thank Thee for the world which Thou hast made and that Thou hast permitted us to dwell in it. Gracious God, grant that we may be ever mindful of thy bounties, ever grateful to Thee for Thy goodness. *Amen.*

WILLIAM G. HAWK
Homestead Avenue United Brethren Church, Johnstown, Pa.

LORD OF A CITY

So built we the wall.—Neh. 4:6

Dear Fred: Soon you will be joining your brothers in bombing attacks on cities and their military objectives. We are all caught in this work of destruction, but let's not forget that God's will for us is construction, the building of fairer cities and lovelier homes.

"That is the work which our Lord undertook in the cities of Galilee and Judea. You may dig these things out of your New Testament as I have tried to do and watch Him helping in the home where He was a Lodger; paying taxes; treating a proud man to some mighty humbling table talk; pointing out to Zachaeus the fact that he was traveling a wrong road; dealing firsthand with various social problems, disease, outcasts, sinners, making a member of a hated and despised race the hero of the world's greatest short story, the Good Samaritan; worshiping in church, "as his custom was," each Sabbath; working on the corporate conscience of each community; teaching the children; weeping in compassion over Jerusalem; and carrying more than His own weight of suffering on that tough road to Calvary.

"Somehow, Fred, we must win His Spirit and keep it in these war days. It is the only hope for our world. And remember that He promised to be with His disciples to illumine their minds, strengthen their moral courage, and share their sufferings."

LORD OF TRUTH, we do not pray for ourselves alone but for those whom Thou hast given us to love. Gather them into Thy tender keeping lest any harm befall them. Breathe upon all the benediction of Thy peace. Our prayer is offered in the name of One who said, "Ask, and ye shall receive, that your joy may be full." *Amen.*

HERBERT BEECHER HUDNUT
Woodward Avenue Presbyterian Church, Detroit, Mich.

COMMITMENT

Commit thy way unto the Lord; trust also in him, and he shall bring it to pass.—Ps. 37:5

A little orphan child left New York City to make her home with a beloved aunt in Minneapolis. There was simply a tag about her neck, announcing her destination, her name, and that she was alone. A kind friend turned the little girl over to the conductor of the through train to Chicago. Soon the story of the little girl was noised among the passengers. Everyone was gracious, thoughtful, attentive and sympathetic.

The conductor and his associates cared for every need she had. Upon arrival at Chicago, the conductor went across the city and transferred her to his colleague conductor on the northern train. She received every attention there as well without undue embarrassing publicity. Her story became known again, and everyone felt for the little orphan. Her way was *committed*; she had a *trustful* little heart. When she walked down the passageway at her destination she saw the happy face of her aunt; and in a moment her little arms were clasped about that loving neck, and tears were falling from both.

On the other side our loving Father awaits. He is our Father in heaven! We all are but children. This simple tale of a little girl touches our hearts because it reveals the friendship and love of our heavenly home, "I go to prepare a place for you."

OUR HEAVENLY FATHER, who hast taught us how good it is to follow the holy desires which Thou hast put into our hearts, give us grace to seek and desire Thy will and Thy best gift to the children of humankind. Forgive us, we pray, for the imperfections of even the best offering we can make to Thee. Kindle Thou our sacrifice by the heavenly fire of Thine own goodness and infinite love. In Jesus' name. *Amen.*

JOHN TIMOTHY STONE
President Emeritus, Presbyterian Theological Seminary, Chicago, Ill.

MEETING DISCOURAGEMENT

And David was greatly distressed . . . because the soul of all the people was grieved . . . but David encouraged himself in the Lord his God.—1 Sam. 30:6

Every person knows hardships, feels limitations, experiences failures, and occasionally becomes discouraged; and the verse from the Bible tells what David did when that happened.

Many people are wondering about God in these times, how it is that He has allowed the world to get into its present fix, where He can be, and what He may be doing. In facing these questions there are two facts to keep in mind. First, it is humanity, not God, that makes trouble. We have been richly endowed by our Creator and have no reason to blame Him for our misuse of His gifts. We must remember that the moral law operates in the universe as surely as does the law of gravity.

Second, we are still moral infants, and if we hurt ourselves in learning to walk it does not signify that God has been careless. Those high attributes of humanity, namely, conscience, morals, honor, social idealism, and a sense of duty, are still in their early stages of development. Our technical and mechanical abilities have outrun our moral controls, and so we have brought trouble upon ourselves. But let us not be discouraged; give God and us time.

OUR FATHER IN HEAVEN, look with sympathy upon the turmoil of our beings in these times. Feel the impulses of our hearts, and bear the words of our lips that carry a deep regard for Thee. Afford us the comfort of spirit that comes from a sense of harmony between ourselves and Thee. Understand the struggles we are making to hold on to our ideals and to keep the faith in these times. And even though we cannot always see our way, may we persevere in the course that seems to be plotted by Thee. *Amen.*

JESSE L. MURRELL
First Methodist Church, Covington, Ky.

ABIDING WITH HIM

*He saith unto them, Come and see. They came and saw where he
dwelt, and abode with him that day: for it was about the tenth hour.*
                                                              —John 1:39

At the very beginning of the public ministry of Jesus some of John's
disciples asked Him where He lived. Jesus said, "Come and see." The
disciples accepted His invitation and went with Him, "and abode with him
that day."

From that simple incident, about which there is nothing startling or
unusual, has flowed unmeasured blessing to humankind. It was the beginning of that personal fellowship with Jesus Christ which has brought peace
and abiding joy to people in all generations since.

Andrew and John and the others did not look like men who were to
initiate the spiritual conquest of the world. But they had found the
Messiah. Jesus had been pointed out to them as the One "of whom Moses
in the law, and the prophets, did write." All their lives they had been taught
about the Messiah, and now they took all their religious teaching and
knowledge and went to spend the day with Jesus. They found Him to be
all that they had learned that He would be, and they determined not to
part from Him again.

The only way to make a good world is through the contagion of a
good life. Only Jesus Christ, living in us, can heal the world of its sorrow.
Apart from Christ the world has no meaning and life no purpose. With
Him struggle is grand and even defeat is victory.

O great and gracious Son of Man,
Most glorious Thou of all I am,
Most potent Thou of all who can—
I give up all to follow Thee. *Amen.*

AHVA J. C. BOND
Dean, School of Theology, Alfred University, Alfred, N.Y.

TWO WORLDS

Whatsoever things are lovely . . . think on these things.—Phil. 4:8

You who are members of the armed forces of the United States find yourselves—as some of us did a generation ago—plunged into a world to which you are strangers. It may have its points, as you will discover someday as you look back upon it. But in the main it is a world of shattered ambitions, frustrated love, haunting fear, and perhaps of hell itself if the heavy burden of killing rests directly on you.

But there is another world which you must keep fresh in memory and aspiration. You have gone out from important sections of that world that others may live in it and that someday you—we hope—may be permitted to return to it. It is the world of home—father, mother, child—where love abides and waits. It is the world of friendship, in which hands and hearts are joined in quiet friendship. It is a world of nature—beautiful, inspiring, majestic with flowers, sunsets, and mountains. It is a world of music and art—the abiding place of beauty. It holds good books and the leisure to read them in store. It has work which one loves to do. It has God waiting at sanctuaries where everything is designed to speak of Him. Allow that world to live in memory and aspiration, that one day it may live in daily experience.

O GOD, help me to live in two worlds at the same time. I would be brave in this grim world of war where I must walk. Help me to play the part of a soldier in it. But help me to live also with the great spirits of the human race—Jesus, Isaiah, and the noble company of the prophets. Give me time for great thoughts which encompass the world. Help me most of all to live with Thee. *Amen.*

VERE V. LOPER
First Congregational Church, Berkeley, Calif.

GIVING THE SWORD OF THE SPIRIT A CHANCE

I store thy word within my heart, to keep myself from sinning against thee. . . . The interpretation of thy words enlightens and instructs the open-minded.—Ps. 119:11, 130 (MOFFATT)

Thomas Fuller, a chaplain of Cromwell's day, has left this comment: "Lord, this morning I read a chapter in the Bible, and therein observed a memorable passage, whereof I never took notice before. Why now, and no sooner, did I see it? Formerly my eyes were as open, and the letters as legible. Is there not a thin veil laid over thy Word, which is more rarified by reading and at last fully worn away?"

Out of his experience Moody declared, "I know the Bible is inspired because it inspires me." A native youth in India, whose zeal and love outran his English, wrote to a friend about a revival they were having, saying, "We are having a great rebible here."

Important as is the Bible in a courtroom, it is more important as personal equipment; it may be used to settle arguments, but better yet it answers the deepest needs of the human heart; it is a symbol of religion, but will point its reader to the way of life; it has long been the bestseller, for no other book offers such comfort, guidance, or inspiration.

> Shine forth, O Light, that we may see,
> With hearts all unafraid,
> The meaning and the mystery
> Of things that Thou hast made:
> Shine forth, and let the darkling past
> Beneath Thy beam grow bright;
> Shine forth, and touch the future vast
> With Thine untroubled light. *Amen.*
> —WASHINGTON GLADDEN

EDGAR T. WELCH
Former President, Welch Grapejuice Co.
President, Methodist Board of Lay Activities, Westfield, N.Y.

CONFIDENCE

Let us run with patience the race that is set before us, looking unto Jesus the author and finisher of our faith.—Heb. 12:1, 2

Maurice Maeterlinck published *Before the Great Silence* in Paris. He has always been a questioner; the mystic has battled the skeptic for the possession of his soul. He has no hope of social immortality because the hope for humanity is a fading gleam. "Humanity will have ceased to be when men have reproduced and exhausted all the inventions of nature— but it is more probable that it will have slain itself with its own hands long before this comes."

This is the mood of many today. It might well be the mood of all, but for our religious faith. Over against such words I like to turn to a man who knew far more of physical distress and suffering than Maeterlinck has known. John Bunyan writes: "In this country [of Beulah] the sun shineth night and day, wherefore this was beyond the Valley of the Shadow of Death, and also out of the reach of the Giant Despair, neither could they from this place so much as see Doubting Castle." In the closing words of the tenth chapter of Hebrews are some great expressions of confident faith: "Now do not drop that confidence of yours. . . . We are not the men to shrink back and be lost, but to have faith and so to win our souls."

O GRACIOUS GOD, who dost sustain by Thy strength those who trust in Thee, be nearer to those on the fields of battle, in the places where soldiers are trained for conflict, in all the homes of our land, and give us that confidence in the triumph of the right and the victory of the good which can come only from belief in a great spiritual purpose in our universe. We ask in the name of Jesus Christ, who came to reveal that purpose. *Amen.*

IVAN LEE HOLT
Bishop, Dallas, Tex. Area, Methodist

BEYOND THE CALL OF DUTY

What do ye more than others?—Matt. 5:47b

The Medal of Honor can be given to any officer or enlisted person who shall "in action involving actual conflict with an enemy distinguish him- or herself conspicuously by gallantry and intrepidity, at the risk of his or her life, above and beyond the call of duty."

One of the distinguishing marks of true Christian character is also the willingness to take risks and go beyond what is demanded by the call of duty. Our Lord Jesus Christ made it clear that He expected this of His followers when He challenged them with the question, "What do ye more than others?" To conform to ordinary standards of decency and respectability was not enough. Jesus intended that His disciples should be the light of the world and that they should go far beyond what was required by customary ideas of duty.

Extra service, the willingness to do more than what is demanded of us, is a measure of reality of our patriotism and the depth of our religion. To go beyond others in acts of courage, loyalty, and kindness is one of the marks of a "good soldier of Jesus Christ."

O GOD, our Father, we thank Thee for the heroic examples of all faithful people who have gone beyond the call of duty in their service to their country and in their service of Thee. We humbly pray for strength for our daily tasks and for the spirit of devotion that goes beyond what is required in loyalty and in unselfish love. *Amen.*

JAMES C. PERKINS
The Federated Churches, Schroon Lake, N.Y.

PERSONALITY INVESTED

The Word was made flesh, and dwelt among us, full of grace and truth.—John 1:14
As my Father hath sent me, even so send I you.—John 20:21

The word *Word* here comes from the Greek *logos*, which means all that we mean by "plan, purpose, intent, end." The plan, purpose, intent, *personality* of God "was made flesh"—concrete, visible, so that we could see Him, how He would behave living under the conditions under which we live.

This "Word in the flesh," Jesus, said to His disciples, "As my Father hath sent me, even so send I you." So we are to invest our personalities and reveal the deepest purposes of our hearts and lives as He did.

Tennyson expressed his in poetry; Shakespeare, in drama; Gladstone, in statesmanship; Einstein, in mathematics; Eddington, in astronomy; Mother, in her sacrifices for home and family; Father, in his untiring industry and sacrificial thrift for his family and church and nation. So each one of us has a way to invest our personality, all we are, the best we are. Who can deny that in the long evolution of humanity and in God's purpose overcoming our sin and saving our free will God is in history? If He is—and I can believe nothing else—there must be a place for all of us to invest our personalities to resist or prevent Satan, no matter how or in whom personified, from being victorious over any inch of ground we can save for our freedom and God's glory—His glory because He always wills that we shall be free and use our freedom for the realization of the highest.

O GOD, help us to follow the example of Thyself in Jesus and invest our personalities, at whatever sacrifice, for the good of others and the ultimate glory of God in human history. *Amen.*

FREDERICK ERDMANN SMITH
Austin Baptist Church, Chicago, Ill.

KNOWING JESUS

Martha, Martha, you are anxious and worried about many things. There is need of only one thing. Mary has chosen the better part, which will not be taken away from her.—Luke:10:41–42 NRSV

In this story, Martha and Mary welcomed Jesus readily into their table fellowship. In the context of the Jewish community, this was a special privilege and intimate kind of relationship. So many centuries removed from the time of Jesus, we also need to prepare to welcome Him into our families and into our intimate company.

The different roles that the two sisters play in this story are important. Martha is busy about the necessary task of preparing the meal. Mary, on the other hand, is serving as the host of Jesus within the household. Inherently, neither of these tasks is more worthy than the other. The living out of our Christian commitments may involve us in different roles in different situations with different combinations of people. Whether our service is some form of manual labor or involves us in a more direct personal encounter, each of these tasks has a dignity in and of itself.

Finally, Jesus uses the minor dispute between the two sisters to emphasize the importance of focusing on His presence and its significance in both of their lives. Knowing Jesus takes time and effort. We need to read the Scriptures, study the theological tradition, and spend time in prayer. In this sense, no matter what our particular roles in life, we need to come to know the Lord with all of our mind, heart, and strength.

O GOD, help me to focus this day on coming to know Your Son, Jesus Christ. Help me in the busyness of life to focus first on the most fundamental things. Help me to pray so that I might have a deep wellspring to draw upon for my service of Your people. *Amen.*

EDWARD A. MALLOY
President, University of Notre Dame, Notre Dame, Ind.

✝

THANK GOD FOR SOWERS

A sower went out to sow his seed. . . . Some fell on the rock; and . . . it withered. . . . Some fell into good soil, and when it grew, it produced a hundred fold.—Luke 8:5–8 NRSV

Have you ever taken a walk in the woods? If so, you likely returned all covered with weed seeds. The next time you have that experience and begin to pick off the seeds, think for a moment about the many subtle ways God has devised to scatter nature's seeds. Not only do human beings distribute the seeds; animals also transport them in their fur. The winds carry them aloft to new homes. Some burst forth from exploding pods. Certain species of pine trees carefully guard their seeds in cones for years until a fire causes the cones to open and scatter the seeds.

Just as He has a plan for scattering nature's seeds, God has devised a means of scattering His seeds of love and Good News to human beings. His followers have been empowered to be the spiritual sowers. Every act of kindness done in His name, each encouraging word to someone in need, and every testimony of His life-changing power to a seeker is evidence of being a sower for God. Some seeds will surely fall along the pathway and simply get trodden underfoot or wither from a lack of care. Yet, many of these seeds will cling to the lives of those in need. In some cases, the seeds may go seemingly unnoticed for years or lie dormant until the heat of a crisis causes them to spring forth. Still others are picked up and carried away to enrich additional lives.

Thank God for His unique ways of planting His seeds among us. In turn, may each of us be a sower of good seeds to others.

DEAR LORD, equip us to be skillful sowers of Your seeds. Give us compassionate hearts and willing spirits that we may be used to spread Your love to all we meet along the pathways of life. *Amen.*

R. CHIP TURNER
Baptist Broadcasting Center, Fort Worth, Tex.

YOU CAN'T BLACK OUT THE STARS

In all these things we are more than conquerors through him that loved us.—Rom. 8:37

In one of the conquered countries, a captain of the conquering army stood before a weatherbeaten farmer and ordered him to turn over certain of his crops to his soldiers. The captain brusquely said, "And if you are stubborn we will take away everything you have." Quietly the countryman replied, "But you can't take away the stars." You can read into that simple reply the most profound philosophy of the ages—for no conqueror can destroy the imperishables of God.

Many people today are fearful that civilization will be destroyed. But humankind's achievements have never depended upon outward circumstances, but always upon the inward power of our minds and hearts—upon the divine image within us. Some will compose music if they live in only a garret. They will paint great art though they be clothed in rags. They will write great literature whenever ideas take fire in their brains. They will cleave to the truth though their tongues be cut from their mouths. Home, love, religion—these are imperishable in our hearts.

We can black out our cities. We can torture each other's bodies. We can destroy our property and our future. We can wreck nations as well as blot out human lives. We can black out our cities and black out our world. But we cannot black out the stars in the heavens, nor the stars of hope and freedom in the hearts of people everywhere.

ALMIGHTY GOD, who art our refuge and strength, a very present help in time of trouble, grant us Thy light to shine in the darkness. Grant us courage to face whatever difficulties, temptations, hardship, or suffering may come upon us. Guide us with confidence in our Lord and Savior Jesus Christ. *Amen.*

DAWSON C. BRYAN
St. Paul's Methodist Church, Houston, Tex.

REALIZING GOD'S CONSTANT PRESENCE

The Lord will command his lovingkindness in the daytime, and in the night his song shall be with me, and my prayer unto the God of my life.—Ps. 42:8

It is good to believe that God is with us day and night, sharing every experience; but it is thrilling to realize that fact through frequent thoughts of Him. Jesus taught that God is ever within human reach, but that teaching is meaningless until we have formed the habit of reaching out hands of faith to touch Him as the hours pass. This was the psalmist's habit: "And my prayer unto the God of my life."

We can begin the day with God by thinking first of Him upon awaking. We can think of Him objectively as "shining beauty, radiant joy, creative power, all-pervading love, purity, and serenity." We shall miss Him if we awake to dread of the day's tasks or fears of the day's perils, but waking thoughts of His care make hard work easier and save us from paralyzing alarms.

At the end of the day, having thought often of Him and spoken of Him, when we are ready for sleep, we can shed strain from body and mind, and give ourselves to grateful remembrances of His love and mercy. Appreciative thoughts of Him as sleep closes our eyes helps us easily to direct our waking thoughts of Him as another day begins. For the best way to begin tomorrow with God is to end today with thoughts of Him.

ETERNAL GOD, our Father, we rejoice that Thou art with us day and night, but we deeply long more fully to realize this blessed fact. Help us this day to deliver our full energies upon our tasks, but as the day goes on may we find moments in which to remember Thee, O Thou who dost never forget us! Keep in our hearts a song of Thy lovingkindness, and make us strong to fulfill Thy purposes through us, in Jesus Christ our Lord. *Amen.*

RICHARD L. OWNBEY
Main Street Methodist Church, Reidsville, N.C.

CHRISTIAN HEROISM

And he that doth not take his cross and follow after me, is not worthy of me. He that findeth his life shall lose it; and he that loseth his life for my sake shall find it.—Matt. 10:38–39 ARV

Those who risk their lives in the interest of a great cause thus win respect and consecrate themselves forever. The elemental human rights and the greatest treasures of civilization—freedom of thought, speech, and public assembly, and the right to worship God according to the dictates of conscience—are seriously menaced. Freedom from atrocity, brutality, and slavery will be had only through the expression of Christian heroism.

Jesus was the most nobly courageous person who ever lived. He consecrated His life to a noble cause. He never did an unholy or unrighteous thing, and he never compromised in the interest of personal comfort or safety. For example, our Master was so gentle that children trusted Him; yet He was so austere as to drive mercenaries from the temple. He could not embarrass a woman; nevertheless, He exposed hypocrites. He wept with bereaved friends; still He was so firm that He told Pharisees they were vipers and sepulchers full of dead men's bones.

Moreover, in the interest of righteousness, Jesus chose the hard way of life. He had no home; His family misunderstood Him; and His neighbors tried to kill Him. In the hour of danger His disciples deserted Him. He was unjustly tried, scourged, mocked and crucified; but He died so nobly courageous that a Roman officer exclaimed: "Truly this man was the Son of God."

ETERNAL FATHER, in this hour of trial we long for Thee. The way is rough and steep, and it is dark. We pray for the light of Thy holy presence. Hold Thou our feeble hands, and guide Thou our uncertain feet. We are Thy children; help us, therefore, that we may know Thy Will and glorify Thy name. *Amen.*

A. C. REID
Wake Forest College, Wake Forest, N.C.

CHRISTIAN FOLLOWSHIP

If any man will come after me, let him deny himself, and take up his cross, and follow me.—Matt. 16:24

Leadership has been the important word in educational and religious circles, and it is well to develop able leaders. But qualities of leadership were not the criterion on which Jesus based Christian discipleship. He prefaced the call to discipleship by asking people to follow. There is always a need for leaders, but only a limited number of places of leadership can exist. However, followers are needed in unlimited numbers—a few generals in an army, but millions of privates; one president of a nation, but millions of citizens to make up a country. For the majority of people followship will be their lot in life. Therefore it is vital and important that we develop the art of being good and worthy followers.

In order to be good followers it is essential that we have a sense of values and the ability to select the kinds of ideals and leaders to which we give our followship. There are millions of youth in the world who have gone after false gods, treacherous leaders, and ideals and aims unworthy of the loyalty of them. The youth of our land must be won to the program of Jesus Christ and become magnificently obsessed with a passion to follow Him through the cross to a Christian victory. It is Christ, and Christ alone, who is worthy of our absolute confidence, and to whom we can surrender our followship with the assurance that He will not betray our trust. "If any man will come after me, let him deny himself, and take up his cross, and follow me."

FATHER GOD, we look up to Thee through Jesus Christ and find Thee to be the Leader whom we can trust. Give us access to Thy resources and insight into Thy ideals, and thus will we be strengthened for the great task of helping to bring in Thy Kingdom. In Jesus' name we pray. *Amen.*

JOHN BRANSCOMB
First Methodist Church, Tampa, Fla.

THE EVER-PRESENT GOD

Whither shall I go from thy Spirit? or whither shall I flee from thy presence?—Ps. 139:7

To the psalmist, religion was a vital thing without which he could not live. He knew, as every person knows, that he could hide many things from people, but not from God, the Creator of the universe.

Eventually every person comes face to face with the spiritual fact of God's presence, and His presence is always a judgment, or a source of courage and cheer. An atheist wrote a book entitled, *God Is Nowhere*. His little daughter gave him a severe jolt when she read the title, *God Is Now Here*. This arrow pierced his unbelieving heart, and the joy of the believer in the Ever-present God became his.

Many have told me that they do not even want to think of a God who knows all and sees all. Of course they don't. It would seriously cramp their style. But God is not so easily pushed aside, for "He that planted the ear, shall he not hear? He that formed the eye, shall he not see? . . . The Lord knoweth the thoughts of man."

What a blessed thing it is to be a child of the Ever-present God who has full knowledge of all of life! Who knows our pure hearts, and who knows our denials and betrayals as does He! "O the depth of the riches both of the wisdom and knowledge of God! how unsearchable are his judgments, and his ways are past finding out!" "If God be for us, who can be against us? He that spared not his own Son, but delivered him up for us all, how shall he not with him also freely give us all things?"

ALMIGHTY GOD, our Father, we have no fear because Thou art on the throne of the universe. Establish us in Thy love and fill our hearts with joy and courage that we way triumphantly meet every experience of life. Through Jesus Christ. *Amen.*

C. G. LUNAN
Third United Presbyterian Church, St. Louis, Mo.

GOD, OUR GUARDIAN

As the mountains are round about Jerusalem, so the Lord is round about his people from henceforth even for ever.—Ps. 125:2

Someone has said: "Courage is fear that has said its prayers." It is more. Courage is fear that has become aware of the ever-loving, never-vanishing God. The panic that is in many hearts at this hour would vanish like darkness before the rising sun if the Eternal Sun once dawned upon their souls. The anxiety that paralyzes a nation or lowers its morale simply cannot plague one who has entered into fellowship with God.

Centuries ago during the terrible Roman persecution, when Christians were being put to death without mercy, one lone follower of the Galilean stood before the Emperor Julian to receive sentence of death. Sneeringly, the emperor asked: "And what is your Galilean Carpenter doing now?" Without hesitation and without a tremor, he answered, "He is building coffins!"

When we are blest with a faith in an unconquerable God, when we know that a coffin is the destiny of every historical movement that denies God, when we are sublimely confident that all souls and all significant values are in God's keeping, when we believe with all our hearts that however dark and disastrous the times in which we live there is "one far-off divine event, to which the whole creation moves," nothing daunts us, nothing can subdue us, nothing can dismay us into surrender to evil.

OUR FATHER, we thank Thee for Thy presence everywhere, for Thy love bestowed so richly upon us all, for Thy mercy which forgives our sins, and for Thy power adequate for every situation. Help us to trust Thee, that we may with undaunted courage meet the ardors of these troubled times and live and die like sons and daughters of God. Through Jesus Christ our Lord. *Amen.*

ALBERT EDWARD DAY
First Methodist Church, Pasadena, Calif.

FORWARD WITH GOD

If thy presence go not with me, carry us not up hence.—Exod. 33:15

The chief factor in the orientation of young people to this confused modern world is their adjustment to the living God. This world of ours belongs to Him. If we fail to adapt ourselves to Him, pain and disaster follow. In this mysterious universe we cannot insist on our own selfish way and find abundant life. The fulfillment of our high destiny demands, as a prime requisite, that we get right with God and proceed with Him.

We need God because in Him and in Him alone can our souls find their final and adequate satisfaction and fulfillment. Do not expect a quiet, uninterrupted course. Your life will not be all calm. God never promised that. There will be storms in your life and in the world about you. But let none of these things fill you with fear. For remember, those who meet life with God can stand anything, and in the fiercest adversity they will know the joy and peace that belong to conquerors.

In the busy and perilous days that lie before you, steadfastly devote some time to the practice of God's presence. An opportunity which God alone can measure is awaiting you. As you advance toward it, pray for grace to see it through the eyes of divine wisdom in order that by the help of divine power you may make the most of it. Keep your vision clear and your hope bright, and walk with the indomitable courage and confidence of one whose feet are set in the highway of God.

ETERNAL GOD, our Father in Heaven, who hast assured us by Thy Son that Thou art with us always, even unto the end; increase our faith in Thee, our devotion to Thy cause and our awareness of Thy blessed Spirit. Give us grace to order our steps that our walk will always be close with Thee. *Amen.*

TEUNIS E. GOUWENS
Second Presbyterian Church, Louisville, Ky.

WE TRAVEL BY PRAYER

After this manner . . . pray ye.—Matt 6:9

In *His in a Life of Prayer,* Norman Harrison tells of a devout ship's master and a man named George Müller who encountered a very dense fog as they were sailing to Quebec. The captain had remained on the bridge for twenty-four hours when Mr. Müller came to him and said, "Captain, I have come to tell you that I must be in Quebec on Saturday afternoon." When informed that it was impossible, he replied, "Very well, if your ship cannot take me, God will find some other way. I have never broken an engagement for fifty-seven years. Let us go down into the chart-room and pray."

The captain continues: "I looked at that man of God and thought to myself, What lunatic asylum could that man have come from? I never heard of such a thing as this. 'Mr. Müller,' I said, 'do you know how dense this fog is?' 'No,' he replied. 'My eye is not on the density of the fog, but on the living God, who controls every circumstance of my life.' He knelt down and prayed one of those simple prayers, and when he had finished I was going to pray; but he put his hand on my shoulder and told me not to pray. 'Firstly,' he said, 'because you do not believe God will, and secondly, I believe God has, and there is no need whatever for you to pray about it.' I looked at him, and George Müller said, 'Captain, I have known my Lord for fifty-seven years, and there has never been a single day that I have failed to get an audience with the King. Get up and open the door, and you will find that the fog has gone.' I got up and the fog was indeed gone. George Müller was in Quebec Saturday afternoon for his engagement."

OUR HEAVENLY FATHER, help us to keep our eyes upon the sunshine and not upon the shadows, upon the reality of Thy Love and not upon the counterfeits of the wilderness. *Amen.*

GLENN CLARK
Macalester College, St. Paul, Minn.

BOUND UP WITH THE HUMAN RACE

I am debtor both to Greeks and to Barbarians, both to the wise and to the foolish.—Rom. 1:14 ARV

Recently I had a most trying day—one filled with responsibilities which taxed my strength to the utmost. Coming from a conference where some community problems had weighed rather heavily, I had forty minutes in which to reach home and eat dinner before having to meet another problem. I was tired and emotionally exhausted.

When I came into the house laughing, my wife was puzzled, for she knew what kind of a day I had had. "What happened?" she asked. I replied, "I have just met a great man." "What's his name?" "I do not know his name, but he is a great man. He runs an elevator in the building from which I have just come. I have just discovered that exuberant good nature is bound up with the human race."

That elevator operator had challenged me with such a merry spirit and with such a good-natured line of chaffing that in one brief moment my whole universe had changed and the burdens of the world had shifted their weight a little.

The contagion of one joyous spirit had made itself felt through the lives of many persons that evening. Our lives are bound up with other lives. The joys, sorrows, and needs of others are a part of us. Our goodwill or our meanness are reflected in the lives of others.

OUR FATHER, show us the importance of our little lives. Help us to see how significant we are in the scheme of things. May others have joy and not sadness because they have touched us in the ordinary contacts of our daily jobs. *Amen.*

H. OTHEMAN SMITH
Church of the Redeemer, Yonkers, N.Y.

KEEPING THE SACRIFICE PURE

The birds of prey swooped down . . . but Abram drove them off.
—Gen. 15:11 (SMITH-GOODSPEED)

Because he had been granted a fresh mission of God, Abraham wanted to offer a sacrifice. According to the customs of his time the victims were killed and kept until evening when they were to be burned upon the altar. But vultures waited in the branches of the trees, and through the afternoon Abraham had to keep driving them away.

We have been called upon to make a great sacrifice in this time of our country's danger and need, but there are birds of prey which are ready to defile that sacrifice. The black buzzard of hatred is waiting in the trees to swoop down upon it. In war it is not hard to hate, but hatred is a poison which harms more the one who harbors it than the one against whom it is directed.

Another bird of prey is the spirit of self-exaltation. Such an attitude not only defiles the sacrifice; it weakens our war effort. So also the spirit of intolerance. We are not entirely right, nor our enemies entirely wrong. Another black buzzard ready to defile the sacrifice is that of cruelty and hardness of spirit. Let us make this sacrifice, but God help us to keep it pure.

O GOD OF RIGHTEOUSNESS AND PURITY, we pray Thee to help us to stand for ideals which are high and holy; but as we fight for right, may we fight in the spirit of Him who taught us to love our enemies. We ask it in His name. *Amen.*

ROBERT N. MCLEAN
First Presbyterian Church, Santa Barbara, Calif.

OUR PRIVILEGE

God having provided some better thing for us, that they without us should not be made perfect.—Heb. 11:40

No one's life is complete in itself. This is a principle underlying our verse. Our lives are a part of what has gone before and a part of what follows after. It is God's purpose to bring forth an order of perfection, and it is a better thing for us to have part in building that order than to enter into it without any work. All who have faith in God and are in unison with His designs have their part in this purpose no matter when and where they live. It is a great thought that even Abraham and Moses cannot attain to completion of life unless we do our part in God's service in our own day.

This thought should give us the correct perspective of life. We have important and essential places to fill in God's designs for a kingdom of perfection, but this gives us no occasion for spiritual pride. We are links in a chain, and important as links, but we are not the whole chain.

It should also provide an inspiration for worthy living. To know that we are in the line of a great succession who have given of their best and utmost for God should lead us to do likewise. Our fathers who suffered for freedom at Valley Forge depend upon us in this day for the perpetuation of their ideals.

O GOD OUR FATHER, we thank Thee for the privilege of joining with all Thy servants of the past in faith and service. We pray for wisdom and strength to serve our day according to Thy will. Give us a sense of our responsibility both to the past and to the future. Help us to live right, serve wisely, and enjoy fellowship with Thee. In Jesus' name. *Amen.*

JOHN C. SILER
Tinkling Spring Presbyterian Church, Fishersville, Va.

THE OPEN DOOR

Behold, I have set before thee on open door.—Rev. 3:8

There is nothing more stirring and pleasant than to feel that life has good things ahead. On the other hand, there is nothing more depressing, more unnerving, than to feel that life holds nothing in store for you. "Is life over for me?" was the question that one who had grown weary by the way asked of a friend and counselor. The answer is found in that immortal promise to the church at Philadelphia, "Behold, I have set before thee an open door." Life is never over for those who follow Jesus.

This is grandly true of you. You have the incomparable chance of youth; you have the opportunity to learn life's great purposes, to learn how to do good. The door is wide open now. Five years from now it will be a little less wide open. In middle life it will be half shut. A little later it will be three-quarters shut, and then, at length, so far as the opportunity to be good and do good in this world, the door will be closed. Therefore, enter it now. "Work, . . . for the night cometh."

But this is a promise of opportunity which speaks not only to youth, but to those in every period of life. It has a great meaning for those who are conscious of past mistakes and omissions. Even the most thoughtful and careful will recall doors which they passed by, opportunities to speak for God and the truth, to warn someone in peril, to encourage and help a troubled soul. But God opens another door. He gives us another chance.

LORD, we thank Thee for the open door, for the second chance. We know that Thy Spirit will not always strive with us, but that so long as there is a spark of yearning in our hearts for Thee, or one chance of winning us from sin, Thou wilt keep the door of repentance open to us. Make us, then, eager to accept the second chance, to begin the new life in Thee. *Amen.*

CLARENCE EDWARD MACARTNEY
First Presbyterian Church, Pittsburgh, Pa.

COURAGE FOR THE TASK

Be strong and of a good courage.—Josh. 1:6

Courage—the very word suggests the valor of the soldier. There are several varieties of courage. It may be the bravery of the soldier who bathes some battlefield with his blood, the intrepidity of the aviator who risks the hazards of the stratosphere, the daring of the sailor who faces the perils of the deep.

These are spectacular displays of valor. By possessing it men and women achieve the rank of heroes and win immortality of fame. Their names are written on the shining pages of history.

The rank and file of us, however, need courage for the daily task, courage to endure, to wait patiently. "Be of good courage, and he shall strengthen your heart, all ye that hope in the Lord."

> God, make me brave for life,
> O braver than this!
> Let me straighten after pain
> As a tree straightens after the rain,
> Shining and lovely again.
> —GRACE NOLL CROWELL

FATHER, God of invincible might, free us from fear. Help us to feel that Thou art the strength of our lives and that though a host should encamp against us, even then may we be confident. Grant us the steadfast spirit of the courageous Christ, who did not flee from the cross, nor flinch in the hour of pain. For His name's sake. *Amen.*

CLYDE K. CAMPBELL
Superintendent, Albuquerque, N.M. District, The Methodist Church

THE NEW CREATION

Therefore if any man be in Christ, he is a new creature: old things are passed away; behold, all things are become new.—2 Cor. 5:17

Who is the new creature to whom all things are become new? It is the one who believes in Christ as personal Savior. It is the one who knows that Jesus paid the penalty for sin on the cross in his or her place.

The change is so great that it is proper to speak of the new creation in Christ Jesus. He or she has new views, new motives, new principles, new objects, and new plans of life. The impure becomes pure, the profane becomes clean; there is a change so deep, so clear, so entire, so satisfying, so abiding that it must be described as a new creation. It is the divine power of God alone which can accomplish so wonderful a change.

Old things are passed away—prejudices, opinions, habits, love of sin, love of the world. Behold, all things are become new. Oh, the joy of it! The mind is centered on God, and the heart forms new attachments. All these things are in the mind and heart of the newborn soul. The new creation in Christ Jesus is born of God.

OUR FATHER, may we give Thee praise from the heart for Thy lovingkindness. Turn our faces heavenward that we may see all Thou wouldst do for us. May we know more of Thy tender mercies, that we may love more in accord with Thy will. In the name of the Lord Jesus Christ we pray. *Amen.*

H. E. EAVEY
President, The Eavey Co., Xenia, Ohio

THE POWER OF AN ENDLESS LIFE

Who is made, not after the law of a carnal commandment, but after the power of an endless life.—Heb. 7:16

"Give me a place to stand, and I can move the earth," said Archimedes, the ancient mathematician. One needs a cosmic setting to deal successfully with this world's problems. It is good for us to plan our lives on an eternal basis. Jesus did. The Master knew He came from God and went to God.

The power of an endless life can do at least three things for us. First, it creates courage by making life qualitative. Our goal is to live well. What of Methuselah's long life in comparison with Jesus' good life? Although it costs us life itself, we take our stand with the good because it is guaranteed by God. Second, the power of an endless life gives us poise. The knowledge that we cannot accomplish everything we desire here does not make us panic-stricken. We also have the hereafter in which to achieve our coveted goals. Third, the power of an endless life sustains us morally. Because we are accountable to God, and because we must live with ourselves throughout eternity, we are careful of our characters. We would rather live with a hero than with a coward, an honest person than a cheat, and a decent person than a moral pervert.

O LORD, who art from everlasting to everlasting the same, we turn to Thee in the vicissitudes of life. Guard us from evil, confirm our worthy desires, and lead us in the way everlasting. In Jesus' name. *Amen.*

L. E. SCHWARZ
Westminster Presbyterian Church, Topeka, Kan.

FATHERS AND SONS

And he shall turn the heart of the fathers to the children, and the heart of the children to their fathers.—Mal. 4:6

This is the last verse in the Old Testament. It was about 460 B.C. that Malachi wrote it. That long ago parents and children did not see things alike; the older generation failed to understand and trust the younger generation; the young people disregarded the wisdom of their elders. The prophet, looking for a new Elijah, felt that surely he would change this.

We have to admit that it is a good thing sometimes that the heart of the children is not turned to their parents. There is a time for "the revolt of youth" when the older generation has worshipped its idols and corrupted the world. But the hope of progress is that fathers and mothers may live constructively, and that sons and daughters may enter into their labors and advance the good causes which their parents have served. The Spirit of Jesus turns the hearts of parents to the children and the hearts of children to their parents.

The Spirit of Jesus accomplishes this by making the home of mutual benefit to the different ages, by bringing judgment on motives and behavior, and by keeping the ideal of the Kingdom of God on earth in the mind and in the heart.

GOD, our Father, we thank Thee for our homes and for the faith of our parents. Where there is misunderstanding between generations, may Thy Spirit direct the way to sympathy and peace. May those who have suffered by the mistakes of their parents so live that their children may receive a truly Christian heritage. Hear our prayer in the name of Christ. *Amen.*

HAMPTON ADAMS
Union Avenue Christian Church, St. Louis, Mo.

AWAITING GOD'S HELP

Make haste, O God, to deliver me; make haste to help me, O Lord.—Ps. 70:1

The psalmist finds himself in an emergency, therefore his urgent plea. He wants to say, "If help does not come soon, O God, I cannot hold out." We also feel this way when confronted by difficulties. Often the need has increased to where we feel God does not want to aid us. If He is on the way to help, it seems He is coming at a snail's pace.

We need to learn that in His good time God will reveal Himself to those who wait patiently for Him. He is greater than any trial. He never comes too late, for He can make up for apparent lost time; and we shall learn that in the end "all things work together for good to them that love God."

We are urged to "come boldly unto the throne of grace, that we may obtain mercy, and find grace to help in time of need." But let us not be discouraged if our petitions are momentarily unheeded. His deliverance and help will surely come.

ALMIGHTY GOD, we approach Thee with boldness to supply our needs, realizing that Thou art able and willing to deliver and help us. Although we plead for haste, we will await in cheerful hope and patience Thy leisure. Since Thou hast never forsaken the soul that trusted Thee in time of need, we feel Thou wilt grant us that which is for our good. We ask this in Christ's name. *Amen.*

FREDERICK R. DARIES
Zion Evangelical and Reformed Church, Indianapolis, Ind.

TAKE CARE OF YOUR HEART

Keep thy heart with all diligence; for out of it are the issues of life.
　　　　　　　　　　　　　　　　　　　　　　　　—Prov. 4:23

When these words were written, it was thought the heart was the seat of the emotions. They mean, then, something like: "Be careful of your emotional life, for whatever moves you molds your future." When we care deeply about a cause or a person, permanent changes take place in the very structure of our lives. If it is a noble cause we serve, if it is a worthy person we love, we ourselves grow better because of our devotion.

How important this truth is in times like these! Our emotions are deeply stirred. Self-discipline is a necessity or our lives will disintegrate. A few minutes each day with the New Testament and prayer will give God the chance to clarify our minds and make more real to us the things we really love and want to see endure.

This is the secret of the joyous life so many deeply religious people live. They are happy with a happiness not affected by changes in outward circumstances. Loving God, they love truth, justice, goodness, which are expressions of God's life in the world. Loving God, they seek to make the world a place where all children of God shall have the opportunity to come to their own highest and best.

Take care of your heart, then, for you will at last become like that which you love.

OUR FATHER, in moments of clear vision we see the road Thou dost want us to follow. Help us, we pray, to follow this road always, doing justly, loving mercy, and walking humbly and teachably with Thee and others. *Amen.*

PAUL QUILLIAN
First Methodist Church, Houston, Tex.

IN THE LIGHT OF ETERNITY

In thy light shall we see light.—Ps. 36:9
The Lamb is the light thereof.—Rev. 21:23

Nothing is seen in its own light. We see the landscape, the running brook, in the light of yesterday. Memory supplies the light.

The psalmist says that to see this world you must look at it in the light of the coming world. For scenes of earth, heavenly light is necessary. You cannot interpret your own life circumstances without it. Most people feel that in the light of eternity earthly objects fade away. The psalmist says that not until we have the light of eternity will earthly objects be in our sight.

It is the Lamb that was slain from the foundation of the world that is the light. We are unable to understand the struggles of this world by any other light. We have nature's abundant light of sunshine, but we retain our pain. We have the wonderful revelations of the artist, but blind eyes miss the scene. The light of the philosopher may seem to illumine, but the light soon begins to fade.

The light thereof is the sacrificial gift of the divine Son. The crowning light of Creation is the Cross. The purest white robe is the robe that has been washed white. It is the Lamb who is the Light thereof. It is in Thy Light, O God, that we see light!

O LORD, let Thy Light be the light of my path. May I view the scenes of earth not by their shadows, but in Thy glorious light. Help me to walk in the light as He is in the light and have fellowship. *Amen.*

G. J. CARLSON
Tabernacle Baptist Church, Chicago, Ill.

LOST IN THE BAGGAGE

Behold, he hath hid himself among the stuff.—1 Sam. 10:22

When the tribes of Israel were selecting a king, they sought quite diligently for Saul and found him by and by hidden in the "stuff"—the baggage. When they brought him out from the stuff, the young man stood head and shoulders above all, and he was declared king. The story portrays exactly the situation you and I find ourselves in so often; the best that is in us, the regality of our lives, the contentment and glory of our personalities, is lost in the detail and confusion of life.

Life has a great deal of baggage. It is seemingly important to have, but after you get by the importance of something, it seems to vanish. We are impressed with the fact, as we get down the road a ways and look back, that we have spent a great deal of energy just "toting baggage." We gather together every convenience to take care of possible emergencies, and these conveniences become so numerous that they themselves become a burden. By this process we become slaves to our baggage and are lost in the accumulations of things.

It is our privilege to find our throne, our place of complete mastery—to extricate ourselves from the multiplicity of interests and live abundantly. Faith in ourselves and knowledge of life values do wonders in lifting baggage-loaded pilgrims from confusion. A constant look into the heavens following the star over the manger will help us daily to get the true values of life and bring ourselves to a destination of worth.

ALMIGHTY GOD, help me this day to be bigger than the many interests that encompass me. Save me from enslavement in petty affairs until my soul loses all its kingly glory. Help me to press toward the prize of the high calling of a child of God. In Thy name I ask this royal blessing. *Amen.*

JOHN G. BENSON
Superintendent, Methodist Hospital, Indianapolis, Ind.

LOVE IS THE BASIS FOR ALL LIVING

Follow after love, and desire spiritual gifts.—1 Cor. 14:1

Life is the gift of God, exceedingly precious—a trust from Him for which an accounting will have to be made. To make a life count most, love must be the basis. Drummond wrote a volume, *The Greatest Thing in the World*, on love to demonstrate this fact. Somehow I like the message of H. J. Heinz, who wrote, "'The Greatest Thing in the World' is humanity, and the greatest need is love."

What a tremendously changed world this would be if love were adopted by everyone as the basis for living. Fear and hate and selfishness and greed would be transformed into faith and joy and friendship and kindness.

To have this love, we must have a "heart companionship" with Christ, the greatest example and demonstration of love—the love of God our Father. To grow daily in this spirit it will be well for us to repeat early every day another of Paul's declarations, "Whatsoever ye do, do all to the glory of God." This will give divine strength and power coming from the Christ who said, "Lo, I am with you always, even unto the end of the world."

ETERNAL FATHER, fill us with Thy love, and implant Thy Holy Word in our hearts to guide us through the life here and fit us for the life hereafter. We pray in the name of Christ. *Amen.*

HARRY E. PAISLEY
Former Treasurer, Reading Railroad
Superintendent, Trinity Reformed Bible School
Philadelphia, Pa.

STRENGTH FOR THESE DAYS

Thy shoes shall be iron and brass; and as thy days, so shall thy strength be.—Deut. 33:25

When the tribes of Israel were assigned portions of the Promised Land, Asher was given the rocky sea coast, with rough roads to travel—but with a promise, "Thy shoes shall be iron and brass; and as thy days, so shall thy strength be."

God has never encouraged His children to believe that life is easy. It was not so for His Son nor for His disciples. The difficulties we face in life are not as important as how we face them and the worthiness of the cause we serve.

This is a very difficult period in our lives. These are days for faith and not panic. God has promised strength adequate for every need. Our Father always makes us strong in the hour of trial.

In the darkest hour of the Revolution, when everywhere the enemy was triumphant, a general said to Washington, "We are lost! Everything is lost!" With flashing eye Washington quickly replied, "Sir, you do not know the resources and genius of liberty." To every prophet of pessimism and fear today let us say with confidence, "Sir, you do not know the resources and genius of God." This is a time to trust our all to the love and wisdom and power of Omnipotent God, who has promised that, "as thy days, so shall thy strength be."

DEAR FATHER, save me from an easy-going religion. Awaken within me a faith that will count upon Thy promise of strength and wisdom as I strive to serve Thee among others. Use me this day for Thy name's sake. *Amen.*

J. W. HAWLEY
First Methodist Church, Pittsburgh, Pa.

NOT FORGOTTEN

Fear not therefore: ye are of more value than many sparrows.
—Matt. 10:31 ARV

The fear of being forgotten lies deep within us. Even in social relationships we are hurt when overlooked. To the person in uniform the thought must come often that he or she is but one of millions; his or her life is cheap; he or she is like the sparrows in an Oriental market, valued at two for a penny! But Jesus said that even a sparrow "shall not fall on the ground without your Father." God's love is so great that it extends to the smallest creatures He has made. No one is overlooked by God.

That is difficult to believe when we consider the millions who inhabit this universe. But observe that God has taken infinite pains in His creation. Your body is wonderfully made, but even so you are unlike anyone else in the world; God has seen to that. Even your fingerprints are different.

So be sure of this: God is supremely interested in you as an individual; what concerns you concerns Him. He has created you for a purpose, and you may accomplish that purpose in the flash of a moment—for which all previous years have been but the preparation.

O GOD, who lovest all that Thou hast made, we thank Thee for our faith that we are not forgotten by Thee. Grant that we, in turn, shall not forget Thee, nor the power of Thy Spirit to sustain us. Save us from the things that would destroy our souls, and help us to live according to Thy will. *Amen.*

VERNON BRITT RICHARDSON
Westhampton Baptist Church, Richmond, Va.

CHRISTMAS CELEBRATION

On earth peace, goodwill toward men.—Luke 2:14

This is Christmas Eve, and tomorrow will be the celebration of the greatest day of the world's history—the birthday of your Savior and mine. You can celebrate it in two ways. First, you can go out and do things you will be sorry for afterward. Yesterday morning on the train were some soldiers. One said to the other, "How did I get into lower six of this Pullman?" and the other answered, "I'll tell you, Buddy—the porter put you there, and the last thing you did was to spray a lady in the opposite berth with your vomit. A nice way to celebrate, Buddy." The other fellow's head dropped in his hands in shame, and he said, "And I promised my girl I'd quit it." That was celebration without cerebration. You can do that with Christmas. If so, then your head will be in your hands at the end, if not literally then figuratively.

There is another way to celebrate—a celebration with cerebration. Take the meaning of this day: He came to be with the world that we might be with God. Then I will truly celebrate that—I'll put its meaning into my life and live it out. I'll have a spiritual birthday on the Savior's birthday. I'll be a new person. The best gift I can send to the folks at home will be the gift of this news—the news that I am new. Then they will have "peace on earth," and I too will have it within me. I'll do it, God helping me.

O GOD, on this Christmas Eve I give in response to Thy gift. I give myself. It's all I have, but it is Thine. *Amen.*

E. STANLEY JONES
Missionary to India

CHRISTMAS DISCOVERY

The Word was made flesh, and dwelt among us.—John 1:14

For centuries people had been totally baffled by the strange writings which were found in Egypt, the hieroglyphics. Then in 1799 there was discovered the Rosetta Stone. Upon that stone were three parallel columns, in hieroglyphics, demotic, and Greek. There was the key. The Greeks knew. Using what they knew, they unraveled the mystery of the hieroglyphics.

Christ has been exactly this to innumerable people. He has mediated to them God. The distant and incomprehensible, for whom their hearts longed, became near and real and understandable in Jesus. "He that hath seen me hath seen the Father."

A mother put her little daughter to bed and turned out the light. The child anxiously asked, "But Mother, am I to be left alone, and in the dark too?" "Yes, my dear," answered the mother, "but you know you have God with you all the time." The little girl replied, "Yes, I know that God is here, but I want someone who has a face."

This is the Christmas discovery—that God has spoken in a language that everyone can understand—their own language, the language of human character. Paul speaks of Jesus as "the image of the invisible God."

OUR FATHER, we thank Thee for the blessing of that first Christmas. Open our eyes anew to the revelation of Thyself in Christ Jesus. May we in humility and gratitude stand again at Bethlehem's manger. Help us to prove our gratitude for Thy great gift in lives fashioned after the likeness of Thy Son. *Amen.*

FRANK B. FAGERBURG
First Baptist Church, Los Angeles, Calif.

ATTITUDE OF GRATITUDE

O give thanks unto the Lord; for he is good: for his mercy endureth for ever.—Ps. 136:1

Gratitude is a fundamental virtue of Christian character. To live in the attitude of gratitude means one must think and talk in grateful terms and act kindly toward others at all times.

Our nation is grateful to you in the armed forces. We who served in previous wars say to you: We are grateful, and we pray every day that God may give you strength and courage to meet your tasks. God bless you!

Gratitude is the basis of reverence. The words "thanks" and "thankful" are found many times in the Bible. Paul said on many occasions, "Thanks be to God." He recognized that all good gifts come from God and that therefore we should be grateful.

When a friend has treated us kindly, we say, "I thank you." Before we eat, therefore, we should thank God for His kindness and His provision for our every want. It is only selfishness that prevents all peoples of every land from having the abundant life. If people were grateful they would be reverent and unselfish. Let us make an effort to develop in our own lives the attitude of gratitude.

OUR FATHER, we thank Thee for Thy gifts. We thank Thee for the men and women who have gone before and paid for what we enjoy today. We pray that we may be led by Thy Spirit in these troubled times. Guide those who serve their country; protect them and keep them in Thy perfect love. *Amen.*

HAROLD R. HUSTED
First Baptist Church, East Orange, N.J.

SELF-CONTROLLED LIBERTY

Where the Spirit of the Lord is, there is liberty.—2 Cor. 3:17
The fruit of the Spirit is . . . self-control.—Gal. 5:22–23 ARV

It would be well now for us to recall a word that Moses is said to have spoken to the people of Israel. Back of them was Egypt and three or four centuries under despotic control. Ahead was a Land of Promise, but somehow they had not been able to reach it. The great leader gave an inspiring word, "He brought us out from thence, that he might bring us in." Out from the settled life in Egypt to wander in the wilderness, but all that they might go *in* to the better and higher way of living.

God has brought us out—out from our security, our easy prosperity, our assumption that our country is already free and right and good for all, and safe from attack—into a desert where all is uncertain, where old things are changing with alarming rapidity, and the new is not taking clear shape.

We have seen one nation after another come under despotic rule. Over against this we set our ideal of liberty. But we have been quite too ready to identify liberty with irresponsibility. It might startle us to recall how many times we have heard, "This is a free country," used to justify what no right-minded citizen should be guilty of. True democracy can be attained neither by control nor by absence of control, but by self-control. Only those able to control themselves can be trusted safely to live without external control.

GOD, give us grace to live worthily and to hold our inheritance as a sacred trust, that we may leave it increased, for those who shall come after. In Christ's name. *Amen.*

WILLIAM PIERSON MERRILL
Pastor Emeritus, Brick Presbyterian Church, New York City, N.Y.

ADVERSARIES MAKE OPPORTUNITIES

For a great door for effectual work is opened unto me, and there are many adversaries.—1 Cor. 16:9

Open doors and adversaries in the same sentence? An open door ought to symbolize entrance into opportunity without barriers. But St. Paul takes for granted that opportunities and adversaries are usually found in conjunction. It is a surprising truth that the things that oppose us in life actually offer us our finest opportunities for growth and service.

Opposition usually quickens our zeal. The early Christians learned that persecution promoted the spread of Christianity. Today, when all of us have come to grips with the difficulty of being Christian, many of us are finding our determination to follow Christ growing daily stronger.

For, you see, it is often adversity that makes us realize our opportunities. Facing now a world gone suddenly mad and the armies of sin and shame mustered against it, our Christianity is shocked to attention. The door becomes "great" when we realize the extent of the opposition. At once we are aroused into a now-or-never desperation of heart! However terrifying the odds against us, the door through which we must enter to relieve the need of the world is squarely before us.

> Lo! the hosts of evil round us
> Scorn Thy Christ, assail His ways!
> Fears and doubts too long have bound us,
> Free our hearts to work and praise.
> Grant us wisdom,
> Grant us courage,
> For the living of these days! *Amen.*
> —HARRY EMERSON FOSDICK

WILLIAM FREDERICK DUNKLE JR.
Old Stone Church, Methodist, Jacksonville, Fla.

THE ART OF HANDLING OUR TROUBLES

*In everything and in all things have I learned the secret both to be filled
and to be hungry, both to abound and to be in want. I can do all things
in him that strengtheneth me.*—Phil. 4:12–13 ARV

When Paul wrote the words above he was a prisoner in Rome. Day
by day he lived chained to a Roman soldier with no knowledge
of what another day would bring forth. But he was not unhappy nor
frightened nor worried.

He tells the Philippians that he had "learned" the great "secret" of how
to be "content" in all kinds of situations, favorable and unfavorable. How
long it took him to learn this he didn't say, but we may be sure it was not
a lesson that could be quickly and easily learned. The word translated
"content" literally means "self-sufficient," or "independent of external
circumstances." So independent of external circumstances was Paul that his
letter to the Philippians is one of the most joyful and most hopeful docu-
ments of the entire New Testament.

What was his secret? A complete committal of his life to God, a deep-
seated faith that God is able to take care of all the uncertainties of the
future, and a constant communion with God which provided him with
inexhaustible spiritual resources.

Someone asked a pastor who lives in continuous danger of persecution to
tell the secret of his calm endurance. He said, "When the house is dark, I do
not try to sweep away darkness with a broom: I light a candle." Prayer is the
light of the soul. When it glows within we may ignore the darkness without.

LORD, initiate us into the secret which enabled Paul to face the uncertain future with noble unconcern and which enabled Jesus to endure the
cross with a shout of triumph. May our faith in Thy great love be so strong,
and Thy hold on us so firm, that we can meet whatever comes with true
Christian courage. *Amen.*

ILION T. JONES
First Presbyterian Church, Iowa City, Iowa

COMPANIONS OF STRENGTH

In quietness and in confidence shall be your strength.—Isa. 30:15

God made the world for the exercise of all our powers. Attainment in the Christian way of life demands effort of body, mind, and soul. Weariness and fatigue are the result of the use of our strength. Events compel us to find resources for renewal and recuperation. When the crowd pressed upon them, near the close of the day, Jesus called His disciples aside into a desert place to rest awhile.

Quietness is always a dependable well of refreshment. In the school of solitude we learn the mightiest truths which can be seen only with the inward eye. "Be still, and know that I am God."

Usually confidence accompanies quietness. Contrast the methods of modern doctors and ancient medicine men who danced and made loud incantations to ward off evil spirits. Physicians are confident because they have walked the quiet path of training and experience.

Jesus undergirded His life of exceptional activity with the power of quietness and an unfaltering trust in His Father's purpose. The door of the infinite power of God is open to everyone who will enter with quietness and confidence.

OUR FATHER, we pray for strength equal to our tasks, for we would be doers of the Word and not hearers only. Renew in us the promise of Thy presence. Through Christ may we be strengthened for all things. In His name we pray. *Amen.*

DALE M. LIMBERT
First Methodist Church, Green Camp, Ohio

CHRIST'S FREEMEN

And when he had seen the vision, straightway we sought to go.
—Acts 16:10 ARV

Dr. Emory Ross once said: "The dominant thing in our day is *movement*." Xenophon, Xerxes, and Alexander the Great marched thousands of men through a mountain pass to "destiny and doom." After them came two lone travelers on foot, Paul and Silas, who marched through that pass to "destiny and life." The two movements, one toward "doom" and the other toward "life," still vie for the loyalties of humanity.

> We serve no God whose work is done,
> Who rests within His firmament:
> Our God, His labors but begun,
> Toils evermore, with power unspent.
>
> God was and is and e'er shall be;
> Christ lived and loved—and loves us still;
> And man goes forward, proud and free,
> God's present purpose to fulfill.
> —THOMAS CURTIS CLARK

Our next steps, to be toward "life," will be spirit-guided. They will be forward! They will be firm! They will be in unison with other forward-moving people of faith and hope.

OUR FATHER, may we move among people as those who know where they go. May those who step where we have trod walk out of darkness into light, from weakness into strength, and from folly into judgment, that Thy way may be known upon earth, Thy saving health among all nations. *Amen.*

NEAL K. MCGOWAN
First Christian Church, Fresno, Calif.

THE TENDER COMPASSION OF GOD

In the tender compassion of our God the dawn from on high shall break upon us.—Luke 1:78

Each morning we rise to face obstacles and opportunities—some days there seem to be far more obstacles than opportunities. Everyday we stand between the darkness and the light—at times there seems more darkness than light. But each moment we are in the presence of the holy ones of all times and places, the communion of saints, those friends of God and prophets.

There is Zechariah, father of John the Baptist, kinsman of Jesus. Like him and all holy men and women of old, we must rise to the challenges of this day, and face the darkness of our own hearts. Together with them, we hope in the tender compassion of our God and look for the light to break upon us, to guide us through this and all our days.

GLORY TO THE FATHER, through the Son, in the communion of the Holy Spirit. As it was in the beginning, is now, and will be forever. *Amen.*

HIS EMINENCE CARDINAL ROGER MAHONY
Archbishop of Los Angeles

†

ANSWERING THE BELL

Jesus answered, "I tell you, not seven times, but seventy times seven times."—Matt. 18: 21–22

A fighter named Sonny Liston won fifty professional fights and knocked out thirty-nine heavyweights, including the great Floyd Patterson twice, but most of us only remember his fight against Cassius Clay (now Muhammed Ali), where Liston stayed in the corner after the bell rang. That one action in his life overshadowed everything else he did.

There are many things to remember about my father, but I suspect that my grandchildren will remember one story I have told over and over about him: the story of how he forgave the man who was supposed to be his father, but who ran away and never answered the bell.

My father went to his father's funeral and bowed before the man he had never met and prayed for the father he had never known. He knelt and prayed for the man's soul. A few days later we were chopping wood when I asked him how he could have done such a thing. My dad put his axe down and leaned against the axe handle as he wiped his brow and squinted at the question.

"Son, when the Scriptures tell us to honor our parents, they don't say to do it if they are good parents. They just say to do it. And when our Lord says to forgive seventy times seven, I don't think He really means us to keep count, do you?" My father not only answered the bell and faced the challenge of forgiving, he turned it into a lesson for his children and their children's children. I hope my children and their children can practice the same measure of mercy.

HEAVENLY FATHER, help us to remember each day that we must forgive with the same fullness as You have forgiven us through the sacrifice of Your Son. Help us to answer the bell. *Amen.*

DONALD A. HUNSBERGER
Attorney at Law, Orange, Calif.

LET YOUR LIFE SPEAK

Do not be conformed to this world, but be transformed by the renewal of your mind, that you may prove what is the will of God, what is good and acceptable and perfect.—Rom. 12:2

What if I told you that you already have everything you need to be successful? You were born with a mind and a heart, a unique individual, and you bring your own very special gifts into the world. Real success does not come from a job or money, but from expressing your authenticity—your inner strength and integrity.

There is an old Quaker saying: "Let your life speak." Parker Palmer, a teacher and author, speaks frequently to groups about listening for your vocation. He says that vocation is not a goal to be achieved but a gift to be received. True vocation (success) comes from listening to yourself.

Each of us must discern the person we are called by God to be. We often listen to others' expectations—it is usually easier than listening and responding to our true selves. If we do not listen to ourselves, we will never be truly fulfilled.

Frederick Beuchner explained, "True vocation joins self and service." What are the things you care most about? How can the world use your talents to meet its deepest needs? The gift of self is the only real gift we have to give. Let your life speak through service to others.

GRACIOUS GOD, help me to use my heart and mind, to listen prayerfully, and serve humbly, that my life story might be Thy will. *Amen.*

ROBERT G. BOTTOMS
President, DePauw University, Greencastle, Ind.

HOLIDAY DEVOTIONS

FAITH FOR DARK DAYS

I know whom I have believed, and am persuaded that he is able to keep
that which I have committed unto him against that day.—2 Tim. 1:12

This is Good Friday. Followers of Christ everywhere are thinking of the events of this last day of His earthly life. It is said that at three o'clock in the afternoon Jesus cried out, "My God, my God, why hast thou forsaken me?" These are difficult words to explain.

God was not putting on a show. This was a real experience of suffering. Jesus' flesh had been nailed to a cross, and the pain was as real to Him as it would be to us if spikes were driven into our hands and feet. The thing that should sober us is that He did it because of His deep love for us.

> Love so amazing, so divine,
> Demands my soul, my life, my all.

Here in Jesus we find the supreme example of faith in dark days. In the face of tragedy He trusted in God.

Donald Hankey, of World War I fame, talked much about betting your life there is a God. Well, he did and won. We need that kind of faith today. Our democratic way of life seems to have its back to the wall and is fighting for its very existence. The future is dark, and we must have faith. Helen Keller was once asked the secret of her victorious life. She replied, "I am very happy because I have faith in God."

OUR HEAVENLY FATHER, we realize our need of Thee. The way ahead is dark and uncertain; shed Thy light upon our path. We do not know what will happen to us and to our comrades; but regardless of what comes, grant that we may put our trust in Thee. This we ask in Christ's dear Name. *Amen.*

BACHMAN G. HODGE
Superintendent, Nashville, Tenn. District, The Methodist Church

RESURGAM

Now is Christ risen from the dead, and become the first-fruits of them that slept.—1 Cor. 15:20

Though grim, resistless death its wrath shall wreak,
Disintegrate my mortal dust, efface
My image from the cosmic clay, erase
My name and title from my place, left bleak
And desolate; nor any voice shall speak
My praise, recount my deeds; and empty space
Shall crown my habitat—by Christ's good grace,
I shall arise, the lost He came to seek!

His pierced, holy hands hold deathless sway;
He is the Lord of life; the shattered grave
Of Easter morn, the trophy of His might;
His Cross has blazed life's ransomed, royal way;
From sin and death th' Omnipotent to save;
His glorious day shall end earth's travailed night!
—W. H. F.

O CHRIST, unto Thee who hast conquered, be glory evermore! Light of the world, splendor of the Father's presence, Son of Man in humility and self-devotion, Son of God in power—Thy risen life is the assurance of our victory! *Amen.*

WILLIAM HIRAM FOULKES
"Homespun" of the Blue Network,
Pastor Emeritus, Old First Presbyterian Church, Newark, N.J.

WHEN IS MOTHER'S DAY?

She shall rejoice in time to come.—Prov. 31:25

When is Mother's Day? Is it but a sentimental date upon our calendars? Or will there be a finer reality that we can more truly realize as Mother's Day?

It is entirely possible for every day to be the day that honors her who gave us birth and surrounded all our growing years with her unfailing love and care. Every day that I am true to her ideals, her love, her faith, her God—that day I honor my mother. Every day that I make one of strength, courage, clean living, and unselfish service—that day becomes a living and shining memorial to my good mother.

But there is a greater Mother's Day yet to be. When by God's help the sons of men win and build a world in which all womanhood is honored, redeemed, and freed; when all of childhood everywhere has the chance in life which God intended; when all of the homes of the world know economic security, social safety, and spiritual opportunity; then the Day of God will dawn for all mothers everywhere. "She shall rejoice in time to come." To that end and in honor of my own mother, I would dedicate my service, my toil, my loyalty, and my life.

O GOD, I give Thee thanks for all Thy blessings to me through my mother. Help me daily to be faithful to the highest and best that she taught me and that she lived in her own life. Give me courage for every day's duty and patience for the long striving. Enable me with others to build a world safe for the dreams of motherhood. Through Jesus Christ. *Amen.*

E. G. WILLIAMS
Western Representative, Presbyterian Board of Pensions

LABOR

I must work the works of him that sent me, while it is day: the night cometh, when no man can work.—John 9:4

Today is appointed to honor labor. It is well, for we often think of labor as a burden. It is a blessing and is of God. In Eden, before they had sinned, Adam and Eve were to subdue the earth and dress and keep the garden. Even then they were to labor "together with God." God commanded labor on six days. Our Lord said: "My Father worketh even until now, and I work," and "We must work the works of him that sent me." There is glory in labor.

All who work any work of good service render a holy labor and should be honored today. Let us resolve to recognize that every laborer is "worthy of his or her hire"; to help order our society that not only shall justice be done, but everyone shall have a sense of vocation, the thrill of the creative spirit, the motivation of service, and the dynamic of love.

Then let us resolve to increase the ranks of those who consciously labor "together with God." How true of our day are the words of Jesus, "The harvest indeed is plenteous, but the laborers are few." Let us come to Him who called all who labor, and take His yoke, which is easy because it fits; and let us learn of Him, and find rest unto our souls.

OUR FATHER, we thank Thee for the privilege of working Thy works with Thee, and for the knowledge that such labor is not in vain. Grant us the wisdom, strength, and courage to do our part. Today we dedicate ourselves to this task. *Amen.*

R. MURRAY JONES
First Presbyterian Church, Inglewood, Calif.

THANKSGIVING AS A SPIRITUAL ATTITUDE

Giving thanks always for all things.—Eph. 5:20

Thanksgiving Day is distinctively American. It is as old as our country itself. Its observance began with our pilgrim fathers and mothers gathering in a special service of thanksgiving, not for prosperity enjoyed, but chiefly for adversity endured and ended. Ever since Abraham Lincoln in 1864 proclaimed the fourth Thursday in November as Thanksgiving Day we have observed the custom.

Thanksgiving Day, so distinctively American, is symbolic of a spiritual attitude toward life which makes us superior to our environment. Gratitude depends not upon where we live or how much we have, but upon what we are. It has little to do with our outward circumstances.

If the Thanksgiving spirit depended upon physical or material well-being, then our first Thanksgiving Day should have had its origin in the Jamestown Colony in Virginia, which enjoyed marked comfort and prosperity rather than in the Plymouth Colony in New England, which suffered untold hardship, misery, and destitution. Thanksgiving has more to do with our spiritual attitude than with a physical and material condition. The thankful heart is found as frequently among those who have little as among those who have much.

ALMIGHTY GOD, who in former times didst lead our fathers and mothers forth from lands beyond the sea into this fair country, grant to us, their children, the grace to face life in our generation grateful and unafraid. *Amen.*

JOHN HOMER MILLER
Hope Congregational Church, Springfield, Mass.

SPECIAL DEVOTIONS

THE OPENING

Praise be to God, Lord of the worlds, the Compassionate, the Merciful, Ruler on the Day of Repayment; You do we worship . . . and You do we call on for help.—Quran 1:1–7

This is chapter one of the Holy Book (The Quran) hence the name "The Opening." It is the most frequently recited chapter in the Quran, being part of the ritual prayers as well as a prayer by itself repeated for any number of times during day or night. In its short span it enfolds the basic principles of Islam included in the Quran, and is therefore also named "The Mother of the Book." First is the acknowledgment of God as Lord of the universe, deserving of all praise, whose mercy is unlimited in duration and magnitude.

He is our ultimate Judge on the day of judgment and the only one we worship and seek help from. We ask for His guidance through our journey in this life, to be in the ranks of those with whom He is pleased, not those who displease Him.

LORD! Let me be conscious of You every moment of my life. Let me walk in Your light and protect me from darkness within or outside myself. Let my striving, my living, and my dying be for Your cause and Your purpose, and let my happiest day be the one when I stand before You for judgment. *Amen.*

Dr. Hassan Hathout
Islamic Center of Southern California, Los Angeles, Calif.

MY GRANDFATHER, REV. TURNER

O mankind! Lo! We have created you male and female, and have made you into nations and tribes that ye may know one another. . . . Lo! Allah is Knower, Aware. —Quran 49:13

I picture him in his clerical robes, framed by the sun rising over the Pacific. My grandfather, the Reverend William Henry Turner, was chaplain of the troopship *President Grant* in World War II. He led the troops in song and prayer. He encouraged the living; he held the dying. He died there, too, when the ship struck a reef, and is buried far from his loved ones, in the Philippines.

I never met my grandfather. Never heard the Reverend Turner preach. But his soul speaks to me always as I prostrate myself before God. I am Muslim and he, Baptist. I felt him watch me as I circled the Ka'aba in the Muslim Holy City of Mecca. I imagined him standing arm-in-arm with my other grandfather, a Muslim, both of them smiling.

My Christian grandfather and I may worship differently, but we are united in our love for Allah, God, and our trust in His plan for us—a plan that doesn't always match our human hopes, a plan that sometimes fills us with fear, uncertainty, and desperation—but also can bring the greatest of joy.

DEAR LORD AND CREATOR, thank You for cradling us all in Your wide-beyond-wide embrace, for Your bigness when we're small, for Your courage when we're scared, for Your company when we're lonely. Thank You for sharing the best of Your creation with me. Help me keep it safe for my children and grandchildren to come. *Amen.*

ANISA MEHDI
Television Producer, Maplewood, N.J.

FORGIVING IS NOT CONDONING

You shall not take vengeance nor bear a grudge against the children of your people. But you shall love your neighbor as yourself, I am the Lord.—Lev. 19:18

The ancient Rabbis taught that it is wrong to harbor anger indefinitely. They explained that an offender is required to ask for forgiveness three times. If, by the third time, the victim refuses to grant forgiveness, the victim becomes culpable and the offender is freed from any further responsibility.

Why do we hesitate to grant forgiveness to someone who has hurt us? We fear that, by forgiving someone, we are condoning the offensive behavior. We fail to understand that forgiving does not mean that we now consider cheating, lying, gossiping, or any other offense committed against us to be acceptable. What is unjust remains unjust. No act of forgiveness can change that fact.

Rather, forgiveness means that our negative feelings resulting from that offense can now be alleviated. By forgiving the offender, we have unloaded our hostilities. We have rid ourselves of those corrosive elements that have brought us down. We have cleaned our souls of their spiritual bacteria. We can then begin to rebuild our relationship with the one whose negative behavior initially caused it to be ruptured.

O GOD OF FORGIVENESS, help me this day to unburden myself of the hurts inflicted upon me. Enable me to forgive the ones who cause me pain so that I can be free of my distress and begin to transform my resentment into a friendship. *Amen.*

SAMUEL M. STAHL
Rabbi, Temple Beth-El, San Antonio, Tex.

AS I LOVE YOU, LOVE ME

You shall love the Lord your God with all your heart, and with all your soul, and with all your might.—Deut. 6:4–9

The question was asked by a philosopher a generation ago—what would happen if everyone on earth was told that they had one hour to live? His answer: we would call everyone else we knew to say how much we loved them. I think of my mother, who was given such a gift. On the day before she died with her hospital room full of family, she chose to call those who meant the most to her, to say good-bye, and that she loved them. She spoke those words with a smile but with resolve.

In our Torah we are commanded to love—to love our God, to love our neighbors, even to love ourselves.

The message of this day and every day is that God loves us even though we are not perfect. If we would be godly and try to live up to our highest level, then we too will love people who are not perfect, because we will never find any others. This day has shown us that we must love God's world, even though there is a lot wrong with it. At times it hurts us, or disappoints us, but we must still love it. Even in our pain, even in our anger and frustration, on this day we come to tell God we love God anyway.

Love is the one door that opens on heaven and the more we love, the wider heaven's door is opened. So don't wait until next week or next month. Turn to your wife, use that cell phone to call your husband, write your parents, e-mail your children and your friends and declare, "I love you, you are important to me. As I love you, love me." For you see, only by loving others do we truly live ourselves.

DEAR GOD, with love you sustain the living, with great compassion give life to all. We praise You, O God, the source of life. *Amen.*

KENNETH KANTER
Rabbi, Congregation Micah, Brentwood, Tenn.

THE LORD'S PRAYER

Our Father, who art in heaven,
hallowed be thy name.
Thy kingdom come,
thy will be done on earth as it is in heaven.
Give us this day our daily bread.
And forgive us our trespasses,
as we forgive those who trespass against us.
And lead us not into temptation,
but deliver us from evil.
For thine is the kingdom, and the power,
and the glory, forever. *Amen.*